W9-AJW-998

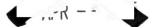

Spirits Rejoice!

SPIRITS REJOICE!

Jazz and American Religion

———◦◦◦———

JASON C. BIVINS

OXFORD
UNIVERSITY PRESS

OXFORD
UNIVERSITY PRESS

Oxford University Press is a department of the
University of Oxford. It furthers the University's objective
of excellence in research, scholarship, and education
by publishing worldwide.

Oxford   New York
Auckland   Cape Town   Dar es Salaam   Hong Kong   Karachi
Kuala Lumpur   Madrid   Melbourne   Mexico City   Nairobi
New Delhi   Shanghai   Taipei   Toronto

With offices in
Argentina   Austria   Brazil   Chile   Czech Republic   France   Greece
Guatemala   Hungary   Italy   Japan   Poland   Portugal   Singapore
South Korea   Switzerland   Thailand   Turkey   Ukraine   Vietnam

Oxford is a registered trade mark of Oxford University Press
in the UK and in certain other countries.

Published in the United States of America by
Oxford University Press
198 Madison Avenue, New York, NY 10016

© Oxford University Press 2015

A copy of this book's Cataloging-in-Publication Data is on file
with the Library of Congress.

ISBN 978-0-19-023091-3

1 3 5 7 9 8 6 4 2
Printed in the United States of America
on acid-free paper

For Nina

Contents

Acknowledgments

IN THE LATE 1990s I wrote an angry letter to the hoary jazz publication *Downbeat*. One of the magazine's more irascible critics at the time, John McDonough, had written a dismissive review of a recently unearthed late recording by tenor saxophonist John Coltrane. McDonough, a longtime opponent of anything that smacked of the avant-garde (as he understood it), panned the record, listing as one of its chief faults the fact that it was mired in incoherent spirituality, a pseudo-religious pabulum whose earnestness distracted listeners from how awful the music was. I didn't want to get into a musicological debate with McDonough (and there were enough letters doing that already, as legions of irate readers were horrified that anyone should pen a negative word about the sanctified Trane), but I suggested that in his dismissal of Coltrane's religiosity he was overlooking something central, not ancillary to the person and the music. If we divorce Coltrane from his religiosity, I wrote, then we have to take it away from Ellington, Mingus, Abdullah Ibrahim, and what kind of jazz would that leave us with? McDonough's tough-guy response to me (in print, much to my surprise) was blunt and self-satisfied: he never really cared for Ellington's "Sacred Concerts" anyway.

It is a long time since that letter was published, but my connection with the music has deepened over the years. Though I have written mostly on political religions and methodology, I have for nearly two decades been working my way toward this book, which resonates with me on multiple levels. What leads me to this exploration of jazz and American religions, a music I love and which is so deeply written into the fabric of American religions? On the one hand, it's because this music is so rarely acknowledged in religious studies and it needs to be engaged responsibly. But the real answer is that the sounds have led me here, echoing continually in my memory.

I remember first those many afternoons in my father's apartment on Capitol Hill, where he boomed music from the house stereo—Bach cantatas,

Beethoven symphonies, occasionally a perplexing dash of Stravinsky or an unexpected Simon & Garfunkel tune. He'd grill my sister and me to pick out notes on his beat-up old Chickering upright, with its cigarette burns and drink stains, and to identify instruments (starting with Prokofiev, of course). I remember falling in love with rock music, first gravitating to its iconography: I had a bad-ass Supertramp shirt (*Crime of the Century*) but they stunk, while Parliament (which was everywhere in D.C. and Silver Spring during the 1970s) and KISS compelled for obvious visual reasons. But each time I heard rock—thumping from my neighbor's tricked-out orange van or with my cousins singing along to Heart or "Afternoon Delight"—the switch failed to flip. It was punk, post-punk, and metal that woke me up as a teen, with their intensities, angularities, and subcultures permitting escape from a ludicrous decade.

I remember finding a stash of jazz LPs in a back room upstairs when I was fifteen or sixteen. They were part of my uncle Bill's collection, which Daddy took home after Uncle Bill died. There was some trad stuff that I never really dug, but I started to fall for jazz via those Bill Evans and Thelonious Monk records. And when I went off to Oberlin College, with its hot music program and player-heavy student body, I plunged into the deep end of the pool. One night my friend Taze Yanick played the mighty Mahavishnu Orchestra for us, at the peak of the high. A drummer named Beaver had to leave the room, saying the music made him dizzy. But I was transfixed, smitten, in love with the sound of John McLaughlin's guitar and with the incredible, impossible lines he played in rhythms I'd never heard. Then it was Coltrane, *Birdland* in particular. After the theme and the long rolling trio section opening "Afro-Blue," when Coltrane took that soprano into the heart of the cosmos—that incredible glissando intro sounding at once like a spirit rocket and the most beautiful sadness you've ever heard—well, that was just it. Forever. Tapes were traded, huge piles of records were sold in order to buy other huge piles of records, and I never looked back. I listened obsessively, practiced guitar as much as I could, and realized after a time that I was a "jazz guy."

Then off I went to graduate school. During my first semester, Robert Orsi wrote the most interesting comment on a paper: "You write like the World Saxophone Quartet." How cool was that? Of course, he was telling me that the "long, looping lines" of my writing made it difficult to read (I'm still trying, Bob). But really, how cool was that? Maybe someday I could write about American religion and jazz, the two things that so stimulated my gray matter. But I continued to think that this was a thing apart from my scholarly life. Despite having written seminar papers in graduate school and given talks under this book's title since 2000, I wanted to keep music in what I imagined to be a "purer" space. After all, my own performance had sustained me since I was a teen (and still does), making music in bedrooms, garages, leaky basements, churches, galleries, pirate radio stations (one of which was invaded by hordes of Santa Clauses chanting "Ho! Ho! Ho!" rather forbiddingly), clubs, restaurants and bars, New Age emporia, rec centers, libraries, a skateboard ramp, warehouses, lofts, record stores, studios, and occasionally a proper concert hall or a park or a pasture. And since 1997, I've also spent hundreds of hours in another kind of cramped space, listening to, thinking about, notating, and writing about music as a jazz record reviewer.

I know well the frustrations of trying to describe a music that not only lacks lyrical content but also evades form. And I know too well the frustrations of trying to communicate through this marginalized music, which many understand to be far more than mere entertainment, and instead as possibly a self-conscious way of recalibrating perceptions and even, sometimes, a different way of being in the world. I began, in the mid-2000s, to think that these things needed to be written about in the academy and that my combined experiences positioned me well to do so. I began to spend more time reliving moments of particularly intense encounters with such strange beauty, collating memories that might make their way into the book: Sonny Rollins parading the stage of Oberlin's Finney Chapel, the sight of Albert Ayler's horn lifted aloft in "love cry," my quickened pulse when first hearing Rahsaan Roland Kirk insisting "Listen! Listen with all your might!" and my bafflement and excitement witnessing Sun Ra's Arkestra moving in procession toward the stage, swinging incense of all things, and—in shiny robes and elaborate headgear—singing "We travel the spaceways, from planet to planet." Notes and examples piled up as I began to plot out the interrelations between such figures and important dimensions of American religions, thinking and listening my way to an alternate sonic history of American religions that I decided early on to call *Spirits Rejoice!* after a mid-1960s Ayler record (a title later appended with an exclamation point by Louis Moholo-Moholo).

That these sounds could exist at all seemed to make lighter my world of dark clouds, all those things I have written about until now. So, too, have the lessons learned through playing and writing about the music: respect and restraint, generosity of listening, other worlds opening up through sound. My hope is that my immersion in the music through recording, touring, and reviewing shapes and enlivens the scholarship, which is my primary goal and the music's desert, since it is no mere accompaniment to important religious developments in the United States over the last century and change but a constitutive element of them. This research and writing have been accompanied by continual interrogation of my authorial position, though I have not theorized it explicitly in the text. As a middle-aged Caucasian male, I've been aware of how white listeners often unconsciously embrace what Anthony Braxton calls "the across the tracks syndrome," where jazz is appropriated as an antidote to squaredom. Contrarily there is the oft-purported existence of "Crow Jim," where African American musicians have sometimes denied the "authenticity" of white jazz playing or criticism for their inability to fully understand the music's wellsprings. Though I am sympathetic with these concerns, I am fortunate that the musicians I communicated with were convinced of my (and my book's) scholarly merit. Perhaps this is also because I have not tried to conceal my secondary goal: having told dark stories about American political religions for so long, I can say honestly that it would warm my bitter heart if readers not only learned something about American religions, thought differently about their sounds and shapes, but rededicated themselves in a commitment to the arts—especially the music—of the United States.

In this and other things, I have been a lucky academic. In the years since my previous book, I've grown more at home in a field I also continue to criticize, and along the way have made many marvelous friends. I've also had tremendous institutional support, amazing colleagues, and a cosmically awesome group of friends and family. Let me sing your song now, good people.

First and foremost, I want to thank the musicians who have so generously given their time, sharing their thoughts and reflections with me. The multiple lengthy conversations I had over the past many years have been some of the most rewarding I can remember, and not just in terms of scholarship. And while a large percentage of those conversations did not end up being quoted at length herein, I am grateful to you all and have learned so much from you. Those who participated most extensively, and with such generosity, patience, enthusiasm, and the right measure of skepticism are Brian Adler, Roy Campbell, Connie Crothers, Stephan Crump, Hamid Drake, Ellery Eskelin, David "Fuze" Fiuczynski, David Friesen, Dennis Gonzalez, Burton Greene, Jason Kao Hwang, Rozanne Levine, George E. Lewis, Francisco Mela, Myra Melford, Sue Mingus, Lawrence D. "Butch" Morris, Ivo Perelman, Sam Rivers, Ned Rothenberg, Matthew

Shipp, Wadada Leo Smith, Ijeoma Thomas, Oluyemi Thomas, and James Weidman. Rest in peace, Roy, Butch, and Sam.

There are a great many others who expressed support for the project but ultimately did not want to participate in interviews. There are others whom I sought out repeatedly but unsuccessfully. Some interviews fell through, alas. And there are others with whom I spoke or corresponded, and whose stories did not eventually make it into the manuscript (or who are only briefly noted), including Don Byron, Kahil El'Zabar, Sonny Fortune, Joe Giardullo, Susie Ibarra, Vijay Iyer, Travis Laplante, Rudresh Mahanthappa, Jim McAuley, Dom Minasi, Toshimaru Nakamura, Tatsuya Nakatani, Larry Ochs, Dave Rempis, Matana Roberts, Adam Rudolph, Alan Silva, Salim Washington, and Jack Wright. Thanks for the encouragement and enthusiasm. And mostly, and this goes out to a cosmos of musicians far beyond just those in this book, *thanks for the music!*

Mind you, I would have had a hard time chasing down some of the above people without the able assistance of those folks who own labels and represent artists. Thanks to Ann Braithwaite, Stephen Buono, Joyce Feigenbaum, Adam Hertz, Daniel Melnick, and Matt Merewitz. Huge shout-outs go to my editors in jazz writing over the years. Above all I'm grateful to Bob Rusch, who gave me a shot way back when, and who for nearly four decades helmed the good ship *Cadence* (now under the guidance of the terrific pianist David Haney). Respect. Much fond gratitude, as well, to Pete Gershon of *Signal to Noise*, Scott Hreha of *One Final Note*, Al Jones of *Bagatellen*, Otis Hart of *Dusted*, Dan Warburton of *Paris Transatlantic*, and Bill Shoemaker of *Point of Departure*. I thank the following travelers in these climes for great conversation about this book's subject matter: Jon Abbey, Nate Dorward, Stephen Griffith, Walter Horn, Marc Medwin, Brian Olewnick, Eric Saidel, Hank Shteamer, Steve Smith, and Derek Taylor. I've also been lucky enough that the following gifted photographers consented to have their work reproduced here: Guy Kopelowicz, Jan Persson, Luciano Rossetti, and Bill Smith (a gifted improviser who for decades edited *Coda* and co-ran Sackville Records).

Dearest to my heart are my own musical collaborators, good friends and brilliant people with whom I've chased the flash for a long, long time. Love to Unstable Ensemble, Micro-East Collective, eNtet, the Impermanence Trio, Polyorchard, Cyanotype, Slugworth, EXO, Congliptious, the mighty M, Sterno, the JBT, and all the other folks who cook up the strange stuff. Special thanks to a cherished subgroup for conversations about this book's subject matter over the years: Martha Bausch, Marty Belcher, Jeb Bishop, Ian Davis,

Jimmy Ghaphery, Tim Harding, Bill McConaghy, Dave Menestres, David Miller, Richard Patterson, Lee Pembleton, Tomas Phillips, Steve Simms, Joe Stone, Nobu Sutoyoshi, Eric Weddle, and Bennett Williams.

In the academy, I've been fortunate to receive significant institutional support in tight times. North Carolina State University still rocks, and I'm much obliged to my college for support and leave on crucial occasions. A special tip of the hat to Matt Shipman, for friendship and for helping build a better megaphone. My departmental colleagues rock hardest, though. Michael Pendlebury is the Platonic form of department heads, and I thank him abundantly for support and friendship on countless levels. The conversations in the Department of Philosophy and Religious Studies are invariably lively, challenging, and enthusiastic, and it's a place I appreciate more all the time. David Auerbach, John Carroll, Tim Hinton, and Mary Tjiattas have been particularly encouraging in the writing of this book. All of my R.S. bandmates keep the engine room humming. In particular, Bill Adler is a great neighbor, font of advice, and fellow sardonicist with regard to academic insanity. Anna Bigelow and Karey Harwood have been super supportive, too, understanding the importance of sonic loves. Most of all, Levi McLaughlin has been an incredible friend and musical wizard, reading this stuff, gabbing about the field, and on occasion heshing out majestically with me. And my good friends Ann Rives and Ken Peters, what would I do without all our uproarious, conspiratorial conversations? You're the best. And big thanks, too, to my musical co-conspirators in other departments: David Ambaras, Katherine Charron, Brent Sirota, Cat Warren, and Ken Zagacki.

It's been a delight to work with Oxford once again, and my deepest debt is to the incomparable Cynthia Read, whose enthusiasm, guidance, and friendship are truly valued (not to mention all those great record recommendations!). The steady hand and able assistance of Marcela Maxfield have been a boon to me, as has the first-rate copy editing of Rene Carman. And I am really grateful to have had such amazing anonymous readers for this book. Thanks for such good observations and for knowing the music so well!

For inviting me to speak about materials related to this book, I'm grateful to Patricia Ahearne-Kroll of Ohio Wesleyan University, Yaakov Ariel at the University of North Carolina at Chapel Hill, Isaac-Davy Aronson of WUNC's *The State of Things*, Brandi Denison and her fabulous colleagues at the University of North Florida, Paul Harvey at the University of Colorado Colorado Springs, and Bart Scott and Jenna Supp-Montgomerie of the American Academy of Religion's Religion and Media seminar. Thanks also to The Immanent Frame for giving me space to workshop some of these ideas.

I've been humbled by the generous thinking and criticism of my friends in religious studies over the last decade as I've slowly assembled this book. These folks may or may not remember how they've influenced the course of my thinking, but I've benefited from my conversations with Andrew Agapour, James Bagwell, Jessica Baldanzi, Courtney Bender, Ann Burlein, Julie Byrne, Chip Callahan, Yvonne Chireau, David Cline, Finbarr Curtis, Curtis Evans, Megan Goodwin, Shane Graham, Rosalind Hackett, Mary Hamner, Titus Hjelm, Stewart Hoover, Steve Hopkins, the inestimable Jeff Isaac, Michael Jackson, Richard Jaffe, Greg Johnson, Sylvester Johnson, Elaine Maisner, Setrag Manoukian, Colleen McDannell, Rich Miller, Kristy Nabhan-Warren, Todd Ochoa, Sally Promey, Mary-Jane Rubinstein, Chad Seales, Lisa Sideris, Tony Stewart, Randall Styers, Winni Sullivan, Ann Taves, Leif Tornquist, Ted Trost, Tom Tweed, Jonathan Van Antwerpen, Grant Wacker, David Watt, Mary Jo Weaver, and Isaac Weiner. In the world of jazz studies, I deeply appreciate the enthusiasm of John Corbett, Ajay Heble, Robin D. G. Kelley, and Ron Radano.

Most of all, this work was lucky enough to receive the consistent engagement, cheerleading, and careful reading of the most bad-ass group of scholars I know: Tariq al-Jamil, Ed Blum, Tracy Fessenden, Paul Harvey (twice!), Jeff Kasser, Katie Lofton, Laurie Maffly-Kipp, Sean McCloud, John Modern, David Morgan, and Sarah Pike. Your friendship means most of all to me, but you have my deepest thanks for all that you have done to help spirits rejoice. In his own category is Robert Orsi, who has championed this book and urged me to write it for as long as anyone I know. Into our third decade of friendship now, the depth, range, and warmth of our conversations abide despite all other changes.

Lastly, friends and family have not just supported my scholarship but have shared my love for the music. James Bell, Ted Leventhal, and Hans Indigo Spencer go back just about as long as I can remember, and the thought of you still makes me smile. Doug Padgett and Marcia Massey still bring the wellness. And here in Bull City we've got a lively, sassy posse but special thanks go to Michael Schaumann and Abbie Schmidt.

Things were tough in the family these last few years, as we suffered the illness and loss of my beloved stepfather, Peter Noerr. Peter did as much as anyone in this life to encourage the work I do, talk with me about it, challenge me, and share my enthusiasms. I miss him, and my late father, Royal G. Bivins, more than I can say; but I'm lucky at least to have had them both. My mother, Kate Noerr, has been unflagging in her strength, wisdom, good humor, and support, and Mom's lifelong passion for music has been an additional boon as I've bounced these ideas around. My terrific sister, Kristina, and brother-in-law, Jeff Hammond, continue to be there and keep it real with good humor, reality checks, and hospitality. Thanks, too, to my wonderful Uncle Lu and Aunt Lorraine and to their daughters, my amazing cousins Nora and Retta, and their rocking husbands, Harvey and Steve. My aunt Sarah Burns and uncle Dennis Gannon are blissfully retired academics whose insight, understanding, fierce support, and righteous good humor are seriously treasured here.

Nina B, once again I do not know how words can suffice to say how you have sustained me and made everything worthwhile. And so very joyful. Over the years, the threads between us intertwine more tightly and I am so lucky to be held in that embrace. Last time out, I sang your praises with a Duke reference. You remain beyond category, but I admit I'm fond of the canon we've been composing together. The future may not deliver on its promise of floating cars or food from a wall, but as long as you're in it (and of course the chows), we can paint the brashest brushstrokes and win all the races together. I la-la-love you.

And one last thing, dear reader. This book is meant to be accompanied by its sounds, so I have prepared for you a chapter-by-chapter playlist here: http://spiritsrejoice.wordpress.com. I hope you listen to and love the music.

Spirits Rejoice!

PART I

I

First Meditations[1]

> *You blows who you is.*
>
> —LOUIS ARMSTRONG

> *I always speak the truth. Not the whole truth, because there's no way to say it all. Saying it all is materially impossible: words fail.*
>
> —JACQUES LACAN, *Television**

Jazz Death

On an early Art Ensemble of Chicago recording, trumpeter Lester Bowie recorded a piece called "Jazz Death." In the self-consciously satirical style for which the group was known, Bowie interviewed himself. Posing as an aloof jazz journalist, Dave Flexingbergstein from *Jism Magazine*, Bowie asked himself "Is jazz as we know it dead yet?" Bowie responded by playing a solo trumpet piece, a rarity in the late 1960s. Brash, splattery, and cranky, his muffled eructations and chortles in the bell of the horn sounded initially worlds away from what most associate with the contentious category "jazz"; and yet its clarion tones and bright phraseology sounded continuous with the exuberance of early Louis Armstrong, even as Bowie peppered such familiar statements with hushed and almost insectoid perambulations that sounded out other worlds beyond our listening limits. He concluded by saying snidely to Flexingbergstein, "Well, I guess that all depends on what you know."

If we take the challenge of "Jazz Death" as a starting point—and it is worth considering how many of jazz's innovations have occurred amid

---

*Jacques Lacan, *Television* (New York: Norton, 1990), 3.

proclamations of its death—what might we *know* about the convergence between the stories of jazz and those of American religions? What can this mostly wordless music, often scornful of reference and criticism, tell us or offer up to "know"? Would things look and sound differently if we turned from Bowie to other figures? What would we see and hear from them?

In late 1980s Manhattan, you might see a middle-aged African American male, recently homeless. Dressed with a bowler hat, clown makeup, and a plastic nose, he warned listeners that worshiping Christ demanded op- posing abortion and homosexuality. Charles Gayle is a saxophonist whose yawps and fierce innovations in the altissimo register seem to match the intensity of his convictions. Few knew that this apparent eccentric stood not just on a random Manhattan corner but in a long tradition of impro- vised music and religions. At Wesleyan University, you might see Anthony Braxton shuffling between classes. His unkempt natural, specs, and frumpy cardigan signify professorially, but the saxophonist/composer has written pieces for orchestras on separate planets as part of his system of musical metaphysics exploring what he calls the ritual and ceremonial logics of "post-Ayler" music. In post-Vietnam South Central Los Angeles, you might see Horace Tapscott teaching piano to neighborhood kids. More than just a charismatic local teacher, Tapscott also founded the Union of God's Musicians in Artists Ascension, fusing jazz, community- building, and religious imaginings of African culture.

And beyond such sights dwell the sounds. Multi-instrumentalist Eric Dolphy once addressed the interpretive challenges of sound, perception, and memory more effectively than most critics could ever dream. At the end of a European concert performance (just days before he died of com- plications from diabetes), Dolphy leaned into the microphone and said, "When you hear music, after it's over, it's gone, in the air; you can never capture it again." Dolphy's words raise provocative questions about the transience of improvised music, a quality regularly ascribed to "jazz" as religious. Could the very abstraction of the music, its elusiveness in terms both commercial and aesthetic, be conducive to the sorts of self-realization, collective purpose, or sense of being-in-the-world linked with religions?

These are the sounds on the air that I attempt to transcribe. Others have proposed models for hearing the "meanings" of contemporary musics. Paul Gilroy has written vividly about the role of the expressive arts in the construction of the "black modern," a changing transatlantic diasporic sen- sibility with important (and complex) sonic dimensions.[2] Ronald Radano has urged scholars to engage in what he calls "insurgent listening," a form of critical receptivity where we hear music—even if it contains no lyrics telling us what to hear—as an "evidentiary body" that reveals in part the makings of cultures.³ And George Lipsitz cocks his ear to the "hidden histories and long fetches" of American music, attending to the cultural locations of sonic creations.⁴ These orientations suggest that the rupturing and fragmentary qualities of sound complicate factors like secularity, the urban modern, and expressive culture.

But what specifically are the possibilities and the dangers of trying to "capture" the music by focusing on its (often-elusive or barely obvious) religiousness? While there is a long-standing contention among many players, producers, critics, and fans that these two terms—"jazz" and "religion"—are intimate, at times even coterminous, Bowie reminds us not to get too comfortable with what we "know" about such matters. From its very first notes, there has persisted throughout the history of this complicated and misunderstood music a belief that certain elements (structural, affective, communal) were either religious in nature or were particularly conducive to religious experience. While academics bristle at notions like "religious in nature," to performers this notion has helped articulate the belief that improvised music is distinct and authentic, a sound that cannot be captured by the market or undermined by racial misrepresentation. Indeed, this concern for authenticity—so indelibly a part of American desires for self-fashioning from the Transcendentalists to the New Left of the 1960s, among many others—is paramount to the musical articulations of religion throughout this book. Significantly, the religiosity of jazz is understood as the register of its transcendence of constraints. Even as the music is surely conditioned, many musicians have held the belief that through the open work of improvisation one can cut through the layers of artifice to encounter some kind of musical enlightenment or becoming. How, then, to carve this formless block?

Sounds Religious

Ludwig Wittgenstein once wrote, "Since everything lies open to view, there is nothing to explain."⁵ Yet with only sound to follow through these stories, we find ourselves in a foggy atmosphere of mystery and uncertainty. There is everything to explain. How do we know what to listen or look for? How do we know sounds are religious? How do we think about and analyze what we choose to focus on? Scholars of religion have started attending more rigorously to the centrality of the senses to religious experience. Rather than simply attending to "the body," attention is now being paid specifically to specific registers like sound and vision.[6] And so religious studies has become more attentive to the role of sound and music in religious worlds: practitioners who hear the voice of divine beings or who make music central to ritual. Scholarly engagements with these expressions have focused often on either "religious music" (i.e., specific song forms belonging to established traditions) or representations of religion in various musical genres (with a consequent focus on lyrical content).

These focuses, however, contain often unacknowledged limits and blindnesses. Stephen Marini notes the "vital functions" of hymns as "a primary vehicle of the numinous": "[s]inging, hearing, or praying upon hymn texts frequently mediated" religious experience.[7] "Sacred music" is posited as "an interpretive lens" (a notably ocular metaphor) through which to understand religions.[8] Philip Bohlman writes that music "*encodes the sacred language* and therefore also contributes critically to the sociolinguistic basis of American religious experience."[9] The languages used to study religion and music are thus often textualist or functionalist in their orientation, noting that music is a "sacred medium" (but presumably not the sacred itself) used and/or experienced by practitioners, or that it is "expressive" of established virtues and norms, or evocative of Clifford Geertz's moods and motivations.[10]

These approaches seem to assume that we know what religion or the sacred is in the adjectival sense; that is, they assume that religious music is music that tells us it is religious by virtue of its texts or its settings. They seem to posit that religions can be included among R. Murray Schaeffer's "acoustic communities," and that music thus occurs *in* religion, that preposition doing considerable analytical work for the interpreter. Might we only pronounce blandly that music is a form of "meaning-making," thus assuming that what people want from their music, and their religion, is fixity and certitude rather than experiential indeterminacy or non-linguistic aesthesis? Sound travels, of course, beyond conceptual as well as physical boundaries; more suggestively, it is as absent as it is present, time-bound, and thus always evaporating from the moment of its articulation. And music is never only expressive of something else beyond itself; it always moves in other directions, on other scales, creating its own context of hearing.

There is no way of avoiding these traps in writing about the senses, perhaps especially non-referential sound. Recall the old canard that says writing about music is like dancing about architecture. Writing about religion and music seems doubly foolish, then, since scholars fret about the impossibility of defining religion. It is because of this very elusiveness that there is so often a privileging of the textual in defining religious music. But the study of religions is always an engagement with multiplicity: notoriously difficult to define, religions sit at the intersection of a wide range of human activities both imaginative and embodied. Their qualities are scrambled, and so we can only be alert to hybrid forms of religio-musical identity, practice, and experience that are written and improvised in the United States.

We look to recognizable institutional or ritual context, or language to contain this hybridity and ground our reckonings about sound. But knowing we often lack these frames, on what grounds might we posit that music is "religious" (keeping in mind Roland Barthes's caution against over-reliance on the adjective in interpreting music)?[11] Must a musician cry "Praise Jesus!" or *"om mani padme hum"* for us to be able to append to it the tricky adjective? Does a melody or chord sequence *sound* different if we can link it with religion via words or other markers of "tradition"? What, in fact, distinguishes religious from non religious music: setting, expectation, the emotional content we bring to it or that the music brings to us? Does something played on harpsichord suggest religion more than electric guitars, sweet melody more than dissonance, regardless of the intention of the musicians or the performance's proximity to a devotional setting?

These questions throw us back on our own processes of projection and fabrication as we attempt to hear what is going on. Crucial to this book's efforts at hearing "religion" and "jazz" together are music's known formal properties, its ascriptions to specific historical contexts, and documentation of its creators and performers' interests and aspirations. Yet even here it is not long until we encounter challenges to our efforts. Composer Edgard Varèse said that music was "organized sound."[12] Musicologist Robert Walser suggests that music "organize[s] the flow of experience."[13] Composer Morton Feldman once observed fascinatingly that "music might not even be an art-form," but instead "built upon primitive memory structures."[14] These formulations suggest that even identifying music's formal fundaments (rhythm, melody, and harmony) is inseparable from our own evaluations (with categories, appraisals, and emotional intensities). And since music is—like religions—situated in polyvalent human cultures of practice and embodiment, the attention to social setting and historical influence adds to the complexity of either crudely formal definitions or intentionally vaporous ones.

So while texts and events share a series of referents, sound and spirits both spill beyond whatever formulation we can momentarily give to them, carried away on the breath—the in-spiration—that creates and steals them both as soon as, as sure as they're born. Of course these observations might well apply to the very transience and incompleteness of language itself, which complicates my claims about music's non-textuality. Yet what I mean is that questions about religiosity cannot be settled only when there is language on which to hook the adjective. And while this poses an authorial challenge it might also be (as Mark Taylor has famously suggested) precisely where "religion" gets most interesting.[15] American religious music is as diversified and polyglot as American religion more broadly and extends far beyond textual settings into disparate domains of human experience, social interactions, performances, and symbolism, activities commonly ascribed to both music and religions. It is no mere accompaniment to the inwardness of meditation, theology, or prayer; nor can it be limited to the basically dialogic features David Stowe enumerates: "a means of communication with the divine; a mechanism for expressing praise and thanksgiving, for petitioning for mercy, protection, and power."[16] It always includes more, from the embodied modes of ritual, communion, celebration, and protest to practices and sensibilities that (like many of the performances discussed below) keep slipping from our grasp into a hazy atmosphere.

This book presumes, then, that there are expressions and experiences in American religion whose musicality both can and cannot be transcribed. And both the transcriptions and their cannot-ness form suggestive, identifiable presences on the American religious landscape. Seeking to give shape to the co-emergence in sound of jazz and religion, I take it as axiomatic that these frustrations and vexatious questions cannot be avoided. Best, then, to embrace them as part of the process of exploration, since they are also integral to the experiences of the music itself, and to how many practitioners describe their religious experience. In this I am at least partly following Jonathan Z. Smith's attempt to imagine "religion" by seeking out its less obvious expressions, locating those sounds and spaces that do not necessarily announce themselves as "sacred" but that still provide occasion for thinking about senses, spaces, and gods.[17] And as I show below, there is a history and a sociology clearly emerging from these considerations, ones that prompt new questions about American religion and how to study it. Underlying the testimonies of the musicians and the evidence of their practice (communities, performances, compositions), there is an overarching concern with perception, performance, experience, and identity, often construed religiously. This is not to say that all jazz musicians have been preoccupied with religiosity, or that every performance of

"Nardis" has sacred significance. But since Ralph Ellison wrote that much of American life is "jazz-shaped," I write of what we might learn by listening for the religious in this formulation.[18]

"A Dirty Word"

What, though, does it mean to be jazz-shaped? And what *is* jazz? To reckon with jazz in American culture is to reckon with a music whose popularity and role in the American imagination have changed radically in its first century-plus: from the street social music of its New Orleans birth (or rather, the intertwining of extant traditions that ultimately came to be called "jass") to the popular music of the swing era, and from there on to bebop, free jazz, and subsequent developments. It surfaces every so often in public media, focused on well-heeled musicians marketed for official recognition of what Dr. Billy Taylor called "America's classical music" (and which bassist Alan Silva once described to me, while wearing a wizard's hat and robe, as "America's national treasure").[19] First Lady Michelle Obama recently praised jazz as "America's indigenous art form," using the shop-worn observation "there's probably no better example of democracy than a jazz ensemble: individual freedom, but with responsibility to the group."[20] Critic Stanley Crouch believes jazz is "perfect for America because...it's about democratic means being used to arrive at utopian ends."[21]

Despite such lofty associations, there is little basic familiarity with the music. One encounters often an academic tendency to compare things that are vaguely fluid and improvisatory to jazz.[22] On the one hand, this may have all the force of saying that water is wet. But it also says little about jazz, since improvisation is common to nearly every musical genre imaginable, from Carnatic music to bluegrass to noise (it is also widely known that composers like Bach and Mozart were renowned improvisers).[23] Even acknowledgments of jazz's specificity can do little more than gesture, since "jazz" may differ audibly and historically from other idioms even as it resists being fixed or known too easily. Does jazz sound like the joyous diatonic song of Louis Armstrong's Hot Fives, the elegant section work of an Ellington ensemble, the angular harmony of bop, or the "love cry" of Albert Ayler? Is it the sound of a Harmon mute on a trumpet, the crack of a Roy Haynes rimshot, of a walking bassline?

The music's very history ducks the question. Indeed, some of jazz's most well-regarded innovators—those who would be included in any canon, of which there are many—despised the word *jazz* itself, sometimes referring instead to "creative improvised music," "our music," or simply "the music." Duke Ellington insisted on avoiding the term "jazz," famously saying that there are only two kinds of music, good and bad. He heard music as "beyond category," noting that "to have a category, one must build a wall" and that a category "is a Grand Canyon of echoes. Somebody utters an obscenity and you hear it keep bouncing back a million times."[24] Pianist Thelonious Sphere Monk said of jazz: "It's about Freedom, more than that is complicated."[25] Guitarist Pete Cosey responded to questions about whether Miles Davis's electric bands of the early 1970s played jazz by insisting, "[D]on't say that, that's a dirty word."[26]

From its inception, jazz was thought by both detractors and advocates to represent a modern, urban, secular America.[27] Critics feared its libidinous urgings and heard in its propulsive swagger the sacred's absence. Supporters championed it as art music, the very sound of progress and sophistication. Yet aside from these and other debates discussed below, what we hear in jazz from its contested beginnings to its multiform present is the abundance of the religious, even—or especially—when this category is difficult to locate and pin down. Blendings of the musicological, the anthropological, and the moral often characterized the alarmed reactions to jazz's emergence, many of which sought to serve as definitions in their own way. Famed revivalist Billy Sunday, the popular advocate of Muscular Christianity, judged with characteristic bluntness that jazz was simply "bunk."[28] Daniel Gregory Mason called jazz a "sick moment in the progress of the human soul."[29] Early critics found jazz to be musically "objectionable" because there was too much "ad libbing," its formal freedoms portending social chaos and threats to musical respectability (and all that it stood for).[30] Others objected on political grounds to "this Bolshevistic smashing of the rules and tenets of decorous music, this excessive freedom of interpretation."[31] Some feared, tellingly, that "jazz could have degenerative effects on the human psyche" or that it might popularize interracial sex (even African Americans occasionally expressed such nervousness, with one journalist wondering in print if jazz might not be a stealth weapon of the Ku Klux Klan).[32]

Jazz was scorned as "barbaric, sensuous, jungle music which assaulted the senses and sensibilities, diluted reason, led to the abandonment of decency and decorum, undermined dignity, and destroyed order and self-control."[33] While it was embraced by marginal figures for these very reasons, jazz's innovations more commonly induced cautions. Varèse announced that jazz was "a negro product, exploited by the Jews."[34] The National Socialist Party of Germany dismissed jazz as the deviant, decadent product of American cultural miscegenation, while critic Theodor Adorno worried that jazz was a low art product of the culture industry, whose "veneer" and "rhetoric of liberation" actually masked its deep conservatism.[35] But most American audiences and observers were less concerned with sociopolitical implications than with the music's alleged libidinousness. Walter Kingsley wrote in the *New York Sun*—echoing the music's early syntactic associations, for example, "jaz her up" or "put in jaz"—that "[j]azz music is the delirium tremens of syncopation."[36] The *New Orleans Times-Picayune* contrasted the rhythmic urges of jazz with the "inner court of harmony" where true music lives (so much for Art Tatum!).[37] Jazz may have been associated with the modern (which brought together seductions and revulsions of its own, including the possibility that jazz was the soundtrack of a permissive secularism), but it was also heard as atavistic and brutish. Anne Shaw Faulkner warned that jazz "might invoke savage instincts."[38] To justify such alarmism, Faulkner insisted that jazz "originally was the accompaniment of the voodoo dancer, stimulating the half-crazed barbarian to the vilest deeds."[39] These formulations of authentic music through the dynamics of wildness and control resemble obviously long-standing characterizations and denunciations of African American religion (or indeed of enthusiastic religion, broadly speaking) as too sweaty, emotional, and erotic.[40] They constitute a field of representational and material constraint that Braxton has called "the reality of the sweating brow," a term I use throughout this book to invoke such religio-racial expectations, and which I theorize explicitly in the conclusion.

This was a music that seemed to spill beyond limits—moral, cultural, musical—and to many demanded a vigorous reassertion of those same norms. Big-band music, while it is now often remembered for its art music aspirations, often had a lower-class or lower-middle-class appeal, and African American churches in particular railed against it, frequently trading in typical "devil's music" discourse. As Ellison recalled, "[J]azz was regarded by most of the respectable Negroes of the town as a backward, low-class form of expression."[41] Fats Waller's father was a pastor at Abyssinian Baptist Church, and as a child "[m]usic and religion became the keystones of Waller's life."[42] But in response to his growing love for rag and jazz, his father told him that such music was "the devil's workshop."[43] Though "jazz" has been subject to manifold misrepresentations that have obscured its musical values and complex cultural sources, its very multiplicity and instability have enabled its creative associations with religiosity beyond these early critiques.

In this, the music simply drew from different religious traditions. Especially following the Great Migration, churches emphasized freedom and solidarity as possibilities to be (partly) achieved through creativity. Jerome Cooper called the connection between the sacred and the creative "the natural law of an artist."[44] Drummer Rashied Ali said "the musician is a kind of preacher."[45] And even Miles Davis, the glowering trumpeter often called the Prince of Darkness or the Dark Magus, recalled the lasting influence of "that blues, church, back-road funk kind of thing, that southern, midwestern, rural sound and rhythm ... [that] started getting into my blood on them spook-filled Arkansas backroads after dark when the owls came out hooting."[46]

Fans and critics regularly asserted the unity of religion and African American music. The 1958 debut issue of *The Jazz Review* published without complication the following statement: "The influence of the Negro church on traditional jazz is obvious in the very sound of the music.... To study the history of jazz is to take the church background for granted."[47] In part this reveals how consistently African American music and religious idioms merged in the urban North as in the South. As Guthrie Ramsey notes, gospel and blues were not relegated simply to church or country settings; from the storefront churches in Harlem and elsewhere issued "weird sounds" that, while often variants of sanctified gospel, were ascribed to "jazz."[48] Even the innovations of the big bands and bebop drew from earlier musical forms that were remade in Depression-era and postwar urban America.[49]

So even the most cursory history of "jazz" reveals its complex entanglements with "religion." The term itself was always contested, always considered deceptive in what it was alleged to reveal about black religion and culture. Yet in the thick of these squabbles over representational politics, jazz also made way for and often nurtured not just anti-essentialist strategies that can be linked to trickster tales and strategic signifying but essentialisms of its own devising that served the needs of musicians and advocates. These features, along with more detailed developmental accounts of the music, emerge more fully in this book's investigation of particular articulations of what I call "spirits rejoicing."

Listen with All Your Might![50]

But if "jazz" disrupts stable identities, spills over its own limits, and generally evades definition in ways suggestively similar to the tricky category "religion," why has so little been written on their collaboration? Think of it like this: if you heard only four bars of John Coltrane's *A Love Supreme*, would you be satisfied, not having heard the whole? Or if you caught only the tail end of a Cecil Taylor solo performance, could you speak confidently about its shape and development? Cultural historians of religion and of music have mostly failed to listen to the whole performance of religions and jazz mutually defining each other over the course of a swinging century. The more you listen, the more clearly do the two articulate in harmony, together forming a powerful interval, and the more suggestively do they intertwine throughout American history (and possibly beyond), playing in cultural space like a polyrhythm.

Much of this lack can be attributed to three assumptions, from roughly different authorial crowds. First is a tendency among many non-academics to dismiss religiosity as either pabulum or inessential to the music (those modernist bifurcations shaping the way other selves and sounds are understood). Second is the relatively undercooked attention to "spirituality" in many otherwise excellent works in jazz studies. Third is a limited approach to what counts as religious, or religiously significant, even by those who acknowledge the importance of the subject; religion, then, fades into the background as only a scant detail. Even notable exceptions like Stowe's *How Sweet the Sound* or Eric Porter's *What Is This Thing Called Jazz?* tend to examine select high-profile individuals like Duke Ellington, John Coltrane, and Sun Ra rather than engaging in sustained, comparative analysis.[51] Fine book-length studies on Mary Lou Williams, John and Alice Coltrane, Duke Ellington, and Thelonious Monk have been published in the last decade and contain valuable information on their own individual religious practice.[52] Others, like Samuel Floyd, Albert Murray, and David Rosenthal, have written cogently about the influence of gospel on jazz musicians, extending the argument that the "black church" shapes vernacular musics.[53] Robin Sylvan has written about representations of the "sacred" in popular music.[54] And Neil Leonard once wrote a problematic book on jazz as an object of religious devotion itself, focused on the perception of jazz as spiritual in a "more functional than metaphysical" fashion.[55] Leonard's focus on jazz's "rituals and myths" or its "prophetic" figures is analytically quite flabby, akin to dull observations that the Constitution is "America's sacred text" or that any adored entertainer is ipso facto an object of "religious" veneration.

An otherwise admirable work, Ingrid Monson and Eric Porter come close to conflating terms like "personal growth," "utopian possibilities," or "emancipatory function" with "spiritual."[56] Many jazz scholars who note the importance of religiosity beyond individual stories—or, occasionally, the role of traditions like Islam—often conclude that an uptick of "spirituality" occurred alongside the civil rights movement of the 1950s and 1960s. As above, it is not that these observations are wrong-headed or poorly substantiated. In fact, they are quite important and have a place in this book. But not only are they incomplete, is there nothing more to jazz and religion than jazz that tells us in the most direct words possible that it is in fact religious? *Pace* Scott Saul, jazz did not just start "going to church" in the 1950s and consequently become "more intense."[57] Both the formal and the ephemeral dimensions of religiosity have been abundantly present in jazz since long before the word *jazz* was popularized. While the music changed in the 1950s, it is mostly unrelated to the evidence Saul cites: the "holy roller" influence in Mingus records, the activist tunes of Max Roach, or the pervading influence of African retentions or church music.

I bring up these limits not as a preface to some academic cutting contest, that dull ritual. But in looking beyond these orientations, and beyond narrow definitions of religiosity coming from outside musical communities and practitioners, we find provocative evidence of a broader history of religio-musical exploration central to jazz. Listen, then, beyond "religious music" or the breadcrumb trail of lyrics and keep jazz in earshot as a way of thinking about, listening to, and experiencing American religions freshly. In telling these sound stories, it is important not simply to describe the sonic accompaniments to important known events—the dog-barking at Cane Ridge, the glossolalia at Azusa Street, the outraged shouts at a protest—but to think carefully about how this music, whose resistance to language is integral to its religiosities, has also constituted a powerful, if elusive, form of American religious experience itself.

Amiri Baraka once wrote, "The notes mean something."[58] Where and how do we locate jazz in the multiple narratives of American religion, and what does jazz reveal about them? Can we talk meaningfully about the development of "jazz" (however understood) without engaging its religiosities? I think the answer is no. Jazz history is woefully understood without making central the role of religion therein, with all of that lone category's deceptiveness very much in mind. At the very least, we miss a great deal of what is meaningful about jazz to its players. Can we talk in fresh ways about American religious history by attending to jazz's sonorities therein? I think the answer is yes. My suggestion is not that it is no longer possible to understand the religions of the United States since

1900 without making central this music. But careful listening to jazz—attentive to the slipperiness of jazz history and canon—enables us to hear fresh things about and among these religions, scrambling familiar notions suggestively. To focus on traditions and individuals is an obviously limited way of conceptualizing the religious and, significantly, an orientation whose limits are explicitly rejected by a considerable number of musicians themselves.[59] Even to go further and focus on linguistic references to religion, or performance in recognizable religious housings, seems to overlook an important range of localisms and particulars that can be sounded out beyond the obvious. So beyond the words the musicians and audiences and critics have pinned to the music, what can be said about histories, communities, rituals, relations with spirits and gods, presence, and cosmologies? These themes are central to the study of (American) religions and are heard consistently in jazz. So below, I look not to a particular religious culture with jazz as my guide; to posit that jazz facilitates religion or vice versa, each the medium of the other's essence, would hold them separate in ways that the characters in this story flatly reject. Rather, I cull from jazz a neglected component of its own narratives and also use jazz to amplify our understanding of religion and music, of subcultural expressions of religion, and of "religion" as a category.

The Chart

Throughout this book, I often use the gerund "spirits rejoicing" as a synonym for "religion" or "spirituality." It signifies the musicians' own understandings "beyond category," and also signals my intention to avoid a number of conventional writing pathways. As noted above, the orientations familiar to the study of religion (church attendance, religious functions, or text adaptations) are useful and interesting ones. But in this project I seek to go beyond them, not simply because of authorial taste but in the name of a more comprehensive understanding of spirits rejoicing. Much writing about jazz has tended to take the form of glorified record reviews or discographies; has focused imperfectly on the sounds themselves, either through impressionistic descriptions or dense musicological analyses; or has written its way out of the challenges by muffling the music to some extent, writing it into institutions or texts that are easier to describe, or reducing it to semiotics. I also avoid constructing a standard chronology (which would risk tying religiosity too closely to specific musical developments, for example, the religion of the bebop era) or focusing exclusively on "exemplary" individuals (which would undermine the comparative resonance of the themes so evident in the music).

My explorations will, instead, improvise on the standard questions and stories that might be told. *Spirits Rejoice!* explores a series of themes, pursuits, reoccurring focuses, and interpretations harvested from the religious and cultural history of American jazz. These themes emerge not just in the musicians' own words (in interviews, liner notes, or journals) but also from the bandstand, audience reception, and critical interrogation. Because this book cannot be encyclopedic, it focuses almost entirely on the musicians (though I regularly contextualize the music's reception by audiences and critics, as with Duke Ellington's heavily debated "Sacred Concerts" or John Coltrane's departure from conventional song-form). Because this is a history mostly untold, my focus is on preserving the musicians' words, stories, and self-understandings as a kind of archive of their religiosities. While I attend consistently to the sound and performance of jazz, and the ubiquity of embodiment to these creations (what is jazz, after all, without the physical disciplines of improvisation?), I seek the words and their resonance within the narrative of themes investigated. In chapter 2, I explore jazz's relation to specific religious traditions as groundings for musical creativity, while also complicating the notion of what constitutes a tradition. Chapter 3 examines how jazz has chronicled American history and religion in musical settings. Chapter 4 surveys jazz communitarianism, exploring the institutionalization of religio-musical practice. Chapter 5 teases out notions of jazz as a practice of ritual or healing. Chapter 6 limns the sound of absence, discussing jazz notions of mysticism, egolessness, and sonic vessels for the divine. Chapter 7 ranges across jazz cosmologies and metaphysics. I conclude by exploring how "the sound of spirits rejoicing" challenges not only prevailing understandings of race and music (framed substantially by the "reality of the sweating brow") but understandings of what we know about "religion" too. This structure moves from fairly obvious expressions of "religion" to less obvious ones, combining, trading off, improvising all the way.

Behind all these explorations is my claim that jazz makes sense in and also complicates known accounts of American religion, finding strangeness in the familiar and familiarity in the outside. *Spirits Rejoice!* adds a different resonance to American religious history since the 1920s. While we know what was happening religiously in 1930s New Orleans, in bebop's postwar Manhattan, and in the cities awakened by free jazz in the 1960s and 1970s, we have not yet adequately understood how jazz has not just been in conversation with religious developments in the United States, but shaped and drawn on them as more than simply their musical accompaniment. For example, jazz musicians participated in the religious exchanges and combinations that have proliferated in the United States since 1965, adopting Hindu gurus, pursuing jazz as an expression of Vajrayana Buddhism, or linking performance to the developmental schema of Scientology. By exploring what Ellison called the "lower frequencies" of American culture—populated by marginal creators, activists, provocateurs, and mischief-makers—we find that jazz registers in some unexpected but meaningful places in American religions. In many ways, *Spirits Rejoice!* accretes these themes as a way of proposing a framework for a cultural history of American religions told in the tones and tales of jazz. While the music itself has often lacked a sizable audience, in ways that directly shape the stories told in chapters to come, a central storyline in American religions and avowedly "secular" modernity has been the engaged, knowing determination of (mostly) African American musicians to trouble the certainties of their religious, musical, and indeed American inheritance. In each phase of jazz's development its innovators and institutions have been improvising with the central religious themes and practitioners of the time as well: Ellington's inundation with the religious creativity of the Harlem Renaissance, Art Blakey's participation in the post–World War II embrace of African American Islam, Horace Tapscott's role in the proliferation of intentional communities in the 1960s (and we will see how regularly it becomes apparent that the 1960s had multiple, particular implications for spirits rejoicing, as it did for American religion more broadly), and the reinvestigation of traditionalism so prominent in the 1980s.

So the stories of jazz are integral to the stories of American religions in the last century, even if I arrange them here in non-chronological fashion. *Spirits Rejoice!* generates overlapping narratives attentive to what Greil Marcus calls the "lipstick traces" connecting disparate phenomena: images, themes, and sounds that resonate multiply, opening beyond themselves to encompass others or be absorbed elsewhere. With each chapter (all titled after jazz records), I open with a sound and a personal reflection. This sound distills the chapter's theme, which captures something about American religion, which in turn articulates a theoretical or conceptual debate in the study of religion. These different elements relate to and play off of each other throughout the text, and, I hope, beyond, capturing what Ellison calls "the complex forces of American life which come to focus in jazz."[60]

I have been conducting research into this project since the mid-1990s.
Since that time I have also spent considerable time in two areas of activity
that benefit me in listening for the nuances in these expressions, knowing
what and whom to consult, and for drawing together themes and materials: I have been a recording and touring musician myself and have reviewed
jazz recordings for *Cadence, Signal to Noise, Dusted, Point of Departure,*
Bagatellen, One Final Note, Paris Transatlantic, and *Point of Departure.* Drawing
on my own experiences, performances, and conversations in music has
proven invaluable as this project has taken shape. In addition to a vast
number of personal conversations, many of which did not ultimately
make their way into the manuscript, and engagement with relevant scholarly literatures, this book is the product of a lengthy immersion in non-
scholarly writing about jazz, including conversations with fellow critics
and the archives of jazz periodicals, and in the music itself. I initially
imagined that the book would focus on how "religion" in jazz enables an
escape of predominantly racial misrepresentation. While this concern
resounds in each chapter, I now engage it explicitly in my conclusion, for
the more research I conducted and the further into jazz I got in my own
life, the more I began to sense the story was far larger: the themes and expressions of religiosity that have compelled jazz musicians are as broad as
those of American religion, and they continually surfaced organically during
my research. While other themes did not make it into this book—such as
religious migration, or jazz and religious protest—the criteria or assumptions shaping the chosen themes have been those of the study of religions.
In other words, I prioritize these themes and name them as religious both
because I recognize them as central concerns in the history of American
religions and also because, underlying the testimonies of musicians and
the evidence of their practice, we see these same religiously construed
concerns overarching.

In wondering how jazz might be heard in light of contemporary religious studies debates, and how "religion" might be understood when
bathed in such sounds, I mostly avoid musicology.[61] Rather, I study jazz in
much the same way as I do religion: as a form of human cultural communication that can be "heard" meaningfully within its contexts, histories,
and according to the self-understandings of those involved in the music.
From these considerations emerge a portrait of how jazz rejoices with
spirits. In addition to describing musicians according to their own self-
understandings, honesty demands I acknowledge my deception at the
outset: I use the word *jazz* in this book, even though many musicians reject

the term outright. To this I can say that one of my primary concerns with both *jazz* and *religion* is their limits, their inability to contain that which they hope to express. I also have taken pains to document and analyze this linguistic discontent as part of this twinned history. For this reason, I work with a fairly capacious understanding of "jazz" and hope that readers will imagine this term continually in scare-quotes throughout, seeing it as useful precisely because it confronts us with its own inadequacy.

In trying to capture a range of the music through my chosen themes, I delineate several portraits per chapter in order to evoke their resonance. Readers may be tempted to see an ideology of "jazz" at work in my musical selections. I include Thelonious Monk but not Frank Sinatra. I write about more avant-garde music than some other authors might (although if one stuck only to New Orleans and jazz funerals, very little would be learned about jazz and religion). And while I have tried to be similarly expansive with regard to jazz's long history, many of my cases populate the period between the 1960s and the present. This is the case for several reasons. In terms of periodization, there is quite simply more jazz being played by more musicians in more local scenes since the 1960s. Self-released recordings and DIY concerts have contributed to this numerical increase, as has the proliferation of jazz degree programs in American universities, and this self-cultivation has paralleled a similar turn in religious practices. For reasons that become clearer below, while many of the cases of "traditional" religious take shape in the 1940s and 1950s, the majority of practitioners contributing to improvisations on ritual, cosmology, and meditation have populated more recent decades (hence my more contemporary focus in these cases). And while some might balk at including Fred Ho, Cecil Taylor, and John Zorn in a book on "jazz," I not only include them in my own capacious sense of what the category makes possible (even in reacting against it) but also note how suggestive it is that the themes I treat herein come up more often among musicians slightly closer to the margins, aesthetically and financially. Here I stand with John Szwed, who argues that all of the expressions usually quarantined as "avant-garde" (away from jazz as museum object) are traditional, with stylistic connections to early jazz and historical gravitas alike.[62] That we cannot imagine, say, Ella Fitzgerald or Stan Getz writing cosmologies or performing musical ritual is a discredit to neither those musicians nor the frame. What is more, it seems mostly irrelevant that many musicians herein are often less popular than others, since much of the discovery that awaits below is akin to coming across a new archive of material or finding a previously unknown family of new religious movements (a resonance that also makes sense given jazz's increased economic and cultural marginality of late). Many of the cases I discuss could probably appear in chapters other than those in which I have placed them: I focus on Sun Ra's historical sensibility, for example, but in an earlier draft ensconced him (somewhat too obviously, I thought) in a chapter on cosmology. Duke Ellington and Dizzy Gillespie appear twice. Some who do not appear in this book might be excellent examples of themes I have chosen. And I have consciously written with breadth in mind, because I see this book as a start, an arrangement of materials that will prompt further investigations.

My understanding of "religion" is similarly capacious, one that musicians themselves often embrace, where the aesthetic experience of the Kantian sublime is understood to be as really religious as any confession or rite. Also of clear importance is the discursive and embodied production of "spirituality," as distinct from "religion," that these musicians pick up on and also shape. With roots in the nineteenth century, this distinction generally presumes that "religion" is social and institutionally organized, while "spirituality" is more diffuse, focused on contact with the divine, and forms of experimental and experiential practice.[63] But "religion" is also in some ways whatever musicians say it is, since it is from these avowals that emerge the lipstick traces, ephemera, and evocations reflecting on the category "religion" itself. In this archive, "evidence" and "demonstration" are not always reliable or meaningful guides, even if a reader craves an encounter with jazz's "sacred" beyond ascriptions and historical locations. Despite the striving of some phenomenologists, I regard it as analytically impossible to pinpoint where precisely "religious" moments are occurring in the performance or the reception of the music. But with the combinative modes of listening I practice in this book, combined with what the musicians say, we can pinpoint and analyze how musicians describe these experiences, what occasions them, and how the sound becomes different because of them. And if readers find musicians' discourse occasionally vague, or even banal, they will at least come away from this book with an understanding of how to contextualize what they are reacting to.

I am sounding out mutually echoing refrains, pointing to overlapping materials, interpolated themes, and shared longings. This is yet another reason why this book, while it examines dozens of individuals, looks away from jazz hagiography to a music taking shape in the thick of interactivity, local scenes, the economic realities of door gigs, the overarching canopy of racial prejudice, all of it as present in notes played as in pieties cultivated. Insisting that these mutual resonances should be heard, as they help us think of and hear American religion in fresh ways, is not to suggest that obscure players like Roy Campbell are as influential as, say, Billy Graham or Bronson Alcott. Rather, looking at the complex floriculture of this music reveals that its sounds, creators, concerns, and communities capture and participate in and play back to some of the most central and engaging concerns of American religions. We hear jazz's historical suites in the tradition of Jacob Oson and W. E. B. DuBois; we observe in ritualized jazz the outer reaches of a broader American experimentation with ritual and sound; we trace the sidereal ruminations of jazz's visionaries to a pantheon of seers including not just Blavatsky and Swedenborg but Plotinus and Ficino; in each case, by exploring the music's recurring concerns, we learn about the new shapes of abiding religious impulses and about the multiple resonances of the music. So as we begin to explore these territories and expressions we see that to understand them we must take up central methodological debates in religious studies about the emotions and the senses, about ritual bodies, and about the shapes of communities and resistance. And to understand the range of these religious practices and concerns, we must learn from jazz studies the ways of listening to and contextualizing with nuance the sounds bearing the weight of these histories and aspirations. *Spirits Rejoice!* is, I hope, no simple gloss on these debates, but a way both to complicate them and to wring from them new possibilities. Its subject reveals a powerful surplus at work in standard narratives of jazz and of American religious music. In so doing, it doesn't show up a fault so much as point beyond moribund analytic categories to a field and a subject that can be as lively and as urgent as Paul Gonsalves at Newport or Albert Ayler at the Village Vanguard.

A Mind of Music

Religion is not always where we think to look; it moves between and beyond those spaces. No matter how often we students of religion remind ourselves of this multiplicity and unpredictability, there is always our knowledge of our own limits in the face of what Robert Orsi writes about as the abundant "more," that surplus flowing beyond the format of academic writing, eluding our categorization.[64] This ineluctability of language's limits is not just a background condition or a grounding we've failed to notice. Rather, however far we have traveled, we are aware that the cosmos still expands; and no matter how often we seek to look with fresh eyes upon the familiar, we know our vision is blinkered.[65]

It is partly in recognition of this unnamed surplus of energies that I explore the soundings of jazz and religion. Just as jazz's pathways to unknown worlds make it so vital, so too is the study of religion most lively and creative not simply when it highlights things protean and improvisatory but when it looks into spaces of real discomfort or where our formulations fall flat. While some of these ephemeralities may be those of music generally, what compels about jazz is precisely its historically identifiable resistance (through improvisation, through its religiosities) to closure as *part* of its pursuit of the sacred. This quality reaches beyond jazz's identifiable sonic and cultural markers (swing or running the changes), and those of religion (pluralism, bodies, or doxology, for example). The gap between these qualities thus underscores how discourse about "jazz" is, to paraphrase Ann Taves, similar to discourse about "religion": rather than relying on a reflective epistemology, or having confidence in ostensive reference to a definable reality "outside" language, each term achieves its reality through the attributions given to it.[66]

So this very fleetingness calls into question what we believe is true of "religion" and "jazz." As Ronald Radano writes of sound and history, this exemplifies Zora Neale Hurston's observation that in order to make a story good one must "lie it up" a bit. This does not entail purveying mistruths but instead calls attention to the inevitable role of fabrication in writing, where descriptions and interpretive frames are constructed through deliberate embellishments, omissions, and stylistic sizzle. Because writing can never be "true" in the colloquial sense—never fully mapping onto what we imagine is "out there" independent of language—the very idea of truths, essences, or stabilities emerges as a "lie" more recognizable than those of style and story. The very categories we trade in—"religion," "jazz"—are useful, pointing to things or practices we might reasonably understand to be "real" or "true." But while they facilitate recognition and comparison, they also frustrate and vex language, their connection to the object obscured in a fog of nuance and complication. When words reveal their limits—in their circumstances, usage, or disciplinary convention—we struggle for metaphor and grasp after "lies." The "lies" in *Spirits Rejoice!* are faithful to complexity and contradiction (whereas "truth" is singular and therefore not true).[67]

Clearly, there is semiotic instability at work here, in the spaces stretching open between order and chaos, form and improvisation, self and other, place and movement. Names and categories do not settle in one place, are not waiting to escape a lone pair of lips; they are exchanged like a drummer and the band trading fours, and they are always disappearing into Dolphy's air. So, too, does identity recede when realized in sound, in the intentionality of improvisation, in the rejoicing of musical spirits. This study follows these fluid traces beyond familiar categories and formations, listening for their echo in the experiential, expressive abundance in American religions, and in the truths and lies of religious studies. I also listen to jazz in its cultural and religious contexts, as I do to music in its religious and historical settings. But I have learned that it is also in these locations that the unseen and unheard manifest regularly.

Because religion is always somewhere else, perhaps never more so than when we look to pin it down with a definable hook or explanatory theory—just like sound is always surplus, circling the line on the page—this investigation is also a provocation to the ways we study religions. This is not meant simply to signify in familiar rhetorical terms—to rely, as too many humanities monographs still do, on the rhetorics of challenges, contestations, overturnings, and a championing of things marginal, that mundane catechism described as daring—but to suggest that because "religion" spills so copiously beyond whatever limits are placed on the category, it may also effectively constitute very little as an interpretative category. There is no writing about religion that does not ultimately turn back on itself; its constitutive terms, however these are enumerated, beg questions about criteria of selection, evidentiary substance, and especially distinctiveness with regard to other qualities of human experience. Our theorizations are always layered with inventions in scholarly desire or provocation. One hopes that openness and attention to the constructedness of our thinking also says something about the human creativity we aim to describe with it. I have learned that this conceptual tangle also captures how, for the musicians herein, the cultivation of "spirituality" or "religion" is indissolubly a manifestation or a pursuit of aesthetic experience as well. Through and in jazz, we see how "religion" as both a category and experience—its very fleetingness always trailing off like its own coda—renders any distinction between "spiritual," "secular," and "aesthetic" fuzzy.

Note, though, that these disciplinary, terminological limits can be strangely edifying rather than limiting; frank recognition of "religion's" limits opens us up to the playful imagination of religions by examining humans and their activities in improvisatory ways. Wallace Stevens wrote, "One must have a mind of winter/ To regard the frost and the boughs/ Of the pine-trees crusted with snow."[68] Perhaps, thinking along with Stevens's reckoning with the limits of language and "the nothing that is," we must have a mind of devotions when listening to jazz, an ear for the changes when listening to American religions. In this spirit I approach the multitudes of jazz and religions in the United States in the hope of locating "data"—sounds, bodies, feelings, and more—that facilitate new imaginings in and of religion. By relating responsively and responsibly to these creations, and imagining that they are "religious," we might provoke new sonic relations to the religions of the United States and also think freshly out what spirits make jazz rejoice. So this topic enables us first to situate familiar narratives in new settings, like a fresh arrangement of a standard that makes you hear the melody anew or reveals a hitherto buried harmony. But it also keeps in mind what composer and theorist George Russell said was the purpose of all art, and certainly jazz: to fuck you up.[69]

These evanescent experiences, like that whisper in Elijah's ear, occur far more frequently in jazz than the flag-wavers that tell you they are religious. How do they get institutionalized and memorialized, given a language, given a lie, since religion is "about what is always slipping away"?[70] If this seems an impossibility in these first meditations, know that the receding of one set of meanings allows others to be heard. As we try to think about and give shape to the relation between "jazz" and "religion," those impossibilities floating away like a note on the wind, we are perhaps confronted more emphatically by the protagonist of Ralph Ellison's *The Invisible Man*, who said of his own musical tastes, "Perhaps I like Louis Armstrong because he's made poetry out of being invisible."[71]

How does jazz make religion both invisible and visible, silent and heard? We could do far worse than turn here to Duke Ellington, whose melodies and chords made audible what had been muffled in African American life. "Hear that chord!" he once instructed, not requested. Directing a listener's ear to the colors of one of his own pieces, the composer continued, "That's the Negro's life.... That's us. Dissonance is our way of life in America. We are something apart, yet an integral part."[72] And yet these articulations were nothing as simple as the self's triumphal realization in American possibility, no easy ascent of "the sacred" from historical struggle. This was also about maintaining identity as "something apart," evading easy resolution in the major chord of the listener who really did not want to understand too much of struggle, of manyness and fluidity. Ellington, for all his accomplishments and celebration, knew this well. Note one anecdote buried in a 1944 *New Yorker* profile, in which Ellington masterfully deflected an Icelandic student's questions about mastery, composition, and art music by "unwrapping a pork chop that he has stowed in his pocket."[73]

The blended elements of spirits rejoicing confound, like the pork-stuffed pocket. And yet they are just life, the long haul of chasing and channeling sound in, through, and as religion. And moment by moment we play, think, and say this surplus, always crafting a relation with history, community, and those absent-present spirits themselves. To musicians, these are no mere associations or post hoc descriptors given to their output; they are substantive, even constitutive dimensions of the music. And that the music lacks a stable referent, that it is in many ways empty of conventional signification of the sort one expects (craves) with so ephemeral a subject as "religion," is partly the point. Benny Powell said of the substance of spiritual music that "some things can't be explained... some things just are, and we just beat our heads against the wall."[74] But perhaps this too is valuable as we dive into sound. Aristotle believed that "[e]ven inarticulate noises do indeed reveal something."[75] And Michel Serres notes that "[h]earing is our heroic opening to trouble and confusion."[76]

In embodying and leading us into such inarticulate noise, such trouble and confusion, jazz is the creative sustenance or background radiation of the sonic universe, not simply a lone planet therein. My evocations of spirits rejoicing strive to evoke those experiences that are germane to the practices of music-making in jazz historically, as well as their slipperiness, as well as (of course) their sound. In this, I have set for myself considerable challenges. As Ned Rothenberg told me, "[T]he thing you're trying to write about, this whole experience, I mean I wish you luck but you're really trying to grab smoke here. I guess what you can try to do is put the smoke in a container so you can look at it."[77] Religion is not simply out there for us to view and grasp and put in whatever container we choose. But if "religion" facilitates understanding "jazz" and vice versa, the containers I have chosen give us different ways of hearing and recognizing jazz in the spaces and stories of American religions, even as these recognitions inevitably fade and drift into smokiness once more, the very ceaselessness of this dynamic also a part of the terrain from which it emerges.

The improvisers who populate the history of this music continually bring these elusive modes of religiosity into being, and it can only ever be in the face of such frustrating (but also edifying) incompletions that we become, and then revise, and then become again who we are. And so to consider spirits rejoicing is to chase down, but never contain, this smoky, at times invisible, but all-enveloping vastness. I seek to evoke and propose in my writing the vitality of the practices that compel this study, to draw something of the musicians' own styles into my descriptions *of* them, to craft text where the religious themes correspond and even blend with their sounds. Whatever purpose there is in the empty grasp of the scholarly formulation, or the note already gone in the air, they establish the kind of relationality (between beings, between moments, between ideas or experiences) that is not simply a matter of reflection or recognition but built "into the very relationships between the sounds [a musician] makes."[78] These sounds are inextricable from religious modes of creativity and expression.

These relations with spirits take so many shapes and forms, but they recur in each phase, in each area of jazz. They bring musicians squarely to the limits of idiom and flesh, and beyond them too. Jazz has always been "a participatory culture, containing a notable capacity to foster the creation of indigenous forms."[79] In this endlessly mutating music, "religion" both focuses down and expands possibilities, the means of circulation and stasis alike. Regarding the containment within institutions or traditions, Lester Bowie once again brings a kind of clarity: "When you're talking about tradition, it's more than a style, more than a method of playing, more than a tempo... it's a whole life. What about the tradition of creativity, innovation, spirituality, individuality, and personality?"[80] Bowie asks of Norman Rockwell's admirers, what about Rothko? Or to the devotees of Lawrence Welk, what about Partch and Moondog? Jazz is not just a zoot suit and a martini, but a part of what Greil Marcus calls the "old, weird America," except of course that it is also new and, if not normal, then at the very least ubiquitous, saturating (whatever record sales or download rates would say otherwise).

And so as we set out to occupy this more, to envelop ourselves in the smoke with the knowledge of our containers' porousness, we look first to the familiar, comfortable location of good old-fashioned religious traditions. A simple tune to hum along to, nothing harmonically too challenging. Right? Except even these deceptively amenable forms contain strangenesses, unpredictable signs and wonders, and new creations. We are overrun with our own languages and expectations, fabricating words and worlds we convince ourselves are true, while at the same time being fashioned by them. I mean with these sentences no drab invocation of Max Weber's "iron cage," nor a perfunctorily poststructuralist confession that we are always being "written upon" by culture. No, by this I mean we are and can only be poets of sound, meaning that when we seek to give shape to this tricky conjunction—"jazz" and "religion"—we attempt to translate what does not want to be, pretending words suffice where they clearly do not. To write about religion is ineluctably to make things up. Let me, then, quote a poet by way of transition and ask you to think and listen with me, here and with each refrain going forward. Let us say together these words of Kenneth Patchen's as a kind of opening invocation: "Pause. And begin again."[81]

Procession of the Great Ancestry

TRADITIONS JAZZ AND RELIGIOUS[1]

I REMEMBER STANDING on my back porch with percussionist Hamid Drake in 1999 in Bloomington, Indiana, taking the night air. He had just changed from the ritual garb he wore during performance into fresh clothes. I asked him how long he had been punctuating his performances with frame drum improvisations and chanted devotions to Allah. He told me he'd been doing so ever since he became interested in Sufism. "But I thought you were into Rastafarianism," I said. "Oh, I still am," he replied, puzzled by my puzzlement. Now regularly recording odes to Kali as part of his Bindu project and practicing Buddhist meditation, it was Drake who got me to thinking about the fluidity of religious traditions in jazz, something that seemed alive in his incredibly expansive, adaptable grooves. As a first take on jazz and religions, I listen to the multiple ways jazz musicians have improvised on religious traditions, the most familiar expression of religion in/and music. The products are unpredictable, flowing beyond known boundaries. But you have to know some standards, and so the first chorus explores the common thesis that "jazz" comes from "the black church," which I explore and then complicate by listening to Albert Ayler and Charles Gayle. From there I look to variations on the theme of jazz and tradition: Islam, Buddhism, the Bahá'í, Scientology, and Judaism. From there, the chapter rides out on a discussion of religio-musical combinations, approaches to tradition as peripatetic and all-encompassing as "jazz" has always been with regard to idiom.

This is a rearrangement of the dusty narratives of traditions by exploring them through the medium of improvised sound, understood by many to have a sacred significance whose very multiplicity captures the protean nature of American religious identities. While there certainly exist jazz settings for religious texts, usages of jazz in religious services, and performances referring directly to deities or sacred stories, we find beyond these parameters a dizzy surplus of themes, practices, and creations in traditions jazz and religious: new bodily practices, music as a vehicle for new experiences of intersubjectivity, and the flowering of religious imagination through sonic eclecticism and combination.

These themes occupy this entire book, but here they reveal how complex it is to know about spirits rejoicing even through traditions. The orientation is an understandable one given that the study of religion has been shaped by denominationalism. It also mirrors the sociological, census-driven orientation of liberal democracies, where rights of recognition often depend on one's ability to identify with established religious traditions. Beyond even commonplace recognition of Americans describing themselves as "spiritual but not religious," which would appear to point beyond conventional traditions to combinative practices, jazz musicians have invented, used, adapted, and discarded traditional lineages in ways that suggestively emulate jazz's musical strategies.[2] These traditions might initially appear to be stable, but on inspection they emerge as place-markers for change that—like the Parmenidean river—never appear to us the same way twice. And so they bid us to invoke a metaphor: think of these traditions as sources of nurture and sustenance, analogous to instrumental styles.

"A Definite Beat!"

Academics do not like essentialism. Recently, a central category of African American religious history has suffered a withering critique. The "black church" has been posited as an analytic framework, a "public sphere," an institutional vessel safeguarding the African past, and more. Eddie Glaude Jr. noted the death of "the idea of this venerable institution as central to black life."[3] He clearly did not mean that the institutional network or its moral languages had ceased being relevant. Rather, Glaude wrote against the "black church" as singular, essential, and unchanging.[4] Yet we encounter continually stories of musical training in church, jazz arrangements of spirituals, and titles name-checking Christianity. What is more, musicologists often posit a single sonic trajectory from the field shouts to the church to vernacular musics.

There is considerable testimony to the idea that jazz is a *function* or *deposit* of this essentialized religious and historical development. Pianist Dr. James Polk notes that "the slaves would be singing gospel...[which led to] a natural progression into jazz."[5] Hugh Brodie said, "[Y]ou go to the church and it's a rhythmic type of thing... like jazz."[6] Lil Hardin Armstrong recalled the influence of the church on Louis Armstrong's Hot Five succinctly as "a definite beat!"[7] Chicago violinist Leroy Jenkins "gave recitals every Sunday in the Ebenezer Baptist Church alongside Bo Diddley."[8] Altoist Julian "Cannonball" Adderley—who, with cornetist brother Nat, played frequently at fundraisers for Operations PUSH and Breadbasket in the 1960s and 1970s—attributed his style on tunes like "Mercy Mercy Mercy" and "Country Preacher" to the phrasing he learned from spirituals.[9] AME-reared vocalist Dianne Reeves remembers that church performance was "where I had this amazing connection with something higher than myself."[10] To Reeves, jazz has the same "spirit" as church music.[11] Pianist Thelonious Monk played in church and accompanied traveling evangelists, "[b]ut I always did play jazz. In the churches I was playing music the same way."[12] Tenor saxophonist David Murray started out "playing with his family's band in a Pentecostal Church."[13] Rapt by the sheer act of playing, Murray—who remains a believer—felt confined by his family's religion since "playing or practicing jazz in our house was forbidden."[14] But as long as he was improvising within the context of a church tune, he could do all the Coltrane or Newk licks he wanted since "it wasn't considered jazz."[15] And Odean Pope formed his Saxophone Choir because he wanted "to figure out what instrument could I use to capture the experience that I had in the big Baptist church."[16]

Some musicians explore the legacies of African American Christianity by seeking out its most specific linguistic forms (gospel tunes and spirituals) and converting part of the African American sacred past into musical repertoire. These have proved immensely popular since the 1938–39 Carnegie Hall concert series "From Spirituals to Swing." Examples include Donald Byrd's "Pentecostal Feeling," Don Byron's *Love, Peace, and Soul*, George Lewis's *Plays Hymns*, Cyrus Chestnut's *You Are My Sunshine*, Grant Green's *Feelin' the Spirit*, and Archie Shepp and Horace Parlan's *Goin' Home*. Pianist Hank Jones and bassist Charlie Haden's *Steal Away* was even likened to "a kind of informal jazz eucharist."[17] Many other musicians have similarly reframed traditional materials, which pianist James Weidman described to me as "participating in black sacred music."[18]

Even cursory research into jazz and religion reveals hundreds of examples. The contours of the "black church's" influence (and its limits) become clear, however, in a discussion of three saxophonists, whose contributions make clear the unpredictable multiplicity that flows from this alleged singularity. Sam Rivers was born into a family steeped in African American religious music. Smitten with big bands soon after his parents moved from Oklahoma to Chicago during the Great Depression, Rivers eventually took up the tenor.[19] After graduating from Boston Conservatory, the bop-obsessed Rivers gigged steadily. On the recommendation of drum wunderkind Tony Williams, Rivers played briefly with Miles Davis and soon recorded a series of experimental dates for Blue Note, featuring his churning tenor improvisations on densely knotted tunes of craggy harmony and driving rhythm. After decades of prolific activity, Rivers relocated from New York to Orlando, Florida, where he explored his grandfather's 1882 collection of spirituals and folk tunes. He told me that his grandmother "was listening to the slaves, listening to the lyrics...[a]nd later on my grandfather became a Bishop in the AME church...he wrote some books on it...and added the music lines for these spirituals."[20] The traveling evangelist was committed to preserving black culture and music, and Rivers's own parents traveled with the Fisk Jubilee Singers and the Silvertone Quartet, whose influence on his own music Rivers confirmed in conversation.[21] Rivers recalled that his parents "considered jazz the devil's music...[b]ut they still took us to see all these master musicians."[22]

Rivers believed his music flowed from this lineage, and from another family trajectory. His uncle in Little Rock, Arkansas, was "the main catalyst in getting Eisenhower to send the troops" to enforce desegregation of public schools.[23] While Rivers worried about art in an America he dubbed "Alice in Crazyland," he believed creativity could still be a kind of life raft. He called improvisation an "ethereal art" containing "uninhibited emotion," "primal forces," and "blissful tranquility," all "a reflection of intrinsic spiritual energy."[24] Even when waxing cosmological and meditational, Rivers emphasized the importance of surprise in art's relation to everyday life, something you could hear in his terpsichorean flute or occasional joyous vocalisms during performance.[25] Music's freedom could transport you from mundane concerns since "[y]ou're the creator; there is no wrong."[26] "Is jazz like life itself?" I asked. Rivers enthused, "It is! Every time it's different, that's what keeps me here."[27] For Rivers, the emotionality and the continual questioning of creativity were not just areas where art became part of one's life; they were also registers of religion, as certain to him as the spirituals were to his grandfather. But to Rivers, a direct extension of this tradition, the lineage reached and resounded beyond itself.

Late for the World: Albert Ayler

Ted Joans called it the equivalent of hearing the word *fuck* shouted in Saint
Patrick's Cathedral.[28] One stunned reviewer described Ayler's music as a
"dualism of horror and euphoria."[29] Another described Ayler's sound as
"intense cacophony the likes of which the human ear has not heard outside of medieval insane asylums."[30] Ayler's music was a barbaric yawp, a
sound beyond the self, a resonance of tradition and memory. Breathy and
ululating, Ayler's tenor sounds equal parts holy shout and Ben Webster
flutter, submitting to and subjugating simple folkish lines—like melodies
from some other culture's pageantry—suspended in a wondrous oscillat-
ing group sound. On stirring performances like "Our Prayer," one encounters melody like a full immersion baptism of sound, something you can
imagine being played at your funeral.

     Ayler, one of the key figures in 1960s free jazz, once said "Trane was
the Father...Pharoah [Sanders] was the Son...I am the Holy Ghost."[31]
Despite the shock and rugged fervor of the soft-spoken man's sound, Ayler
believed that he "soared with the spirits" because his music was contributing to a larger propagation of truth that would lead humanity to a new age.
He sought to use recognizable musical forms (especially the gospel tunes
of his youth and his faith) to find freedom within sound, saying, "I'm not
trying to entertain people, I'm playing the truth for those who can listen."[32]
"[T]he Ayler boys grew up surrounded by religion" in postwar Cleveland.[33]
They were reared in the Baptist Church, where Albert learned to improvise at length in services, saying later that he was "trying to communicate
with a spirit."[34] Ayler began studying religion more purposefully after
enlisting in the army. And upon hearing "the call" while listening to Coltrane,
he plunged into American vernacular music and religion.[35] His style grew
toward huge swooping notes, deep pitch bending or raw barks, and an intense quaver that "replaced notes with glossolalia."[36]

     After his discharge, Ayler "distance[d] himself from the Baptist church"
and began to see himself as a sonic missionary of sorts, a jazz prophet put
on Earth to play healing music.[37] Though the sound sources of Ayler's upbringing remained audible—altoist Marion Brown compared Ayler to renowned Pentecostal saxophonist Vernard Johnson—they were now absorbed
into Ayler's dream of a holistic music.[38] Ayler believed jazz had the unique
musical power to tap into the universal, improvising through the particulars of each culture. While many listeners remarked on the radicality of the
collective improvisation heard in tunes like "Spirits Rejoice," Ayler insisted

that this style—which he called "rejoicing collectively to the spirits"—had roots as strong as Dixieland.

He believed that "he had found the real music and the real religion, and it had a lot to do with God."[39] Many religious traditions have constructed great musical architecture with oscillation and timbre: think of Qawwali or Tibetan Buddhist chant or throat singing in shamanic traditions. Vibrations are also central to a horn player's tone, and Ayler sought to use his to focus us on the vibrations of the cosmos. As he put it, "You have to purify and crystallize your sound in order to hypnotize."[40] The Aylers not only appropriated vernacular themes as the soundtrack for universal consciousness, they also committed to the aesthetic power of single notes: attack, duration, or multiphonics dancing around the tonal center like a congregation. It was the sheer immediacy of his full-throated, ecstatic cries that stunned listeners, even if they were also said to possess "sermonlike qualities."[41] And you find yourself humming along with Ayler, diving into the wide vibrato and harmony, major thirds and fourths stacking up like folk traditions, the whole sounding "like a Salvation Army band on LSD."[42]

When the Aylers toured Europe, some listeners wept solemnly while others were aghast: the BBC destroyed a recording of a performance, so disturbed were producers.[43] But the Aylers were convinced that "[o]ne day everything will be as it should be."[44] Their sheer intensity of purpose was grounded in the belief that the spirits worked through them, their music itself like the body in spirit possession. Back in the States, work was elusive. But after forcing his way onstage at an Elmo Hope gig and grabbing the attention of fledgling label ESP, Ayler said of his religiomusical mission, "People are going to the moon. It's time for music to change too."[45] His prophetically titled songs sounded universal and somehow ancient, expressed idiomatically but free of convention. It was a ritual; it was a flood.

Coltrane observed approvingly that the Aylers were taking the music "into even higher frequencies," and Ayler agreed, insisting "it's not about notes anymore."[46] Instead, it was only about music's "spiritual dimension."[47] The guttural power of Ayler's first recordings attracted the notice of producer George Wein, who placed him on a 1966 European tour with mainstream luminaries Dave Brubeck and Stan Getz. Perhaps improbably, the tour was met with such enthusiasm that violinist Michel Sampson likened it to the reception of the Beatles. During this period, Ayler obsessed over inner purification and tested his physical limits through playing and

FIGURE 2.1. Albert Ayler, Donald Ayler, Sunny Murray, and Charles Tyler at the recording session for *Spirits Rejoice*. Photograph copyright Guy Kopelowicz.

touring with evangelical fervor. "All I do is meditate," he said, so he could become "the universal man."[48] He described this state as "a being in spiritual communion, whose ideas are in total harmony with God," to which the supplicant can only give thanks with joyful noise.[49]

While the language of Ayler's public statements in his last three years grew ever more perambulating, he insisted that "[o]ur music should be able to remove frustration, to enable people to act more freely, to think more freely."[50] He referred consistently to the presence of the Holy Ghost in his music, but invoked correspondential language familiar to Swedenborgians and developed interest in Egyptology and hermeticism as well. Despite a contract with the influential Impulse label, Ayler had only two gigs in 1968, including one ambitious performance with vocals, "Songs of Zion—New Opera: Universal Message: Songs of David." Ayler's last two records even embraced pop music in his desire to reach wider audiences. Hearing his signature sound atop pedestrian grooves jarred, as did Ayler's own yodeling and ululating (on *New Grass*, he even sang free associative quasi-mystical lyrics backed by a gospel choir).

Ayler stilled played what sounded like testifying tenor. Indeed, pianist and harpsichordist Call Cobbs insisted he played in exactly the same style with his boss as he did in his church: "The music was like a Bible to Albert."[51] Yet Ayler subverted any attempts to house jazz neatly in a single continuous tradition. In 1969, his letter "To Mr. Jones—I Had a Vision" was published in Amiri Baraka's journal *The Cricket*.[52] Ayler described seeing Jesus's sword and multicolored flying saucers (which he likened to "the flying scorpion that I had read about in the chapter of Revelation"), hearing the angel Gabriel "sounding the warning" in his neighborhood, and referred often to the Nation of Islam.[53] He warned readers to avoid blasphemy, to "[e]at only the green things," and to pray fervently before the coming of the New Jerusalem. Were these fulfillments of his universalist vision or deviations from it?

Ayler seemed haunted in his last months. In one interview, a sweaty, shirtless, glassy-eyed Ayler stared into the camera and said, "[T]he music that I am playing, this is what keeps me going in life, like my imagination is beyond the civilization in which we live. I believe I am the prophet."[54] He was seen wearing a green leather suit or "a fur coat, gloves and Vaseline on his face in the heat of July."[55] Despite his optimistic pronouncements, he seemed unable to separate himself from his eschatology, telling interviewers "it has become late for the world."[56] He even told paramour Mary Maria, "[M]y blood has to be shed to save my mother and my brother."[57]

And then in November 1970, "psalm-swinging," soul-shouting Albert Ayler plunged into the murk of the East River.[58] His death shocked and saddened his peers. Charles Tyler recalled, "That 'old-time religion' was what caused his sadness; it was in his music.... I wouldn't be surprised his religious background followed him through to the end."[59] Some interpreted his death as somehow related to the exhaustion of 1960s optimism, the loss of the political change and enthusiasm African American religions had heralded. Donald Ayler spent years in a mental institution "because I was into Yoga too deep...there were so many vibrations out there not knowing what it was all about."[60] But it was Albert Ayler himself who said, "We are the music we play."[61] He had channeled his childhood experiences with the root sources of religious music to provide a soundtrack for rejoicing, seeing in the particularities of that experience something broader, a sound resonating across times and spaces, as intimate as the human heart and vast as the universe. Ayler the traditionalist was also the rebel. Written into and out of tradition, Ayler's sound—quavering, yawping, prayerful—resonates still. As Amiri Baraka wrote, "Albert was *mad*. His playing was like some primordial frenzy that the world secretly used for energy."[62]

Set the Record Straight: Charles Gayle

Unlike Rivers's chain of historical influence and Ayler's universalism, Charles Gayle's Christianity is a cry of critical force. Buffalo-born Gayle began his musical tutelage in a Baptist church. To listeners untutored in the demands of out jazz, the startling, at times almost unhinged power of Gayle's upper-register excursions may sound far from the testifying of the church. But when I first heard Gayle, on 1993's stunning *Touchin' on Trane*, I was knocked out by the sheer relentlessness of his energy, the way he combined a ferocious array of extended techniques with a deep commitment to emotionalism that could be equally at home in church or on a late Coltrane side. Never especially enamored with the term "free jazz" (he says he plays music in order to *live* freely), Gayle suggest the music "started in old churches...they would play a motif and then go off and do their own thing."[63] Jazz is just "the way people sing in church...all vibrato."[64] His is the sound of the stentorian prophet delivering a jeremiad, each phrase seeming to resound with musical traditions marked by the cry of the possessed, those "falling out," or the ecstatic shriek.

In his teens, Gayle buckled down on tenor and grew in his conviction that each note was dedicated to God. Gayle was compelled by the "new thing" of the 1960s, which he heard as the natural expression of civil rights and Christianity, a soundtrack to social change "rooted in the church."[65] No sacred/secular distinction mattered for Gayle since music flowed organically out of people's experience in different ways, spanning distinctions like one of his own jaw-dropping intervallic leaps atop a maelstrom of arco bass and furious snare patterns. But after floating around the loft scene of the late 1960s and early 1970s, Gayle simply disappeared. He was living a life that he recalls being inconsistent with his beliefs, scrambling for rent gigs and playing music that he did not feel. Gayle believed that rejecting the hustle was "the only honest alternative for a black musician."[66] In the hardscrabble Manhattan of the day, Gayle frequently busked in subway stairwells or on street corners and was homeless for nearly two decades. By Gayle's reckoning, though, divesting himself of all encumbrances removed all barriers between him and the immediacy of God's music.

Gayle and those who know him claim that his abiding Christianity held together his passion for music and hope for humanity during these street years. To Gayle, finally receiving the sponsorship of the Knitting Factory's Michael Dorf in 1987 was confirmation of the taken path, his uncompromising sound now reaching more than the ears of passersby. Early albums *Homeless, Repent,* and *Kingdom Come* showcased Gayle's rough melodicism, and song titles like "Jesus Christ and Scripture" signaled the sound's religiosity. Gayle described his music as a form of witness to gospel truth, since jazz is by its nature religious: "when you play free improvisation, God is there too...whether you like it or not."[67] He even suggests that this very relationship supersedes the sound that produces and announces it: "I'm not a musician, man."[68] The intensity of this conviction was also visible at Gayle's performances, where he sometimes displayed a stigmata set against a Pan-African flag.

But for the most part Gayle's politics have been expressed differently. Following his ascendency among the free jazz cognoscenti, Gayle began appearing on stage wearing clown makeup, a bowler hat, and a red plastic nose. This was his Streets the Clown persona. Beginning to feel a bit disconnected from his recent turn of fortune, Gayle recalls that he wanted not to "think of Charles so much."[69] When he became Streets, he felt completely free onstage for the first time, ripping up a paper heart or mugging a sad clown's face during an elegiac improvisation. Was he clowning jazz itself? Calling attention to jazz fans' (sometimes unconscious) replication of the tropes of minstrelsy? "Obviously," Gayle says, "it was about the streets."[70] It was a way of "acting out...love, pain, joy, and things that happen in life."[71] He began to include skits, "little props," or "pantomime": "playing wasn't enough for me, especially since I've been on the street,"

Gayle explained.[72] In time, Streets began to talk very explicitly—too much so for some of his audience, who occasionally shouted at Gayle to shut up (another echo of audience expectations for black musicians to be silent yet emotive)—about Christianity, and specifically about the "sins" of abortion and homosexuality as Gayle understood them. After all, "[w]hy are we tight-lipped about the rest of life? You're hardly working anyway, so what've we got to be afraid of?"[73]

Amid the polytonal fury of Gayle's performance, one senses the sheer conviction of his playing, a relentless commitment to realize values he insists are borne of love for God. Consider a performance of "In the Name of the Father," where Gayle announces, "We're gonna talk about abortion. . . . We're gonna talk about God."[74] Gayle challenged the jazzbos: "you couldn't love John Coltrane if you didn't understand that his music was about the Holy Ghost."[75] For Gayle, this meant listeners must reckon with their own shortcomings before God: "[w]hether you being a homosexual, you drinking, you lying. . . . I'm not trying to do nothing but set the record straight."[76] If he wouldn't abandon these principles while on the streets, he certainly wouldn't water them down in the clubs.

Gayle claims of this stance that "it's in my heart—and God will make that decision of whether I'm a phony or not."[77] Critics piled on Gayle, calling him a paleo-conservative, and some engagements were canceled. (Gayle scoffed, "I ain't no right wing nothing! I ain't got no wings!")[78] He professes not to understand why audiences "got uptight" and "bent out of shape" since "I just said 'We can think about these things,' that's all."[79] But for Gayle the reality of these truths is as undeniable as his music is uncompromising, and "[i]f the Bible's wrong, I'm wrong. I'll go for it."[80] After all, "[t]hey hung Jesus, so what are they gonna say about me?"[81] At the very least, there is a great deal more to say about "the black church" than that it is an unchanging institutional locus, whose sensibility and music has flowed unbroken into "jazz."

Truth Has Come: Islam and Jazz

What other variations on tradition are possible? How does the "instrumentation" of jazz play other traditional materials, and how do these traditions affect the music? The most significant non-Christian tradition in jazz history is Islam. On one level, this simply expresses a centuries-long religious history of people of African descent. Not only did a large percentage of the West Africans brought to America with the slave trade practice

Islam, throughout the twentieth and twenty-first centuries millions of African Americans have converted to Islam for a variety of reasons. Recently, Christopher Chase, Robin Kelley, and Eric Porter have made important contributions to understanding Islam's role in jazz, a counterpoint to the "black church" thesis. Chase notes that Islam has "given Africana jazz musicians the opportunity to locate their subjectivity in a different prophetic salvation history."[82] Beginning in the 1930s and 1940s, jazz musicians responded in greater numbers to the rise of Islamic religious options in the American urban north, seeking to "forge an audial soundscape of a global, race-neutral unity—the Islamic *ummah*."[83] Kelley notes that it was owing to the influence of the Ahmadiyya movement (an Islamic improvisation founded in 1888 by Mirza Ghulam Ahmad, an Indian who claimed he was the Mahdi) that Islam began to attract bop players. Trumpeter Idrees Suleiman had joined an Ahmadiyya group called the Muslim Brotherhood, whose aesthetic and historical sensibility "bestowed upon black American culture a sense of dignity and nobility, which appealed to the creators of the new music."[84]

It was through a small network of Ahmadiyya players that Islam began to spread among players. After drummer Art Blakey was beaten by cops in Albany, Georgia (after refusing to address an officer as "Sir"), he sought "a better way of life…[since] Christianity had fallen down on the job'."[85] Not long thereafter, trumpeter Talib Dawud recruited Blakey to Ahmadiyya, after which Blakey "took an Islamic name."[86] The two "started a Muslim mission out of Blakey's apartment," eventually moving to a mosque on Thirtieth Street.[87] Here they started a Qur'an study group and a rehearsal band that later evolved into Blakey's legendary Jazz Messengers. As Chase and Ingrid Monson note, the term "messengers" signifies quite strongly in Islam generally and in Ahmadiyya specifically that music was a form of prophecy, with jazz understood as something specifically American in its democratic promise and simultaneously embodying Islam's universalism.[88]

It was common for jazz converts to Islam to embrace its otherness from American culture and its universalist ethos in equal measure, the latter understood to partly fulfill an egalitarian promise so evidently absent in the clubs and the streets. Jazz was a mode of emotional commitment to and performance of these ideals, sometimes expressed through collective improvisation or by using non-European instruments like the shenai or the ney. At times the music resounded with the timbres of recognizable devotional musics like the Gnawa; but for the most part, Islam was experienced as a legitimation of fresh musical development. New sounds became new histories and new identities. Conversions like those of Nadi Qamar, Ahmed Abdullah, Muhammad Ali, and Billy Higgins were understood as musical decisions, too, since embracing Islam was understood as coextensive with a deeper commitment to communication, a more intense realization of musical developments, or a sense of mission. These tendencies are exemplified in two famous pianists' conversions to Islam.

As soon as I first heard Abdullah Ibrahim's incredibly distinctive rhythmic shapes in the middle register on "Toi Toi"—with its emphatically punched E-flat, township shuffle, and lovely Ellingtonian arrangements—I was hooked. Reared in South Africa as Dollar Brand, Ibrahim was brought up in an African Methodist Episcopal (AME) church. He was preoccupied with the combination of voice and drum, which he heard as the root of African music, and which would anchor his vision of jazz as a music of "cross-cultural borrowings" from gospel, chants, and street music.[89] To Ibrahim, such combinations reflect the polyglot backgrounds of musicians as well as the shoulder-rubbings of culture itself. As he later noted, "[M]usic can provide a conducive atmosphere for all other daily activities, as it does in more traditional societies."[90] So to Ibrahim, whose great-grandfather was a Khoi medicine man, being able to name his music "jazz" is less important than what the music can accomplish or realize socially. He named his first group the Jazz Epistles because "like the early Christian teachers, he believes that he is writing Epistles."[91] Music is for Ibrahim an expression of divine truth, whose purity and directness exemplify what "Allah says in the Koran," which is that "the truth has come and falsehood has vanished."[92]

The universalism of the Ummah certainly proved attractive to Ibrahim, a convert in apartheid-era South Africa (which he and wife Sathima Bea Benjamin left for Switzerland in 1962), and his music has also been shaped by his specific understandings of Islamic music. Ibrahim has regularly included devotional pieces on his records: *Africa—Tears and Laughter* features the lengthy vocal piece "Ishmael," offered in thanks to Allah; *The Journey* includes "The Hajj"; *African Space Program*'s "Jabulani—Easter Joy" features a devotional chant section; and *Echoes from Africa* includes the moving "Zikr," with vocal intonations of "Allah" and "Salaam." As Chase says of the latter tune, it works like Ibrahim's other pieces to reorient the listener and the performer in a "proper relationship with God," which when achieved can purify or heal the audient or player; indeed, Chase hears Ibrahim's exuberant playing on "Imam" as an imam leading a community in prayer.[93]

But again, traditions are never as simple as they seem. After apartheid, he and Benjamin opened the music school Project M7 in Capetown, combining music, dance, meditation, health, and martial arts. Ibrahim has avidly pursued the latter, whose emphasis on concentration and readiness for the moment he sees as parallel with prayer and meditation in Islam and with jazz spontaneity. What knits together these various pursuits is, for Ibrahim, that they are "what God commands me to do" and the hope that "one day I'll be able to play 10 seconds of pure beauty."[94] Ibrahim sounds traditionalist in his conviction that "whatever comes to you comes through grace."[95] However, this understanding of God's grace is also influenced by martial arts and Noh theater: "the eventual state of bringing the mind, body, soul—bop!—together at one point. The Japanese say Mu Shin, No Mind."[96] Ibrahim links this mentality to the "high" he gets from improvisation and from prayer, explaining with the buoyancy that inflects his playing that "jazz comes from what we call in Islam Tariqa, a state of trance."[97]

Philadelphian McCoy Tyner converted to Islam after having a "spiritual awakening" around the age of eighteen.[98] While he and his boss John Coltrane shared a Christian background, it was Tyner's association with Hassan Ali that started him down the path to Islam. He took the name Suleiman Saud, and with Coltrane Tyner developed a very personal style of modal pianism, with heavy comping, that produced a kind of hypnotic effect within the surging music. Tyner's music does not signify in ways as explicitly Islamic as Ibrahim's; but it is nonetheless informed by his devotion and his sense that "God still speaks to man" through musicians.[99] Upon leaving Coltrane in 1965, Tyner explored introspective and meditative music. His 1967 composition "Contemplation" was described as "the sound of a man alone...reflecting on what religion means."[100] Tyner said that "Search for Peace" "has to do with a man's submission to God."[101] Yet like Ibrahim, Tyner also developed a fascination with Japanese culture, linking its "[o]vertones of serenity, peace and contemplation" with his own Islamic devotions.[102] To Tyner, the desert imagery of *Sahara* represented "the infinite, open-ended possibilities available to any man who 'stays spiritually in tune with life and with nature'."[103] Fusing such naturalism and meditation with universalist conceptions of a musical Ummah, Tyner believes jazz can perhaps uniquely awaken modes of connection among musicians and listeners that can generate social harmony as well as a "rapport with the cosmos."[104]

Back when he was Bill Evans and playing in Dizzy Gillespie's Afro-Cuban Big Band, multi-instrumentalist and composer Yusef Lateef perhaps had an inkling of how far his omnivorous musical and religious curiosity would take him. He later recalled, "[I]f I was to continue making music, I would have to...stud[y] the music of other cultures."[105] Reared in Detroit, the reedist was working in Chicago in 1946 when he was introduced to Islam through Talib Dawud. Lateef, who had read avidly about religions throughout his life, officially became part of the Ahmadiyya movement in 1948 (and legally changed his name in 1950).[106] He felt that Islam encapsulated the virtues of all other religious traditions. A stint in Blakey's Messengers solidified his belief that improvising was a gift from God. Lateef became deeply pious, learning Arabic so he could read the Qur'an in its original language. His interest in studying Middle Eastern, African, and Asian music—begun in the 1950s and continuing after his 1960 tenure with percussionist Babatunde Olatunji—was also borne of a deep dissatisfaction with the associations of "jazz" itself.[107] He bristled at the term's "connotations that debase the art and belittle those who play it."[108] For Lateef, the compassion and universalism of Islam yielded "music that inspires listeners and puts them in touch with themselves."[109] Music was more than art; it was a form of generosity that can manifest the interconnectedness of various levels of the created order, whether biological, aesthetic, or spiritual.

Lateef's use of new instruments and idioms in his own vision of "jazz" sounded out the resonance of beliefs and practices he considered basically Islamic, while also pushing the musical envelope. "Islam has a saying," Lateef explains, "that life from the cradle to the grave should be a search for knowledge. That gave me the encouragement to go wherever I had to go to find it."[110] But early records like *Prayer to the East* also found him appropriating modes, scales, and rhythms from different cultural and religious traditions. On the one hand, Lateef used double-reed instruments to invoke the Muslim *adhan*.[111] But he also intended to create respectful combinations of sound that to him embodied the universalism of Islam but could be performed in multiple fashions.[112] In 1970, he began to describe his approach, which he would codify in his 1981 text *Repository of Scales and Melodic Patterns*, as "'autophysiopsychic' music, that is, music from one's physical, mental, and spiritual self."[113] It is not so simple, then, as hearing Lateef as playing "Islamic music," since this terminology signified Lateef's belief in the harmony between culture, biology, and sound, knit together by "invisible forces" and "spirit power."[114]

The musical expresses the biological, which captures a religious and social implication: "we are all part of nature...clouds, trees, grass—they look different but they blend. It's the same with humans."[115] Just as different notes occupy a chord, and natural elements the same space, humans and their religions can harmonize too: "[a]t the core of the tones, the essence vibrates love."[116] Lateef links these ideas to a larger sonic awakening captured most perfectly in Islam, whose purpose he says is to awaken us to a beauty "not due to the thing itself...[but to] God the Beloved, Who has bestowed upon them the beauty which they reflect."[117] So the creation of and openness to beauty situates the musician not only in a moral universe— where generosity exists at the center of a meaningful life—but prepares one for mystical understanding that humans are "on a small scale, all that exists in the external universe."[118] Music thus must have a trajectory toward healing, and players "must strive to gain the highest level of consciousness and awareness by developing his mind, body and soul."[119] Yet far more than merely leading to insight or a kind of musical "therapeutic," Lateef's Islam speaks through metaphysical categories that exist at the intersection of Ralph Waldo Emerson's "Over-Soul," Warren Felt Evans's divine mind, and Emanuel Swedenborg's many and watchful angels. Traditions are not what they seem.

Into the Unknown: Buddhism and Jazz

This is true, too, for Buddhism, a tradition that attracted players like J. R. Mitchell in growing numbers beginning in the late 1960s. Mitchell, who was Muslim, recalls, "There was a gig coming up and because I wasn't a Buddhist I wasn't able to get the gig. So I said, 'wow, let me join this religion if it's gonna help me get some gigs'."[120] But what might it mean to think about jazz as Buddhist, fresh gigs or not? If we saw with Islam that the universalism of the Ummah is seen as a model for communication and receptivity to the divine, how might Buddhist meditation, vows of prostration, or compassion shape jazz?

Players have been drawn to Buddhism for many reasons, most stemming from the post-1965 (the year legislation ended previously extant immigration quotas) flowering of interest in Asian religions in the United States. Mahavishnu John McLaughlin plugged into Sri Chinmoy and Marshall stacks. Charles Lloyd played odes to the lotus. And legions of Coltrane acolytes took from the imagery and titles on the master's albums an injunction to investigate non-monotheistic traditions. Such interest in Asian traditions continues today. Guitarist David "Fuze" Fiuczynski, for example, described himself to me as a "non-practicing Taoist."[121] Attracted by the "profound simplicity" of Indian and Chinese music, Fuze finds "something about the openness, the fluidity of Taoism" conducive to improvisation, "where people take strength from [it] and turn it into creative energy" (even as there is an effort to "purge the ego").[122]

Drummer Terri Lynne Carrington, who believes jazz is inherently "spiritual," was introduced to Buddhism by trombonist Robin Eubanks and saxophonist Wayne Shorter, who led Carrington to Soka Gakkai International. She acknowledges that Buddhism has shaped her aesthetic in relating to musicians and audiences from a position of compassion. And the discipline of meditation has influenced her playing, its breath patterns integral to her sense of rhythmic flow and focused concentration. "[Y]ou can affect your environment, as opposed to letting your environment affect you," she explains. "That's actually a Buddhist concept."[123] Through jazz, she continues, "I feel in harmony with most things, in large part because of my beliefs in Buddhist philosophy, the spiritual world, and nature in general."[124]

Pianist Marilyn Crispell plays jazz because she is compelled by experiences that surpass the mundane.[125] After an adolescence defined by what Crispell recalls as not fitting in with mainstream conceptions of femininity, music opened her up to her own identity: "I remember bursting into tears and crying for hours because it was such a relief."[126] She began to study Buddhism and Tibetan culture as a way to realize this identity consistently and had what she recalls as an awakening experience while listening to Coltrane's *A Love Supreme*: "I felt a presence. A very loving, powerful presence.... It was total inspiration...like a loosening of the spirit."[127] Alto saxophonist Bobby Zankel has practiced Nichiren Shoshu Buddhism since 1973. As regularly as he runs his scales and changes, he chants "Nam Myoho Renge Kyo" from the Lotus Sutra. A way of bringing his inner dispositions into harmony with his actions—and specifically with his improvising—Zankel claims Buddhism has helped him manifest "compassion for other people," a generosity that is conducive to collective improvising.[128] He also believes that "chanting awakens you to yourself" and "tap[s] into our wisdom and creativity."[129] Harold Land, who has chanted daily with family for more than two decades, feels similarly about Zen Buddhism. He claims he "didn't realize that it influenced my music until different people began to say...'there seems to be another source of energy'."[130] Land explained to them that it "was the result of my chanting two times a day—from the *Daimoku*. It's the eternal law of life."[131]

But then there is Newk. It is difficult to imagine a tenor saxophonist more consistently divinized and more regularly frustrating than Sonny

Rollins—divinized because of the effortless mastery of his playing, and frustrating because of his lengthy and sudden departures from the scene. Most famous among the latter was a years-long hiatus from performing that found a Mohawked Rollins regularly practicing alone on the Williamsburg Bridge. During this interval, the Moravian-reared saxophonist had become a Buddhist. Beaver Harris recalls looking for Rollins and was told by Albert Dailey, "Newk is an Indian and he's been chanting."[132] Ira Gitler notes that when Rollins returned to performance in the late 1960s, he continued his focus on meditation. On tour in Japan he made a point to stop and meditate near Mount Fuji. He spent time in an ashram in 1968, contending that "music is something very spiritual to begin with, and if you are a deep thinking person...you really want to use music as a vehicle of expression of your religion."[133] This is why during his periods of greatest musical exploration Rollins also studied yoga in India and Zen in Japan, where he was told by a teacher, "[W]hen you play your horn, that in itself is meditation."[134] But Rollins approached Buddhism as he would one of his famously discursive improvisations, saying, "Trying to draw specific lines to [Buddhism] doesn't work for me. I've studied some Zen and yoga. My music is my yoga...to play my instrument, to concentrate and get inside myself, is my way of doing all of these spiritual things."[135] He would like to believe in God, he said, "but it is so deep I can't talk about it."[136] And so he plays on.

Pianist Herbie Hancock's career has been as wide ranging as one of his solos—extending from the rump-rolling funk of "Watermelon Man" to the electric sizzle of *Headhunters* or the synthed out "Rockit" and beyond—but for forty years he has followed the constant of Soka Gakkai's Nichiren Buddhism. Unlike some players, Hancock did not come to his tradition out of a sense of crisis or contemplative insight. It was Buster Williams's bass solo that did it. At a 1972 Seattle gig where the energy was high, Hancock called the tune "Toys," which features an acoustic bass introduction. Williams killed it, knocking listeners for a loop with his flow of ideas, his commitment, and technique. After a "magical" set, tearful audience members rushed the stage to thank the musicians. Hancock asked Williams where he got such energy and focus: "Hey, Buster, I heard you were into some new philosophy or something and if it can make you play bass like that, I want to know what it is." Williams replied that he had "been chanting for a way to tell you about this" and in time Hancock joined him in chanting "Nam myoho renge kyo."[137]

Hancock describes jazz as "a wonderful example of the great characteristics of Buddhism...[b]ecause in jazz we share, we listen to each other, we respect each other."[138] Improvising is to Hancock a non judgmental way of openness to the other and to the universe, through creativity that contributes to the order of things and its ceaseless development. Moving forward through the flow of time is itself a creative act, to Hancock, so in turn the creative process becomes a form of life. Following his adoption of Buddhism, drummer Mike Clarke recalls, "Herbie was trying to *shaka-buku* [convert] everyone."[139] He told musicians and audiences that chanting draws upon and connects to the universe's fundamental energy, and the musician in touch with these realities can channel those energies in performance. Hancock also contends that chanting enhances perception in ways consistent with improvisation's focus on form and detail: "when you start...acknowledging the beauty of the smallest things and acknowledging the full elements of something outside the box, it gives you a chance to grow" individually and collectively.[140] After all, "[m]any of the attributes of jazz are wonderful attributes for living: there's a lot of hope in jazz, there's sharing, there's living in the moment."[141]

Hancock's friend Wayne Shorter arrives at like conclusions somewhat more elliptically, a personality trait Hal Miller once described as follows: "I once asked Wayne for the time. He started talking to me about the cosmos and how time is relative."[142] Shorter was reared Baptist, but unlike many other musicians he found church music "negative and gloomy."[143] He sought a different kind of lift off, into fantasy and imagination. On his earliest records, Shorter wrote pieces reflecting his interest in religion, and by the 1970s was preoccupied with the idea of "cosmic consciousness," an expansive spirituality linking nineteenth-century metaphysics with the Age of Aquarius. Regular tours of Japan with Weather Report enhanced Shorter's interest in Nichiren Buddhism, and he developed a network of contacts who plied him with books and advice. He was attracted to Buddhist goals of compassion and openness, and to its disciplines (which resonated with his musical regimen). In time he followed Hancock into Soka Gakkai and began pursuing "the idea of 'the eternal self,' and...this whole thing called eternity."[144]

Taking joy in conceptual conundrums, Shorter uses creativity to tweak the taken-for-granted in the name of open-ended discovery. As with Hancock's music, one hears comparably little in Shorter's playing of the particular devotional modes or instrumental timbres of traditional Buddhist music. While one might point to the flow of ideas in Hancock's playing or the emphatic silence between Shorter's notes as derived somehow from Buddhist aesthetics, it is on the adaptability of Buddhism to music-making that these players focus rather than overt musical signifiers. As Shorter puts it, when jazz improvisers play, "we know our grasp is further than our reach and we go for it, into the unknown."[145] To him, this is realer than the everyday world of appearances, where even Buddhism dissolves as just another illusion concealing the eternal. It is a tricky thing to realize the dissolution of that heftiest of illusions, the self, in a musical tradition so focused on individual expression, and one cognizant of Dolphy's reminder that sound is always already gone. But to Shorter, this is less a problem than an opportunity, since the improviser is "in on the actual creation of life," imbuing performance itself with ritual significance, with experiential weight.[146] Music is thus inevitably about more than itself, in Shorter's reckoning, a momentary flare in a vast cosmos. And asked about the best idea through which to realize this ever-changing same, Shorter nods to Stephen Hawking's Grand Design and exults in the possibility of multiple histories, multiple humanities, all of whose existence is more real to him than the drab everyday. In both jazz and Buddhism, he notes, you are "reaching for a higher and higher life force in everything you do."[147]

Channel Musical Light: The Bahá'í

At the core of Bahá'í belief is a related gaze beyond the present, to a future shaped by the unity of humankind, religions, and God. Since humans are understood to be of one body, Bahá'í ethics foreground mutual obligation and selflessness. These notions of spiritual unity, interactivity, and listening without offense have been understood by Bahá'í jazz practitioners as constitutive of their improvisational practice. Though there are fewer Bahá'í than Muslims playing jazz, this tradition has also steadily gained adherents since the 1940s. Foremost among these converts was Dizzy Gillespie, who would become a worldwide ambassador for the faith.

Gillespie became famous in the 1940s for his association with Charlie Parker and bebop. Beyond his beret and mugging persona (Dizzy ran for president in 1964 and sang about the "land of oo-blah-dee"), the trumpeter was a fierce advocate for African American rights. The music was no gimmick; its very exuberance shouted "no!" to a society that sought to constrain black creativity. As he grew more outspoken in support of civil rights, Gillespie studied religions more avidly too. On tour in the 1960s, Gillespie was charmed by Milwaukee fan Beth McKintey's musical passion and learned that she was traveling to spread the word about the Bahá'í. In subsequent exchanges with McKintey and her husband, Gillespie warmed to the religion's teachings and spent time studying its history. After a despondent period following Martin Luther King Jr.'s assassination, Gillespie reawoke to the possibilities of music as a vehicle for communicating divine wisdom and universal fellowship.[148] He believed jazz players were the most in tune with the universe and began peppering his amiable stage banter with references to Bahá'í concepts like the "contingent world" and the "spiritual realm."[149] He did not imagine that music would become the universal language or the social glue prophesied by the Bahá'í, but understood that music's ability to cut across social and linguistic divisions—like one of his glorious, swooping trumpet lines—made it uniquely useful in awakening human spiritual sensibilities, predicting that "in the future, a groovy number of Bahá'ís [will be] composing music praising God."[150]

What did the trumpeter think playing jazz as a Bahá'í actually meant? At the 1971 Bahá'í Caribbean Conference, Gillespie announced that his playing was informed by the lineage of musical messengers from different traditions, "like it's one big master painting."[151] This relationship, he elaborated, was like different sections of a band, a composition, a society: "[o]ur music depends on rhythm, and when we're not together we're out of it."[152] His musical aesthetic grew steadily to embrace the Bahá'í category of unitive purpose, likening instruments to different elements of a painting,

FIGURE 2.2. Dizzy Gillespie at a recording session, with his signature bent trumpet. Photograph copyright Jan Persson.

parts to a whole that could only be realized collectively.[153] And in its own development, jazz itself is "like a religion...you have the bellwether...then you have the main messenger himself...[t]hen you have offshoots of these guys."[154] So the Bahá'í had taught him that jazz and religion were effectively different emanations from the same place: "[t]hey just come from different intervals in our spiritual development."[155] Messenger after musical messenger would arrive, then, clarifying and awakening.

Many Bahá'í musicians—from "Doc" Holladay to singers Betty Carter and Hazel Scott—have little direct connection with Gillespie. Yet many more, like singer Carmen McRae, embraced the tradition based on the trumpeter's enthusiastic conviction that jazz expressed Bahá'í teachings on unity.[156] Jazz musicians joined in growing numbers, attracted to the Bahá'í belief that music is a form of spirituality, and that "work performed in the spirit of service is a form of worship."[157] Mike Longo, who leads a Gillespie commemorative band at the New York Bahá'í center, believes that "[t]here's natural music out there in the universe, and you just go and get it."[158]

Longtime Gillespie bandmate James Moody was attracted to the message of universality, which he believed translated easily into music, which "involves everything...[a]nd the person that does it is influenced by everything."[159] Vocalist Flora Purim embraced the Bahá'í while on tour with Gillespie, attracted by its racial egalitarianism and commitment to social reform. Purim was impressed by Gillespie's clarity of perception and became convinced that jazz epitomized Bahá'í spiritual unity.[160] Drummer Cindy Blackman became a Bahá'í just out of high school and claims "music is so sacred that once you're playing music you are doing the work of prayer."[161] Vocalist Tierney Sutton, who converted at age eighteen, sees music as a form of cultivating joy beyond the material.[162] The possibility of transformation through communication is what Sutton believes jazz and the Bahá'í share: "[u]nity changes the way you do everything."[163] For her, music itself bridges the gap between the longing human being and the unknowable essence of God: "society sucks us into basically selling our souls...[but] we get glimpses of something really beautiful."[164]

Reedist Oluyemi Thomas and singer Ijeoma Thomas of Oakland's Positive Knowledge play free jazz, their intense cries (and elaborate colored robes) expressing Bahá'í ideas differently than Sutton or Gillespie. Oluyemi believes the practice of improvisation and the very existence of music confirm human spiritual potential: "music comes from the world of beyond...to convey collective reality."[165] He first became aware of the

Bahá'í in 1970, and "in 1972 I had a dream and what I'll call the spirit of truth...announced to me, now is your time."[166] He has since striven to "channel musical light," with positive transformation possible because "this earth world is a reflection of the invisible world."[167] He links jazz to the Bahá'í belief that souls seeking reunion with the Creator can build a new creation, crafting organization from chaos, as long as principles are sound: just like improvising itself. Thomas begins each musical performance by attempting to "lay it out prayerfully," since the sound is not coming from the musician but "from silence, which is really the Creator...you're having a conversation with God, which is prayer."[168]

Oluyemi also infuses some of these more basic Bahá'í sentiments with a very particular understanding of neo-Platonism, sound, and spatiality. He talks about the journey "beneath tone floor": "there's several levels of the beneath...it's pre-thought or action." I asked him about the importance of relationality and energy exchange, and whether listening was the art of the divine. "Yes!" he exclaimed. "We think [sound] came from us, but it really came from the pre-silence of the tone world." Human existence is inherently spiritual and musical, related to the mysteries and generative properties of nature. Invoking Gillespie's imagery, Oluyemi notes, "It's all part of the wonders of our creation...like an orchestra." For Oluyemi, the movement between opposites—above and below, form and chaos, physical and spiritual—reflects the exchange of energies, which is how progress occurs musically and otherwise. Ijeoma feels similarly, describing the purpose of art as facilitating personal transformation and social betterment: "[t]he more we can talk about it and celebrate it, the better off we all are...because we're all connected anyway." The artist must continually reinvent herself, which Ijeoma sees as linked to a larger spiritual cycle of "freeing yourself of certain things." Part of what it means to be a spiritual being, she explained, is breaking down opposites and understanding the unity of things, in common purpose like good improvisation. With such art, "we can have what Baha'ullah calls a divine civilization.... Step by step we go: word by word and note by note."[169]

This Moment's Forever: Scientology

Another optimistic and futuristic tradition, Scientology on some level could not be more different from the Bahá'í. It is impossible to encounter the tradition outside the derision that so often accrues to it. While some jazz reviewers savaged records simply because of associations with the tradition, players like saxophonist Lee Konitz explained that Scientology helps "[keep] me as productive as possible and to live as meaningful and spiritual a life as I can."[170] The story of jazz and Scientology focuses mostly on Boston-bred pianist Chick Corea, whose dazzling technique and gift for thematic playing landed him gigs with Cab Calloway, Herbie Mann, and the irascible Stan Getz in the 1960s. Corea's big break came when he was hired by Miles Davis. In 1968, Corea was introduced to L. Ron Hubbard's *Dianetics* and was immediately compelled by principles he saw as directly analogous to jazz (and shared by Hubbard and Miles): "[f]ree-dom to communicate, and freedom to think how you want to think."[171]

He recalls this period of searching, saying, "I thought for a long time that the freedom I was seeking was a wholly personal thing."[172] At the time, Scientology was engaged in active recruitment among the counter-culture and creative seekers of Corea's age, playing up concepts like "affinity" and "communication" and even inducing males to auditing sessions via young women in miniskirts (in a suggestive parallel to the Children of God's "flirty fishing").[173] Corea found in Hubbard's writings a tradition, a framework, and a method for progress and self-improvement, claiming "music has always been the dream of a better life."[174] And for Corea, in jazz "the attainment of freedom was a group activity."[175] He struck up a correspondence with Hubbard, and with his trio A.R.C. (Affinity, Reality, Communication) Corea first began to apply Scientological principles to improvisation. In the quartet Circle he explored the possibility of total communication in (mostly) free improvisation. Each member of Circle was a Scientologist for a time, and Corea described their music as "what we are as spiritual beings outside of space and time in this moment's for-ever."[176] This rhetoric resounds with Scientology's promise of freedom from the prison of MEST (matter, energy, space, and time), but reedist Anthony Braxton recalled years later that the band's demise came largely because of other members' distaste for Scientology and Corea's decision (which Braxton attributed to pressure from Scientology) to go commercial.[177]

Corea did indeed change his music with Return to Forever in the early 1970s. Taking up jazz-rock fusion and adding to it a prog-rock, sci-fi sensi-bility, RTF's albums sported titles often cribbed from Scientological litera-ture or Hubbard's sci-fi writing. Corea's embrace of new musical technologies and the fantastic taps into a deep vein of musical futurism in America (from the experimentalism of Henry Cowell or the keyboard trance of Terry Riley all the way to P-Funk and Devo) that resonates more generally with the sonically adaptive propensities of American religion (from electric guitars wailing in megachurches to Hare Krishna rap). After RTF disbanded in the late 1970s, guitarist Bill Connors lamented Corea's leadership style: in the name of helping bandmates realize their potential, Corea "got more demanding, and I wasn't allowed to control my own solos."[178] Saxophonist Joe Farrell says that he left RTF because of "that Scientology shit."[179] Corea simply insisted, "I require a certain amount of ethics from anyone I work with."[180]

During the 1980s, Corea became more outspoken in Scientology's defense, as it attracted regular scrutiny. Corea was described as part of "a star-studded roster of followers" taken in when Scientology "regally pamper[ed] them at the church's 'Celebrity Centers'."[181] In 1993, Corea was labeled a "propagandist for the Scientology sect" and forbidden from performing at a government-funded concert in Stuttgart. Other German states banned him after promoters and government authorities were told of Corea's vocal advocacy in public appearances. The German government justified this by describing Scientology as "a totalitarian, business-driven organization," "non-religious," "a potential threat to democracy," and "guilty of significant human rights abuses."[182] Since the 1990s, Corea has been less outspoken but no less committed to Scientology. And he continues to apply Scientological ideas to music-making, enamored of the tradition's dream of "a world without war," its espoused commitment to human rights, and its technologies for awakening human potential. He dismisses sensational allegations about Scientology's feud with psychotherapy and its sci-fi paraliterature, saying simply that "Scientology is a strong promoter of religious tolerance."[183] The infinite nature of art and expression, for Corea, bids us to look beyond the limits of the body and time to realms of pure possibility. And this is why he ultimately sticks to jazz: "you can't pin it down, and it's a spirit of spontaneous creativity."[184]

Some Nasty, Urban, Ethnic Shit: Radical Jewish Culture

In 1994 a friend said I just had to hear John Zorn's Masada, describing it as "Ornette Coleman playing klezmer." Perhaps there was something in the air in the 1990s, marked by heated debates about "multiculturalism," if even jazz was becoming identitarian. A secular Jew from New York City, Zorn briefly attended St. Louis's Webster College, where the young alto saxophonist was exposed to the Black Artists' Group.[185] Taken with the 1970s avant-garde, Zorn's catholic musical tastes found him exploring not only different improvisational idioms—European free jazz, then-forgotten post-bop masters like Sonny Clark, or "No Wave"—but also Western soundtracks, surf tunes, and hardcore. In the tradition of American mavericks like Charles Ives, Harry Partch, or Frank Zappa, Zorn's "jazz" bands confronted audiences with grindcore; his "rock" bands played George Crumb fragments; his "chamber" ensembles scandalized listeners with hyperspeed Ornette Coleman nuggets. Zorn's attitude to orthodoxy seemed exemplified in his composition "Perfume of a Critic's Burning Flesh." What, then, was downtown's leading bad boy doing getting all comfy with Judaism?

It was an association with at least some precedent. Many early big band practitioners were reared Jewish and noted frequently the kinship between Jewish vernacular music and early jazz. The lilting, reeling dance music klezmer was actually called "Jewish Jazz" by some, "jazz" still functioning as a catch-all term for naming the musical (and by extension the cultural) other.[186] David Stowe notes that Judaism's resonance in jazz's early period "was consistent with the adaptive tendencies of Jewish music over many centuries."[187] While some of jazz's most famous Jewish players between the 1930s and the 1950s—like Benny Goodman and Dave Brubeck—seldom engaged the more ribald, theatrical dimensions of contemporary Jewish music, there were occasional expressions of audible Judaism in jazz, as when Ziggy Elman brought klezmer to Goodman's band in the 1930s, or when Cab Calloway imitated cantorial vocals. It was beginning in the 1950s that these themes began to resurface, not as something essentially "Jewish" or "jazzy" but in what Josh Kun calls "the aurality of Jewish difference."[188] Drummer Shelly Manne's *Steps to the Desert* celebrated the commonality of music-making in Jewish history, featuring pieces (including "Hava Nagila" and "Yossel, Yossel") that exemplified the variety of Jewish music as it influenced American culture.[189] This inaugurated a tradition that continues in more explicitly devotional contexts today. Reuben Hoch's Chassidic Jazz Project uses only liturgical melodies in its repertoire. Dave Chevan's Afro-Semitic Experience provides instrumental settings for music from Jewish High Holy Days, occasionally working with cantors in temple services. Pianist Ben Sidran has performed entire sets featuring Jewish liturgical classics and his own traditionally inspired originals (like the awfully titled "Shofar Shogood").[190]

One of the most interesting figures from mid-century, though, was cellist Fred Katz. In addition to his work with Chico Hamilton, Katz scored Roger Corman and Sidney Poitier films, taught jazz to Benedictine monks (he used to jam with a nun who played bongos and a sax-playing priest, to whom Katz used to enthuse "Father, you're a mutha—"), and was a professor of anthropology and comparative religion. Katz's 1958 *Folk Songs for Far Out Folk* rearranged American, Hebrew, and African traditional songs. Katz linked this souped-up, combinative traditionalism to his own religiosity. His father was a "self-taught Kabbalist," which Katz also studied. He described himself as an atheist and a practicing Buddhist: the front of his California home embodied his scrambling of cultural idioms often kept separate, with a Buddhist rock garden and a welcome mat beaming "Shalom."[191] Katz said, "I respect the search for God, the search for understanding...[t]he rest is make it up as you go along."[192] Just as some folks say about jazz.

Yet as we see everywhere in our explorations, spirits rejoicing enacts the difference that the term "religion" cannot contain either, perhaps even staging a further reversal whereby the religiousness of the music performs what the word *jazz* cannot. This kind of code-scrambling of "Judaism"— whether or not made "minor," as Deleuzians would say—is at work in African American clarinetist Don Byron's long-term engagement with klezmer music. Byron's 1993 *Plays the Music of Mickey Katz* was not only a sonic crossover but a mash-up of two schtick-happy traditions of American performance. Byron intended not only to celebrate klezmer but to complicate the memory of the mid-twentieth century as "a time of cheerful and harmonious pluralism."[193] Byron saw in Katz a musician who understood the ludicrousness of such entertainments, wanting to skewer their ersatz versions of "Jewishness" and present instead a Jewish American identity equally traditional and mischievous. To Byron, klezmer was no safe, NPR-ready folk music: "It was some *nasty, urban, ethnic* shit, B."[194]

Zorn's shit is pretty nasty and urban too, a polyglot music of the Lower East Side reckoning with that neighborhood's twinned histories of immigrant Judaism and experimental music. The downtown scene of which Zorn was the poster child took root in hoods where, before mid century, "lofts had not yet been converted from sweatshop factories and warehouses" and "the white ethnic immigrants who worked there had not yet moved out to the suburbs."[195] Zorn's disparate projects can be seen as his bucking against the way specific musical "contexts" (notes and implied harmony, for example) "are resolvable into systems" such as those that have long characterized Western composition; indeed, we might also hear his reconfiguration of religious tradition as analogous to such musical irresolvability.[196] Feeling himself very much a cultural outsider, in 1987 Zorn moved to Japan for several years and during this period began reflecting on his Judaism (motivated by experiences with anti-Semitism on tour in Germany and by his father's death).[197] His engagements were less metaphysical or conventionally ethnic than an attempt to figure out why so many of his contemporaries gravitated to experimental music: "[i]t was like, wait a minute, how come all these cats are Jewish?"[198]

In 1992 Munich sponsored a "Festival for Radical New Jewish Culture" (RJC). There Zorn explored his new interests, in a typically iconoclastic way. The powerful *Kristallnacht* blends furious free improv shrieking, Hitler recordings, and—during "Never Again"—layer after layer of the sound of shattering glass (the tintinnabulation is purposefully brutal, which Zorn intended to remind listeners that these events cannot simply be buried in the past). Always a combinative thinker, Zorn became compelled after this performance by the variety of possible answers to the question "What is Jewish music?" and saw in this multiplicity the fecundity, rather than the limits of tradition.[199] Over the next fifteen years, Zorn and fellow musicians began to explore the question under the aegis of the RJC series on Zorn's label Tzadik (which means "righteous one" in Hebrew). In 1993, at the cramped and wonderfully scuzzy old Knitting Factory on Houston Street, Zorn held the first RJC festival, which, along with the Knit's seders, became an annual event. There, one could spot Zorn in his trademark combat boots, leather jacket, and fatigues, now wearing a tallis and tzitzit beneath his clothing (though never a yarmulke).[200]

Many of the acts initially featured on Tzadik—including Zorn's multiple manifestations of Masada—were rooted loosely in klezmer sound, with its infectious melodies, bright dances, aching laments, and distinctive use of harmonic minor or Phrygian scales. Zorn sponsored Ben Goldberg's New Klezmer Trio, David Krakauer's Klezmer Madness, Marc Ribot's Yo I Killed Your God, Anthony Coleman's Selfhaters, and a series of provocative interventions by Richard Teitelbaum ("Golem"), Erik Friedlander, Marty Ehrlich, Shelly Hirsch ("O, Little Town of East New York"), and others. The series' stylistic range seemed to reflect Zorn's ambivalence regarding his own Judaism. On the one hand, he firmly opposed any kind of essentialism (to the point, as Jeffrey Matthew Janeczko observes, of lower-casing terms like "jews," "jewish," and "judaism").[201] Yet he also appeared to ascribe such consistent exploration and creative pluralism to the tradition itself. As Zorn and other RJC musicians explored these ideas throughout the 1990s (outside the RJC axis, pianist Narada Burton Greene, a student of Swami Satchidananda living in Amsterdam, had performed

klezmer since the late 1980s), participants and audience members came
to see the Knit as, in Michael Dorf's words, "a sort of shul for Jewish musicians who don't feel comfortable in the usual Jewish settings."[202] Tamar
Barzel described RJC efforts as creating a "conceptual space" for reassess-
ing religious and musical identities as consistent with the improvisatory
self-determination of Jewish history.[203]

Traditionalists thought RJC was too iconoclastic in a world where anti-
Semitism still thrived. Others saw "Jewish self-consciousness," however
cannily qualified, as a step back into enclave identity.[204] But like the other
traditions explored here, it is perhaps better seen as an improvisation on
religious identity through a different kind of boundary work, exploring not
just the capaciousness of tradition from the inside but the porousness of
apparent divisions between genres and cultures. If "Judaism" and "jazz" are
such unstable signifiers, why not play heavy metal like Yoshie Fruchter, or
Roberto Rodriguez's Cuban-Jewish hybrids, or reggae like David Gould?[205]
Did this music only become Jewish with the inclusion of Gershom Scholem
and Isaac Bashevis Singer quotes in the liners? Zorn once said "a Jew
is someone who naïvely believes that if he gives selflessly to his host culture he'll be accepted."[206] Performing this difference, this nonacceptance,
then, could constitute a Judaism whose identity was at best provisional, its
ironies and eclecticism kicking at steady moorings. It is transcribable, re-
peatable under the proper circumstances, but perhaps fully exilic and improvisatory to the last.[207] As Zorn wrote in a kind of RJC manifesto: "[j]ust
as jazz music has progressed from dixieland to free jazz and beyond...the
same kind of growth should be possible" for Judaism.[208]

Possible futures come, for Zorn, not from vigilant adherence to a specific canon but from the plunge into that point "where the objective and
the subjective begin to overlap," where individual idiosyncrasies remap tradition.[209] In several projects since 2000 he has woven his interests in
Kabbalah into a broader engagement with esotericism, ranging from
Aleister Crowley's Temple of the Golden Dawn to hermeticism to an almost
Swedenborgian fascination with angels. Zorn's Aleph-bet Sound Project
"acoustically explores the Kabbalistic principle that the ancient Hebrew
alphabet is a spiritual tool full of hidden meaning and harmony."[210] As part
of his "Book of Angels" (the second major phase of his Masada compositions), Zorn has often arranged a "Kol Nidre" to be performed with the specific sense that creative (or creator) angels are invoked in the ritual of
performance.[211] And in compositions like "Necronomicon," "IAO: Music in
Sacred Night," and "Songs from the Hermetic Theater," Zorn has found in

the unifying but fluid thematics of his own interpretation of Judaism a way to bring together the variety of his own musical interests.

This interplay between what John Brackett identifies as tradition and a Bataille-like impulse to transgression also characterizes other RJC musicians.[212] While many share musicological similarities—Janeczko identifies the recurrence of traditional compositions alongside modes like the Misheberakh—their understandings of Judaism vary considerably.[213] Guitarist John Schott says, "[T]hose three words [*radical, Jewish, culture*] are very contested ground."[214] Anthony Coleman explores affirmations of identity amid anti-Semitism in his combo Selfhaters, saying, "My Jewish experience *is* a palimpsest...the Jewish experience is atomized."[215] For Coleman, RJC is neither ironic nor kitschy but instead a vehicle for exploring the experiential difference of Jewish identity.[216] Trumpeter Frank London and his Klezmatics bandmates were miscast as iconoclasts when they "stripped away...[a]ll the schmaltz, kitschy nostalgia, the corny elements, all the *Fiddler on the Roof*."[217] With albums designed to raise consciousness about gay rights and other issues, the Klezmatics wanted to restore klezmer's authentically radical dimension, rooted in social activism. To London these seemingly disparate explorations of avant-garde jazz, political activism, and religious tradition are simply part of a Jewish multiplicity that can be heard in a single rhythm. He sees no relevant distinction between his study of Arabic or Ethiopian music and his involvement in cantorial *hazònos* or Hasidic *nigunim*; for London such combinations flourish in "spiritual Jewish music" that requires no texts or institution as long as it possesses "spiritual intensity, a meaning, *kavana*."[218]

Clarinetist Ben Goldberg formed the New Klezmer Trio in Berkeley in 1987 explicitly to reimagine klezmer "in an avant-garde way."[219] To Goldberg, if klezmer could not develop then perhaps neither could Judaism. Tenor saxophonist Greg Wall's Later Prophets pursues a similar sense of historical updating, combining idioms from traditional Azhkenazic music to funk. Linking their improvisations to the practice of Torah cantillation, Wall credits his tutelage of a Lubavitcher Hasid as opening him up to a deeper exploration of his own Judaism. In their sax lessons, "Wall began davening mincha, or the afternoon prayer service" and became involved with a Jersey City minyan, where he saw in this "true 'lunatic fringe' of Judaism" an obsessiveness and idiosyncrasy that mirrored his own.[220] He got deeper into prayer and Torah study and stopped taking Friday night gigs in observance of the Sabbath. Now an orthodox rabbi, Wall even performs (in both liturgical and improvisational settings) on the shofar, or ram's horn, contending that "[t]he sound of the shofar emanating from the heavens was heard at Mt. Sinai" and responding to its sound "is a mitzvah."[221]

Trumpeter Steven Bernstein contends that music is made Jewish by either playing traditional materials (regardless of style) or playing with what one considers to be the spirit of Judaism.[222] Paul Shapiro has written for the "Saturday morning liturgical melodies" he recalled from his youth, for the Kabballat Sabbath, and in commemoration of mealtime among Yiddish-speaking Jews in New York.[223] Shapiro waxes in the style of Mircea Eliade when observing that, in the transition from mundane to sacred time and place, music evokes "something that is deep inside yourself that excites yourself, [and] good music comes out."[224] Yet he also believes Jewish liturgy is fundamentally musical: "when they're praying...[people] sing or hum to themselves...everyone is moving forward, at different speeds...like sort of an Ornette Coleman approach to free jazz."[225] Vocalist Jewlia Eisenberg's iconoclastic Charming Hostess reminds audiences that vernacular Judaism is a repository of women's prayers and sensibilities. Her Bowls Projects recites inscriptions from Babylonian incantation bowls to tell "stories about female desire, spirituality, and the power of magic."[226] Seth Rogovoy hears Charming Hostess as an extension of midrashic tradition, "layering commentaries upon stories, and stories upon commentaries."[227]

The varied, capacious RJC community even accommodates an evasion of Judaism itself. While some see this as paradigmatically Jewish, others—like winds player Ned Rothenberg—see it leading to a kind of dissolution of classification. An Oberlin religious studies major in the late 1970s, Rothenberg developed as an improviser alongside his exploration of Watazumido-Shuso's shakuhachi music.[228] Rothenberg—who described himself to me as "kind of the agnostic here, bordering on atheist"—might seem an unlikely candidate to contribute to RJC.[229] While he uses differing ensembles in ways that mirror RJC focus on the fluidity and polymorphousness of identity, Rothenberg long resisted Zorn's entreaties for a "Jewish record," since he is a secular Jew with reservations about cultural identity.[230] But on *Inner Diaspora*, he chronicles the movement between cultures and an opposition to what he provocatively calls "spiritual materialism."

Rothenberg is not entirely sold on the frequent avowals that improvised music can create trance or "spiritual" states, or even necessarily on the ritual quality of music-making. He says instead, "I just call it presence....This is something nobody can own....Maybe when I'm playing solo I'm more like a priest or something but I don't own it." By contrast, what he calls "spiritual materialism" is "all these people competing with each other to jump through the highest hoops, whether it's orthodox Jews talking about how many fibers they have in their coats or whether it be Shiites and Sunnis arguing.... You might as well play baseball."[231] So instead of quasi-mystical ruminations about experience, and explicitly against "spiritual materialism," Rothenberg's tentative identification with Judaism refers more to "a personal, historical thing" (rather than what he calls "the experience thing") whose very "Jewishness" he hopes will be downplayed (even as he admits that this music could likely only have been written by a late twentieth-century/early twenty-first-century agnostic urban Jew).

Imaginary Folklore: Jazz's Rovers

Traditions, then, are not always comfortable in their own housings or unidirectional in their implications for music-making. Even a cursory survey of American religious traditions reveals their pliability, ceaseless change and adaptation (even when declaring themselves resistant to change), and tendencies to develop newer, denser branches. Jazz is most clearly shaped by the combinative, fluid tendencies of American religious traditions. Ranging from African American Christianity to RJC, we see a consistent, improvisational instability in even the most purportedly stable expression of "religion." These qualities are consistent with jazz, and with a subset of American religious practitioners sometimes called "seekers," those who rove between traditions, combining them or linking them together in a kind of holism. Beyond the role of jazz in new religious movements, or musicians who convert from one tradition to another, the importation, fusion, and multifaceted appropriations of post-1965 America reveal different dimensions of how traditions get "jazzed." By "rovers" I mean those religious "seekers" who travel from location to location, changing and combining fragments of religious traditions to facilitate the changing needs of self-realization. While this might sound functionally analogous to New Age practitioners—who might blend reiki palm healing with sweat lodge ceremonies—for musicians like Don Cherry and Hamid Drake, these explorations evoke a more apt analogy to a well-constructed improvisation that interpolates elements from different idioms (always with the understanding that this, too, is temporary and revisable).

Crucial to this moment in jazz is the increased presence of musicians who trained outside the United States and brought the aesthetics of other musical traditions (almost always with cultural and religious assumptions) into jazz circles. Examples of these performers include oudist Rabih Abou-Khalil, percussionist Zakir Hussain, and vocalist Sainkho Namtchylak. Alongside this development are a growing number of players who, like so many Americans in the late 1960s and 1970s, appropriated and adopted new religious idioms from Asia, Africa, or elsewhere. Here, musicians fashion self and sound from these expressions of religion, and new religious formats from sonic exploration: harvesting new sounds from nonstandard instruments like the erhu or the djembe, positing the religiosity of the encounter between different musical communities jointly exploring communication and creativity, or embracing "jazz" as music that could, in its very openness and mutuality, realize the principles of peace or spiritual enlightenment. Saxophonist Hafez Modirzadeh writes of these tendencies that jazz's "inclusivity" is a chief reason that it has so often sought to explore and/or absorb various "world musics."[232] Examples of these tendencies abound, especially in the musical extensions begun in the 1950s and 1960s: Ahmed Abdul-Malik's introduction of the oud into jazz, Yusef Lateef's popularization of then-exotic reed instruments like the shenai, Kali Z. Fasteau's multi-instrumentalism, and Miles Davis's use of Badal Roy's tabla.[233]

Few did as much to popularize this kind of musical/spiritual voyage as Don Cherry. Known for his puckish improvising on pocket trumpet, Cherry was the son of a Choctaw woman and African American man from Oklahoma. He spent his formative years in Los Angeles, singing in a Baptist church choir and keeping an ear cocked to the city's influential Central Avenue music scene.[234] An early acolyte of bebop, he absorbed as much music as possible, something that reflected not just his omnivorous love of jazz but his sense that musical communication at any level possessed growth possibilities. With Ornette Coleman's pioneering bands, Cherry's often startling lines sounded like they wanted to vibrate their way out of their quasi-bop syntax into pure velocity, the perfectly pinched contrast to Coleman's deep, bluesy inflections. They sounded like prophets portending a new musical covenant, or at times like what novelist Thomas Pynchon (who famously nodded in the direction of two jazz eccentrics, Coleman and Monk, with the sax-playing character McClintick Sphere) would years later describe with the iconic opening line to Gravity's Rainbow: "A screaming comes across the sky."

Cherry set off on his own and to explore associations and musical idioms that reflected his religious curiosity. Often called a musical gypsy, Cherry announced that "jazz is indeed an international language," with improvisation a kind of common tongue that could overcome discord and distance.[235] Playing with an international coterie of musicians, Cherry began to use what some called "Third World" instruments to reflect the spiritual growth he thought improvisation facilitated.[236] He received State Department funding for trips to Africa, where he studied traditional rhythms and instruments like the doussn'gouni.[237] This notion of spiritual realization through slipping the bonds of home and identity is on the one hand written deep into the American religious imaginary; Cherry and wife, Mocqui, flirted regularly with establishing a green utopia around their home Tagarp in Sweden, an organic farm that served often as a house of hospitality for children and traveling musicians, and which prompted many to compare Cherry to Thoreau.[238] But it was also a means of reconstruing the entire world, even the universe itself as one's home. And it was in the wandering and the wondering that one became enlightened. So the hitchhiking Cherry emerged in the late 1960s as a jazz Bashô whose purpose was "to play different instruments in...natural settings like a catacomb or a mountaintop or by the side of a lake."[239] Such a "musical gypsy" was Cherry that he sat in with actual gypsies in France, as part of his attempt to prostrate himself continually before different musical teachers, be they traditional gurus like Ustad Zia M'Digar (with whom, Cherry professed, he had to "humble" himself), or the Native American saxophonist Jim Pepper (whose father was a traditional singer in pow-wows and with whom the quarter-Choctaw Cherry had a deep affinity).[240]

He sometimes saw himself as constructing an "imaginary folklore" for future humans.[241] Cherry's sense of music's peaceable kingdom, and its enlightenment possibilities, was thus reflected in his growing internationalism and embrace of pan-global spirituality (signaled in titles like "Nu Creative Love" or "Om Nu"). Cherry believed "jazz" (or "organic music") now had to be realized with nontraditional instruments so it could be fully interactive and also realize its meditative aims, which Cherry described as "the discovery of one's inner self."[242] After the apotheosis of free jazz, many heard in Cherry's different path a way out of the fractured 1960s, an impression that led some players and listeners to regard Cherry as a kind of shaman or guru. By 1973's *Relativity Suite*, Cherry had been studying karnatic vocals with Pandit Pran Nath and was incorporating Hindu devotional chants into his performances. He adapted ragas, recited sacred texts, and cribbed from gamelan and other musics. He wanted to "make [performance] space as holy as he could," by laying down a rug and "draping a cloth wall hanging behind him decorated with the Sanskrit scale."[243] Vibraphonist Karl Berger recalled Cherry's belief that "gamala taki rhythm training" and group chanting "could connect improvisers with the musical traditions of any culture."[244] His subsequent *Eternal Now* tipped its hat to the burgeoning New Age moment, its title referring to growing interest in mindfulness and total awareness (linked by advocates of New Age to not only a heightened perception—as located in meditational or shamanic traditions—but to the realization of positive human futures).[245] Cherry's was as synthetic a vision as one might encounter in the overstuffed aisles of the "metaphysics" section of the growing number of New Age bookstores in the United States and Europe, though he also insisted that the Tibetan Buddhism he practiced tied it all together: "the dharma is everywhere."[246] And while his newly tranquil, meditational music seemed distinct from "jazz," his groups' "sense of one-world optimism" reflected sonically the hopes of many listeners still invested in that category.[247]

Cherry was not the only player seeing cultural and geographic exploration as necessary accompaniments to musical seeking. Horace Silver's *Silver n' Percussion* was a "tribute to the gods: side one of the Yoruba, Masai and Zulu; side two the Indian gods of the Incas, Aztec and Mohican" (Silver was also involved in Transcendental Meditation at this time).[248] In 1978, Maynard Ferguson began making annual pilgrimages to "a place in South India that embraces all the faiths."[249] Percussionist Dan Weiss studied with tabla guru Pandit Samir Chatterjee. Harris Eisenstadt has studied with African percussion masters, reflecting his interest in spiritual inclusivity (he claims his percussion playing is inspired by the example of Mohandas Gandhi and *ahimsa*) and instrumental specificity.[250] Saxophonist Avram Fefer, from a family of European Jews, notes, "[M]y own recent Jazz spirituals" are informed by his early studies of Krishnamurti.[251] Others associate their music with specific devotional or textual lineages as a way of acknowledging what they understand to be the sacrality of their pursuits. Ravish Momin's Trio Tarana plays an amalgam of "Japanese Taiko drum ensembles, Afghani folk songs, Hindu chant and North Indian rhythms."[252] Former theology student, vocalist Kurt Elling has set Rumi poems to jazz song. Bassist/ composer Dave Holland (whose legendary recording *Conference of the Birds* is, in fact, *not* inspired by Attar, though vocalist Jeanne Lee once wrote such an adaptation) has composed tributes to Vedanta mysticism and also transcribed and arranged "a traditional song of the Ba-benzele pygmies of West Africa."[253] Billy Fox has arranged Rabindranath Tagore compositions. Deepak Ram chose the flute because of its association with Lord Krishna. Mixing jazz standards with devotional tunes, Ram seeks to realize the musical effect of Krishna's own flute: when followers heard it, Ram notes, they "forgot their own individual identities and found themselves running to the sound, which is the ultimate truth or reality."[254] The Prana Trio seeks to "probe the mysteries of improvisation and the spirituality of classic poetry from ancient Persia, India, and China...to convey deep feelings and mystical power."[255] And trumpeter Roy Campbell took Cherry's cue and used improvised music to break down cultural barriers.[256]

One of the most spirited exponents of this tradition is percussionist Hamid Drake. Born Hank Drake in 1955 in Monroe, Louisiana, the percussionist moved with his family to Evanston, Illinois. Inspired by revolutions in rock, Drake picked up drums. Influenced by a wide range of musical idioms and performers, Drake played everything from mainstream jazz to reggae. Meeting Cherry in 1978 proved to be one of the most significant moments in Drake's life. They worked together until Cherry's death in 1995, exploring "music's spiritually infinite transformational possibilities."[257] The drum's folk associations and cultural functions seem to Drake to be written directly into music's spiritual registers. Yet he is not even sure he would commit to a distinction between music and spirituality, "because music to me is a spiritual force and...the people that I hold high in the music world I feel have also been spiritual forces."[258]

Drake is attracted to improvised music's evasion of fixed linguistic formulations, genres, or spiritual housings. He suggests that "one of the great forces that is motivating the whole thing of course is love which also allows us to enter into the magical play of mystery. This is a place without definition, without boundaries."[259] Though he has explored Sufism, Hinduism, and Rastafarianism intensively, Drake is currently studying with Vajrayana Buddhist teachers Traktung Rinpoche and A'dzom Rinpoche, and links these qualities of improvisation specifically to Buddhist teachings about "the empty nature of form."[260] He explains further that awareness of sound's infinite possibilities should lead to a sense of "interrelationship."[261] Music's implications for ethics and spirituality, then, are shaped by his Buddhist teachers who say that "there's an aspect of me that dissolves so I can be in a place of maybe not having so many preconceived notions."[262] It is the responsibility of the musician not to foreground merely personal expression but to understand that music can promote egoless awareness and thus a kind of healing, which Drake says is really "the enlightened role of the musician."[263] Drake also relates this ethic/aesthetic to the Sufi maxim "die before you die."[264]

These are, for Drake, philosophical and spiritual universals that can be accessed through multiple traditions of inquiry and expression. When one pursues questions of meaning, Drake believes that one finds "something deeper to life than what we always perceive, that's just right in front of us."[265] He adds that in thinking about these matters, "[i]t's not that we have to become hardcore religionists"; but contemplatives, musicians, and others who try to "reach those high peaks" can feel "this other energy starting to pervade their whole body and their whole stream of things," whether one calls "[t]his life force" prana, chi, Brahman, or God, to cite the examples Drake notes.[266] Seeking out this "divine source" through music brings the seeker in touch with "something that's inside of us...almost like this door that's waiting to be opened."[267] He likens the experience of improvising in this manner to what happens with "different meditative techniques," where "we push ourselves past that point that we think we can't go any further," to the point where "[t]here's this juice, this electricity, that's kind of flowing."[268] This is Whitman, he says; this is Emerson. Music and one's own mantras—or Drake chanting hymns to Allah as he plays frame drum—allow one to get "tapped into a whole other mind stream...to tap into this deeper sense of life."[269]

One finds here a sense of the aesthetic, where one encounters the other (in the divine, and in one's fellow players) with a sense of awe and responds with ethical motivations to "become better human beings...[and] show a little more kindness and compassion."[270] These sensibilities come to Drake through, and are sustained by, the specific teachings informing him. From Sufism, he says, comes "this expression that there's only one being, but that one being does have different faces...all we have to do is find a way to allow it to unfold."[271] Indeed, it is importantly through the very roving itself that these sensibilities are inculcated. But they also come through the specifics of musical practice, sonically, generatively. Drake told me his Bindu project pursued such specificity, using "different form[s] of music" as it "focuses on the spiritual in music."[272] Drake adapts devotional chants from Northern India, qawwalis, and fuses them together in reggae or swinging jazz, in order to evoke what he calls sensuality and "the science of rhythms."[273] And Bindu dedicates itself to various spirit inspirations (musicians and more recognizable deities) in its ongoing effort to "create open environments."[274]

WE COME TO a pause in this book's early improvising on "religion," an "open environment" where we might look at religious traditions anew. Unconsciously, we understand traditions as stable things distinguished from other static entities, religion against music, say. But their complexities and breakdowns put the lie to any simple sociology of community or denominational study. This is not to say that traditional boundedness of and orientations to community play no role here, since they clearly matter for some musicians. But we see more regularly a flouting of convention and a ceaseless playfulness with traditions that has become steadily more observable in American religions generally. If all we do when asking "what is a tradition?" or "what is jazz?" is provide names that posit a false coherence, we miss out on this shifting expanse of multiplicity so integral to jazz and the protean nature of American religions too. They are deceptive signifiers, and yet fundamentally interwoven.

Since any consideration of jazz and religiosity must also be a consideration of an American racial habitus—"the reality of the sweating brow," as this is experienced by African American performers—it seems reasonable to wonder how and where the engagement with religious traditions points beyond material and experiential constraints. Standing amid a cultural and historical context of degradation and marginalization, where black expressivity and subjectivity have been denied or undermined, religious belonging of the sort permitted by traditional identification creates possibilities for living outside the "reality" of conventional institutions, expectations, and representations of music-making. Is this not the story of American religions sounded out among and by jazz musicians? It is a story produced not by trite, one-dimensional links with putatively stable traditions, pieties, or institutional locations, but rather through a wending, densely combinative, and surprising riot of ideas. Like jazz. Like America. Now, what stories does jazz tell about itself and about America, and how does religion figure in them?

3

Shadows on a Wall

JAZZ NARRATES AMERICAN RELIGIONS[1]

JOHN CARTER WAS from Texas but spent the majority of his musical life in Los Angeles. One of jazz's most dazzling clarinet innovators, Carter's major statement was a five-album chronicle of African and African American history, *Roots and Folklore: Episodes in the Development of American Folk Music.* The fourth album, *Fields,* focuses on slavery and its conclusion, "On a Country Road," features Carter's clarinet accompanying a recorded front porch conversation with his uncle, who recalled traveling muddy country roads on a busted buggy. Carter worked a fifth alongside the chatter, capping it with a woody minor third trill. Like this clarinet phrase, the narrative is a dissonance to the bright tonic of America's song of self-understanding; its chronicle of pain, dislocation, and inhumanity a rejoinder to the smiling face we show the world.

This moment resounds in a broad tradition wherein musicians have chronicled their experiences and cultural roots. Jazz narrates itself in ways I regard as central to the American religious imagination, and especially to long-standing traditions of African American sacred historiography. Clearly, jazz's archives are filled with creations that celebrate, bemoan, and interrogate American history. Some see jazz as key to completing the American experiment. Others see improvisation itself as an "exchange of histories."[2] Jazz might be a lost history, or a technique for recovering it; jazz might be a tone parallel to America or a counter-melody. Is jazz democracy in miniature, a countersign to a history of white privilege, or perhaps something else? In each formulation, though, jazz is "an ongoing medium of memory."[3] Its sounds are "the alternative archives of history," in which "musicians have discursively transcoded the hard facts" into specific sonic constructions.[4] The music's religious reimagination of (mostly) African American history and identity obviously employs critical declamation. But these retellings also employ strategies of evasion designed to counter attempts to control and commodify "jazz" and "religion" alike; they contend with racialized aesthetic formations that demand sweating exuberance from black musicians; and they produce alternative narratives wherein an African past is invoked as counter-sign and critical lever against America. Improvised music and religiosity jam together in forming, reflecting, and challenging modern understandings of religion, nation, and race.

Religious narratives of the nation are a familiar topic, ranging from Protestant providential musings to Mormon sacred history to dystopian renderings of America as Babylon. While jazz has regularly chronicled its own history or paid tribute to revered figures in African American religious history (Anthony Davis wrote an opera for Malcolm X and many others, from Julius Hemphill to Christian McBride, have written odes to Martin Luther King Jr.), a strong undercurrent exists in the music that attempts to establish history, place, and tradition in jazz by framing these categories religiously or in relation to something called "religion." This chapter explores three such modes of exploration.

The first narrative mode criticizes what Charles Mingus once called "A Holding Corporation Called Old America." This mode is exemplified by Mingus's, Max Roach's, and Archie Shepp's works during the civil rights era, and more recently by saxophonist Fred Ho's criticism of American Christianity and capitalism. A second mode resounds in what Sun Ra called the "Astro Black" dimensions, where Afrocentric history and futurism blend in music designed to facilitate and explain religious experience. Finally, composers like Duke Ellington, John Carter, and Wynton Marsalis have also narrated African American religious history itself. Each mode makes religion the subject and object of musical and cultural narrations. Jazz remembers and writes via the religious, its sounds continually made and transformed. Fats Waller may have once sang, "Mr. Christopher Columbus sailed the ocean with rhythm as a compass," but these histories resound more clearly in Ellington's differential chords.

A Polyphonic Past

It can be said with some confidence that a peculiar self-consciousness has shaped American religious and national sensibilities since before something called the United States existed. This tendency to engage in historical self-reflection has regularly been accompanied by religious self-imaginings too. Of particular importance to spirits rejoicing is a confluence of traditions in which African Americans have imagined and narrated their complex relation to the United States and the African past. These narratives have been liberatory and fatalist, apocalyptic and reformist, marked by immanent democratic critique or Pan-African rejectionism. This deep history of religio-national imagination has shaped and is reflected in jazz history since the mid-twentieth century. This is not to suggest that the works discussed below can be reduced to their narratological or political properties, as if the sounds are mere accompaniment to text or ideology. Instead, the sounds themselves simply *are* the history, the religion, and the politics they aim also to evoke.

Early attempts to set African American experience to music (from Scott Joplin and William Grant Still to Duke Ellington) reckoned regularly with Africa as a source of freedom and culture. The construction of a "usable past" took place in religious traditions, civic institutions, and the expressive arts, as narrators and creators wrote their way into and out of society, grappling with the central dynamic of freedom and constraint in the religious imaginary and democratic life. As Curtis Evans, Eddie Glaude Jr., and Laurie Maffly-Kipp show, the construction of black sacred histories is complex and nonlinear even as it often privileges singular categories. In the eighteenth and nineteenth centuries, African American figures like Jacob Oson and Alexander Crummell proposed a common history for those who were ripped from their homes, suffered through Middle Passage, and were renamed "slaves." Narrations of lost Africa were important means by which African Americans came to understand their condition, consciousness, and culture; and these constitute a tradition of reflection that (re-)emerges in jazz's historical soundings. Through a series of associational networks emerging in the 1770s, many of these narrations expanded their territorial and thematic concerns to extend to Masonry and Egyptology, fascinations that would last well into the twentieth century as formative influences on figures from Noble Drew Ali to Sun Ra. The narratives (coming from figures like Henry Highland Garnet, Martin Delany, Henry McNeal Turner, W. E. B. DuBois, and later figures such as Marcus Garvey or W. D. Fard) shared a focus on autonomy and self-determination, nascent Afrocentrism, a geographical contrast that reveals the importance of space to these historical longings. Distance both real and imagined was central to reckonings with America, and voyages into the past served as attempts to shape the future. The powers that collapsed the distance between Africa and America were the same powers lending to black creativity a pronounced religious power, a truthfulness and authenticity, an emotional or expressive energy. Qualities such as these, of course, were also those which critics and colonialists seized upon to pronounce African American culture wanting in relation to both European and traditional ("real") African cultures.

As Maffly-Kipp shows, these narrations "gave African Americans control over their identities, allowed them to refute the pervasive dictum of black inferiority, and affected their ability to shape the future."[5] These narratives were usually religious and thus "gave birth to a worldview and a way of interpreting circumstances that imparted meaning and value" to the experience of slavery and oppression.[6] The narratives led often, as Glaude shows, to upended assumptions about and values of blackness, often shading into exhortations to freedom and self-determination.[7] More than this, though, these narratives both contained and stimulated interest in music and ritual, in griots, in cultural borrowings and crossings, the very improvisations that would later constitute in sound the narrative themes first written on nineteenth-century pages. More than a flat historical consciousness, then, the narratives reveal and promise an Ellingtonian polyphony and discord.

These projects have been extended and complicated by jazz composers. Just as histories of black culture, though they may express themselves in what Maffly-Kipp calls "familiar, racially-derived styles," cannot be "fixed" and pinned down in a comprehensive narrative, so too does black sound— perhaps especially jazz, which largely eschews lyrical content and lives in improvisation—elude settled formulations, constantly leaping past those patches of turf where it can be notated, essentialized.[8] The messiness of the past, its polyphonic details and complex voicings, challenges attempts by outsiders to locate and preserve a "presentable" form of blackness. More than just DuBois and Garvey and Malcolm X, the marginal or subcultural expressions that populate African American historical sensibilities reveal a series of complex, interstitial expressions of religion, race, and culture. And sound.

Jazz also emerged as *part* of this history, struggling to be heard amid the clangor of American self-congratulation and assertions of religiosity. Jazz has been shaped by, and partaken in, American narratives about national progress, public life, modernity, and religion/secularism. Its musicians have improvised on larger traditions of American meaning-making, as both critics and caretakers. Theirs are histories made new, and in them "religion" is recast audibly not as a category in someone else's teleology but something emergent in timbre, rhythm, and the lilt of melodies, ever changing onward, resisting the notion that anyone in particular has the final say about its meanings.

A Holding Corporation Called Old America

Even narratives not marked by "religious content" often turn on some formulation of the religious: as a spiritual principle underwriting democracy, as an assumed cultural-musical wellspring, or as the vital absence that makes possible an art like jazz. This self-consciousness is central to a critical mode wherein jazz composers have assessed their own history and religion so as to measure America's worth. Against "A Holding Corporation Called Old America," musicians disrupt the history of "religion" in the name of other principles, or use religious tropes to challenge the corporation's tale.

Jesus Christ and Guy Lombardo: Charles Mingus

When one thinks of bassist and composer Charles Mingus, a collection of whose recordings is aptly titled *Passions of a Man*, one thinks first of an eruptive temper. There are those stories, after all. He once met his landlord carrying a shotgun beneath his overcoat. Mingus was no fan of the rent. He legendarily excoriated his audiences: "[W]e are distracted by your noise. Don't even take any drinks or rattle the ice in your glasses, and no cash registers ringing."[9] Mingus was no fan of distractions. He terrorized his band, pushing a musician offstage, mocking their screwups ("that's why we call it a workshop"), even breaking trombonist Jimmy Knepper's jaw onstage.[10] Mingus was no fan of indiscipline. But Mingus's joy, tenderness, and sorrow were equally renowned, from loving tributes to Duke Ellington to riotous, jubilant defiance of social convention on "Oh Lord, Don't Let Them Drop That Atomic Bomb on Me" ("Don't let 'em drop it! Stop it! Bebop it!"). What brought together such rage, melancholy, and joy? Mingus was no fan of America. Only, he was.

Mingus was reared in Los Angeles and, like so many other players, profoundly shaped by his exposure to religious music, especially that of "the Holiness church, which was too raw for my father."[11] But this was the raw sound and emotion that grabbed him: the quaver of church sonics, and the riffing quality of the preacher's cadence. Beyond this, Duke Ellington's music "excited me so much that I almost screamed."[12] Following stints with vibraphonists Lionel Hampton and Red Norvo, Mingus began to explore first the bass's melodic possibilities and the use of layered tempi in composition. This signaled an independent streak also manifested when, in 1953, Mingus helped organize a series of Jazz Workshops at Brooklyn's Putnam Central Club. Restless with jazz orthodoxy, too, he began to reinvestigate religious music and its foregrounding of feeling over technique. This was part commentary on the routinization of society, which occluded the spirit in favor of technical rationality. The use of vernacular materials also evinced a historical sensibility that conferred authority on the fiercely critical tone of his music. Mingus believed that jazz was "the individual's means of expressing his deepest and innermost feelings and emotions."[13] Feeling became both aesthetic and ethic. Consequently, the larger the thematic material Mingus explored, the more he heard his reckonings with African American history and religion as vehicles for the expression of enthusiasms and passions that signified against a dead, conformist society.

The scope of Mingus's ambitions was announced with *Pithecanthropus Erectus*, a meditation on humanity's decline, which he saw in an America defined more by its antagonisms than its promise. The wide-ranging piece exemplified his belief that "all music is one," its resistance to category not just an aesthetic lesson but a religious one, since sound could not be contained any more than spirituality.[14] Mingus saw *PE* as a means to catalyze feeling, galvanize the shared work of improvisation, and set the spirit moving. Yet its declension narrative held that "this *machine world* we see would never have been . . . if not for the religious fanatics and white slaves who thought it was their idea in [their] quest for freedom and ventured to America as pilgrims."[15]

Rejecting the association of jazz with the modern, Mingus fulminated that even white jazzbos seduced by jazz's passion (as an antidote to dullsville cold war culture) participated in an essentialism that acted as racial constraint. Throughout the 1950s, he experimented compositionally and often sought to conjure "soul" in his music, now more powerfully evocative of the blues and gospel. He wrote using a complex rhythmic language whose multiple tempi became vehicles for thematic juxtaposition. Setting different musical materials against one another, with a boiling rhythm section that made your heart leap, was no simple act of musicology; for Mingus, the "dissonant intensity" and "swelling and fading tones" of these efforts were meant to call attention to the clash of opposites and sublimation of passions in American life.[16] It is meaningful, then, that records like *Oh Yeah, Ah Um,* and *Blues and Roots* brimmed with church influences: a low-end gospel tremolo; complex antiphonal work, trading phrases back and forth in a knowing echo of the call-and-response dialogism of African American music (Mingus claimed to be gifted with "extrasensory perceptions" and said of his near telepathic rapport with drummer Dannie Richmond, "It made me start to believe in God"); and a use of guttural, vocalic textures that connected New Orleans to the avant-garde.[17] Mingus shouted encouragement to his bandmates, the stage his pulpit. He described tunes like "Wednesday Night Prayer Meeting" as a sound from his childhood, where parishioners "sing and shout and do a little Holy Rolling."[18] On some tunes, Mingus even confessed from within the ensemble: "Oh my Jesus!" or "I know I been wrong, yeah, I have."

It is too simple, though, to hear in such multitudinous music only the call-and-response patterns of "the black church" or the emotional enthusiasms audiences demanded of "black music." Like the music of Charles Ives, another great American compositional maverick, Mingus's music aimed to jar the senses, scramble convention, and sound out new cultural, political, and religious meaning. Yet many authors have narrowed the parameters of Mingus's sound by calling his use of hushed dynamics "reverent" or "confessional," or suggesting that his use of collective improvisation parallels the "oral tradition" of African American religiosity.[19] These hearings are too credulous, mistaking Mingus's preacher guise on these famous pieces for a one-dimensional authenticity, absent of irony, critique, or complexity, recapitulating an audience's desire to hear an uninterrupted flow of "black religion" through improvisations that could be edifying but not troubling. But Mingus's music *was* history, the music of past, present, and future roiling together in an "imagined church service."[20] Like James Baldwin, he often lambasted the tradition others would habitually link him to. He said of "religious minds or primitive minds" that "[t]hey tend to go on luck and feeling and emotion and goof."[21] And he fretted that "black people of America don't have a folk music, unless it be church, which is pretty corny."[22]

Similarly, others see in Mingus's responses to the civil rights movement the limit of his critique. This is not to deny the power and importance of the social commentary Mingus regularly delivered by the late 1950s (and after all, Mingus pointed out this connection to his listeners quite bluntly). When Mingus wanted to be direct, his music throbbed with singular purpose, as with "Freedom" (a dirge set to the sound of chains: "freedom for your brothers and sisters, but no freedom for me"), "Prayer for Passive Resistance," or the undeniable intensities of "Haitian Fight

Song." Most emphatic was the controversial "Fables of Faubus," a swipe at the Arkansas governor who forcibly prevented school integration. Mingus wrote lyrics that his ripped, righteous quartet brought alive:

> *Name me a handful that's ridiculous, Danny.*
> *Faubus, Nelson Rockefeller, Eisenhower*
> *Why are they so sick and ridiculous?*
>
> *Two, four, six, eight:*
> *They brainwash and teach you hate.*

"H-E-L-L-O!" Are you listening, America? The point was to be heard. The centrality of the voice to this formatting of "religion" is not coincidental, and it resounds too with imaginings of democratic self-determination. The riotous self-creation of a whooping Mingus small group—the bass in your face, Richmond's ride tapping out possibility, indomitable horns singing new bodies—was cited as a model for the freedoms sought by the civil rights movement (less, though, was made of the more authoritarian Mingus of larger ensembles). The pulse at the heart of Mingus's music linked it not only to African idioms like Ghanaian highlife but to the glorious propulsion of Bach, whose music made Mingus swoon and which he insisted made it possible to imagine lofty human achievements like the moon landing. Ultimately, though, his music resounded with his nonconformity, his thumping, swinging enthusiasm a quickening of the pulse that made the words and the critiques as urgent as the polyrhythmic sound. As Jennifer Griffith notes, Mingus's playfulness with genre meant he would not let his audiences become complacent. He famously pissed on their self-satisfaction: "you think you're important and digging jazz… [but] [y]ou don't want to see your ugly selves, the untruths, the lies you give to life."[23] Here we see an ambivalence about "jazz" as pronounced as that regarding "religion." While he dreamed that jazz—"which is religiously involved, without the Christian tones"—might one day be recognized as "a sacred music for our people," even become a kind of church itself, he also asserted "[j]azz means 'nigger': if you can't get a job in a symphony you can get a little job over here where you get a lot of write-ups and no money."[24]

Of course, Mingus meant it when he displayed his ambivalences and multiple personas, and there is no imposing a false cohesion on his personality or his composition of religio-historical elements. Among the things Mingus was out to make audible were these very limits of genre, the artist's persona, and religious identities. Mingus was also out to make religion audible and the most consistent subject of these efforts was the riot of African American history itself, a clash and a jumble greater than his personalities, a narrative that could not contain itself and could not hope to represent the variety of experience callously ignored by audiences and government. He could only direct it, like his shotgun, at a holding corporation named old America. (Mingus once literally took aim at the holding corporation's racist expectations, when he showed up to Columbia's accounting department with "safari suit, helmet, and shotgun.")[25]

Into the mid-1960s, the voluble bassist strove to create his most sheerly beautiful music as a sign against the violence and naked degradation he felt around him. The large ensemble record *The Black Saint and the Sinner Lady* synthesized post-bop arranging, Latin rhythms, and collective polyphony. Yet in typically Mingusian fashion, at the heart of this rapturous music was an accompanying libidinous rant about soul and Freud and detestable critics, his response to "living in a society that calls itself sane ... [where] we should be blown up to preserve their idea of how life should be."[26] In channeling various pasts (beauties and critical principles alike) against a nasty present, Mingus himself was drifting further from any balance between his hope and anger. His groups of the mid-1960s explored his fury at Watts, Malcolm X's assassination, and Congress's inability to change life for African Americans. Mingus sharpened his historical articulations in compositions like "Once Upon a Time There Was a Holding Corporation Called Old America" and "They Trespass the Land of the Sacred Sioux." But by 1966, emotionally strung out, he dropped out of the scene altogether. His outlook was reflected in a dark, menacing 1968 improvisation on the Pledge of Allegiance: "I pledge allegiance to the flag, the white flag. . . . I pledge allegiance to seeing that someday they will live up to their own promises to the victims that they call citizens."[27]

In 1970 it became apparent what Mingus had been doing during much of his "retirement." As the bassist put together a cracking new band and began to perform again, his "autobiography" *Beneath the Underdog* was published. The book played with multiple identities, genres, and "truths" in much the same way his music long had. It was here, in the last decade of his life, that "religion" emerged most vividly. Far outside the simple, deceptive identification with Christianity, Mingus revealed what was in his music all along, a complex brume of the sacred, beginning with his early prayers outside the principal's office (disobedient from the first, Mingus worried that God might be a "boogie man") and his suspicion that

FIGURE 3.1. Charles Mingus, in rebellious profile. Photograph by Teppei Inoguchi, copyright Jazz Workshop, Inc.

he himself had "mystic powers."[28] The bassist recalled, "I could always hypnotize people...we're nowhere as good as Jesus Christ was or even Buddha or Amenhotep. Swami Vivekananda is closer to my league....I know I was born with something mystic."[29]

Even while dutifully attending church, Mingus had read "everything he could find in the library that went beyond his Christian Sunday School training—karma yoga, theosophy, reincarnation, Vedanta."[30] He felt himself outside of his own context, America and the church, even while pinned to his blackness. The world taught you cruelty, and America made the world in its image. The same holding corporation that had subsisted in slavery and economic exploitation also ground down creativity, evicted artists from their lofts, and dismissed criticism as mere "black rage." About the two words Mingus encountered most often in his musical narrations of self and culture, Mingus simply said: "Fuck 'Negro.' Fuck 'jazz.'...I want to be accepted as an American now with all the rights—or forget it and I'll show Krushchev how to guide his missiles due South."[31] And in that great unfolding story of black people in America, oh what the church hath wrought. He doubled down on his satire of Christianity: "HEAL BROTHER JOHNSON!...Reta goosa la-po co-ro da-le!...Talk in tongues, brothers! Get that devil Death out of here!"[32] Mingus was no fan of faking it. And he thought culturally normative religion was a scam. It was more than just the hypocrisy or racism of religious people that convinced Mingus: "God is white, 'cause the white man's the only thing I know can cause, make or force people to do his bid."[33] But still, to renounce the spirit altogether was to renounce beauty, to renounce life itself: if "you believe there ain't no God, you're fucking yourself."[34]

Mingus believed in his own multitudes and in his own beliefs, heard in the arc of his music. The same Mingus who hurled lightning bolts at "old America" said "[s]omebody—the God of love or someone—seems to believe the world can make it with all these races here or things wouldn't have gone this far."[35] If "[t]here's no better test for Biblical life than American society," this was also the country birthing the music that might heal its own madness.[36] The same Mingus who told jazz to fuck off preserved it from thievery, challenging his audiences: "You had your Shakespeare and Marx and Freud and Einstein and Jesus Christ and Guy Lombardo but we came up with *jazz*, don't forget it!"[37]

Believing in jazz meant occupying its limits, turning them inside like an alternate take in the studio of history. In his imagined conversations with Fats Navarro, the bassist is told, "I say you believe more than the believers who can't bear to think that there might *not* be a God."[38] One could read this as a hipster's Pascal's wager, perhaps. But with Mingus's powerful socio-historical sensibilities in mind, we might see such belief as the register not just of the disciplinary gaze but of an authentic self, one whose very existence seems lied up by the holding corporation world. Mingus's own beliefs held that "I'm as old as time and my knowledge of all the worlds express an Edison, Buddha, Christ, or Bird" come to teach America about itself through sound, with religion a key factor in the riot that Mingus documented.[39]

Even after he was diagnosed with Lou Gehrig's disease in late 1977, Mingus took the stage in a wheelchair. And when President Jimmy Carter gathered jazz musicians to the White House in 1978, and walked across the White House lawn to hug the hobbled bassist, Mingus wept. Was this a rapprochement with the machine? A beatific experience of legitimacy? Perhaps Mingus sensed the fullness of his own life, those things few knew in their rush to celebrate the simple equation: Mingus + church = civil rights. After a period of holistic treatment in Cuernavaca, Mexico, Mingus passed away at the age of fifty-six. It was rumored that fifty-six whales beached themselves on the Pacific coast of Mexico that day, as if Mingus's revenant was singing the old Dock Boggs lyric "the whales will fuss over me" in some great beyond sending postcards to the "old, weird America."

But why did this "holy-rolling" jazz man have his ashes spread in the Ganges? Recall that the young Mingus on Central Avenue dreamed of mystic powers, psychic insights, mystic transport beyond the body, and more. He read William James's *Varieties of Religious Experience* and began a lifelong preoccupation with Vedanta. When he and Sue Mingus were wed by Allen Ginsberg, the ceremony was accompanied by bells and dance and chants to Krishna. His widow recalled that Mingus "believed in the Hindu religion because he felt it was fundamentally democratic"; she explained to me that in this Mingus "was as democratic about religion as he was about social issues," and he would regularly "call out 'ALL the prophets!' on the bandstand."[40] And yet, "Charles was his own church."[41] His catholic tastes and reading can certainly be mapped onto the postwar American mood, but it is also evidence of an abundance and generativity seldom acknowledged in African American religions. Like his music and his criticism, Mingus's links to religions and historical narratives subverted expectations and subverted themselves, in the name of a constantly refreshing self-authentication. So many different Minguses populated this church, juxtaposed and overlapping like his tunes. But as the man himself said of his selves, "They're *all* real."[42]

Tender Warriors: Max Roach and Abbey Lincoln

It didn't get more real than drummer Max Roach's nimble polyrhythmic swing, which made him one of the central figures in the bop revolution. Max was still making wax in the 1960s, but was playing a more layered, free, African-influenced style that accompanied a shift in Roach's public persona. A defiant leader both on and off the bandstand, with 1960's *We Insist!* Roach and his wife, vocalist Abbey Lincoln, both chronicled and contributed to the civil rights movement. Their role in this is well known and widely discussed by scholars like Ingrid Monson, Eric Porter, and others. Yet the grain of religiosity in their work has seldom been discussed outside of expected acknowledgments of the movement's obvious links to African American Christianity.

Roach was born in 1924 in Newland, North Carolina, into a family of gospel performers who moved to Brooklyn when he was four. Roach first played drums at the summer Bible school of Concord Baptist Church, and began to gig steadily at the tail of the big band heyday. He had an epiphany hearing the godfather of bebop drumming, Kenny "Klook" Clarke, who eschewed the kick drum–driven sound of the big bands in favor of a brisk, riotously fast sound focused on the ride and hi-hat cymbals. Roach then helped create a drumming style filled with crisp accents (sometimes called "dropping bombs"), polyrhythms, and an urgent drive that suited bop's harmonic density and angularity. Bebop was understood as a dramatic expression of black musical independence. As Monson notes, "It was about developing a singular and personal voice, without saying in words so much what the critique was about."[43] While bop was also seen as an aesthetic epitome of the urban secular, its players often fused self-determination, musical innovation, and committed forms of religiosity. As Roach led prominent ensembles, he showed flashes of the fierce independence that made him so controversial in the 1960s.

Lincoln grew up Methodist in rural Michigan. She often performed religious music for relatives, but also followed the North Star of Billie Holiday's vocals. She understood early that "a song is a prayer.... [I]t will manifest in my life one way or another."[44] As the civil rights era dawned, Roach and Lincoln sharpened bop's conjunction of religion, politics, and aesthetics into a new narrative about America itself, one emphasizing the possibilities in African traditions, the liberatory potential of American traditions (particularly African American religions), and the growing openness of jazz itself. In 1958, they worked with Kwame and Elombe Braithwaite to form the African Jazz Art Society, which many observers saw as the precursor to the Black Arts Movement most commonly associated with Amiri Baraka. Poet and activist Kalamu ya Salaam recalls the couple's intensity and purpose as resembling "the power of a secular Holy Ghost, a terrible Shiva-force that destroyed you to renew you.... This was not just jazz. This was a religious experience."[45]

Roach was invited to compose some music in advance of the centennial of the Emancipation Proclamation. Like many musicians, Roach's experiences of racism in the music industry had deepened his frustrations with the moment. He and his collaborator, lyricist Oscar Brown Jr., saw little use commemorating a nominal freedom they rarely experienced in American life. Monson explains that their original intention was to follow a narrative that began in Africa and concluded in contemporary America (Roach also planned "a long work titled The Beat that would 'tell the story of the African drum'").[46] But while Brown favored nonviolent integrationism ("I was preaching love"), Roach wanted the music to address political issues more directly, even aggressively.[47] While the influence of King's movement grew, Roach turned his ear to the powerful counterpoint of resurgent Pan-Africanism and the Nation of Islam.

We Insist! was no mere accompaniment to a social movement, nor was it simply a political work. Rather, the record was a meditation on the power of Africa in the diasporic imagination, in narratives of the American experience, and in spiritual sound. The slightly edgy rattle of Roach's snare drum (each strike meant to be heard as a whipcrack) opens the incendiary "Driva' Man," with a steely Lincoln recitation about slave life: "ain't but two things on my mind, driva' man and quittin' time." Dark harmonies, a spare 5/4 tempo, and a sense of bitterness open the album before the graceful, lithe swing of "Freedom Day" announces "throw those shackling chains away." But did democratic vistas, voting rights, and shared water fountains lie beyond? Roach announced different conclusions with the album's remainder, toiling musically through anguish before concluding in African territory. Following the powerful "Prayer," where Lincoln intones wordless vocals that evoke the shout tradition and the spirituals, the album's most shocking and defiant piece is "Protest." Lincoln screams in a refusal of silence, a declaration of intentions to radicalize. After the balm of "Peace," the suite's final two pieces found Roach taking up internationalism. On "All Africa," Lincoln and Nigerian percussionist Babatunde Olatunji recite the names of African culture groups (Lincoln in English, Olatunji in Yoruba). No mere multicultural celebration, this invocation of a spiritual and cultural lineage also commemorates tribes that were pillaged by slavers who banned the drum. The concluding "Tears for Johannesburg" is a pounding ostinato that signals solidarity between African American and African freedom struggles, with Roach here honoring those who suffered in the Sharpeville Massacre earlier in 1960.

Jazz had come to hear itself as part of these broader musical and religious histories and contexts. Roach and Lincoln's subsequent *Percussion Bitter Sweet* opened with an intense, heavily syncopated 7/8 groove called "Garvey's Ghost." The mordant "Mendacity" (where Lincoln sings bitterly about a morally unresponsive political mainstream) and the swaggering "The Man from Africa" reflected Roach's agreement with Malcolm X that you had to understand the Congo if you wanted to understand Mississippi.[48] Despite skepticism about the likely success of the civil rights movement, Roach still dedicated "Tender Warriors" and "Praise for a Martyr" to the nonviolent freedom fighters and to those who "sacrificed their lives fighting for their individual and collective freedom."[49] Throughout the 1960s, the couple did benefit concerts for the Nation of Islam, Congress of Racial Equality (CORE), and Student Nonviolent Coordinating Committee (SNCC), while Lincoln independently "led an organization called the Cultural

Association for Women of African Heritage."[50] A 1961 demonstration in response to the assassination of Patrice Lumumba "partially originated from meetings held at [their] penthouse apartment."[51] They fraternized with creators in the Black Arts Movement and with Malcolm X himself. Farah Jasmine Griffin notes that Lincoln, one of the first female musicians to wear an Afro, was widely understood as echoing a black womanist spirituality heard by DuBois in the spirituals, or by Jean Toomer growing up in Georgia.[52] Roach's refusal to temper his radicalism got him blacklisted by the recording industry for several years during the 1960s, when he was ostracized "because I said that music can be used for something other than entertainment."[53]

While Roach and Lincoln split in 1970, their music continued to fuse politics, religion, and music in a historically grounded aesthetic that narrated African American experience through jazz. In 1971 Roach recorded a gospel album, *Lift Every Voice and Sing*, to demonstrate the comprehensiveness of African American religious music. He subsequently formed the all-percussion ensemble M'Boom, described as "pancultural music,

FIGURE 3.2. An insistent Abbey Lincoln performing. Photograph copyright William E. (Bill) Smith.

which falls somewhere between that of a classical percussion orchestra and an African drum choir," fusing gamelan, swing, mariachi, and funeral music in ways that recalled the stylistic amalgam of early jazz.[54] This move obviously signified narratologically for Roach, who understood the links between different eras of black music, culture, and religion (and his emphasis on the centrality of percussion resounds across traditions, from Taiko drumming to the Native American Drum Religion, from the Yoruba to Neopagans). Indeed, on his album *Chattahoochee Red*, Roach accompanied a recording of King's, "I Have a Dream" speech, suggesting the dream is the drum, a spiritual sound that cannot be pigeonholed in a distant African past or written off as an exotic musical curiosity.

Lincoln recorded several heavily Afrocentric albums like *People in Me* during the 1970s. Despite an occasionally chilly critical reception, she remained popular, especially with women. Singer Cassandra Wilson called her "a culture-bearer...a griot."[55] Lincoln grew further into this sensibility and talked about dedicating her music to ancestors, who in her reckoning pass into the light and become "miracles."[56] While some might hear this as New Age rhetoric, Lincoln insisted on the importance of Africa, where on a 1974 trip she received the name Moseka ("a god of love in the form of a maiden").[57] She saw African cultural-spiritual traditions like naming as integral to music's own comprehensive function: "[w]e used to dance and sing and play instruments and tell stories...to feed your spirit and to help you live in a hostile environment."[58] And Roach concurred, saying, "See, the illusion is that art is for the sake of art, that it has nothing to do with the rest of the world...[h]ow could [jazz] *not* be political if you live in a society like the US and you're black?"[59] Music and religion are both the record and the substance of these convictions.

A Lily in Spite of the Swamp: Archie Shepp

Tenor saxophonist Archie Shepp once noted, "I'm worse than a romantic, I'm a sentimentalist."[60] Shepp came to prominence as the 1960s "New Thing" was reconfiguring the cultural politics of jazz. While Shepp is not known for his own religious transformations, he regularly used elements from African American vernacular history in the service of a musical and social radicalism. Some listeners recoiled from Shepp's cries and shrieks through his horn, but there was something lush in his sound, with its warm vibrato, that looked back to Ben Webster and Lester Young. This

oscillation between deep roots and cutting edge revealed a sharp historicism to Shepp's music-making, which was also his radical intent.

His aesthetic was as satirical, theatrical, and sentimental as it was transgressive. While Shepp shared with some of his contemporaries the conviction that African religious and cultural principles were revolutionary, he was
equally insistent on blurring boundaries (between genres, or between Africa
and Europe). Shepp was one of many musicians taking part in the 1964
"October Revolution," intended not simply to assist musicians in organizing
for better working conditions (Shepp called clubs "crude stables where black
men are run until they bleed"), but to revolutionize the category "jazz" itself.[61]
Shepp expressed the view, typical of the time, that jazz was no mere entertainment but instead a vehicle of revolutionary solidarity. Jazz is "anti-war,"
he insisted; "it is opposed to Vietnam; it is for Cuba; it is for the liberation of
all people ... [b]ecause jazz is a music itself born out of oppression."[62]

Acutely aware of the music's racial habitus, Shepp insisted, "If we continue to call our music jazz, we must continue to be called niggers. There,
at least, we know where we stand."[63] But while "jazz" functioned racially,
the word could not contain the intensities or narrative conceptions of
musicians like Shepp. Some in Shepp's circle, like percussionist Beaver
Harris, preferred the term "Black Music," "because this way you have all
of your history to draw from."[64] But Shepp kept using "jazz," since it
allowed him to playfully articulate a critique alongside his exhortations.
"Jazz," he once said, "is a symbol of the triumph of the human spirit, not
its degradation. It is a lily in spite of the swamp."[65] Shepp linked such
affirmations to his confidence in the transformative power of art. As
Baraka wrote, while Shepp's music intended primarily to "make you *feel*,"
it was inevitable that "your reactions will be *social*."[66] New combinations of
references or genres could cajole a listener to new feelings and experiences of the "social." Exploring the juxtaposition of the beautiful and the
caustic, the contemporary and the traditional, Shepp used pieces like
"Rufus (Swung, his face at last to the wind, then his neck snapped)" to
direct attention to historical episodes in African American culture and
religion. His aesthetic was inseparable from this historical sensibility,
taking place within and alongside the civil rights movement like other jazz
from the period: not just Mingus and Roach but the echo of Billie Holiday's
"Strange Fruit," Nina Simone's "Mississippi Goddamn," Coltrane's "Alabama,"
and Louis Armstrong's 1957 excoriation of Governor Orval Faubus.[67]
Religious materials were part of Shepp's broader interest in vernacular narratives and histories (ranging from church holy-rolling to venerations of

Malcolm X to Pan-Africanist anthems), which he collectively positioned against the deadening effects of modern culture.

While Shepp's music was manifestly political in some ways, it was also characterized by a surplus that jarred expectations (a Broadway tune or folk song a kind of sentimental curveball) and a refusal to be pigeon-holed. For example, Shepp's band once took part in a benefit for Stokely Carmichael where dozens of reporters scrutinized each musical detail for signs of racial signification. Harris recalled that the band played regular gigs in Harlem, where "the brothers" raised their fists and proclaimed "play your ass off, Abdullah." A tickled Harris and Shepp began to use the gesture to signal to each other onstage, which prompted audiences to mimic them under the assumption that the band was repping Black Power.[68]

What politics were audible in Shepp's music were more historically dialogic. *Fire Music*, from 1965, responded to that year's Watts Riots and Malcolm X's assassination. Alongside "Prelude to a Kiss" and "The Girl from Ipanema," versions both bruised and lush, Shepp delivered the riotous "Hambone" and the tone poem "Malcolm, Malcolm, Semper Malcolm," in which Shepp professed X's immortality. *On This Night* contained a dedication to W. E. B. DuBois, wherein Shepp announced his dreams of "the day of liberation." "The Pickanniny" looked back to the demise of Jim Crow, while the title track (subtitled "If That Great Day Would Come") could be a soundtrack to the writings of Henry McNeal Turner or DuBois. Listeners continued, despite Shepp's public disagreements with Amiri Baraka, to associate Shepp with the notion that jazz was an "extension of the black nationalist movement."[69] But Shepp himself cautioned that "[a]ppearances can be deceiving. People expect you to come onstage in a dashiki and fez, well I say 'You know the C.I.A. is wearing all that stuff now.'"[70] Flirting, winking, revering, or declaiming, it was the very multiplicity of Shepp's relations to blackness and to America that constituted his personas in the 1960s, all of them eternally returning to the ubiquity of religion in African American historical narrative. As if to make the point, Shepp was fond of saying that his education was in Marxism and Southern Baptism, which together gave him a good view of America.[71] Yet while the church sustained a kind of cultural identity for many African Americans, Shepp also claimed "the burden is on the white man to prove the morality of the entire Judaeo-Christian tradition."[72]

Shepp articulated this on "The Wedding," where atop the groaning arco basses of Donald Garrett and Lewis Worrell he described the link between racism, the market, and religion: "They had been born in a Christian climate and capitalism had picked them clean." Of the swaggering *Mama Too Tight*, Shepp described its mix of "the poignancy of the blues and the jubilant irreverence of a marching band returning from a funeral" as an interpretation of slavery's legacy, or "the feeling of being subjected to a 'haunt.' But the victims have their ghosts too."[73] Shepp thus theatricalized black history and religion themselves, which accompanied his increasing focus on ritualism. He wanted to play music that could facilitate the "transmogrification of one's entire biological, sociological, political being into a single living line—so that the moment of performance is less a technological feat than a prayer" in which the musician "steps to the altar."[74] This ritual depended, however, on Shepp's ongoing historicism, drawing together a sense of the African past with a focus on the integrity of African American culture forms. So on *The Magic of Ju-Ju*, Shepp featured Frank Charles playing "talking drums," signifying that the illegible musical codes of the nineteenth century had meaning for black musicians in civil rights–era America.

For a time in the late 1960s, Shepp left the United States to travel in North Africa, identifying with DuBois and Turner in his sense that African American history might eventually have to drop the suffix in order to avoid riots, discrimination, and state suppression of radicalism. But the saxophonist, a reader of Fanon, was also enamored of postcolonial oppositional movements in Africa, seeing in them not so much a model for American liberationist movements as the common culture for people of African descent globally. He later recalled how his music was altered by the experience, saying, "I have exactly the same feeling as I would in a village playing a sacred hymn."[75] While Shepp still performed pieces like "There Is a Balm in Gilead" in his sets, one observer noted that he "could well be one of those sorcerers who carry their amulets with them . . . a saxophone reed imbued with some supernatural power to blow out the utopias of Marcus Garvey's UNIA."[76] Shepp, always willing to engage stereotype to turn it inside out, concurred: "I'm a ju-ju man, a ju-ju man, that's for sure!"[77]

Records like *Yasmina, A Black Woman* deepened this ritual sensibility by pursuing repetition and increased duration to create trance-like states.[78] Yet Shepp ultimately returned to the didactic approach, still sensing that vernacular forms like gospel, vaudeville, or a funeral band were most effective in distilling historical traditions of empowerment. In the context of Pan-African reinvestigations of history, his performances strangely evoked not just the tradition of African griots but Lorenzo Dow's sendups of

Calvinism at Second Great Awakening camp meetings, or the Chautauquas. Both individuals and communities could be transformed, Shepp believed, through exposure to "the vital force, African roots."[79] In the 1970s, his records returned vigorously to a critique of American racial injustice, combining fierce social commentary with messages of cultural and religious uplift. *Things Have Got to Change* was intended to be structured like a tent revival, with an unwavering beat (including the African percussion Shepp had used since *Juju*) and the repeating chorus "Things gotta change, God dammit!" *Attica Blues*, a direct response to the Attica prison riots, featured outraged lines like "only when nature doesn't take its toll am I worried with the human soul" and appealed to divine intervention to transform human consciousness. *The Cry of My People* fused out jazz with gospel roots, the spanning of historical eras drawing together themes of religious resistance and emotional appeal. And *Kwanza* celebrated the then-new African American holiday.

Shepp subsequently investigated tradition in a different key. Though he had consistently maintained interest in the blues and spirituals, he had rarely explored them directly, as he did on his duets with pianist Horace Parlan, *Goin' Home*. But while Shepp's investigation of the materials was heartfelt, he also said of jazz musicians who take teaching gigs and record traditionals, "I think in a sense we're guerrillas: we hide in trees, with camouflage, and we must be there until we and our music are respected."[80] As if summing up the entire trajectory of his music, Shepp continued, "[T]he African-American religious experience takes a direction of its own; there's a whole body of music connected with it and a meaning attached to that which has socio-political implications."[81] Music evades the language that constrains and generates the language that evokes and sustains. Perhaps this is why Shepp said, "Listen to [my music] on my terms. I will not let you misconstrue me."[82]

Be the Poem: Asian American Jazz and Resistance

Fred Ho was naked and painted green. Representing his Green Monster Big Band, which signified viciously on pop culture stereotypes, Ho stood afflicted by cancer (which would claim him in early 2014) and defiant. A longtime socialist, Ho believed jazz can only be understood as the product of people who "suffer from their history, identity, and culture being defined, (mis)represented and explicated by [their] oppressors."[83] Ho's music railed against another holding corporation and celebrated "the people's struggle" in pieces like "Beyond Columbus and Capitalism" (with subsections "My God, My Gold," "The Huge Farts of Red Meat-Eating Imperialists Foul the Earth," and "Ghost Dance on the Grave of Capitalism"). These tell a tale of indigenous cultural and religious identities being quashed and rising again in revolt against white religion, like some raucous echo of Chief Seattle's "Oration."

When he was young, the future radical actually served in the Marines. He was dishonorably discharged for decking an officer who had made a racist comment to Ho. The event radicalized him and in time he "became one of the first non-Blacks to join the Nation of Islam, although he balked at taking the name Fred 3X, arguing that his given name was Chinese and therefore not a slave name."[84] As he began fusing music and activism, Ho's investigations of American religion (via *The Autobiography of Malcolm X* and other works) convinced him to intervene in its history by exploring the possibility of organizing Asian American musicians, saying, "We looked to the black experience as a reference, as a metaphor to our own."[85] A student of the Black Arts movement of the 1960s, Ho specialized on baritone sax and apprenticed with Shepp and Cal Massey. Ho was shaped by a vibrant West Coast activist scene which, in the late 1970s and early 1980s, sought to reclaim identity from American triumphalist narratives and bland melting-pot injunctions. Activists and musicians displayed and played these identities using Taiko drums, martial arts, and traditional ceremonialism.[86] While Ho was influenced by early movement milestones like Chris Ijima's band and the Boston collective I Wor Kuen, he was careful not to essentialize or totalize traditional music, wanting to avoid the reception dynamics he calls "chop-sueyism" while underscoring that music "is the basic truth of humanity."[87] Following the First Asian American Jazz Festival, in San Francisco in April 1981, Ho began to write pieces like "Underground Railroad to My Heart" to "compose a new reality" or a new history.[88] His alternate archives included the suites *Journey Beyond the West: The New Adventures of Monkey, A Chinaman's Chance, Warrior Sisters: The New Adventures of African and Asian Womyn Warriors,* and *All Power to the People! The Black Panther Suite,* which Robin Kelley describes as sharing "the power of the trickster" to "expose the limits of terms such as multiculturalism," doing so by "[d]rawing on a vast musical well, from spirituals to Chinese opera, blues to Filipino kulintang."[89]

Rooted in his belief that "the journey of discipline is inherently more spiritualizing" than inherited options, Ho concocted in sound—the surging low end of the groove and his horn, the mashup of a cartoon theme song and folk music—a history co-inhabited by jazz mavericks like George Russell and Rahsaan Roland Kirk, religious activists like Malcolm X, and the forgotten "sheroes" of women's history.[90] More than just the sound of immigrant music resounding in American street blendings, Ho's musical-historic imagination may not have constituted a kind of surrogate spirituality, but its fierce idealism sustained Ho's faith in alternate futures.

To articulate this critical history, Ho immersed himself in traditional Asian music and contemporary pop culture in order to "build a pan-Asian identity" that confronted white liberal audiences with their own stereotypes, which he hilariously called the "Putamayo coffee-table guide-book" approach.[91] As a counter-religionist, Ho still shaped understandings of "religion" via his music. For Ho, "religion" and "spirituality" were not pieces of some Chinese cultural essence, since he had no truck with "jazz and I Ching" exotica. Rather, Asian identity was a base for solidarity and organizing for revolutionary struggle, which regards all essentialisms with suspicion. To the extent that spirituality functioned positively in Ho's work, it was largely aesthetic, evoked with traditional instruments and in alternate histories. The musical stories of Buddhist monks like Xua-zang or "the mythic primate superhero Sun Wukong" would expose the contingency of imperialist narratives that naturalized Christianity and capitalism.[92] Ho was reluctant to use the term "jazz," because of its racialized associations. But he still heard the music as liberatory, believing that some of this power came from its capacity (as an improvised art) to "reflect the changes" of history.[93]

Contemporaries of Ho's have pursued similar projects with slightly different understandings of religion and history. Anthony Brown sees "identity formation" as the link between jazz and politics, and toward this end has helped form the organizations Cultural Odyssey and United Front to sponsor musical and cultural pedagogy.[94] His efforts at identity formation involve revisiting history, complicating the idealized past by, for example, performing the big band charts of George Yoshida, a Japanese American interred during World War II.[95] Violinist Jason Kao Hwang has since the 1970s participated in cross-cultural organizing and improvising. With his Far East Side Band or his operas *The Floating Box* and *Immigrant of the Womb*, Hwang creates music that engages history and culture as "a recognition of spiritual survival and evolution."[96] His early involvement with Asian American identity movements in New York taught Hwang about "awareness of one's own existence as a cultural and ethnic being, an element of a much broader array of vibrations."[97] In ongoing projects like Burning Bridge or text-based projects that are part oral histories, Hwang seeks to represent tradition and spirituality in sonic modes that capture the complexity of ethnic identity in what cultural theorists call hyphenated existence. From the base of the particular, Hwang seeks to "grab nutrition from the air like a whale," to "help people understand themselves" through music, and to "be the poem" that represents his aspirations for his own spiritual development.[98]

Pianist Jon Jang draws from the lineage of spiritual resistance running through Mingus and Roach. Jang sees his Pan-Asian People's Arkestra as "a vessel to preserve and protect precious commodities against the elements that would destroy them."[99] Using traditional Chinese instruments and post-Ellington section arranging, Jang distills specific moments in Asian American history to connect with other American liberation movements and to realize jazz as universal democratic music. A devout Christian, Jang is "dedicated to modes of regeneration through music and culture."[100] He claims, "My Christian faith is very important to me in terms of being faithful to the music," which he regards as a subversive joy well suited to challenging histories of oppression.[101] Radicalized through his encounter with Malcolm X and Paul Robeson, Jang wondered "what happened when the Chinese came to the United States to build a railroad? Did they bring their songs?"[102] Writing or rearranging the songs from this dissipating past has been an act of faith for Jang. "God's love is always abundant," he says, "[s]o in terms of me trying to do my music or us providing an alternative vision, we have to look at that."[103] Jang looks also to the sorrow songs of African American history, hearing in their resonance with Asian American history the possibilities of linking people through sound, realizing through new sonic-historical sensibilities a sense of roots, place, and meaning that dwells in the particular and rises above it too. Along with Francis Wong and others, Jang is uncomfortable with conventional "political jazz" because "it rarely includes spiritual concerns"; indeed, Wong criticizes the separation of politics and spirituality in contemporary life more broadly.[104] In their fusion of these categories, challenges to the "holding corporation" are manifestly a part of American religion, most obviously in their accompaniment of civil rights but also in their representations of religion in American history from the vantage point of disparate moments and possibilities.

"Astro Black" History

But history, too, can be arcane. In what he called the "Astro Black" dimensions, the bandleader Sun Ra blended Afrocentric history with futurism in adventurous improvising designed to promote religious imaginings of black creativity. The very futurity of these imaginings, when tied to the authenticity posited in hidden histories, establishes these temporal chronicles as critical ones.

For much of the twentieth century, Chicago vibrated with simultaneous musical and religious improvisation. The same population changes that brought disparate religious groups together (beginning with the post-Reconstruction migrations "Up South" and the subsequent promise of work in the industrial economy) contributed to a jazz scene unparalleled outside of New York. Many of the musicians who fueled the territory bands of the 1930s and 1940s, and fed into Chicago's own vital scene, lived on the South Side. There, one maligned and provocative figure was Sun Ra, a keyboardist, composer, and bandleader who combined experimental charts with communitarian living and a worldview encompassing Gnosticism, Egyptology, New Thought, numerology, and myths of interplanetary travel, all knit together in his idiosyncratic reading of the past.

Ra insisted he was no earthling, but a native of Saturn. His Earth town was Birmingham, Alabama, "the Magic City," and his terrestrial name Herman Poole Blount. The young Ra became obsessed with studying the Bible and other religious literature. Briefly attracted to the Seventh-Day Adventists, he discovered his destiny in what he described as an encounter with angels and demons. But he claimed these were not characters from the Bible but "space men" who "wanted me to go to outer space with them."[105] They told him about the secret truths woven into ancient sacred texts, and about what disciplined study could achieve: "I call it transmolecularization," and an ascent into spheres of celestial beauty.[106] This made sense of his own alienation, and he began to say he was no earthling, since "[a]s a man thinketh, so shall he be."[107] John Szwed compares this experience to a conversion, "where God calls the chosen by means of lightning bolts, shafts of sunlight, moving stars and celestial music."[108] Ra attributed his earthly presence to sidereal influence, claiming his arrival occurred because "the stars were...[i]n a position where a spiritual being can arrive."[109] He continued his studies at Birmingham's "Black Masonic Lodge."[110] He also threw himself into music, though he "rejected the Gospel music" of his milieu, since it represented the meekness of Christianity; he felt that "the Black people of America needed an awakening," one that could be accomplished through new sounds and a new sense of the past.[111]

Ra plugged into the territory band scene and accompanied Fletcher Henderson as a copyist. But he also claimed to have been apprenticing with "a secret organization—American Woodman. They showed me orders, discipline, how to be a leader."[112] He envisioned the big band itself as a kind of secret society, a vehicle for deliverance from subjugation through sound and knowledge. He was drafted in 1942 but refused to serve on the basis of his religious beliefs (which he identified as "cosmic philosophy").[113] He pleaded his own case in court using religious and esoteric literature, but ultimately had to serve a short stint in prison. Even more convinced he was not of this world, after his release from prison Ra spent the next decade establishing—in name (which he changed in 1952 to Le Sony'r Ra, a "member of the angel race"), music, and lifestyle—that "outer space is a pleasant place."[114]

He relocated to Chicago, where he found work in the surviving "black and tan" clubs from decades past, subbing for bandleaders or backing blues and doo-wop singers. Even as early as 1951, Alton Abraham and Ra—who together founded El Saturn Records/Research to document Ra's work—conducted research into human origins, astrology, and various forms of esoterica or sacred texts. Abraham recalls that their purpose was "to prove to the world that black people could do something worthwhile."[115] These themes resonate powerfully in American religion and in Chicago's history. Ideas about self-betterment, the spirit, and community organizing had roots not only in obvious religious sources like Garveyism and the Nation of Islam but also in traditions of associational democracy such as those found in Saul Alinsky's Industrial Areas Foundation.

Saturn Research held that transformations in hearing and historical perception would yield interpersonal results that could ultimately change community life, aspirations that Graham Lock links to religious imaginings of utopia. These activities were fueled by the active exchange of ideas on the South Side. Just after his move, Ra was given a copy of Theodore Ford's *God Wills the Negro*, which picked up on long-standing beliefs (in David Walker, George Wells Parker, and Marcus Garvey) that African American suffering was a vehicle for redemption and chosenness.[116] Ra became obsessed with substantiating these ideas historically, but outside the conventional Christian orbit. He read John G. Jackson's *Ethiopia and the Origin of Civilization*, and from Godfrey Higgins's *The Apocalypsis* he encountered the widespread worship of Sun deities in world religions.[117]

Ra and preacher's kid Abraham read comic books and sci-fi along with such treatises (a life-long habit for Ra, who later judged that *Star Wars* was "very accurate"), and soon began a street-corner discourse in Washington Park, alongside evangelicals, the Nation of Islam, and others.[118]

In capes and headdresses, Ra espoused the connections between robots and the pyramids. His "secret reading group" with Abraham had turned up not simply lost pasts, but the wisdom-seeking, star-gazing dimensions of esoteric traditions.[119] Under the aegis of Thmei Research, Ra's street-corner disquisitions were stuffed not just with bizarre biblical exegesis but with what saxophonist John Gilmore recalled as "Solaristic Precepts" that underscored the Egyptological roots of world religions (Israel became "Is" "Ra" "El") and the star-stuff found throughout the Nile delta. America was doomed, Ra said; but unlike the Nation of Islam's warnings, Ra did not foretell God's destruction of white people but said they would "be sent a teacher."[120] Ra intoned prophetically that "[t]he Bible is a dangerous book," but also rejected its doctrine of "salvation through sorrow, suffering and shame."[121] This has led African Americans to ignorance and lack of culture and appreciation for beauty, a state Ra summed

FIGURE 3.3. Sun Ra, deep in contemplation. Photograph copyright William E. (Bill) Smith.

up as "nothing": and "[t]here is no place in God's universe for nothing."[122]
Ra waxed Platonic in saying that the typical human is "just a reproduc-
tion" and must learn "to create himself by simply rising up out of the re-
productive system into the creative system."[123] He handed out leaflets
emblazoned with sentences like "Today is the shadow of tomorrow because coming events cast their shadow before. 'The music is alive,' it is not
the shadow, it is the reality in a prevue form."[124] Ra was "talking about all
these double versions of the Bible, turning all that stuff around, everything I'd ever heard, he was just saying the opposite."[125] Szwed, Lock, and
John Corbett have written about the centrality of inversions to these
notions of self-transformation and deliverance: shackles made freedoms,
outer space transforming inner self, and madness as true sanity.[126] But Ra
specifically pitched these insights into religion as secrets dredged up from
the true past, whose secrets would liberate as they do in so many other
American new religions. The past itself emerges as "prevue" and evolution beyond the blind faith of Christianity to a cosmic awareness that he
realized in increasingly advanced musical settings.

While Lock and others identify Ra's links to traditions of signifying
tricksterism and abiding interest in Egyptology, Ra scrambled the codes of
what counted as "religion" as much as he used religious notions to scramble
historical understandings. Ra and his growing circle of musicians read
P. D. Ouspensky, the Theosophists, and George G. M. James's 1954 Stolen
Legacy, all pointing to a cosmos alive with sound but covered over historically by the deceptions of narrow monotheism. Hear Ra on "Alter Destiny":
"What is the power of your machine? Music." Robotic voices spoke the
secrets of Egyptian sun priests, whose mystery religions Ra insisted were
suppressed by Christians. What is more, "jazz came down from the sun
priests. . . . They had music, they could heal people."[127] He claimed to possess these historical secrets, technological blueprints, and other esoterica
in tomes filled with language and symbols common to hermetic traditions. For example, one that Ra cherished in his final years was The
Information Book (given to him while he toured Turkey in 1989), stuffed
with allusions to secret brotherhoods, "luminous and flowery paths," numerological codes for unlocking the secrets of religions, invocations of
cosmic beings "from a medium where the spiral vibrations end," whose
healing sound most earthlings could not yet hear, and even what Art Hoyle
said was an "equation for eternal life."[128]

In the thick of dominant conceptions of black religiosity, Ra forged a
different path, a religio-sonic idiom where musicians are angels, priests

are demons, and the adoption of alien personas was no mere survival strategy but a declamation of truth. Beginning in 1960, his Arkestra began to wear spacesuits and Egyptian robes for their heavily ritualized performances. These qualities drew the band much ridicule (and later, titillated attention from *Rolling Stone, Saturday Night Live,* and *Nightwatch*). Yet Ra saw in the imaginative possibilities of the space age a recipe for reaching the impossible, drawing down futurology into a mythic past newly vibrating with alternate meanings. They chanted, sang odes to the cosmos, covered albums with photos of nebulae or drawings of famous astronomers, and projected images of space behind the stage. A serious student of Helena Blavatsky who would also regularly announce, "I AM" (perhaps a nod to Guy Ballard and Alice Bailey), Ra told his band, "You all are playing God's music."[129] Ra believed he was "a secret agent of the Creator," using the big band as "the instrument on which [truth] would resonate."[130]

Space meant more than abstract freedom; it meant fluidity among different knowledge bases. Szwed notes that traces of Ra's Baptist upbringing survived in the imagery of chariots and leaving earth for the heavens, where "Afro-American folk religions are used as sacred technologies to control virtual realities."[131] But while Aristotle, Hermes Trismegistus, Georges Gurdjieff, and others may have posited a similarly enchanted universe, to Ra it was in "Astro-Black" history that these notions achieved their truest distillation. In their silver-robed processions, electronics-laden big band jazz, and futurist aesthetic, Ra's ever-shifting Arkestra played music that looked back to big band sonorities as Ra did to the pharaohs, but used angularity, horn polyphony and wailing, overtones and esoterica, because Ra said, "I like all the sounds that upset people."[132] But as wild as the sounds could be, none wilder than Ra's dense waves of mashed electronics, he rejected the category free jazz, insisting instead that his intensities "were meant to represent the chaos that would ensue on earth without Ra's divine intervention."[133] The band was thus an actual ark, one catering to the musicians' belief that the history Ra taught was nearing its calamitous end.

From Chicago to New York to Philadelphia, where they lived mere blocks from John Africa's MOVE, Ra's Arkestra avoided the jazz mainstream and pursued disciplined living through sound until Ra "went home" in 1993. In the 1960s, Baraka regularly brought them to New York for performances, including the soundtrack for his "A Black Mass," which parallels the Nation's tale of Yacub. Occasionally Ra's rhetoric recalled Sweet Daddy Grace or Father Divine, as in the 1974 film *Space Is the Place,* when he claims "[e]verything you desire upon this planet but have never received will be yours in space."[134] But this was no prosperity gospel; since black people were not real to Americans, but only served myths of domination, Ra invented alternate myths in order to ask, "If you are not a reality, whose myth are you?"[135]

Discipline would expose the myth and make real the histories sonically recast for the future that screamed our way. In 1971, Ra was appointed as a lecturer for one semester at UC-Berkeley, teaching "The Black Man in the Cosmos." He assigned the *Egyptian Book of the Dead,* nineteenth-century astrology, slave memoirs, Blavatsky, and the *Book of Oahspe,* often beginning class with "permutations" of biblical texts and ending with music. He announced, "I am a scientist of justice" who used "equations" to point out the lies of Bible and government.[136] Improvising on Nation of Islam cosmology and fusing it with a neoconservative emphasis on discipline, Ra told black people they "could sound magnificent if they had the correct composer or arranger."[137] Freedom was bunk to Ra and only deluded people into thinking the current system could be improved. He dismissed political equality since "[t]here is no equality in nature...[and] [m]usic is not based on equality—the chords and the notes are all different."[138] Self-realization could only come through looking away from an empty present, since—as the Arkestra chanted—"it's after the end of the world. Don't you know that yet?"

In a world of false consonance, Ra spent his life on Earth preparing ears to receive "these sound waves" that would scramble brains, doing so by locating ordering principles within the flat or atonal space of the American twentieth century: a tone, a melody, a structure to things even if it is not audible to some, even if it made a lie of culture's bogus harmonies.[139] Humans could ascend beyond the body, like the aliens who visited Ra, like Theosophy's mahatmas, like spirits on the astral plane. Bodies were sonic, too, combinations of vibrations that could resonate with the essence of things underlying the forms. By fitting ourselves to the universe, through the ordered relation of its intervals, we also help make it, becoming divine ourselves. But if the Arkestra's joyful noise was to help listeners achieve spiritual liftoff, it would require disciplined inquiry into the secrets of the past so as to unlock the mutable energy of all things. Despite the links between Ra and other religious visionaries, there is also trouble and mischief in his historical futurology, blasting past anything as neat as a lineage like one of his pitch-bent, tone-mangling synthesizer mashups. There is "religion" here in a clearer sense than in some other improvisations discussed in this chapter, but in terms of the broader patterns of cosmos, spirituality, and sound, Ra is also distinct in his intuiting an order to the past and the starry beyond. Yet even here, Ra mordantly, playfully linked his sense of divine purpose with the improviser's lot: "I want to be the only thing I could be without anybody stopping me in America—that is to be a failure. So I feel pretty good about it, I'm a total failure."[140]

Roots and Folklore

Back on Earth, jazz has narrated African American religious history itself, in ambitious song cycles like Duke Ellington's *Black, Brown and Beige*, John Carter's *Roots and American Folklore*, and Wynton Marsalis's *Blood on the Fields*. These three composers are not the only practitioners of these narrative arts. Where Mingus, Roach, Shepp, and Ho invoked the sacred past, and the sacred in the past, to articulate critical principles, and where Ra's hidden histories birth future possibilities, these chroniclers self-consciously set the past itself to music, preserving it but also showing thereby that the past contains revelations. African American composers have often set history to music, most famously in Scott Joplin's *Treemonisha*, William Grant Still's *Afro-American Symphony*, and James P. Johnson's *Yamekraw: A Negro Rhapsody*.[141] Jazz musicians have similarly responded to challenging social conditions by declaring that historical identities are preserved better in sound than in fallible institutions. Yusef Lateef arranged prison songs and nineteenth-century vernacular music for his *African-American Epic Suite*, which he described as "an odyssey attributed to the African Americans 250 years of servitude in America."[142] Lateef included a section focused on the Second Great Awakening, after which he wrote "African-Americans were involved in...ideas [of] love for all, freedom for all."[143] From this trajectory, Lateef suggests, jazz and civil rights emerged in "a very homogeneous sound."[144] Saxophonist Oliver Nelson also engaged the meeting place of deep history and civil rights with his *Afro-American Sketches*, which began with the sonic chaos of slavers in Africa and concluded with a bracing song for the Freedom Riders. Sonny Rollins downplayed the politics of his *Freedom Suite*, insisting that it was about musical freedom as much as Emmett Till. Dave Brubeck wrote an oratorio using different singing styles as a model for "black/Jewish relations."[145] Anthony Davis's opera *X* used musical repetition "to reflect the way black people create their own version of history in the telling and retelling of certain stories."[146] For such narrations, Davis insists, "your ultimate audience...is God."[147] And saxophonist Matana Roberts has written the *Coin-Coin* suites based "on the life of Marie-Therese Coincoin who rose from slavery in Louisiana to become a wealthy land owner."[148] But three examples of telling history through music loom largest, especially for their representation of religion.

Come Sunday: Duke Ellington

Growing up in D.C., my earliest familiarity with Ellington was via the bridge and the school bearing his name. Duke and history made sense. Part of D.C.'s black middle class, the church-reared Ellington was exposed to African history as a child, and as a teenager was deeply influenced by DuBois's stage production *The Star of Ethiopia* (whose depiction of millennia of African history shaped Ellington's insistence on his music's cultural groundings). After moving to New York, Ellington began writing works (like "Black and Tan Fantasy") celebrating the distinctiveness of black culture, buoyed by the Harlem Renaissance in his desire "to take the themes of supposedly primitive jazz, blues, and plantation melodies, and transform them into orchestrated, conventionally Western works of art."[149] Ellington polished his compositional style at the Cotton Club, and though neither he nor any bandmate had ever been to Africa, that continent compelled him as it did so many in the same Harlem shaped so indelibly by Garveyite celebrations of Africa. His writing used what he called the "weird, queer effects of primitive Negro melodies," signifying on the "primitive" label outsiders appended—with delight and revulsion—to his swaggering sound.[150] Ellington professed that he was not merely innovating in a still marginal idiom, but rather "endeavoring to establish unadulterated Negro melody portraying the American Negro" in celebratory ways that undermined racial stereotype.[151]

Part of Ellington's growing compositional historicism included his consistent linkage of art and religiosity, noting that they were inseparable in African cultures, even when transplanted to America. In a sermon based on a Langston Hughes poem, Ellington wrote that African Americans were "the personification of the ideal begun by the Pilgrims."[152] And he began to write suites illustrating this sacred privilege and aspiration. He composed fragments for what he thought of as his "African Suite," a "symphonic saga of the African race"; the opera *Boola*, a "graphic illustration of the pain of slavery"; and his mid-1940s masterwork *Black, Brown and*

Beige.[153] He had as early as "Black and Tan Fantasy" worked on sonic creation stories, where Adam and Eve were represented by Boola and Voola, the narrative culminating in God's creation of song.[154] He read Roi Ottley and James Weldon Johnson while writing *BBB* (he noted "[t]he audience didn't know anything . . . but the cats in the band did") and saw his compositions as the realization of what Paul Gilroy calls the "potent historical memory" of diasporic cultures.[155] Ellington's early written scenario for the work cribbed from Franz Boas and DuBois in its depiction of African civilizations. The scenario's tone was more confrontational than the produced version, and its initial portrait of the Middle Passage was "rendered in gorier and more disturbing detail, including a story of mutilation of the Africans by the whites in charge of the ships."[156]

BBB's first section, *Black*, explores work songs and spirituals. Ellington's original intention was to use Boola's performances of vernacular music not only to inform audiences about its historic uses ("a smokescreen to comfort the white slavemasters" or a palliative to pain), but to bring attention to contemporary black agency and suffering.[157] While his scenario for the spirituals section prefigured the integrationist themes Ellington would later explore, depicting a white woman giving Boola a Bible, the actual performance of this section centered on a peerless Johnny Hodges statement of "Come Sunday." Ellington's historical delineation of African American religiosity did not always exclude religio-political activism and violence. *Brown* celebrates "the contribution made by the Negro to this country in blood," nodding to Haitian freedom fighters, leaders of slave revolts, and others during the piece's portrait of abolition and the Civil War.[158] Even in its celebratory passages, with their stirring horn section work, a darkness is audible: the musical rendition of the "Emancipation Proclamation," for example, throbs with a blues undercurrent, that recurrent dissonance of what Ellington spoke so cogently.[159] With *Beige*, Ellington looked to contemporary Harlem to highlight what he optimistically identified as "the common view of the people."[160]

Ellington's endeavors were heard as resonating clearly with the growing cries for civil rights after World War II. He was asked repeatedly to consider becoming more outspoken. His nephew Michael James dismissed this, saying, "You don't put Beethoven on a picket line."[161] Ellington believed his music was contribution enough: "I made my statement in 1941 with *Jump for Joy* and I stand by it."[162] And he kept writing. In the thick of misrepresentations of blackness, that fog of sensualist projections and belief in the lies of black religion's "simplicity," even Ellington's adumbrated history sounded out new dimensions of the past in order to realize what he announced with the title of another 1940s work, "New World A-Comin'." It was a sensibility that shaped much of his writing in this period: the mute work and portamento of his trombone section (which he dubbed "God's Trombones") simulated field shouts; the mid-1940s piece "A Gathering in a Clearing" denoted the tense but exuberant hush arbors; and "Three Dances" sang freedom songs of self-determination by interpolating folk music, Latin music, and spirituals.

Ellington's *Deep South Suite* from 1946 went further into the same history and was criticized by some for excessive romanticism. Yet Graham Lock contends that the piece's bucolic imagery was intended explicitly to reveal Ellington's "belief that the 'dream picture'...was a total lie."[163] Even as Ellington continued to notate African American history in subsequent works (the *Liberian Suite* or "A Tone Parallel to Harlem"), he declared, "I've never been interested in politics in my whole life...the only 'Communism' I know is that of Jesus Christ."[164] The band toured the Jim Crow South, and while Ellington vocally supported anti-lynching laws and championed racial harmony, he confessed publicly that the country "ain't ready" to accept civil rights legislation.[165] In hot water for this comment, Ellington redoubled his celebrations of black culture. Rejecting both romanticism and essentialism, he penned *A Drum Is a Woman*, a "fairytale-like tour of the history of jazz," which cast the music as "a historical and cultural link between African, African American, and Latin American peoples," positing this diasporic unity with the use of multiple idioms tracing the development of characters Madame Zajj and Caribee Joe.[166] Ellington insisted that he was doing just music, but suites like this one and *The Queen's Suite* "used images of nature and divine power" to tether music's supra-political power to "the cause of civil rights."[167]

With the 1960s, when he began composing his *Sacred Concerts*, Ellington began attending sit-ins and adding more explicit social commentary to his interviews. His composing reflected these changes. With "My People," Ellington "felt he was making a racial contribution" by portraying African American history in sound.[168] Paying tribute to Reverend King (and criticizing Bull Connor) with pieces like "King Fit the Battle of Alabam," Ellington asserted that he had "pioneered the social movement with the history of the Negro in America."[169] It is not simply that Ellington educated audiences with his historical suites, though he certainly layered among his melodies and chords lessons in religion and culture; many heard these compositions as religious practices themselves. For as Monsignor John

FIGURE 3.4. Duke Ellington, conducting from his piano bench. Photograph copyright Jan Persson.

Sanders noted about Ellington's second rendering of *BBB* (which featured a stirring Mahalia Jackson reading of "Psalm 23"), even without the specific coding of references to God and Scripture, "as you listen to it—it is spiritual" in the moods it summons, the emotions it provokes.[170]

This Song of Pain and Sorrow: John Carter

In the 1990s I regularly performed a solo guitar piece I called "Wynton Marsalis Got John Carter's Pulitzer," a lament that Carter's *Roots and Folklore*, the five-record suite chronicling the African journey to the "New World," had not been recognized as one of the most magisterial works in the history of jazz. Carter performed the discursivity of history literally from the bandstand and in his signification on jazz's limitations and uses in reconstructing black musical identities. Carter was up to more than simply bringing "religion" to life through sonic narrative; he sought to "stage" history, using improvisation to "jazz up" what appears at first blush to be settled, both recognizing and reimagining it.

Born in 1929 in Fort Worth, Texas, Carter took quickly to music after exposure to his parents' record collection and the performances at his Baptist church.[171] As an adolescent, he worked the North Texas R 'n' B circuit and quickly established himself as an improviser of some renown.[172] After receiving his MA in music education, in 1961 Carter and his wife moved to Los Angeles. The Central Avenue scene was drying up, and though Carter occasionally found work with Hampton Hawes or Harold Land, it wasn't until he met trumpeter Bobby Bradford that his music took off.[173] The two had a similar upbringing and some friends in common. Bradford had played for a time with Ornette Coleman, who facilitated an introduction to Carter, and their immediate musical connection led to a lifelong partnership.

Long before punk's DIY ethos was a glimmer in the cultural eye, Carter and Bradford, along with poet Jayne Cortez, decided after the August 1965 Watts Riots to transform Studio Watts into a community workshop cum rehearsal space cum performance venue. They eventually were joined by bassist Tom Williamson and drummer Eldridge "Bruz" Freeman, coming together as the New Jazz Art Ensemble (NJAE). Each Sunday, they held "Cultural Afternoons" for multimedia arts features accompanied by the NJAE, its sound as indebted to new music as to Ornette Coleman. Carter wanted his compositions to facilitate deep listening and interaction, and for the improvisations to evoke "the mood and movement suggested by the theme."[174] In time, Carter would develop this as a way of thinking about history too. His increasingly distinctive compositional imprint featured bracing lines suspended over a free pulse, and an attention to grain and timbre that was comparably rare in "free jazz" at the time. With their floating tempi and intense melodic figures, Carter's tunes were shot through with what John Hardy aptly called a "blues sorrow for the neglected and ignored."[175]

Carter's overriding goal was to craft vehicles for the interdependence of individual voices, a democratic aspiration that harmonized with his developing historical range. The NJAE could bring the heat on sprinting freebop tunes like "Sticks and Stones," but their more compelling moments came in those forecasts of Carter's future work: the burnished, at times fractured lyricism against woody bass thwacks on "Karen on Monday"; the abstract, mournful "The Village Dancers"; or the loping, swaggering "Song for the Unsung." They played waltzes, strolling blues in the vernacular, free ballads, shifting in mood and color from antic to clarion bright to slightly sour lyricism. In 1968, Hardy contacted the group about recording for Revelation Records, and 1969's *Seeking* was a major statement. "Call to the Festival" sounded like a kind of ritual summons, abstract and probing in its coordinated statements. "Abstractions for Three Lovers," whose stair-step theme and sectional development revealed Carter's compositional ambitions, brimmed with lightning-fast transitions between free playing and composed material, and the use of arresting pauses and wide dynamics.

In time the Angelinos received acclaim for their ability to "tap jazz roots and bring forth new relations between familiar things."[176] This, too, is a metonym for Carter's growing concern with history and identity. Fiercely committed to his local scene, to education, and to musical exploration, Carter chose to name the group's third record *Self-Determination Music*. At the dawn of the 1970s, the group was not only familiar with the more radical and explicitly Afrocentric wing of the avant-garde; they also regularly interacted with Pan-Africanist, Black Panthers, and Black Arts radicals in their community. The music's self-determination yoked folk music to free pulse: swing and abstraction, counterlines and unisons, blues feel and extended techniques seemed together to capture a range of possibilities and ideas, drawing together chains of influence from across history into single expressions like "The Sunday Afternoon Jazz Blues Society." It was an idea that stuck with Carter, as the group explored meditative balladry, bright freebop themes, and intense open-ended scuffles—Carter and Bradford's avian lines coordinating above a churn—that spotlighted the instrumentalists' arresting techniques. An altissimo squeal might leap out in the middle of the warmest *chalumeau* burble, as if Carter were directing the ear to those Ellingtonian dissonances once more. Here, he seemed to be saying/playing, is a "Funky Butt" or a "Rag," but it is no mere entertainment.

Robert Levin heard in the music "the black-American's liberation from four-hundred years of uncertainty regarding the worthiness of his identity."[177] Despite their accomplishments, Carter and Bradford still had to slog through day jobs. Carter worked on his important solo records, *Echoes from Rudolph's* and *A Suite of Early American Folk Pieces*. On the latter, Carter's original compositions are in the style of folk idioms. He described "Fast Fannie's Cakewalk" as "a kind of early American dance," and "Johnetta's Night Song" as "kind of a ballad" (on live versions, as Carter summons woody overtones like ghosts hovering around the story being told, some of his melodic extensions sound positively Copland-esque).[178] He married traditional dance forms like "Buddy Red, Doing the Funky Butt" with demanding extended technique.

In the early 1980s, Carter began to develop a larger vision for this presentation of historical American music. With a larger ensemble, each different

group of instruments or overtones series could convey multiple resonances to the phrase, the line, the timbre, the pulse. The presentation of
history in sound captured "something that we want to say...about what's
happening, politically, and socially, spiritually."[179] Coordinated to interlocking parts, it could also be understood as a different kind of musical
technique.[180] Carter's titles were often generic, hinting at formalism and
giving a sense of how he was arranging history. Tunes were not simply
artifacts but had a didactic purpose. One hears echoes in places of songs
like "Frere Jacques," of gruff birdsong or bright clarion reels, of NOLA
street music: "Echoes from Harlem" sounds like lost voices escaping from
Duke's airshaft, while on "Woodman's Hall Blues" Bradford plays second
line against bustling free pulse with the occasional lone "ah-ooh-gah!" But
they rarely sound content simply to evoke a lone idiom or emotion; theirs
is the style of the multitude, the experience that cannot be summed up, as
lines and colors bloom everywhere: Carter's leaping registers or tightly
controlled multiphonics, Bradford's vocalizing with mutes, all forming
episodes of color and density as much as compositional device.

On *Night Fire: An American Folk Suite* (whose title nods to the history
of the hush harbors), Carter leaned further into historical specificity. He
used close harmony and furtive, sprinting lines to reimagine "Juba Stomp,"
his take on the Juba dance, the hambone, or the Pattin' Juba performed in
plantation settings by slaves. Carter evoked the possibilities in traditional
forms rather than simply aping repertory versions of them. On the intensely moody, at times incantatory title track, Philip Wilson's low toms
conveyed a ritual mood, winds doing call and response in the night. The
voicings—Carter's low, woody burble and Bradford's sass—transpose 1930s
techniques onto the nineteenth century via the sensibility of the late twentieth. Carter had found it. And he began writing *Roots and Folklore*, a project he had mulled over since 1974, when he was taken aback when hearing
about his son's trip to West Africa. Carter was struck especially to hear
about "castles in Ghana that had been used as holding pens for Africans
before they were sent on slave ships to the Americas."[181] Carter sought in
part to "dismiss ideas that had been presented to us about what the African
brought to this country."[182] For the first act of his five-part chronicle of the
African journey to the "New World," Carter chose to delineate musically
the life of great African civilizations, establishing the lifeways that would
be rended so completely by the slave trade.

Dauwhe was named for "an ancient African Goddess of music and the
arts."[183] Though Carter had spent a decade composing pieces inspired by

dances or rituals, the opening minutes of the title track—with its ominous swirl of arco bass, bowed cymbals, and spectral winds—portended a coming darkness soon ushered in by the lower-register theme. Carter paired this with a bright, consonant declamation so that the piece constituted a shifting palette of emotions in ways characterized of *Dauwhe* as a whole, a portrait of repose that cannot help being heard in light of the horrors to follow. With "Enter from the East," Carter blended pre-American source materials with contemporary experimentalism, a multi-vocality captured by Carter's occasional singing to himself through his clarinet. Amid a thicket of woodblocks, a traditional melody emerges; elsewhere, blue notes and tight harmonies (a minor second here and there) sound like pre-echoes of jazz. But the point was Carter's integration of multiple styles, collapsing different periods of history into a single musical expression, seemingly united in Luis Peralta's voice, performing as the talking drum of West Africa in a series of dialogic exchanges.

Carter may not have seen himself as anything like a griot so much as a chronicler of the sacred. But his ability to summon and distill is powerfully at work in this music. As one listens to Carter play against the pulse, digging into melody then shucking it off, one is convinced that he is playing the multiplicity of the music and the history themselves. "The Mating Ritual" opens with a percussive crash, rising and falling from there on a sawing pedal point and rat-a-tat triplets from steadily climbing winds. This is Carter evoking cultural majesty, a last unfurling of free limbs before the closedown, the composer's clarinet bright and unbowed above the group. More than mere aesthetic richness and complexity, Carter's music was beginning to function *as* history and not just its transcription.

On the urgent, haunting *Castles of Ghana*, Carter documents the dissolution and descent of West African kingdoms with the beginning of the slave trade. His group's range and imagination provided the means to conjure and illustrate the historical settings compelling the composer. Andrew Cyrille, a serious student of traditional African percussion, opens the record authoritatively, with an invocation that gives shape to the fanfare of horns, gathering voices to their number. Against this backdrop, it is Carter as ever who tells the tale: using circular breathing, he repeats an insistent low note and generates birdlike triplets that spring nimbly into the upper register. The music seems to run riot with polyphony and counterlines, as the band's full palette seems to convey the instability and disbelief of the record's setting. Then a stirring drone opens "Evening Prayer," whose lush clarinet melody is so sorrowful, abject, and lost, it is audibly searching its way through an unknown future. With each turn of a phrase, though, close harmony gathers to block its way (half-steps, almost microtonal in their quavering effect) or dampen its hopes. The listener momentarily senses coherence and purpose, as an ominous chord is made from the whole; but this is made a ruin by a jarring, dissonant blast that is like an invasion. In the aftermath, Carter sobs through his clarinet alongside Terry Jenoure's tremulous vocals, their frantic exchanges seeming to ask of each other "what do we do?" In the next scene, the music is chock with glissandi and melisma, as madness overcomes "The Fallen Prince" (played drunkenly by trombonist Benny Powell) who changes the use of the castles. Following the bluesy, keening cries on "Theme of Desperation," the album concludes with the harrowing, fractious "Capture." As a segue to the subsequent record, Carter announces: "The journey facing these captives would prove to be truly arduous and eventful, a journey that would— before its completion—interrupt and redirect the dynamics of human existence on our planet."

This reckoning is perhaps too sober when measured against the atrocity of the slave trade. Yet Carter's music hopes to rescue something from the horrific past. Religion resonates literally and figuratively in the third suite, *Dance of the Love Ghosts*, which documents the Middle Passage. Carter wrote that "[t]he ghosts of those lost loved ones dance in eternal rhythm to the song of a desperate people who would never again view their homeland."[184] How could this experience be notated, and with what audacity could one possibly improvise on it? The title track launches the record forth as if on a listing ship. Carter squeals, raging to be free, while a babel of different voices pulls in multiple directions as the composer conveys the coexistence of different language groups, whose difficulty of communication we know was intended by the slavers. "The Silent Drum" is a creation story and a theodicy. Against a distant-sounding, mournful line intoning against the deep, The Ashanti Drummers chant in Swahili: "They have taken our father away and his drums are sitting in a corner idling." From this section, Bradford and Powell begin a halting dialogue as if attempting to find a common language, and Carter writes that this piece looks ahead to "one of the great social experiments in the history of mankind . . . the melting pot that is to become America."[185]

It is deeper into this pain that Carter ventures on *Fields*, which shows how "[t]he roots and folklore of this early life put into motion the beginnings of the art form we now enjoy."[186] The record opens with the haunting "Ballad to Po' Ben." Grouped horns are just a semitone off, creating an anxious effect as recorded voices moan in the background's historical atmosphere:

> *There was a good man, worked all the time.*
> *Gone on to glory, left us behind.*
> *Gone day and nighttime, he never cried.*
> *Doubt all his lifetime, but I'm there beside.*

In a stunning aesthetic moment, Carter uses a recording to create not just a musical but a historical effect: Powell playing defiantly against a stentorian preacher's voice, in what I can only hear as a distillation of the official Christianity of the slaveholders contrasted with Powell as the invisible institution. Whether or not these are intended effects, Carter's evocations and historical engagement provoke such associations. As if to confirm this musical portrait of growing assurance, there is even a bit of swagger to the lively "Bootyreba at the Big House," before Carter brings the listener into an urgent atmosphere of forest sounds on "Juba's Run." Jenoure whispers, "Run, Juba, run!" intensely, evoking a hush harbor as things rush by, felt but unidentifiable, clusters of horns occasionally sounding an alarm. On "Seasons," Carter makes clear how he understands this context and its lasting historic effects. On "Seasons," Jenoure recites once more, amid steadily gathering horn darkness:

> *What melody sings this song of pain and sorrow?*
> *Am I enduring some intense drama, judging my own right*
> *   to my own initiative?*
> *Or am I the prisoner of some ungodly historical circumstance?*

Carter answers with "Fields," fading in that recording of his uncle John, who rambles through family and regional genealogy. Another buried voice chants in some African language, a ritual fragment here distilled for our listening and accompanied, almost miraculously, by children singing a playground song. The gathered voices capture the multiplicity and representational range Carter intended. And when he laid his emotional cards even more obviously on the table with a recording of his own grandchildren playing a clapping song, the moment is almost overwhelming: joy and agony, past and future, all held together in those tensile spaces between notes, nuance coaxed like the grain of the voice, that singular clarinet speaking history itself. For Carter, the use of these recordings in his compositions commemorated the power of storytelling in African American culture. These were the tales told when Uncle John played cornet in a marching band and dance group around the turn of the century, and in the music played at funerals and church services. This music of the fields "was witness to the labor, grief and pain...[but] also cradled the beginnings of national music."[187]

With the final record, *Shadows on a Wall*, Carter documents the transposition of this culture in the Great Migration. What Carter aims to show here, to *play* here, is how the music of the fields was not only a mode of cultural survival for African Americans; it was only in the industrial North that "these innate and engrained elements of their music [would] have an opportunity for unhampered development."[188] It was in the cities that African American improvisation would develop not just in its customary musical formats—gospel, blues, or jazz—but in the necessarily improvisational encounter with new spaces, new modes of bodies in contact with one another, new beliefs. Packed densely into Carter's libretto are references to freight trains, popular songs, hymns, dreams of cosmopolitanism, and more, in an overstuffed monologue that is a distillation of the riotous city itself, idioms crowding together like different worshipers in a storefront church. It is clear in these settings that this is where the music and the story have been headed.

The album's centerpiece is the towering narrative "And I Saw Them," whose mournful, powerfully affecting drone background captures the feeling of being stunned before this new vista, uncertain of one's place in it. Dark horn harmony sounds like the still-present past and all the sour notes of any future dreams. Jenoure sings and recites her way through the whole of the suite, the whole of the history that is Carter's purview:

> *And they were exploited and became as shadows of the*
> *Original*
> *Men, women, children of the earth*
> *Shadows on the wall of Timelessness...*
> *I am the Mississippi delta and Times Square,*
> *Central Avenue and Rodeo Drive.*
> *I was at Abijon and the Castles*
> *I remember 1619*
> *I fired the first shot at Harper's Ferry*
> *And I watched at Gettysburg*
> *I am 1929, I am the rent party*

The model A Ford—I am the Cadillac motorcar...
And I saw them forge a national music on
Saturday night and Sunday morning,
And I saw the world come to know and love
That music.
I am the Blues.

It is a marvel, one of the most moving and sheerly ambitious performances I know of. The balance of the record is nearly as intense. The traditional hymn "Yes My Jesus Lives" is used as a background to "52nd Street Stomp," underscoring the unitive nature of the music that has shaped and emerged from the history Carter documents. The piece swings madly as a chorus can be heard testifying in the background (but not *too* far in the background):

Yes, My Jesus lives
I know he lives in me everyday
As I walk along,
I know he's there; I know and I pray.

It is this juxtaposition of jazz in its early pomp and more conventionally recognizable sacred music that captures Carter's entire aim in *Roots and Folklore*: it "shows [that] [s]ometimes the secular and sacred are separated only by text—*Yes My Jesus* could as easily be—*Yes My Baby*."[189] Even when genre music does not obviously code the sacred, then, it may nonetheless ineluctably resonate with it, or even become it. An obsession with only the familiar signifiers of religiosity may stop up our ears to its superfluity. So as his final contribution, Carter gives us the bustling, swinging "Hymn to Freedom" as a concluding fanfare of sorts, a multi-voiced declaration of his aesthetic and cultural and religious principles.

Carter's concluding image of standing together is an apt one, not just for its intended sociopolitical resonance but for its embodiment of Carter's aesthetic, holding together different idioms and ideas in utopic hope: "when the world is saved, it will be us and our idealistic notions that will save the whole thing."[190] As Paul Gilroy writes, "The contemporary musical forms of the African diaspora work within an aesthetic and political framework which demands that they ceaselessly reconstruct their own histories."[191] But spirits rejoicing historically involves more than mere reconstruction, with all the historic freight that term carries. Linking composition and performance to themes of history, community, and religiosity would not compel as much if all it did was rearrange the funky butt. The histories being performed here are themselves often highly discontinuous, and evade simple formulations just as do the slippery central categories of "religion" and "jazz" themselves. Carter heard clearly that what makes the music's spirits rejoice is, in Art Lange's suggestive formulation, how "[i]mmediacy and intensity equate in the vernacular as messengers of the spirit."[192] Carter's contribution, then, was not simply to document once more how central music is to everyday African American history and religion. With each thrilling swoop of his clarinet, he spoke through sound of "[m]usic as an evocative, expressive, and ecstatic condition of existence."[193]

Wynton Marsalis: A Coda

With the arrival of Wynton Marsalis as a commercial and critical force in the 1980s, jazz looked backward defiantly. In sartorial style and sound, Marsalis's music initially recalled Miles Davis's 1960s quintet. At the end of the fusion era, and with pronounced disdain for the avant-garde, Marsalis intoned that jazz players had to focus on "learning and mastering the elements like blues and swing" that once made jazz great.[194] This lament resonated mightily in the nostalgic 1980s, and Marsalis also exuded that decade's braggadocio when he charged that nobody was "man enough" in the 1960s and 1970s to own up to the responsibilities of form.[195] Embracing the role of standard-bearer, Marsalis even opined, "[T]he music business is controlled by people who read the Torah . . . [and it] has declined in its negroidery and purpose."[196] Over time, Marsalis grew closely affiliated with the Lincoln Center Jazz Orchestra and the writers Stanley Crouch and Albert Murray (who abjured all jazz lacking swing and the blues as they understood them). His albums in the late 1980s reflected his curatorial interest in Tin Pan Alley compositions, in the musical mélange of his hometown New Orleans, and in Ellingtonian themes. He began to expand his orchestral palette with *Blue Interlude*, the ballet commissions *Citi Movement* and *Jazz (Six Syncopated Movements)*, and *In This House/On This Morning* (whose structure paralleled that of a church service).

By his 1994 oratorio *Blood on the Fields*, then, Marsalis had developed a polished music interpolating styles from ragtime to the present. And while Crouch is wrong to claim that "[n]othing quite like it had ever been written," it is obvious that Marsalis's historical sensibility situates his efforts alongside those described in this chapter.[197] Using a fifteen-piece ensemble and three singers, Marsalis explored slavery as part of what Ben Ratliff identified as "the history of black Americans and the notion of cultural survival."[198] The long piece opens its depiction of the Middle Passage with the group intoning "crimes against the human soul, far too large for any words to hold." With flashy arrangements, Ellingtonian ensemble effects, and a regular nod to African music, the piece is almost self-consciously grandiose in places (though knit together with bravura instrumentalism and moments of intense beauty and discord alike).

Vocalists Cassandra Wilson and Miles Griffith play the parts of commoner Leona and prince Jesse, who announce the unreality of their arrival in the violent world of slavery. Drawing on idioms from spirituals to prime Duke, Marsalis flexes his orchestral muscles in documenting Jesse's attempted escape, their encounter with Juba the wise man (Jon Hendricks), and their shared quest for freedom. It is Juba who ultimately speaks for Marsalis, telling the couple that to survive the future they must love their new setting, "learn how to sing with soul," and achieve a new identity as free people.[199] The ambitious and wide-ranging writing vividly evokes the slave marketplace, the grind of plantation life, the evolution of the work song, and spirituals like "Oh What a Friend We Have in Jesus." The recitations punctuating the suite strive to show, in Crouch's words, that "slavery is a prismatic metaphor... [for] every inadequacy that was allowed to exist in the United States."[200]

The rousing success of the piece earned Marsalis a Pulitzer Prize in 1997 and led to subsequent works like the church-oriented *All Rise*, the post-Katrina *From the Plantation to the Penitentiary* (where he calls for "strong black leadership" while lamenting hip-hop and materialism), *Abyssinian*, and a central expository role in Ken Burns's documentary *Jazz*.[201] Eric Porter deftly reads this success against Marsalis's earlier celebrity, noting that with his early record *Black Codes from the Underground* the historic function of "black codes" was reinvented as part of a bid for artistic legitimacy in Reagan's no-social-safety-net America.[202] In Porter's estimation, Marsalis, Crouch, and Murray sought to reverse jazz's disrespect at a moment when they believed there were no cultural standards. The survival of the music thus depended on paring it down to a specific aesthetic tradition, one that only acknowledged pain and discord if tethered to some triumphal overcoming. Indeed, Marsalis has been forecasting such visions for jazz since his 1992 dirge "Death of Jazz" segued into "Premature Autopsies (Sermon)," where none other than Reverend Jeremiah

Wright excitedly recited Crouch's prose celebrating the majesty and determination of Ellington, and consequently of jazz.

IT IS LONG since past that jazz is the music of America, but it remains a
music *about* America and its religions. That music cannot evoke precisely
what words can is partly the point, since music exists as it exists—in all its
complexity—precisely because *words fail.* These historic modes, then, reveal what "religion" might be and how it fits in particular sonic forms of
memory. Each represents (and sometimes also facilitates) "religion" in its
score of history, reflecting larger cultural ambivalences about this central
mode of identity since these are not happy stories concluding in the enjoy-
ment of will-formation or recognition. And the prominence of the voice,
the declarative tone, and suite forms capture in sound what the music also
denotes. "Religion" is a root character in some of these narratives, a
feeling/principle/aspiration animating them, even occasionally a radical
absence in them. These creations are not, then, narratives in a conventional sense, nor are they "religious narratives" set to music; indeed, the
centrality of improvisation to jazz complicates the use of teleology in ways
that the cases in this chapter have shown. Rather, a powerful tradition in
jazz has found composers consistently engaging and sounding out the
entirety of African American experience through long-form pieces. Sound
itself becomes a medium by which to understand and express the complexities of African American history, including religions in all their
slipperiness.

Narrative does more than simply function; it is also constitutive, a practice
construed often as sacred (though not by all the historians herein). And perhaps the recognitions and connections these narratives generate are considered spiritual as well. At the very least, we see that rewriting African American
sacred history has been central to jazz. The words we bestow on things and
the order of their arrangement are fundamental not just to religious ways of
knowing but to inhabiting worlds of meaning. These sonic chronicles not only
partake of the historical self-consciousness with regard to religious or secular
destiny that goes back to the American colonial era, they also contain religious
reflections on the limits of sacred nationalism and of glorifications of jazz and
America. In these histories we find more, in other words, than the symbolic
content of narratives or their cultural politics vis-à-vis black religion.

In these reckonings with nation and religion, jazz was long depicted as
black and bohemian in a political context as uncomfortable with "outsider"
religion and politics as with bumptious sound. But Americans tell our own

stories incessantly, so jazz naturally improvises on this complex machinery of religio-national self-regard (both narcissism and perennial self-authoring). This connects, too, with an abiding belief in historical change and betterment, improvisational impulses here conjoined with a narrative teleology hoping to bring such beliefs into being.

And so, as Cecil Taylor said, "The exploration of history is a spiritual process, in order to be able to judge one's self."[203] History is a secret identity, an actualized sound of self and ideal community, an angelic medium for overcoming itself. Jazz makes use and takes stock of the past, judging what "religion" means for music and America, or what America means for "jazz" and "religion." But even here, with fixed narratives or abstract reckonings alike, "religion" blurs and drifts away. Ellington may well have had this peculiar conjunction in mind when he wondered "[w]ho is enjoying the shadow of whom?"[204] Narratives cannot pin religion down, much less self-evidently become it. Nor are these sonic tellings simple expressions of that academic lowest common denominator, "identity." They are means by which to organize and imagine through sound, and they are also alive, vitally and relationally present in the playing. Sun Ra said, "When they started history the truth couldn't move, 'cause they put a lot of lies in there too."[205] Jazz plays history and religion past this immobility, but can it institutionalize them comfortably?

4

Urban Magic

JAZZ COMMUNITARIANISM[1]

HORACE TAPSCOTT'S LEFT hand was indomitable. Some ears are drawn to the filigree and flourish of the melodic right, or the hypnotic compulsion of the cell-like structures on which his style is built. But the lower register, the ostinatos, those three notes snaking out of the pianist's southpaw immediately transport you as he opens "The Dark Tree." Tapscott was one of those talented Angelinos who forsook opportunities in New York's *axis mundi* for local community, where neighborhood musical pedagogy was linked to political critique and self-cultivation. Since the 1960s, the Los Angeles music scene has fragmented and multiplied. And among this sonic ferment, the Union of God's Musicians in Artists Ascension (UGMAA), the organization Tapscott cofounded and led until his death in 1999, institutionalized the exploration of sound, community, and spirituality for generations of improvisers. Like many of the examples discussed herein, the UGMAA was what Norman Weinstein called a "dream of an Afrocentric counteracademy and Chautauqua rolled into one."[2]

Musical communitarianism in America has a long and wonderfully eccentric history. Compounds, recording studios, practice spaces, lofts, schools, galleries, and installations abound in the history of musical subcultures, serving often as spaces wherein the like-minded seek to opt out of "the mainstream" to cultivate their individuality, their own sound, their own scene. Examples include La Monte Young's drone installations, Andy Warhol's Factory, Washington's Dischord House, and Baltimore's Tarantula Hill (once a memorably strange and difficult tour stop for this author), among many other spaces that nurture outsider music by institutionalizing their otherness. Such dogged commitment also runs deep in jazz history in the United States, in Chicago's Association for the Advancement of Creative Musicians, St. Louis's Black Artists' Group, the UGMAA, San Francisco's Saint John Coltrane African Orthodox Church, and Alice Coltrane's Sai Anantam

Ashram. This chapter sounds out the religious expressions in jazz communitarianism, its concern for alternate modes of dwelling, and its religio-musical pedagogy. These efforts are woven into the more familiar history of new religious movements but they also show jazz's own religio-political sensibilities, in another boundary blurred through expressive sound.

A Place for Us

What makes people establish counter-institutions? To what are they "counter"? How should we historicize and interpret those moments when conventional patterns of domestic life, public participation, music-making, and devotion appear insufficient? Many institutional alternatives have been fashioned in the context of long-standing debates about the scope of the state and the desirability of locating democracy in small, robustly deliberative communities that flourish in those spaces between conventional (read: liberal) demarcations of "public" and "private" spheres. Standard notions of political representation in democratic societies, critics have historically contended, only imperfectly capture or institutionalize citizens' democratic power. Such concerns go back to the Revolutionary War period and it is no overstatement to say that American public cultures—their acrimonies and civic rituals alike—have emerged amid these tensions, the irresolvability of these arguments. Intentional communities are thus responses to or flights from these debates, parallel histories that imagine their singularity. In some ways these communities constitute what Jeffrey Isaac calls, following Hannah Arendt and Vaclav Havel, "oases in the desert," loci of spontaneous activity or civic initiatives not wholly determined by the logic of the managerial state or the market.[3] It may be that the very idea of freedom from these conceptual and practical constraints is fictitious or a product of the very logic from which it seeks to escape; yet the search for such freedoms in counter-institutions constitutes a centuries-long American tradition of intentional withdrawal from or resistance to convention. With each wave of centralization or period of political-economic realignment, Americans have—in varying numbers and for diverse reasons—built cultural moats. Whether railing against "bigness" with echoes of populist traditions, retreating into agrarian communities, or establishing organized resistance to the state (in examples ranging from the Hutaree to the American Indian Movement), American self-fashioning has often involved the establishment of different spaces and places to cultivate virtues hard won in a corrupt "mainstream."[4]

This reveals something more than the truism that resistance to political authority is written deep into the American grain; rather, by foregrounding these themes at the outset, we see how religio-musical communities are situated in a constellation of improvisational efforts to enact selves and societies on terms other than the given. Walt Whitman's vistas and barbaric yawps, Herman Melville's character Bartleby preferring not to, the MC5's kicking out the jams, all operate on a frequency of creative refusal that is alive in jazz communitarianism. As George Lipsitz writes, engaged listening to local sound practices reveals them as a kind of "grass-roots theorizing about complicated realities."[5] This interrogation of the world can only occur "in the venues that are open" to participants.[6] So it is in warehouses and living rooms, church basements and coffee shops, community centers and storefronts that sounds come into being and fade into air, that musicians play into being experiences that simply by their existence are radical in McWorld.[7] The communities of spirits rejoicing do not simply seek recognition or legislation, but aim to make certain religiosities audible through their links to place, memory, religion, and sound.

If we saw earlier how the sounds of American religion spill continually and unpredictably from church interiors, it is in the streets of Chicago and St. Louis, San Francisco and Los Angeles, that musicians heard the multiplicity of American religious sound and housed its manyness. The establishment of actual spaces for religio-musical practice, and a persistent reliance on spatial imagery, resounds in what Graham Lock identifies as a "long-standing African-American tradition of...'imagined elsewheres.'"[8] These social spaces for jazz renegotiate the value of art and religious practice, and in so doing, according to Sara Evans and Harry Boyte, "become free spaces, breeding grounds for democratic change."[9] In these spaces, musical and religious performances express utopic possibility, and American religious experience resounds in new sonic institutions.

There may in fact be something about being religious in America that, to a certain sub-tradition anyways, means living against dominant strains of Americanism. In each chronological and geographical corner of American history, we find religious practitioners striving to establish a regenerate community or purified tradition against a society or "system" defined by, for example, commodification, sin, homogenized identity, artistic or intellectual atrophy, or corruption. In this history we find not only the familiar actors in chronicles of American new religious movements—the Oneida perfectionists, Hopedale, the Moorish Science Temple, the Shakers, the Branch Davidians, or the International Society for Krishna Consciousness

(ISKCON)—but also communitarian initiatives often described as "quasi-religious," "spiritual," and many indeed nonreligious by any reckoning. Might we not think of John Africa's MOVE, the Black Panthers, or even the Occupy movement as drawing sustenance from this well? Do not political religious examples like Clarence Jordan's Koinonia Partners or the Plowshares movement manifest the reformist or resistant edge so often defining the impulse to self-organize, institutionalize, and self-create? The sheer range of these examples also creates a rich opportunity to think about the role of music in communitarianism, in ways obvious (Shaker dance or ISKCON chanting as embodied, sensory registers of identity) and subcultural (for example, the Process Church of Final Judgment or the early Grateful Dead House).

Of course the differences in these communities' social analysis, organizational structure, and ritual life obviously outweigh similarities. And we cannot collapse these presences into one another simply because their devotion has been partly sonic. But the very regularity of such endeavors in American religious history challenges us to think of the continuity, rather than the separateness, of music, religion, and politics. This tradition of withdrawal, new religions, and intentional communities is part of the standard repertoire of American religion, and by acknowledging its co-resonance with political critique and musical subculture we can sound out jazz's improvisations on this established (if complicated) theme in American cultural history.

"Survival Is Your Only Defense"

Jazz musicians have regularly sought to avoid mishearing and misrepresentation by taking to self-organization. DIY efforts proliferated in the 1960s, prompted initially by questions about where to play experimental music, since mainstream outlets were unreceptive. In independent labels like Candid or the alternate Newport Festival in the civil rights era, the focus was often on keeping the music itself from being watered down. But with the 1964 October Revolution, Bill Dixon, Archie Shepp, and others aimed to confront the racism and poor working conditions of the jazz scene. They formed the Jazz Composers' Guild "to awaken the musical conscience of the masses of people to that music which is essential to their lives."[10] Dixon was resistant to forming a permanent organization after the event (preferring to see it as an opportunity to cultivate the music's "will to self-actualization" and self-reliance).[11] Refusing to play in "saloons," since they did not promote the spiritual connectivity that linked African American with African music, Dixon rejected all of the essentialisms of "jazz" and said of music that "[s]urvival is your only defense" against those who would define you in terms not your own.[12]

By the end of the 1960s, declining urban infrastructures forced many jazz musicians to migrate to lofts and community centers for performance. And in these spaces, jazz cultivated dreams of "the reform of the spirit, and the reform of society."[13] In Detroit there was the Hastings Street Jazz Experience, The Tribe, the Creative Arts Collective, and The Positive Force; in Chicago Frank Derrick shepherded the Total Experience; Billy Taylor began the Jazzmobile in Manhattan, while decades later there emerged the Musicians of Brooklyn Initiative; just outside the city was Woodstock's Creative Music Studio (once called a "jazz ashram"); and in San Francisco the Asian Improv aRts was formed.[14] Among New York's loft venues in the 1970s were Studio Rivbea, Environ, Jazzmania, LaMama Children's Workshop, the Brook, and Ladies Fort, which formed a small but influential scene where, as violinist Billy Bang said, "We shared a common experience which allowed us to effortlessly enter each other's universe."[15] In this organizational firmament, several communitarian projects shone more brightly than others.

"The AACM Was My Denomination"

Chicago's South Side in the early 1960s was religiously eclectic, politically active, and economically hard luck. With few formal educational outlets for jazz, many musicians joined the armed services in the 1950s and 1960s, since service bands were good places to develop chops and make connections. Chicagoans returning home from enlistment found common cause with others seeking musical employment after high school, but this vibrant, growing group of players had few outlets for performance. During this period a highly restrictive nightclub licensing act made it extremely difficult for entrepreneurs in black neighborhoods especially to open and maintain performance venues. So musicians went looking for new spaces.

Composer and pianist Muhal Richard Abrams invited younger musicians to his home on Mondays for jam sessions. Many of them were attracted to the experimental music of Mingus, Ornette Coleman, and especially John Coltrane, who embodied disciplined self-expression. But Abrams encouraged adepts to think about collective improvisations and pedagogy as well, a shift that signaled communal, political, and philosophical changes as well as aesthetic ones. He assembled his "Experimental Band," a setting for not only musical exploration but for thinking through the intersections of racial consciousness, community building, free improvisation, and religious imaginings of democratic life.

In the early 1960s, many of the young musicians who would join the Association for the Advancement of Creative Musicians (AACM) had ties to the Congress of Racial Equality (CORE), whose focus on institutional racism dovetailed with the neighborhood's long-standing community activism (some tied to the Alinsky tradition, and drawing from a lineage reaching back to Jane Addams's Hull House and the Progressive Schools). As Ronald Radano notes, churches were intimately involved in these South Side activities (and in musical training), creating "a nexus for sacred/sonic linkages."[16] What united these efforts was a focus on self-determination, a resistance to racist limitations on performance, and the interplay of difference and cooperation both culturally and aesthetically.[17] This refusal to be unheard by a society deaf to black creativity led also to efforts at religious renewal and self-creation. Abrams's search led him to Paramahansa Yogananda's *Autobiography of a Yogi*, which "awakened something in me that needed awakening."[18] From there, Abrams read widely in esoteric literature, and subsequently "hooked up with the Rosicrucians."[19] Many of the players flocking to Abrams's apartment, a functional salon for what George Lewis calls "alternate pedagogy," had religious backgrounds that remained instrumental in their development.[20] Charles Dinwiddie's father was a traveling evangelist; Roscoe Mitchell's family was devout (though he enjoyed the music more than the homilies); Amina Claudine Myers played organ in her Arkansas sanctified church; Reggie Nicholson's family was AME for a spell, but his father eventually embraced "the Black Hebrew Israelites"; and Henry Threadgill had been "playing his tenor saxophone for the Lord" with evangelist Horace Shepherd.[21]

Emerging from the Experimental Band's cultivation of self-expression were visions—primarily from Abrams, Jodie Christian, Steve McCall, and Phil Cohran—of an organization that could assist musicians in their independence, teach music as a "tool for personal growth," and counter the musicians' sense of cultural theft and loss around them.[22] These goals were realized through new musical explorations, like the collective's circle improvisations, where people "take impromptu solos as the spirit may move."[23] Rejecting the term "jazz" for "creative music," the AACM chose its name partly for numerological reasons, since "[w]e think and feel in a

spiritual manner about what we're doing."[24] They elaborated "nine purposes" of self-determination, one of which was "[t]o stimulate spiritual
growth in creative artists."[25] Cohran believed that musical exploration would
"awaken in my people their heritage," while Abrams noted the desire "to
awaken the psyche, through originality, not only feelings."[26]

So from a small musical workshop on the South Side emerged a multi-
generational organization that has thrived on tensions, including the performative (incorporating ribald satire and serious chamber music), spatial
(between localism and a more international ethos, as many of its members
have relocated), musical (composition or improvisation, avant-garde or
populist), historical (moving between an explicit Afrocentrism and a reliance on American traditions of democratic activism), and religious (at
times eschewing religion altogether, or elsewhere shifting between a pan-
traditional combinative idiom and a sometimes ironic embrace of particular traditions). Amid these creative tensions, the AACM's and its musicians'
religious sensibilities have often served as prisms through which to view
complex and shifting positions with regard to the freedom and constraints
of race, community, democracy, and music itself.

The organization has placed considerable emphasis on educational initiatives and other elements of grass-roots community-building, all linked
through the notion that music encompasses the collective aspirations, ideals, and musical practices of peoples of African descent. Its urban activism
could almost be heard as a local enactment of Mississippi Freedom
Summer or Bob Moses's subsequent Algebra Project, establishing new
networks and institutions to foster organic, immanent change that was
simultaneously political, religious, and aesthetic. The AACM looked beyond jazz to other musical sources that might help them articulate the
communitarianism they wanted to underpin both musical and religious
exploration. The overarching goal was to unite the importance of improvisation as a form of self-determination with a less narrow approach to
music-making than was currently associated with "jazz"; an expansive approach to the possibilities of sound itself would broaden perception, consciousness, and spirit. The AACM drew on John Cage's insistence on the
meditative qualities of aleatoric music and his embrace of the sounds of
everyday life. In terms of the latter, the AACM became known for the use of
so-called little instruments: varied sound generators that would also mimic
the sounds of the city (like Threadgill's hubkapphone). Their new sounds
blended idioms and sheer noise, resonating in the lineage of intentional
communities and urban ministries that ring those bells for change. Anthony

Braxton recalls the shock of his first performance in this musical milieu: "I say, I'm going to show these motherfuckers what it's all about—thirty-second notes, Coltrane, Cecil Taylor: I finish my solo, and [Joseph] Jarman stood up and said [sings] *Bwaaaah!* [silence], *Oom* [silence], *Pfffft!* I said this motherfucker is totally out of his motherfucking mind, and this is the baddest shit I've ever heard in my life."[27]

The common denominator was a turn away from the formal conventions of postwar jazz in favor of texture and collective improvisation. Music was lived, not simply performed; and performance was an occasion to reflect on one's life and larger cosmological, existential, or spiritual concerns, not just to wail and blow. The musical changes in the air were inseparable from an expansion of spirit. Abrams believed that "the spiritual plane was best approached through the abstract" and that jazz's obsession with "harmony stood as an aesthetic barrier that restrained black musicians in their search for spiritual unity."[28] While there remained a desire to foreground African sources, the AACM developed in fascinating ways to engage theater and satire, and most important to frame all activities as spiritual pursuits. The process of developing one's own musical language was seen as a kind of spiritual rebirth. Jarman recalls that before Abrams's "ministerial influence," he "did not *care* for the life that I had been given," until in music "I found the first something with meaning/reason for doing."[29] Braxton sought to "bring spiritual awareness" to art.[30] Kalaparush Maurice McIntyre realized "there are spiritual laws governing life," which could be realized musically.[31] Threadgill, who has performed Church of God liturgical music and reads creation stories for inspiration, averred that spirit and society are "connected symbolically in the tones."[32] Douglas Ewart explored the implications of the multi-religious milieu of his Jamaican upbringing.[33] Alvin Fielder spoke for the whole, saying, "Music is my church and...the AACM was my denomination."[34] Second-generation members like Ameen Muhammad and Ernest Khabeer Dawkins came to the AACM through their exploration of political radicalism and alternate religions (Dawkins read Mao and the *Bhagavad Gita* alongside Malcolm X before becoming Muslim in 1970).[35] And Nicole Mitchell has recently written sci-fi–inspired explorations of "ritual, trance, and meditation as a way to connect with the inner self."[36] Mitchell (who has written pieces for Gaia and Octavia Butler and who did a Lakota vision quest to connect with her Native American heritage) exemplifies the AACM's fascination with universals resonating through particulars, reflected in Abrams's contention that music "encompasses the universe itself."[37]

Aside from the influence of traditions, there is a ritualistic quality to AACM activities: this began with the group's naming ceremony, its consecration of parliamentary procedure (here invested with improvisational spontaneity, where deliberation moves as the spirit moves you), and the regular use of circle formations, prayers, and invocations. All early activity was ceremonial in nature, including regular prayer, invocations, and meditations, though Abrams insisted "[y]ou could be any faith you wanted."[38] What mattered was linking through the spirit to culture and art. Over time the AACM's musical ethos, spiritually and idiomatically inclusive, was institutionalized in a charter school, a national council, and a reliance on parliamentary procedure in pedagogy and outreach.[39] This interactivity also shapes the AACM's exploration of multiple genres. The organization's mantra "Great Black Music—Ancient to the Future" is thought by most members to eschew cultural and historical essentialism, its capaciousness and flexibility linked instead to what Wadada Leo Smith identifies as music's "ancient, and immediate, past."[40] George Lewis notes that despite the insistence that dialogism and multi-instrumentalism reflected heterogeneous black identities in the diaspora, the AACM experienced some tension in debates about gender equity or black nationalist sentiments. Yet there remains the tendency to frame musical models—care for the self within a collectivist context, the unity of difference and harmony, or a resistance to hierarchy in the name of experimentalism—as religious. The focus on cultivating an ethos of respect and trust, first nurtured as musical virtues—do not play too much, be generous with space on the bandstand—is situated in a larger civic ethos of mutuality and accountability. Experimentation and preservation work together—in music, in history, in community, in religiosity—in what saxophonist and bandleader Ed Wilkerson describes as a tradition with "purposes beyond 'good music.' It has function in people's lives."[41]

One cannot hear in the AACM or its music an explicit theology or creedal formation; there is no common sacred text, ritual, or place of worship. Yet its pedagogy of self-creation, community development, and future-oriented memory are described by members as indelibly linked by active spirits. Building on almost Garveyite themes of self-help and cultural pride, the AACM has continually drawn on the deep religious ties that were clearly part of the associational network of the South Side. Yet the organization has remained equally reliant on "images of the musician-seer in tribal Africa," with the conviction that spiritual depth would be accompanied by "improve[d] political awareness."[42] More than simple group therapy or psychological quest, the very abstractness of the music is understood to move you to "an unknown region beyond the boundary of accepted thought," a realm of mystery where traditional aesthetic, social, and spiritual distinctions broke down and where, through cooperation and ritual performance, new meanings can be elaborated.[43] Here, "'transcendence' referred to a kind of intellectual and emotional catharsis," which made it possible to learn true history, break out of mental chains, and ultimately reach the "spiritual plane" where "through collaborative creation, intuition and intellect meet."[44]

The AACM has embodied and articulated many, if not all, of these themes, using improvisation as a vehicle for religious devotion, not just as a kind of sonic accompaniment to previously generated ideas but as itself a kind of ritual, a sounding-out of human relations to whatever is considered divine. Understanding musical practice to be a sacred mystery, a conduit to the self, and a model for democratic community, the AACM clearly manifests the links between bandstand experimentation, history, community, and religiosity. Its belief is that culture can best be preserved precisely through change, improvisation, and adaptation, modes of connecting to the past, channeling emotion, and opening up connections and creativity. And again, the elusiveness of the formal category "religion" is precisely what demands that through music you break down and then build your own system. Perhaps this gives the player, the listener, the reader too little to hold onto. But as Abrams said, "I can say 'God,' 'Allah,' 'Jehovah,' but all people don't relate to that. Everybody relates to change, and I think change is synonymous with any conception of the deity."[45]

An Act of Giving: The Black Artists Group

While the AACM sought explicitly to create its own institutional pedagogy and historical sensibility, practicing a musical inclusivism it connected with cultural and spiritual abundance, St. Louis's Black Artists' Group (BAG) saw multimedia experimentation as a recipe for institutional and identitarian change. Inspired by the AACM, BAG knit together varied modes of expression in a sensibility that was both Pan-Africanist and global, believing that the arts served the purposes of cultural and spiritual reawakening. At the end of the 1960s, optimism about integrationism and racial uplift had faded, leaving many to turn away from aspirations for national policy change and embrace grass-roots efforts to transform neighborhoods. In St. Louis, exposure to music (especially religious music) was common among African Americans.⁴⁶ BAG activists focused on arts as a means to tap these sources to facilitate institutional and personal reform. Dance and music were understood as rituals to awaken consciousness and sustain activist motivation. Multimedia street art was seen as a way to expand the context of the expressive, spilling beyond the clubs and galleries into the streets. BAG summarized its goal as "the spiritual and cultural liberation of black people" through establishing communities of sound and vision.⁴⁷

Religiosity, then, flowed through the cultural lineages and institutions of BAG players, amplifying the associations through which musicians developed their instrumentalism as well as their social networks (like the city's famed drum and bugle corps). The music made by this shifting collective of mostly African American players (a multiform free jazz of the sort that was still confrontational and jarring during BAG's heyday of 1968–72) was sonically and institutionally distinct, owing to its multimedia collaborations with poets (especially Shirley LeFlore and Ajule Rutlin), dancers (led by Georgia Collins and Luisah Teish), directors (notably Malinke Elliott), and painters (like Oliver Jackson).

BAG's specific aesthetic and spiritual expressions identified African culture as generative and sustaining without clinging to any kind of racial essentialism.⁴⁸ Similarly, BAG's collaboration across genres reflected its inclusive spirituality, instantiated in both artistic productions and organizational interactions with neighborhood institutions. With only a handful of performance spaces, the BAG scene took shape through a small group of key performances by influential players who, like Oliver Lake and Julius Hemphill, began considering the prospects of coalition-building and organizing. Actor Malinke Elliott had been brainstorming with local teacher Russell Durgin about establishing an organization that could harness the city's young artistic talent and link it to both community development and spiritual self-realization. They wanted initially to explore experimental theater networking and create "some kind of common experience working together"; but when Lake proposed multimedia collaboration, the seeds of BAG were sown.⁴⁹

The multimedia presentations "Sons" and "Ancestors" signaled the group's inclination to look to the African past in sounding out an African American future. The program described the performances as a "calling forth of the spiritually dynamic forces and powers of the cosmos...[to awaken] that harmonious existence which perpetuates itself as the African Continuum."⁵⁰ The LaClede Town neighborhood (the epicenter of BAG activity) reflected these aspirations at the time, with its blend of political activists, artists, and religious communities. And as more performances were held at the Circle Coffee House, citizens came together in these arts space with increased frequency. After multiple performances during the fractious summer of 1968, BAG coalesced around a collaborative ethos and an expressive style that was confrontational without being blunt, and materialist even as it explored spirituality, ritual, and cosmology. Many listeners were nervous about the mix of often discordant free jazz and political theater. Although some players, like Hamiet Bluiett and Hemphill, were deeply steeped in blues and R 'n' B, audiences "thought we was a bunch of wild animals, not real musicians," according to James Jabbo Ware.[51] BAG players felt their music was being dismissed as an entertainment sideshow to St. Louis's steamboat traditions, and they avoided any situation requiring them to play music they felt was beneath them. This eschewal of cheap sound and expectation was an integral part of their community outreach, arts pedagogy, and activist networking in what Lake called "an experiment in 'socio-economic liberation.'"[52]

In its warehouse on Washington Boulevard (which they rented for a lone dollar annually), the organization was a model for the vitality of urban arts. Like many urban religious communities have done, BAG sought to contrast their cooperative spirit and creative purpose with the blasted landscape surrounding it. This same amalgam of context and concern was reflected in the thematic content of its performances, in its refusal for art to "play nice" in its designated spaces. In its belief that creativity could be the substance and the medium of neighborhood regeneration, BAG echoed the AACM's insistence that cultural history grounded spiritual pursuits and community work. Unexpected grants from the Rockefeller and Danforth foundations helped BAG provide for several years of initiatives (they also benefited from President Lyndon Johnson's anti-poverty funding, and BAG incorporated as a nonprofit in 1968).[53] The warehouse became an organizational, performance, and living space, where members slept, gave lessons, and held rehearsals, their lives part of the larger multimedia event. Seeing themselves beyond idiom and even beyond "art," BAG members called themselves "cultural aestheticians" or "poets of action."[54] The BAG-AIR center, the group's free music school, sought to "make black people more aware of their creative potential" as part of an integrated life.[55] The idea of dispossessed people reengaging history, educating themselves, and controlling the political tone of their immediate environment certainly drew on extant themes of the period and the widespread desire to forge new diasporic identities. But BAG was distinct in linking these notions to new sonic explorations of "open tonality and form as well as unmetered rhythmic momentum."[56] These creations were further linked to musical and personal disciplines: ideas were work shopped rigorously, and most members forswore pork and drugs.

In time, BAG began to document its music. Lake's first album by his NTU troupe, *The Point from Which Creation Begins*, reflected his (and BAG's) broader cosmological concerns. BAG was well versed in African culture, which it sought to refract in performance and in their efforts at racial uplift and grass-roots urban engagement. Religious institutions were central to BAG's neighborhood, and Berea Church especially encouraged experimentalism; even though BAG's spirituality was inclusive, artistic pursuits continually took place in concert with established religious institutions (though also sometimes with nationalist groups like the Warlords or the Black Egyptians).[57] Visual artists worked regularly with CORE and SNCC (facilitated by Charles Koen's Black Liberators, which he saw as an outgrowth of his ministerial study), producing works like the Wall of Respect mural designed "to bring on black awareness and black consciousness of black history."[58] Stylistic and genre shifts were seen as part of the ongoing ritual of self-creation, expanding the social and political context in which these imaginings occurred.

BAG's arts education would counteract the "erasure of cultural memory."[59] Their efforts in this area were widespread, inscrutable, and usually subversive. At times the initiatives took familiar form, as in the November 1969 "Festival of Creation, a daylong arts event at the city's high-church Episcopal Christ Church Cathedral."[60] But often BAG presented more challenging fare. Leon Thomas's productions were known for "invoking a pantheon of jazz masters as 'Sturdy invisibly hooded holymen,'" as if great musicians formed secret societies of sound like Theosophy's grand masters.[61] Their free jazz accompanied plays (Elliott called them "total theater in the streets") featuring stock characters like corrupt cops and preachers: one restaged Nat Turner's rebellion; "The Pigs" showed a police station with a sign out front reading "We Buy Souls"; and many were, like "The First Militant Preacher," performed in churches with the intent of bringing Panther-style radicalism into the pews to promote "black humane revolutionary change" (even if parishioners were often uncomfortable with such radicalism).[62]

Yet for every production honoring George Jackson as a warrior/poet, others looked to religious and philosophical traditions for sustenance.

The poem "The Dream Time" used Mother/Goddess imagery and marks a shift from 1960s political radicalism to 1970s expansion of religious creativity and consciousness; this shift occurred in the service of what Oliver Jackson called "a sense of clarity about the spiritual state."[63] Teish was among those who insisted on injecting ritual into all BAG productions, improvising on traditions by "weaving in strands of mysticism, Egyptology, and her own versions of African rituals."[64] In this she picked up on a strong undercurrent in the group's fifty-odd members, drawing on African cultural history as she crafted a localist, ecologically oriented spirituality that was womanist ("that forgotten power") and inclusive at once.[65]

Texas-born Hemphill moved in similar directions, "reliving the journey past and plotting out the route ahead."[66] He took inspiration from the West African Dogon, diving into their "cosmology, religions, and...[especially] dance ceremonies."[67] His *Dogon A.D.* and *Coon Bid'ness* investigated his childhood exposure to rural blues and church music.[68] With long, looping repetitions and a sound that used the avant-garde to link West Africa and the Delta, Hemphill also winked knowingly to the role of secrecy in ritual. He was fascinated by how the Dogon tribe decided at one point "to reveal some of their sacred dance ritual" in order to gin up tourism, and by their identification of Sirius's companion star even without scientific equipment.[69] Hemphill located this link between intuitive knowledge and concealment in the Dogon's fable-spinning, exemplified in their suggestion that "they were visited by star people" who bestowed this knowledge on them.[70] Hemphill often followed suit with the process of dissembling and storytelling that produced "religion" as an imagined past of sorts. He played at being Blind Lemon Jefferson, invented characters like Roye Boi, signified on the racism of the music industry with *Coon Bid'ness*, and composed suites like "The Long Tongues: A Saxophone Opera," "The Last Supper at Uncle Tom's Cabin: The Promised Land," an undocumented adaptation of Ralph Ellison's *The Invisible Man*, and the epic "Drunk on God" (which features BAG colleague K. Curtis Lyle's shamanic poetry).[71] Typical of BAG sensibilities, Hemphill identified the common core of these diverse efforts as "an act of giving, coming out of an intensely religious tradition."[72]

But because of poor publicity and dwindling opportunities, many BAG members left the 'Lou and by the mid-1970s BAG existed "only on a spiritual level."[73] While groups like the Solidarity Unity and Children of the Sun remained in St. Louis, many key figures in BAG split for New York or Paris after the funding ran out. As Rutlin put it, "[T]he experiments and investigations were abandoned short of their goal which was/is to find a way to re-establish the natural harmony of the Spiritual World."[74] Since BAG's dissolution in 1973, the musicians have continued to investigate religiosity as part of their self-fashioning. Some collaborated with Senegalese percussionist Mor Thiam on traditional Wolof songs. Lake has published poetry, accompanied recordings of Martin Luther King Jr. speeches, and performed Navajo chants and gospel tunes. Bluiett has performed Yoruba chants and African American spirituals. And LeFlore has been involved with the multimedia ensemble Spirit Stage and founded the BAG-inspired Creative Arts & Expression Laboratory in St. Louis.[75] The investigation of folk and religious musics from Asia and the Middle East reflects a common sensibility in the 1970s. BAG artists took to chant and incantations, symbols and rituals from Native American cultures, India and Nepal, and Sufi practice, ostensibly in order to express "the unity of one world of black culture."[76] But as Lake put it, "[W]ords have been used to separate and catalogue and divide, and consequently they divide the people from listening to the music"; the spirit would reunite them.[77]

Common to these efforts and the group's inception was the attempt to generate languages of artistic and spiritual self-creation that were publicly engaged but resistant to cooptation or easy interpretation. Part of this elusiveness means that, though the community itself sponsored investigations into religiosities and worked with religious institutions, it is difficult to call BAG a "religious community." But this elusiveness and resistance to conventional formulations of "religion" is also written into the history of American communitarianism, as with Fruitlands or Indiana's Lothlorien, and into the panoply of American multimedia street religiosity, from the Hare Krishnas to the Reverend Billy Talen. And Parran noted that as part of artistic self-creation and collective involvement, there was "another sort of spirit."[78] BAG was also, as Lipsitz writes, an "alternate academy," one squarely in the tradition of jazz that asks what jazz is, asking religious questions about what religion could be.[79] They played in tongues of fire, built institutions that reached beyond the neighborhood even while creating new ways of listening to and inhabiting it. Music not only organized socially but did so perceptually and religiously, arranging the ongoing flow of time as one occupied it in a small corner of the Vietnam-era Midwest. In BAG's short lifespan, it established a synthetic performance style that was self-consciously ritualized and historicized, its "religion" generated in the tropes and aspirations of artists working at the intersection of what Benjamin Looker identifies as "music, death, and minstrelsy."[80] If the AACM explored what Jarman called the "non-cognitive aspects of the city," then BAG's poetry of action conjured "religion" from its atmosphere of experimentation with art and politics, seeking to realize a situated flow of ideas fully of and beyond its time and place, the languages of the spirits signifying both the surplus and the situation.

The Giant Has Awakened: The UGMAA

Horace Tapscott (1934–99) was born in Texas to a family equally committed to music and community service. They moved to Los Angeles in 1943 to find work in the shipyards, and young Tapscott immersed himself in the famous Central Avenue music scene. He studied luminaries like Coleman Hawkins, Dexter Gordon, and Charlie Parker, later woodshedding on trombone while stationed with the Air Force in Wyoming. Upon his discharge, he landed a gig with Lionel Hampton and, after years on the touring circuit, was introduced to Coltrane by Eric Dolphy in 1959. Weary of the touring life, Tapscott was inspired by these forward-thinking musicians to return home with a change of musical purpose: "[I] started thinking about putting the Arkestra together.... I wanted to preserve and teach and show and perform the music of black Americans and Pan-African music."[81]

Switching to piano, Tapscott began composing and organizing in earnest just as jazz was hybridizing further, often in explicitly pedagogical and spiritual directions. By the early 1960s the Central Avenue scene was crippled by exorbitant rents, rising crime and police brutality, and demographic changes. The neighborhood's musical and cultural pluralism remained, sustained by education, unionizing, and collaborations (e.g., with "cool" players affiliated with Howard Rumsey's Lighthouse or Shelly Manne's Manne Hole). But with suspicions of communism surrounding African American political efforts and with the increased economic segregation faced by non-commercial players, there were changes. A radicalized Tapscott responded by committing to local organization. He found additional inspiration in the ascendant Black Arts and Black Power movements, whose focus on community survival and development was particularly influential in California.[82] These sentiments coalesced amid a network of extant churches and neighborhood institutions, and in an air of spiritual inquiry that piqued Tapscott's organizational interest.[83]

Recalling how community work flowed from the pews of his childhood church in Houston, Tapscott felt that local churches were neither tapping into musicians' spiritual interests effectively nor doing enough neighborhood service. In any serious church, Tapscott believed, "You've got to have the music all of the time" and must ensure that children are "taught about African American history."[84] Horrified when "those four little girls died in that church bombing in Birmingham," Tapscott decided to form his own counter-public to serve these purposes."[85] Away from the pressures and compromises of commercial music, Tapscott founded the Underground Musicians Association, a stylistic and a sociological designation signaling the music's radicalism. Renamed UGMAA in 1963, the group explored explicitly Afrocentric pedagogies and was supported by the United Clergymen of Central Los Angeles for its efforts at neighborhood improvement and education.[86] Tapscott centered many of these efforts on his Pan-Afrikan People's Arkestra: "'Pan Afrikan,' because the music would be drawn from African peoples around the world, and 'Arkestra'...[because] [w]e would preserve the music on our ark, the mothership."[87] While communitarian ventures and politically oriented intentional communities were common in the 1960s, Tapscott saw UGMAA as a religiously grounded (but non-creedal) alternative to conventional music-making that was also a locus for community organizing. UGMAA's "turn to African American and African tradition" was a response to the debasement of human aspirations in a commercial, corporatist society (felt acutely by improvising musicians).[88] Art and spirituality would be cultivated in places illegible to the "cultured" eye that could not see working-class black populations. And "the Ark" would be the vessel of an authenticity and self-realization that was cultural, religious, and sonic.

The organization's inception changed Tapscott's music, now shot through with an outpouring of community emotion and "those sounds that expressed what we were all feeling."[89] This was the sound of UGMAA as a surrogate church, and Tapscott sought to bring this joyful noise to the city's underprivileged through children's education and community art and music classes. In these early years there were "cats going around teaching older people how to read and write," a senior citizens program called Medimusic, and an arts outreach to the mentally ill.[90] They often charged no admission to shows other than a can of food and encouraged children to attend for free (Tapscott recalled kids skipping down the street humming "The Dark Tree" after shows).[91] But though UGMAA was contextually responsive to the civil rights movement, the organization did not reflect its relatively optimistic strategies of conveying critique via common symbols and narratives, opting instead for a quasi-separatist, diffuse Afrocentrism also recognizable in movements as far-flung as the Black Panthers and the

Nation of Islam. While UGMAA was never tied to a particular religious tradition, nor was it as militant as either the Panthers or the Fruit of Islam, the group's social critique and ethic of self-determination enjoined musicians to organize their institutions, sounds, and pedagogies based on differential identities and values.

This difference crystallized following the wake of the 1965 Watts Riots. Tapscott wanted UGMAA to provide for Angelinos a cultural affirmation, where the arts could directly serve as part of people's self-determination music rather than simply accompany tepid liberalism. Daniel Widener locates Tapscott's efforts in the lineage of "the radical participatory democracy of Ella Baker."[92] But the emphasis on community revitalization also places UGMAA on a continuum lineage with Sojourners, the Catholic Worker, and Progressive houses of hospitality, here the subject of specifically African American improvisations on shared critiques and social practices. Steven Isoardi suggests that UGMAA was successful in making such connections because it grounded its efforts in "aspects of West and West Central African cultures" that placed music at the heart of all social activity.[93] In a moment when conventional ideas about personhood were being questioned and new perspectives on African history emerging, UGMAA drew inspiration from a past where, as Isoardi notes, "among the most significant guilds of artists were the griots and griottes, those most responsible for maintaining the history of their people."[94] Artists were central figures, but beyond this, visual and musical expressions were integral to religions, giving form to ritual and also serving as vehicles by which religious feelings were enacted, ideas circulated.

The notion that religious worlds are formed through sound, that the relation between the human and the divine is sonically mediated, helped UGMAA articulate "a range of goals, from supporting artistic integrity and creating performance spaces, to participating in the preservation and betterment of their culture and communities."[95] UGMAA regularly collaborated in these efforts with local religious institutions and was shaped further by members' own spiritualities. The music had to come from and be available to those very people to whose experience it spoke. These relations with religious organizations emerged organically from UGMAA's atmosphere of conceptualism and spiritual inquiry. Saxophonist "Black Arthur" Blythe recalls how he "got exposed to Elijah Muhammad, Malcolm and Dr. King and Adam Clayton Powell" through UGMAA, which emphasized cultivating "feelings musically and about political things, spiritual things, social things."[96] Neighborhood folks were attracted to the coopera-

tive, street social spirit of the Ark, and its regular sponsorship of workshops and teach-ins. Members were encouraged to pursue multiple forms
of artistic expression, to read and converse when not creating, and to seek
out opportunities for community enrichment. As Leon Thomas put it,
"We were like a big Sun Ra family."[97] UGMAA also made considerable
room for women in leadership roles. Members Amina, Avotcja, Linda,
and Danyel were prominent teachers and creators, often described as
muses. Danyel described Linda as "mystical," "connected to some spirits
or sources of the unseen world."[98]

Indeed, there was something about the group's mixture of history,
music, religion, and activism that many members felt cultivated such intense spirituality, making the very atmosphere of the UGMAA conducive
to the transformation of the self. Such sensibilities were understood by
fellow Angelinos and UGMAA members (or associates, like Jayne Cortez,
who had worked with SNCC) to be linked to the expansion of political
consciousness. As UGMAA became a more established neighborhood
presence in the late 1960s, the boundaries of the political seemed everywhere expanding; the Black Panthers, the US Organization, and the
Nation of Islam were regular presences in the streets where UGMAA
made its sounds, usually with police watching fearfully. Tapscott had seen
the riots coming and hoped the Ark could insert itself into this combus-
tible social mix (following the example of proto-rappers and street preachers the Watts Prophets) and calm things down. Here the Ark was inspired
by the African tradition of *mafundi*, or street artists. But the dance and
celebration the music inspired panicked the police, who alleged that the
music was "inciting" violence.[99] Tapscott only further underscored the
music's sociocultural resonance. The Ark ended every concert with "Lift
Ev'ry Voice and Sing," and Tapscott—knowingly connecting his efforts to
long traditions of African American religious freedom struggles—recalls
"[e]very time we'd play 'The Giant Has Awakened,' the audience would all
stand up, salute; some would be crying."[100]

Some UGMAA members responded to unrest by becoming directly involved in the NOI, and "[o]ne member worked with a small group of militant Muslims that advocated military-style confrontations with the LAPD to
combat police brutality."[101] Others identified strongly with the goals of the
Panthers (whose Elaine Brown was featured on the Arkestra's *Seize the Time*
album, and who with Tapscott cowrote "The Meeting," which became the
Panthers' anthem).[102] But Tapscott always insisted that the group's goals of
self-organization and self-determination, allied with their identification

with African cultural and spiritual traditions, did not require any affiliations outside the UGMAA. When asked if the UGMAA was a Muslim group, a Panther offshoot, or something else, Tapscott took delight in confounding expectations, insisting, "'We're black Americans, and want to live in the American way.' You dig?"[103]

UGMAA's songs and grass-roots initiatives together made visible and audible the contrast between spirituality and cultural debasements like racism, police brutality, and economic injustice. This was consistent, in Tapscott's mind, with what religious counter-publics had always accomplished for African Americans. By yoking the group's purposes to God's, "we were going to ascend through the arts to bring about recognition and understanding of each other."[104] So the "Ascension" in the group's name signified in meaningfully religious ways to members who still belonged to traditional African American Protestant denominations, to those who had become Muslim, and to those inspired by the pan-idiomatic spirituality increasingly popular among young Americans. But it also hearkened back to Garvey's exhortation "Up, you mighty race!" and the notion that black culture would rise through self-determination and self-expression, the up-lift both sociological and religious.[105]

Though some neighbors were unsettled by the group's Africanisms, worrying that this "radical group of musicians" was performing "hate songs," the UGMAA eventually became integral to the community.[106] Residents attended Sunday Ark concerts after church services, and Tapscott regularly added speakers to the program so that he could educate his neighbors about politics and culture, helping them when they had to "go back into the war zone."[107] As the decade turned, the group's long-standing "interest in the history and spirituality of African and African American traditions" seemed to be resonating elsewhere, as with emerging black studies curricula.[108] Nearby, Ron Karenga formed the study group The Circle of Seven at the Aquarian Bookstore and Spiritual Center, where he and wife, Bernice, were involved in what they saw as "maintaining ancient teachings and passing them on to the next generation."[109] Changes in name and clothing went along with religio-philosophical investigations that UGMAA members were used to pursuing, linking historical study and improvised music with their participation in the NOI, orthodox Muslim communities, Christian churches, or traditional African religions.

The Ark drew from and also fed these changes. Its composition book contained originals, jazz tunes from across the spectrum, and many spirituals. They regularly performed a polytonal workout called "The Sun," which Dadisi Sanyika recalls was "about cosmic consciousness."[110] They collaborated with the Watts Prophets, performed spirituals at church services, and recorded music for the movie *Sweet Jesus, Preacher Man*. Their ranks swelled, now including former Los Angeles Jubilee Singer Adele Sebastian (who described the attractions of the Ark, saying, "It's a way of life, and you live it, and you breathe it, and you are it, and you don't sell out"), Earth, Wind & Fire's Gary Bias, and Marla Gibbs, who played Florence on *The Jeffersons*.[111] The Ark that "serve[d] as a life raft for black history and culture" traveled too, as Tapscott took it wherever he thought the sound might resonate most fruitfully, for the ears of the needy in prisons, hospitals, schools, parks, and churches.[112] While the UGMAA gave away food and clothing along with poems and music, the outspoken Tapscott was blacklisted by mainstream music outlets in the early 1970s, called a "dissident" and an "employment risk."[113] Tapscott, unbowed, continued his activities and began a period of sustained creativity and documentation.

In spring 1973, an "old Jamaican brother" named Reverend Wolfe donated his print shop to the UGMAA, and there they were able to develop their music with great rigor.[114] That same spring, the Ark began an eight-year artists' residency with the Immanuel Church of Christ, "part of a church-sponsored, community program called 'The Seed.'"[115] Tapscott had foreseen in a vision his partnership with Reverend Edgar Edwards, whom he subsequently "fell in love with," calling him "a real deal preacher" who served the community as a whole.[116] The unceasing outreach of the church dovetailed with UGMAA's own, and their regular performances—in the sanctuary, on the lawn, in the streets—drew people to the flock too. Neighboring pastors filed noise complaints and bemoaned blasphemous sound, to which Edwards responded, "Well, I read out of the same Bible that you read: 'And I heard the trumpets sound. Let the trumpet sound, let the sound of music roar.'"[117]

Roar the Ark did, making joyful noise through thickets of percussion, snaking ostinatos, and soaring horn sections all the way through Watergate, OPEC embargoes, and wars abroad. In 1974 Tapscott was invited to Dar es Salaam for the Sixth Pan African Congress. And in 1975 he successfully registered UGMAA as a California nonprofit. With an infusion of youth into the Ark, Tapscott emphasized that the music was less about refinement or technique than "tell[ing] the truth about everything," which extended increasingly to matters religious.[118] Always "perceived as a strongly spiritual organization," and not just for its tendency to play church music in the LA streets, musicians came to see performing with the Ark itself as a form of devotion.[119] Roberto Miranda, a devout Christian, "would go there to play/pray."[120] In an extended series of programs, Tapscott steered the Ark to a new goal: to teach "what the African American spiritual is about."[121] To Tapscott, spirituals reflected the range of diasporic experience and submerged history. To feel deeply in a cold society was like a revolution; to think rigorously about one's cultural inheritance was subversive. Bob Watt described the Ark's performances of these materials: "there was the touch of God there...[in] music strong enough to cut through all the stuff that's happening today, all the lies."[122] With Tapscott's insistent piano as bedrock, the Ark's horns leaped and the rhythm section throbbed polymetrically, with rousing lyricism unwavering in the center. History itself was audible in this very sound, in which one member said, "[Y]ou could hear everything from field hollers to tin roof church revivals."[123] Craggy but elegant, bluesy but avant-garde, sensitive but defiant, the music contained multitudes.

The Ark was thus part of what Tapscott called SWU, Sidewalk University.[124] Its lessons were taught by musicians considering themselves griots, operating in part as "cultural historian[s]" so that, as Sebastian noted, the "music [can] be truthful, spiritually motivated and meaningful."[125] The Ark's music sounded out history itself; according to Joshua, "there's a unity within it...that has to do both with the exodus from Egypt and Harriet Tubman."[126] And for Kamau Daaood, "In the music is the emotional history of a people."[127] It is this emotionality that held together self-realization and community unity. As reedist Sabir Mateen put it, "[T]he spiritual side of music" makes self-realization possible; but these processes also generate an ethic, such that group membership is "like following God's plan" by "treating people a particular way."[128] Mateen identified these as Christian categories (where the ideas are "played as a prayer") and saw the effect their realization had in the neighborhood's connection with the Ark.[129] Mateen was given a pass by members of the Crips gang, who said, "Don't mess with that guy. He plays in that group around the corner."[130] And Tapscott was once asked by a wino, during a period of Ark inactivity, "Hey man, where's our band?"[131]

Unity was dangerous. Enshrining it in an intentional community that challenged social convention with music was even more so, since it "reflect[s] the natural rays of creativity, the essence of our existence."[132] This fusion of history, community organization, and spiritually inspired opposition is familiar in the history of new religious movements, though sound is usually left out of these chronicles—and nowhere are the indelible presences of jazz. For the UGMAA, though, music simply came from "the whole everyday thing—from your basic ideas about life."[133] It was constitutive, sound as ubiquitous as the sky's canopy. But in ways tantalizingly like "religion" itself, "music *names* them [experiences] and in doing so celebrates...what has been denied."[134]

Cleaning the Mirror: The Saint John Coltrane African Orthodox Church

The story of saxophonist John Coltrane (1926–67) is near mythical. Born in Hamlet, North Carolina, Coltrane was reared in an extremely religious family, under what he called the "militant" supervision of his grandfathers, both African Methodist Episcopal Zion (AMEZ) preachers.[135] By the time Coltrane's family moved to Philadelphia in his early teens, he had already developed obsessive practice habits and a discipline that some called monastic. After cutting his teeth in hard bop, the budding star was invited to join Miles Davis's first great quintet. By the mid-1950s, though, Coltrane had developed a serious heroin addiction. It was at this point that he experienced what he called a "spiritual awakening." At his lowest point, Coltrane asked God to give him the capacity to bring joy through music. From this point, Coltrane gave up heroin and alcohol, and vowed to "dedicate his music to God, in whom he believed with increasing involvement."[136] His sound opened up into new vistas made possible, he contended, by divine mercy and inspiration. On both soprano and tenor, Coltrane played vertically with such rapidity that he could navigate several different permutations of a single chord—arpeggios, scales, improvisations—during a single measure, creating an effect famously described as "sheets of sound."

In the early 1960s, Coltrane put together his seminal quartet—with pianist McCoy Tyner, bassist Jimmy Garrison, and drummer Elvin Jones—and over the next several years explored music with an increasing abstraction and expansiveness that paralleled his changing religious inclinations. As he got further from established chord structures and harmonic constraints, the shy Coltrane read alone and practiced for hours on end. He began to sense that his obsession with harmonic permutations was like "looking at music from the wrong end of the telescope" and started hearing sound as emanating from someplace, possibly from an agentive power, beyond him.[137] He read Edgar Cayce, Helena Blavatsky, Cyril Scott's Theosophical text *Music: Its Secret Influence Through the Ages*, scientific

FIGURE 4.1. John Coltrane improvising on soprano saxophone. Photograph copyright William E. (Bill) Smith.

and mathematical theory, and Hazrat Inayat Khan's *The Mysticism of Sound and Music*.[138] He became influenced by the ancient notion that transformative insight could come through establishing correspondences between temporal-physical locations, musical tones, and celestial spheres. From this point on, Coltrane's life was shaped by the proposition that human thought, behavior, and experience of the divine could not only be accompanied by sound but realized through it.

Coltrane began assimilating *maqamat*, ragas, and Gnawa music into his sound.[139] He believed authentic existence required seeing beyond all distinctions, sonic or religious. And if all experience was sonic, then all sound was devotional. Coltrane described his increasingly fluid religiosity by saying, "I am [Christian] by birth...[but] truth itself doesn't have any name on it"; and when asked what he would like to be later in life, he said simply, "I would like to be a saint."[140] His artistic growth resonated with developments in American religion, including the civil rights movement. Coltrane recorded *Live at the Village Vanguard* on the night Attorney General Robert Kennedy forcibly ended segregated bus terminals in the South. Many heard this concert's moving "Spiritual" as a plea against the fractiousness that so troubled the gentle saxophonist.[141] But despite the urgency of his playing, Coltrane made few direct commentaries. Some listeners thought they could detect in "Alabama" (written to honor the four African American girls who died in an infamous church bombing) the cadences of a Martin Luther King Jr. speech.[142] But the saxophonist made only elliptical comments, which eschewed the prophetic in favor of pleas for joy and compassion.[143] Against those who would hear the sound of black militancy in his music, Coltrane humbly insisted that jazz "does not have to worry about a lack of positive and affirmative philosophy."[144]

His comportment and music grew steadily to reflect the conviction that in serving the creative urge one gave thanks to God. This outlook was announced most powerfully in 1964's *A Love Supreme*. The quartet moved beyond elongated modalism into a sound defined by its own motivic urgency and propulsion. Consisting of four movements—"Acknowledgment," "Resolution," "Pursuance," and "Psalm"—this record marked the beginning of Coltrane's movement, over his final three years, into a galvanic, questing, at times stratospheric music. On 1965's *Transition*, Coltrane performed a suite that paralleled his regular meditational practice: this music was about "that feeling you have when you finally do reach an awareness...a feeling of peace."[145] And it is difficult for the observer of American religions to peruse titles like *Stellar Regions* and *Sun Ship* without noting the resonance with a charismatic African American tradition linking Sun Ra with Father Divine, who described himself as a messenger of God "in the degree of the Son Ship."[146] These musical changes led the great quartet to disband: Jones eventually left after Coltrane brought second drummer,

Rashied Ali, into the group; Tyner was supplanted by Coltrane's second wife, Alice; only Garrison held it down until the end.

Audiences were compelled as much by the unswerving direction of the music, which rocketed ever outward, as if seeking to escape gravity, as by Coltrane's presence. Much to the consternation of club owners, Coltrane's audiences were often too absorbed to buy drinks. He often drew predominantly African American audiences after Malcolm X's assassination, often including Black Panther members and other militants. Everyone seemed to understand that, in synthesizing various religious ideas with his musical experiments, Coltrane made improvisation itself into a form of worship or ritual, whose duration, intensity, and purpose were understood to be geared toward the transformative. This ritualistic quality to his music was widely remarked upon. Saxophonist Dave Liebman recalls that, by the mid-1960s, it was common for Coltrane performances to incorporate chanting (or even, at a famous 1966 Temple University performance, near-glossolalia from Coltrane himself).[147] At the beginning of *Om*, Coltrane and his bandmates employed handheld percussion as they chanted from the *Bhagavad Gita*: "I am the mantra, the clarified butter...I am Om."[148] His gestures were likened to Sufism, "Eastern religions" generically, Native American and West African traditions, and, more predictably, to that analytical homology "the Black Church." Yet beyond musicological connections with spirituals or ragas, what listeners responded to in long-form works like *Ascension*, *Om*, or *Kulu Se Mama* (based on an Afro-Creole poem) was the "breath-stopping physical impact of the pure sound," a "ritual dance" enabling all who heard the music to "reach beyond the imperfect recordings to touch the spirits that made them."[149]

Coltrane proclaimed that his music now sought "the expansion of time" and was grounded in the sound of "Om" as "the first vibration...that sets everything else into being."[150] Music was about consciousness and awareness expanded. Once freed from the restrictions of conventional harmony and pulse, improvised music is encountered like an aspirant before Rudolf Otto's numinous, an experience David Wild described as like "a supplicant facing religious immensity."[151] Coltrane said of the encounter with transformative sound, "Once you become aware of this force for unity, you can't ever forget it."[152] Performance itself was a form of meditation and uplift, and Coltrane described its aims succinctly: "I want to be a force for real good."[153] He still read vociferously, from the *Bardo Thödol*, Krishnamurti, Yogananda's autobiography, and material on Kabbalah, yoga, and astrology. He had begun taking LSD regularly in 1965, and some recall that his introspection was so intense that he even had to be guided back to the stage after breaks between sets.[154] Coltrane believed his LSD experiences confirmed ideas he had encountered through his studies: "I have perceived the interrelationship of all life forms."[155] The implications for music were considerable, since "[t]here are always new sounds to imagine"; musicians must "keep purifying these feelings and sounds so that we can really see what we've discovered in its pure state" by "cleaning the mirror into the self, going as far through the looking glass as possible each time."[156] He was going beyond music, into mathematical areas described by Alice as focused "on rhythmic structure and the power of repetition," those sonic "elementals" from "the first manifestation in creation before music."[157] He became obsessed with numerology, believing that scientists and improvisers both sought the essence of the universe in "the ultimate vibration."[158]

Reactions to Coltrane's explorations consistently used religious language too. Drummer Jones called him "an angel on earth," believing that "[i]f there's any such thing as a perfect man, I think John Coltrane was one."[159] Multi-instrumentalist Joe McPhee said, "I thought I was just going to explode" at a 1965 concert; "[t]he energy level kept building up, and I thought, God almighty, I can't take it."[160] Liebman recalled: "cats started to put their hands up to the ceiling and the whole place stood up. It was like those holy-roller meetings."[161] Archie Shepp thought "it was like being in church.... [Coltrane] raised this music from secular music to religious world music."[162] Another listener said it was "like something out of the book of Revelations...Cosmos Shattering."[163] Yusef Lateef "could hear, semantically, the songs of Islam."[164] Marcus Strickland described the late records as "almost like getting a sermon from a preacher."[165] And trumpeter Charles Tolliver said simply, "He was God."[166]

Some listeners even began to make Coltrane himself (now sometimes called Ohnedaruth, Sanskrit for "compassion") the center of their religiosity. After Coltrane's death in 1967, Doug Ramsey started encountering "shrines with the centerpiece a print of the cover photograph from Coltrane's album *A Love Supreme*."[167] Miles beyond the simple veneration of an aspect of "popular culture," Coltrane came to be seen not only as the avatar of spiritual unity but a canonical figure in a specific tradition. By 1971, the "days of rage" characterizing the late 1960s had morphed into a generalized fractiousness, as left social movements began to dissipate, right social movements to coalesce, and a long process of disengagement from conventional sociopolitical and religious institutions deepened. Especially in "counterculture" locales like Greenwich Village or Haight-Ashbury, the old tradition of American intentional communities resurfaced in efforts to organize communal living projects, arts initiatives, or new devotional centers.

It was in this socially fluid milieu that Franzo and Marina King founded the One Mind Temple Evolutionary Transitional Body of Christ. The small space in the Haight was inspired by Franzo King's moment of awakening at a 1965 Coltrane set, when King claims he felt "the presence of God" in a "sound baptism."[168] The Kings saw Coltrane as a messenger of God's love and power and embraced a mission to spread this sonic message in the church and in the streets. Other churches, most famously Manhattan's St. Peter's Lutheran, have used jazz music in their ministry; but here Coltrane's personal example and the promise of inner peace and human unity become the substance of community themselves. For a time the community even revered Trane as one of God's incarnations.

For more than three decades the church was on Divisadero, in a neighborhood as colorful as the walls inside the church, though not as sonically boisterous. The congregation is generally mixed in terms of race, age, and gender, with a majority of African Americans mixed in with musical aspirants, hipsters, and other well-meaning visitors. Some wear African robes and headdresses; others priestly vestments. In a quasi-Byzantine portrait that is the church's visual centerpiece (a black Christ is also visible, along with Mary and fellow horn player the angel Gabriel), Coltrane is the saint he sought to become.[169] In this image, flames leap from his tenor and the saxophonist holds a scroll reading, "Let us sing all songs to God."[170] Now relocated from its former storefront space, the church is bright with natural light. With colorful murals, reproduced lyrics, Coltrane sayings, and Bible verses visible everywhere, musicians and dancers perform, with varying levels of skill and energy, during the course of a service. At the center is the lean Bishop King, an assured saxophonist wearing magenta vestments and a skullcap, leading the music.[171] There is Bible reading. There are sermons, peppered with occasional quotes from Malcolm X or Cornel West.[172] There is ritual: in the call from behind a wall announcing, "let the procession be formed"; in acknowledgments of Christ's divinity and Trane's sainthood; in call and response from the congregation; in making the sign of the cross.[173] But it is the house band that announces and leads the central sonic rituals of Coltrane tunes, traditional hymns, and other materials (the occasional Bob Marley song) made sacred by their intonation in this intimate space. Whether playing Trane's "Spiritual," providing music for the congregation's recitation of Trane's lyrics, or jamming at length with congregants' participation, all assembled understand their creation to form "a traditional Christian liturgy, comprised of prayers and confessionals."[174]

The community got to this point in a curious, untraditional fashion. After his 1965 epiphany, the Pentecostal-reared King reports that he co-experienced Trane's own insights before thinking about community. He saw Trane as "beyond culture" and that God, too, was "in the sound" that could not be contained by tradition, institution, or norm.[175] This was like Christ's transgression of worldly law, and as King put it, this "consciousness level, that opening, is evolving. Baptism is what it is."[176] King had to share the news. First he turned part of his house into a worship space, inviting people to arrive at midnight on Tuesdays, when they would commence twenty-four hours of prayer and fasting by listening together to *A Love Supreme*.[177] Soon the group started thinking of itself as a community, calling itself the Yardbird Temple (a reference to saxophonist Charlie Parker's nickname). Members were determined advocates of the poor and in the early 1970s Haight their identity throve alongside an ISKCON group, the Grateful Dead house, the Hendrix Electric Church, and the Diggers. This was a ferment that King recalls as a "new expression of God consciousness that was taking place."[178] He wanted the group to pursue activities they found lacking among mainstream congregations. They had continued using *A Love Supreme* as a form of outreach, playing it for receptive listeners as a kind of sound evangelism, and began cultivating musical performance within the community. Marina King organized a women's choir for the church and "solicited church donations at the SFO airport."[179] SFO staff donated lost-and-found items to the church, which soon established the Coltrane Memorial Outreach Programs to distribute these goods, provide meals, teach, and offer counseling to the needy. Some outsiders began to associate the group, derisively called "the Coltrane cult," with other new religious movements of the time (it would have been more accurate to link them to the Black Panthers, with whom they regularly worked on community efforts). But the church continued its sonic-social activism throughout the 1970s (with King calling himself Ramakrishna King Haqq) until, in 1981, they were sued by Alice Coltrane. Having previously given the community something of a benediction, she charged the church with "exploiting her husband's name and infringing on copyright laws."[180] King believed the music could not be owned, that its social fruits and healing powers should obviate any charge of exploitation. He even tried to have *A Love Supreme* named the new national anthem.[181]

It was into this controversy that the African Orthodox Church stepped, suggesting to King that he might assist the Catholic-derived denomination with establishing a congregation in California (and thereby sidestep the lawsuit). In 1982 the Temple officially affiliated with the African Orthodox Church, which had been founded by the Universal Negro Improvement Association's George McGuire. As Harvey Cox noted, the church "claims its apostolic succession through Ignatius Peter III, the Patriarch of Antioch" and its services blend Catholic and Eastern Orthodox formalism with African cultural sensibilities, African American spirituals, and formal creedal statements (e.g., the Apostles' Creed).[182] Once assured they could maintain focus on Coltrane (although avoid referring to his divinity), the Kings returned to San Francisco in 1984 with divinity degrees and began incorporating the church's sacramentalism into what King recalled as "this hodgepodge of things" they had been practicing in the 1970s: "Sanskrit chanting, things we got from the Holy Ghost, things I brought from the Pentecostal movement, somebody else brought from their Catholic expression, somebody was a Buddhist."[183] The church's solution was to set Catholic prayer to Coltrane's music: "The Lord's Prayer was chanted to Coltrane's 'Spiritual.' 'The Lord Is My Shepherd' was sung to the sax line from 'Acknowledgement.' "[184] Such combinative gestures are widespread in American religions, especially since the 1960s. This particular fusion did not generate the kind of controversy similar efforts had in Catholicism following the Second Vatican Council, and *A Love Supreme* remains the center of the church's daily worship.

Though King still claims to celebrate "the ancient African liturgy," he avers, "We don't hold a monopoly on John Coltrane," whose sainthood he claims is recognizable to all traditions.[185] The sound is sanctified and might signify as the Holy Ghost, the voice of ancient Africa, or any number of associations one might improvise upon hearing it; but ultimately King says, "When you listen to John Coltrane, you become a disciple of the anointed of God."[186] The core members of the community continued their outreach steadily after joining the AOC. At one point they "distributed to schools loaves of bread bearing Coltrane's picture."[187] They ran a soup kitchen, understanding that giving out food and clothing was part of the anointment celebrated by all "ministers of sound."[188] Such work is not only grounded in Scripture; it was a conviction of Coltrane's as well, who admired those who were despised for attempting to rebuild a broken world.

This work is sonic, too, focused on "dispelling evil spiritual influences and menacing spirits through the Sound Praise."[189] Jazz thus sounds out the immanent divine, the experience of whose beauty nourishes fellowship and practices of mercy or resistance. Indeed, one of the church's hallmarks is the belief that conventional religious categories are fundamentally sonic.[190] Deacon Mark Dukes insists that one need not even attend the church to experience sound baptism; it can come even to those who just "dig it."[191] Yet unlike Alan Watts, whose Beat Zen satori could be achieved by slugging cheap wine and digging Bird, Coltrane's music is still realized with special clarity by virtue of its housing in a community focused on sonic experience "in spiritual harmony with God's purposes."[192] The very music obstinate critics once dismissed as "anti-jazz" here becomes, in its focus and searching urgency, an extended song of praise. Sound still cannot be captured. But as Coltrane said late in life, "[T]he music is rising into something else, and so we'll have to find this (new) kind of place to be played in."[193]

Truth on Your Instrument: Alice Coltrane's Ashram

Alice McLeod remembered a youthful musical awakening at Mount Olive Baptist Church in 1940s Detroit: "[t]here was such a God feeling. The people in the audience were so overcome with the spirit."[194] She recalled that from her church playing, informed by such experiences, she drew "the rhythmical aspect" of her style and understood music as an offering to the divine.[195] As Franya Berkman suggests, Coltrane sought forever after to re-create this experience; and she heard her future husband for the first time "like some kind of inner knowing."[196] The Coltranes sought to realize "[t]ruth on your instrument," to be a vessel for healing sound, to bathe in "music, light coming from the ethereal, heavenly realms."[197]

These inquiries were consistent with a prevalent thirst for new metaphysical religions, a harmonial impulse that many sought to realize in conversation with putatively "non-Western" sources of religiosity. For Alice, her husband's transposition of this quest into music constituted a reach beyond extant sonic and spiritual possibility to something universal. Music guided by this goal could realize what she called "higher experiences in spiritual life and higher knowledge."[198] Their ecstatic, long-form improvisations were little concerned with adherence to "jazz"; they were, instead, sonic poems to the One. After John's death, she was no longer even interested in musical expression as such but in music as devotion and offering.

In 1969 she began an association that shaped the rest of her life, leading her to establish a different kind of place in the lineage of jazz communities. She became an adept of Swami Satchidananda, who had come to the United States in 1967, after successfully establishing "several branches of his master's Divine Life Society" in India.[199] He deepened Coltrane's awareness of South Asian music and literature, and she began rigorous study of the *Vedas* and the *Upanishads*. She identified as Hindu, thereafter taking several pilgrimages to India with Satchidananda. After moving her family to California, in 1972 she founded Agoura Hills, California's Vedantic Center, and subsequently its Sai Anantam Ashram. There Coltrane crafted ambitious amalgams of ecstatic jazz, Hindu devotional music, and African American spirituals, increasingly set to sacred texts and serving as the heart of community ritual. In 1976 she had a revelation that she should be the ashram's Swamini, a role she fulfilled until her death in 2007. In that time she published four books—*Monument Eternal, Endless Wisdom I & II*, and *Divine Revelations*—examining "the soul's realization in Absolute Consciousness and its spiritual relationships with the Supreme One."[200]

Coltrane focused her musical energy on *bhajans*, a traditional devotional song that "helps the chanter establish a personal relationship with God, calms and focuses the mind as a form of mantra meditation, and offers the chanter an experience of totality or universal consciousness."[201] Satchidananda had encouraged her early interest in *bhajans*, and after her first trip to India, her record *Universal Consciousness* revealed her own growing musical engagement with these idioms. She wanted to manifest "extraordinary transonic and atmospherical power . . . illuminating worlds of sounds into the ethers of this universe."[202] Bassist Cecil McBee recalled their performances growing ever more ritualized, in darkened rooms with burning incense, atmospheres designed to accentuate a spiritual gravity that McBee remembered "was just there."[203] During the early 1970s, Coltrane underwent what she felt was "a period of spiritual purification . . . on the path to spiritual enlightenment."[204] She had several religious experiences that she described using the term *tapas* ("a yogic concept for spiritual austerity").[205] She fasted, went without sleep, meditated at length, and tested the limits of her bodily and mental perceptions so as to understand the relationship between self, sound, and spirit.

While her experiments sounded initially like further modal explorations of basic musical forms, her embrace of multi-instrumentalism over subsequent 1970s records helped Coltrane realize her broader ideas. She consistently opened performances with dedications to spiritual beings, hoping to signal that the music was "a form of meditation and a spiritual awakening for those who listen with their inner ear"; it would, if successful, help realize "impersonal love" that can transport "devotees across the vicissitudes and stormy blasts of life to the other shore."[206] Her *World*

Galaxy, from 1972, juxtaposed a Satchidananda recitation about cosmic love with passages from *A Love Supreme*; yet in wide-ranging sound, from drone to funk to saccharine strings, Coltrane also explored Yoruban musical idioms. This fluidity reflects the Coltranes' long-standing conviction that commitment to one strand of religiosity should not close one off to the insights and beauties of the others. But beyond this, Coltrane continued to employ the sounds, images, and categories of multiple traditions as a way of illustrating what Berkman rightly notes is "the Vedic notion that the paths are many, yet the destination one."[207]

On *Lord of Lords*, Coltrane used an orchestra to perform the traditional "Going Home" and a fragment of Igor Stravinsky's *Firebird Suite*, which she claims was inspired by a visit from Stravinsky in his astral form. This was far from an isolated event for Coltrane; and indeed, the notion of receiving counsel or blessings from spirit visitors is a common one in American religions. Coltrane claimed to receive most of her musical ideas through such communication with divinities or avatars. In describing them, or in characterizing the "Great spiritual battle" between the ego and the purified self, she continued to foreground Hinduism even as she cited numerous non-Hindu sources (Taoism, Mary, Zoroaster, Moses, or Coltrane himself).[208] Music provided an experiential medium in which these notions could all hang together, working toward the transformation of the self. Music glorified God but was also, as with "Oh Allah," "a prayer for peace, unity, and concord."[209] And such prayers required their proper housing.

As she began in the mid-1970s to live full-time in the ashram, her music went beyond announcing religious convictions to serve devotional purposes for ashram members practicing Vedanta. She arranged traditional chants like "Hare Krishna" and "Sita Rama," certain that their sonic power could promote perceptual transformation. Orange-robed and perched before her Hammond B-3, Swamini led her community through music whose extended sections for improvisation connected jazz and African American church music with the improvised traditions of South Asia. Rooted in the ashram's particular practice, the music interpolated multiple idioms: Coltrane used the *alap* form, practiced *kirtan*, sang *sadhanas*, composed her own hymns, and brought to it all what one resident called "a kind of jazz element."[210] Her burbling, expansive, near trance-like playing of the period was understood as an attempt to "stretch thoughts over to Shiva-Loka, one of the highest points of the universe."[211]

Members of the community (prominently African American at this point) chanted on the albums *Radha-Krsna Nama Sankirtana* and *Transcendence*, where Coltrane's organ gives the chant and traditional percussion a kind of funky foundation (even as she abjured "jazz" as seen from a certain perspective, her departure from "jazz" is clearly part of the music's story itself). Her infrequent recordings now featured devotional music exclusively, almost entirely shorn of the string sections and musical density she had once favored. Underlying this shift was her sense that "divine music shall always be the sound of love, the sound of peace, the sound of life, the sound of bliss."[212] By the time of 1995's *Glorious Chants* there is even comparably little improvisation in the performances. This was not jazz, perhaps not even music so much as what Coltrane called a "transcendental path of light" leading to a "great dimension of consciousness, revelation, of spirituality."[213]

These are understandings unlike those of the AACM, BAG, and even the UGMAA; they are ritualistically and iconographically distinct from the Coltrane Church as well. Yet this was a clear extension of the jazz explorations with John, perhaps even their realization in what she called "the entire experience of the expressive self."[214] What must this feel like, this sense of the heavens pouring into your fingertips, out of your mouth, opening up your ears to the "extraordinary transonic and atmospherical power" of divine sound, "illuminating worlds of sounds into the ether of this universe"?[215] Many listeners turned away from her music, hearing in it only a kind of more committed New Age (slightly less musically banal by being more referential). Yet for Coltrane and those in the ashram, this was the sound of "Absolute Consciousness," of Hinduism's experience of union, of the bliss experience in the embrace of the cosmos, and finally of "God-realization."[216]

RITUAL AND TRANSFORMATION emerge as common contextual factors in the spaces described herein, though we also see in these communities the opening up of new modes of sociality, new networks and affinities constituted through sonic performance. Community is thus, in Ingrid Monson's apt formation, not so much a location or stable identity as a process, very much like jazz and religion, both flowing continually into and beyond the shapes we superimpose on them.[217] Josh Kun writes of how musical performances are "almost-places of cultural encounter that may not be physical places but nevertheless exist in their own auditory somewhere."[218] In these musical spaces, "religion" is a flexible mode of understanding the occasion, the purposes, and the direction of these institutionalized modes of improvised encounter.

These somewheres resonate in the vast history of alternative musical subcultures practicing political resistances, communal improvisations, and

bodily disciplines that feed into and emerge from religio-musical performances. Consider the masterful dissemblances of Vaclav Havel and the
young Czech dissidents of the late 1970s, inspired initially by the political
theater of their Frank Zappa–inspired rock band the Plastic People of the
Universe. Note the oppositional perceptual practices defended by Japanese
no-input mixing board improviser Toshimaru Nakamura, who once explained
to me his commitment to the super-silent music he plays, suggesting that it
forces the listener into a mode of attentiveness that makes possible a different
way of living in the din of Tokyo.[219] We see in these examples, and those of
spirits rejoicing above, improvisations on conventional political attempts at
self-determination, new arrangements of spirituality defined as resistant and
sounding out freedom.

In jazz communitarianism, "religion" is constructed through musical
techniques and sensibilities developed among the like-minded, just as music
is shaped by a range of religiosities: the large ensemble exercises, interactivity, and pedagogical exercises themselves capture the larger theme of
developing new modes of being-in-the-world through collective purpose.
As Sarah Pike writes of neopagans, we see here "a conscious performance
of who one is and wants to be," nurtured pedagogically in religio-musical
institutions.[220] The complex enactments of identity emergent therein recall not just the more defined intentional communities of American religious history, from the Shakers to the Oneidans to the Branch Davidians,
but also those assemblages borne of elective affinity, like Spiritualist conventions, Chautauqua, and camp meetings.[221]

These communities foster modes of education and self-creation, opportunities for feeling and experience whose very outness and protean form
(sonically and institutionally) constitute critical soundings against orthodoxy, here resonating in multiple registers of piety and reverence. This ato-
nality to the world's tonal constraints is consistent with a history of religious
attempts to bring into existence an ideal society in the belly of the American
beast, succeeding to the extent that they can ritually suspend the obliga-
tions, certainties, and truths of the sonically flat everyday.[222] The communities challenge extant social contexts and strive to create new ones, with
spirits rejoicing both creating and heightening identification with these
new contexts and associations through the spontaneous generation of
feeling. By teaching young musicians what the historical and religious context of the music is, these communities emerge as scenes of creating new
selves in a larger arena of place, memory, and social hope.

The existence of these religio-musical communities confronts us with questions about what makes a community "religious," a self-referring problem that is not simply a conceptual conundrum but the very substance of the pedagogy at work in these shifting institutionalizations of "jazz." The housings of religion here go beyond varied narrative representations, or improvisations on traditional lineages, to a point where musicking is understood to be central to the development of religiosity even as it is unmoored from the fixity of attributions or categorizations. In this, these communities not only assume a place alongside those religious movements and institutions with avowedly religious goals and practices; they also enact and sound out modes of religion that spill beyond the walls of community, unsettling our patterns of recognizing the religious, suggesting with these very community members that self-determination and organization may themselves be practices of religion. More than merely an addition to American narratives about religious outsiders, these presences on the landscape of our reckoning call us to even more radical modes of self-creation in spirits rejoicing.

Pause.
And Begin Again.

PART II

5

The Magic of Juju

TWO ENDS OF the line and the same song between us. I was on the horn with the righteous Cuban drummer Francisco Mela, and in our long conversation about ritual and pulse we were trading shared loves. Mela loves Roy Haynes *this much*, as do I, and we were singing Ornette Coleman's "Law Years" together. "Jason!" he exclaimed. "In Cuba we call the drum the kitchen, because that's where everything is cooking!"[2] Nearly a century before we spoke, Baby Dodds said, "You see a band dead: a drummer can liven up everybody, make everybody have a different spirit."[3] So how does one make this spirit, and for what reasons? Alto saxophonist Bobby Zankel once responded, with some skepticism, to an interviewer's question about jazz music inducing states of "calm." He noted, however, jazz's links to mental and physical transformation through "dance and the African line of spirituality involving trance-like states, where you're connecting with elemental forces."[4] By example, Zankel noted Coltrane's fascination with meditation and pianist Cecil Taylor's observation that "you play for a long time until you reach a kind of state of possession by Spirit."[5] Musicians seek these states through pre-performance ablutions or physical regimens, circular breathing on horns to induce trance states, preceding and punctuating performances with recitations, or even coordinating the circulation of blood itself with sound production.

This chapter concerns the ritualization of jazz, and the use of jazz in ritual. Having complicated some of the more obvious articulations of "religion," with this focus on ritual we begin to see an experiential/perceptual expansion of what counts as religious. While ritual can certainly be mapped anthropologically and historically, and signifies in some expected ways, this chapter marks a transition from the first three cases to a more phenomenological or experiential focus in the book's second part. Crafting from the unknowable openness of improvisation a housing for what is construed as sacred is at the heart of much improvisation; but spirits also improvise joyfully on ritual beyond the confines of genre, plunging into open sound as a confrontation between form and formlessness, as a search for the self's limits and powers at once. Below I explore the ritual and the performative in jazz in order to give shape to the immediacy of musical experience in jazz traditions, to see in ritualized jazz a resonance with ritual improvisations in American religion, and to think about sound as the ritual medium of religious transformation. We find among the music's practitioners an awareness of otherness, of extra-physical presence in sound, and of consecration in performance.

There is no thinking of religions without their sonic properties, and bodies in ritual make plenty of sound. They move, feet dragging across floors or stamping out rhythm on them. Joints crack, hands clap. Small moans escape the throat unconsciously, and vocalisms consciously. A floorboard creaks, a microphone feeds back. The intentionality of such actions in the ritual space is motivated and accompanied by the sense that by undertaking them one enters the presence of the sacred. Sound is a producer of or vehicle for these heightened moments, and a mode of response to them. In the felt, embodied, immersive sounds of religions, sound is no mere vehicle but instead is experienced as the constitutive element of ritual in motion, and its expressive sacrality.

This is not the place for a comprehensive survey of ritual experimentation and sound in American religions. But a brief overview of these expressions situates spirits rejoicing in the broad range of American religious experimentation. Ritual is, as Catherine Albanese writes, "the site for *embodied* spirituality."[6] It is thus nearly ubiquitous in American religion, in the dances, offerings, and dream reenactments of Native Americans; the displays of Puritan "visible saints"; the improvised enthusiasms of the early revivals; the ritual dramas of emergent "civil religion" in the mid-nineteenth century; the expressive cultures of African American Protestantism; the liturgical reconfigurations of nineteenth-century Catholicism and Judaism; in abstentions and indulgences, altar calls and astral travel, parades and faith healing, direct action and therapeutics.[7] Religious rituals dramatize and commemorate. They reinforce or sometimes suspend the lessons of authority. They discipline the body or deliver it into new states of ecstasy or transformed consciousness. They establish settings and sounds enabling performers to become "mediums of the gods" or to undergo "ceremonial possession" for a time.[8] They are the vector and the substance of improvisations on identity and community.

Music's role in religious ritual lies beyond the mere sonic articulation of creeds and scriptures. Sound is experienced in bodily registers, and has contributed to the transformation of ritual, in various traditions. But there is the perceptual immediacy and strange fluidity of jazz to consider. If we emphasize ritual's similarity to drama, we find that jazz tears up the script. If we draw on standard analyses of embodiment, we risk getting sucked into well-worn arguments about discourse and representation, losing not just the sound but the situated meanings of jazz's rituals. Clearly there are significant epistemological, phenomenological challenges in thinking through these subjects. At the heart of these considerations is the obviously intersubjective quality of performance, the meanings and directions of embodiment therein, and the problem of attributing meanings or aspirations to music that is not only often devoid of lyrical content but even resistant to other forms of signification. Religious studies has since the 1970s engaged the difficulties of such analysis by paying "more attention to the actual 'doing' of religion."[9] Yet even with the phenomenological focus on intentionality in action, it is tempting to retextualize religious experience by generating from practices a narrative or lexicon we fool ourselves into thinking is "religion." Agents must certainly reckon with extant social scripts. But as Marshall Sahlins, Sherrie Ortner, and others have written about the textualization of "social drama," ritual manifests significantly in "open-ended forms of communal performance" and change across time.[10]

The very inscrutability of sound, perhaps especially jazz, seems to express such orientations. If the multi-sensory, dynamic qualities of music "produce a culturally meaningful environment as opposed to simply communicating ideas," then music is not just a form of meaningful action but also helps make such action possible.[11] Its realization in real time—through senses, motility, and interaction—shows the tenuousness of form and the power of formlessness. The setting and occasion for performance may constrain, but performance is also a resource of practical knowledge and relationships that make a virtue out of necessity, transforming the bent note of endless time into a moment marked, an error converted to beauty. It becomes ritual not, then, through the regurgitation of regularity but in the focus and clarification of the moment where sound is produced and understood as sacred. For as Jonathan Z. Smith wrote, "Ritual is, first and foremost, a mode of paying attention. It is a process of marking interest."[12]

Absent an interpretive frame or narrative structure in which gestures and various signs identify the religious, we must attend to occasion, expectation, and post hoc descriptions if we want to hear the jazz religious in ritual. Musicians certainly pray and dance and recite on stage, and they regularly tell us what they mean. But the very ungraspability of improvisation's sensualism, emotionality, and immediacy is what often leads to the conclusion that one is co-participating in the production of a sacred world that takes shape and then dissolves in sound. For all we might look to structural parameters and audience expectations, the spontaneity and unpredictability so central to jazz suggest that rupture, flouting expectations, and subversion, rather than drab "liminality," may be ritual's salient characteristics. We focus on the moment when the breath is about to be exhaled, the suspended pulse about to beat again; we dwell amid rests, pauses, fractures. If ritual is Baby Dodds's drum, then to experience it is to be behind the beat, that always urgent expectation in which the ear awakens to the intensity of time marked, time gone.

In other words, improvised musical performance facilitates becoming religious, just as religious self-understandings can facilitate becoming musically fluent. This twinned experience is captured in Judith Butler's observation that "identity is performatively constituted by the very 'expressions' that are said to be its results."[13] Open-ended, subject to contingency and revision, something about improvised music gets to the very staged, unstable qualities of religion as it structures and eludes identity. The musicians below seek to create the conditions for spirits to manifest: in music written specifically for institutional rituals, in appropriations of Yoruban ritual in jazz, in ritualized theatricality as audience confrontation, or as healing practice. They are played and experienced as distinct (in occasion, intent, or theatricality) from other human actions. Trombonist Bob Brookmeyer once supposed that jazz is "ritual gone mad."[14] Mad or not, below we see ritual as a kind of actualized living for sound. If Taylor is right to note that "practice is preparation for the celebration of the entrance into the temple of invention," then performance itself *creates* this temple improvisationally.[15]

Hidden in His Music: Duke Ellington

Ritual happens in church, though, and jazz sometimes does too. Richard Brent Turner shows how integral some of the musical practices of New Orleans are to that city's religions.[16] Jazz funerals, for example, feature the tradition of "cut[ting] the body loose," where the band playing a dirge aside the hearse lines both sides of a street to "start playing joyful music," marking life's transition with jazz.[17] But thinking of ritual in the above sense of focused attention on the sacred in musical time, what happens when jazz music is written for a specific ritual setting? James Reese Europe used "religious music alongside the protojazz he performed."[18] Subsequent efforts included Ian Douglas Mitchell's "American Folk Song Mass," the 1962 Episcopal National Council of Churches' use of a jazz quintet, Don Ellis's *Frontiers in Worship*, and Yale Divinity student Tom Vaughan, who "created a jazz liturgy with drummer Charlie Smith entitled 'A Musical Offering to God.'"[19] In 1959, clarinetist Ed Summerlin wrote "a jazz setting for Methodist founder John Wesley's liturgy."[20] In the years leading up to the Second Vatican Council, experiments with popular music and liturgy became more commonplace, as with Anglican Geoffrey Beaumont's "Twentieth-Century Folk Mass" and James Tatum's mass for Detroit's parish of Saint Cecilia.[21] George Lewis wrote *Jazz at Vespers*; Lalo Schifrin and Paul Horn cowrote *Jazz Suite on the Mass Texts*; David Amram and Langston Hughes wrote a "Jewish cantata," "Let Us Remember"; and Vince Guaraldi wrote music for the Episcopalian Eucharist at San Francisco's Grace Cathedral.[22] And in certain institutions, jazz became integrated into services: the famous "jazz priest," Father Norman O'Connor, was most visible, but similar integrations were shepherded by Episcopalian Father Tom Vaughan, Father John Gensel of New York's Advent Lutheran, New York's Church of the Ascension, Newark's Bethany Baptist Church, and New York's famous Saint Peter's Lutheran, the "jazz church."[23]

No setting generated more influence or controversy than Duke Ellington's Sacred Concerts. While American religions have frequently created new musical vehicles for praise, from Shaker songs to Swedenborgian hymns, Ellington's music challenged understandings of "proper" religion and of what was really "jazz." His musical settings of history certainly shaped his understanding of religion, but equally important was the personal crisis he underwent following his mother's death in 1935.[24] He began rigorously studying Scripture and wrote an "elegy" for his mother, which he described as "church music."[25] Ellington began reflecting on how the respect and generosity he learned growing up in church were musical ethics as well, a notion O'Connor later extended by remarking that "the intensity in religion was similar to the intensity of creative jazz."[26] Ellington began using his gift for long-form composition to distill ideas culled from his regular study of religious materials. For decades he kept his personal sentiments concealed, saying only vaguely that religion "gives you strength."[27] But he was remembered by bandmates and associates as having "not so much organized religion...[but] a respect for the church, a love of the Bible."[28] Herb Jeffries believed that Ellington's entire career was "a great ministry"; it was simply "hidden in his music" for several decades.[29]

Only in 1958 did Ellington state publicly how "deeply religious he was."[30] In the context of his growing identification with the civil rights movement, and the public power of African American religion, this comment resonated powerfully. Ellington noted suggestively that when composing music, "one runs into the spiritual aspect" of existence; but he also confessed of his earlier works, "I've written words, but I don't know if the words are adequate."[31] He was surprised to receive commission from Grace Cathedral, since religion was "a personal thing with me, not to be mixed with a theatrical performance."[32] But he also loathed pigeonholes, and decided to write music as an offering to God, explaining that "[e]very man prays in his own language, but there is no language that God does not understand."[33] The piece drew on African American musical aesthetics but addressed "the basic, essential state of mankind."[34]

The First Sacred Concert was performed at Grace in September 1965, and Ellington understood each church-housed performance of his music to possess the gravity of formal ritual. In a kind of critical creation story, Ellington's libretto wrote that before God created the world, there was "no poverty, no Cadillacs, no sand traps," and thus no human conflict.[35] While the concert contained multiple scriptural references, some were unnerved. Longtime vocalist Joya Sherrill, a Jehovah's Witness, declined participation: "I just did not go along with religious jazz concerts."[36] Sherrill articulated a widespread uncertainty as to whether this music was religious at all (dancer Bunny Briggs was also nervous about dancing on an altar), since it did not openly evangelize or map onto known liturgical forms. But, Ellington asked, "Isn't that exactly what Christ did—went into the places where people were, bringing light into darkness?"[37] After the Second Sacred Concert was held on Boxing Day, 1965, at Manhattan's Fifth Avenue Presbyterian, Ellington explained even more suggestively that "everything is a part of God's world, and that the old, arbitrary separation no longer makes sense."[38]

Yet the notion that religion could embrace "secular" music, and respected no attempts to quarantine it, proved inflammatory. Some felt that while the music was not "truly liturgical" it was emotionally resonant; some could accept a sole performance but worried about lasting musical change in religion; and others dismissed the direction as an effort "to have fun shocking a few old fuddy-duddies" or simply a sideshow from "this sin-sick world."[39] Nonetheless, "[c]hurches all over the country were inviting the band to play" the Sacred Music.[40] The Ellington Orchestra took the music on the road, beginning at Brooklyn's First AME Zion, whose Reverend Ruben Speaks enthused, "Christ never attempted to compartmentalize.... There is no rhythm, tune, or melody that is not acceptable to God."[41] Ellington concurred, saying, "You don't *have* to play sacred music only in church."[42]

Perhaps it was the very erasure of the sacred/secular distinction that made some aghast at the spheres of sanctum and stage made porous, even as others praised the music's non-creedal affirmations of love. As Rabbi Sanford Shapero put it, "Surely God will rejoice in having an offering so sincerely and beautifully presented" outside of social and cultural limitations.[43] Amid those elegant section voicings, seductive rhythms, and lyric choruses, all drawing together idioms in a classically Ellingtonian manner, perhaps this music (which Ellington avowed was his very best) was the truest embodiment of his claim that music was "beyond category." The Second Sacred Concert featured a wider range of musical influences and greater attention to lyrical content. "Almighty God" blended spirituals with lyrics describing angels who announced the Ducal categorical imperative: "the freedom to be whatever you are."[44] He called "treating people with love and respect" a "moral freedom."[45] As his health failed in the early 1970s, Ellington became obsessed with writing a Third Sacred Concert. Wracked by the pain of cancer, Ellington took final stock of war and racism and division around him, and in somewhat more conventional music returned again to love as the foundation of ethics. With "The Lord's Prayer/My Love" and "Is God a Three-Letter Word for Love?" Ellington invoked particulars while continuing to insist that he "didn't have any denomination in mind."[46] The music was more searching, too, and many heard in it the composer's suffering. But Ellington remained unbowed even at the end, delivering his message with characteristic panache and defining his own devotional context, saying, "[R]acism ain't strong enough to kill this music; if I'm going to die, I'm ready. But I'm going out playing 'Sophisticated Lady.'"[47]

Mary Lou's Mass

While Ellington wrote for a ritual setting, his Sacred Music was not enacted liturgically. Mary Lou Williams, however, wrote an actual mass. Mary Elfrieda Scruggs's family noted her early musical aptitude when she played the family organ, stabbing out spirituals or rags while propped on her mother's knee.[48] As a young pianist she fell for piano titans Earl "Fatha" Hines, Jelly

Roll Morton, and Fats Waller, whose sounds were both inspiration and refuge: "I began building up a defense against prejudice by...working hard at music."[49] As an adolescent she played vaudeville and carny shows before marrying saxophonist John Williams. On the strength of her distinctive pianism, she quickly entered jazz's innermost circles. She spent a brief period with Ellington in New York, and directed her husband's Kansas City territory band before the two joined Andy Kirk and His Twelve Clouds of Joy. She was a star soloist with Kirk, recalling that when she sat down for a boogie-woogie tune, "things would jump."[50] Her arrangements and compositions drew attention from Benny Goodman, Cab Calloway, and Tommy Dorsey, who extended commissions to her. Remarried to Shorty Baker, Williams relocated permanently to New York in the early 1940s.

From there, she developed associations with beboppers like Dizzy Gillespie (for whom she wrote the fabulous "In the Land of Oo-Bla-Dee"). She led her own bands, and at one point even had a fan club. Yet something gnawed at Williams and held her back from personal fulfillment. She began long-form composition, hearing in this format a way to channel her ambitions to write her name into American music, even to transcribe the stars themselves. Williams's "Zodiac Suite" assigned to each astrological sign a jazz musician who had been born under it. The suite fused the language of bebop with these twelve musical personalities and a commitment to progress that was never merely social but also ideational and cosmic; jazz itself was the song of human destiny. Williams also composed the more biblically oriented "Elijah and the Juniper Tree," though she did not yet dream of liturgical jazz.

Williams all but relocated to Europe between 1952 and 1954. There, she experienced a jarring event, struck in a Paris club by what was later called her "dark night of the soul."[51] The pianist found herself immobile, unable to formulate ideas, and stranded in silence. She abruptly left the stage and entered a period of great personal turmoil. What had happened? In the midst of that club, she "got a sign that everybody should pray every day."[52] And so right there, mid-measure, "I couldn't take it any longer. So I just left—the piano—the money—all of it."[53] Vocalist Hazel Scott encouraged her to begin Bible study. Williams responded positively to her immersion in Scripture, and in 1954 had a pivotal experience of silence and meditative calm: "I found God in a little garden in Paris."[54] She subsequently sought to translate this experience into her music and devotion.

On returning to New York, Williams suffered several emotional and religious crises between 1954 and 1957, retiring from performance altogether for two years. While she had "never felt a conscious desire to get close to God" during those tough years in Europe, Williams now searched avidly.[55] She "went through all the religions...Muslims and everything"; she read *The Watchtower* and briefly joined a Baptist street ministry.[56] She came to feel more at home in her neighborhood's Catholic church, Our Lady of Lourdes, and was taken with the comprehensiveness of Catholic liturgy. Under the tutelage of Father Anthony Woods, Williams was baptized a Catholic in 1957.

Williams resumed performance with a new emphasis and purpose. She saw music as a source of healing and a liturgical vehicle, and she also began to minister to musicians. These convictions led her to initiate prayer meetings, aid sick or poor players, and invite musicians to church (Thelonious Monk brought a bottle of wine and napped). She established the Bel Canto Foundation to further these goals, and became increasingly involved with the civil rights movement. By the late 1950s, members of the hierarchy (anticipating the musical and liturgical changes to come from the Second Vatican Council) had begun encouraging her to write a jazz mass. As Tammy Kernodle observes, Williams's Catholic "jazz for healing" was also part of a tradition of "Africanizing" rituals that had begun in the 1930s.[57] Williams understood these works as faithful not just to Catholicism but to jazz itself, which she believed was a gift from God to African Americans: "God did blacks a favor by creating jazz especially for them. God helps people through jazz; people have been healed through it. It has happened to me."[58] The soul that infuses African American music, Williams explained, "came through the church and suffering."[59]

Father Peter O'Brien called Williams's musical synthesis "the statement of her intertwined beliefs about faith in God, faith in black people, faith in America, and faith in jazz. It was her civil-rights statement."[60] These passions were exemplified in the dedicatee of Williams's first major suite, St. Martin De Porres. She was "[d]eeply touched by the dark-skinned saint's devotion, humility, and religious conviction."[61] If her portrait was successful, Williams thought, "it can be counted as a prayer."[62] And from the opening notes of *Black Christ of the Andes*, the music's authority and emotional conviction sound as if powered by just such purpose. As the choir intones "Saint Martiiiiin," big band arrangements blend with antiphonal voicings in Williams's customary style, jazz expanding traditional liturgy while underscoring its meanings. The choir offers up Williams's prayer, with minor thirds here, an augmented chord there: "Oh, black Christ of the Andes, come feed and cure us now we pray." But the piece bursts unexpectedly into a *habañera* rhythm (a nod to the saint's rhythmic milieu), with Williams's almost Monk-like piano flourishes and close harmonies driving the chorus. In several pieces, Williams uses suspended chords and a lack of resolution indebted to Gregorian chant, from which overtly jazzy sections rise triumphantly as if she is answering her own prayer.

The suite's most memorable sections are those that improvise on traditional liturgical settings. The surging 6/8 recitation of "Anima Christi" gives the devotional text new vibrancy, sacred brio. "Dirge Blues" is meant to accompany the sacrament of last rites.[63] And the concluding "Praise the Lord" announces the "invocation of the Holy Ghost," adapting its lyrics from Psalms 148 and 150. Williams's genius was in such integration of African American materials (blue notes, specific motifs like the "Amen cadence," or portions of known spirituals) with Catholic traditional forms (like the *Pater Nostra*). The mass premiered, to considerable acclaim, on the feast day of St. Martin de Porres, November 3, 1962, tucked after the official liturgy.[64]

Williams was encouraged by the hierarchy to compose more explicitly liturgical music. She wrote the "Pittsburgh Mass" between 1966 and 1967, seeing it as another contribution to Catholicism's *aggiornamento* but also

FIGURE 5.1. Mary Lou Williams in the studio. Photograph copyright Jan Persson.

part of an effort to rescue jazz from the avant-garde, whose "cultic" qualities she denounced: "[w]e're on the verge of losing a great spiritual music."[65]
She performed the "Pittsburgh Mass" at that town's cathedral, and in 1968
began work on her "Mass for the Lenten Season," which would be performed "for six Sundays during Lent" at "the mother church of the Paulist
Fathers."[66] From this piece, Williams harvested some material for her subsequent work, variously called "Music for Peace" or "Mary Lou's Mass." In
1969, she met privately at the Vatican with Pope Paul VI, and was there
commissioned by the American Monsignor Joseph Gremillion to write
this third mass, for which the Vatican gave her "the liturgical texts of the
Votive Mass for Peace."[67] This piece debuted at Columbia University in
1970, and in 1971 Alvin Ailey requested a new arrangement for the City
Center Dance Theater. While her first two masses possessed what some
described as "quiet, reflective qualities," this third piece "became a swinging
mass," owing both to Williams's own assurance and to the dancers'
accompaniment.[68]

The *New York Times* found it possessed of "a spirit that cuts across all
religious boundaries to provide a celebration of man, God and peace."[69]
Far more important to Williams, though, was its resonance within Catholicism. The mass was performed at Harlem's Lady of Lourdes.[70] Soon
thereafter, it was performed semi-regularly at Catholic churches across
the United States (and at the National Cathedral in Washington, D.C.),
once at Rome's Church of the Jesu, and in 1975 became the very first "jazz"
to be performed at New York's Saint Patrick's Cathedral. Williams saw the
increased exposure of her "actual liturgy" to be a way of musically reaching young Catholics.[71] While "Mary Lou's Mass" is now less often performed
as part of a liturgy, Williams's convictions in jazz as "the greatest religion
of them all" (which, if played correctly, is like "praying through my fingers") inspired related compositional efforts.[72] Drummer Louie Bellson
wrote his own "Sacred Music." Pianist Dave Brubeck wrote settings of
sacred texts for the pope, among other religious pieces.[73] Heikki Sarmonto
wrote a "New Hope Jazz Mass" for Saint Peter's Lutheran Church. Kitty
Brazleton has written a jazz "ecclesiastes."[74] And trumpeter Mark Harvey
is a minister who uses jazz regularly in his Boston church. Perhaps most
notable is pianist Deanna Witkowski, who, as musical director for Queens'
Church of the Redeemer, inflects ritual setting with vernacular music (not
just "jazzing up the hymns" but turning others "into salsa tunes").[75] Her
recordings incorporate her own religious lyrics and a "setting of the
'Sanctus' that concludes the Preface in the Catholic Mass."[76] Citing Martin

Marty's avowal that improvisation "provides a metaphor for the Creator's acts toward the creation and toward human creators," Witkowski claims "all my music is an offering to God."[77]

The Drum Is Magic: Afro-Cuban Jazz

But do we always know which God, and which ritual? Ellington and Williams wrote for rituals in buildings. They shared a sense of "jazz's" fluidity, if not of "religion's." But listening elsewhere, we hear that Baby Dodds's drum is also a consecrated drum, its sound coming from a long tradition of spirits rejoicing in Afro-Caribbean sound. It is widely known that Latin musics, whose rhythmic complexity Jelly Roll Morton famously called "the Spanish tinge," were integral to early jazz. But as the music took shape in 1930s New York, a different drum was heard in its development. There had been a growing interest in Cuban music specifically, with its strong, infectious polyrhythms. Audiences swooned to 1931's "The Peanut Vendor," by Don Azpiazu's Havana Casino Orchestra, and some bands featured Cuban soloists to capitalize on the pulse and the lure of exotica.[78] Yet though the "otherness" of the music was immediate, little was known then about the rhythm's roots in Yoruban culture, specifically in the Cuban practices of Santéria, the "way of the saints" wherein ecstatic music and dance serve as ritual offerings to the *Orishas*.

In Cab Calloway's hot big band, a young Dizzy Gillespie played next to Cuban Mario Bauza in the trumpet section, their work together yielding one of jazz's earliest religio-cultural exchanges. Bauza, who soon became musical director of Machito's Afro-Cubans, had been stunned by America's racism (he recalled rent signs reading "No dogs. No Negroes, No Spanish").[79] Musicians like Machito and Bauza saw the embrace of specifically Cuban music as a response to the singling out they were already experiencing negatively.[80] Gillespie was not just a fan of this music; he was acutely aware of its cultural history, noting specifically that when slaves were robbed of the drum they had to communicate only orally (one factor shaping the development of call-and-response patterns). He heard this history's multi-vocality when comparing Caribbean and African American polyrhythms: "[o]ur music is based on a monorhythm, a backbeat that goes, boom-cha, boom-cha. Their music is based on multirhythms, four or five drummers doing different things."[81]

Bop's rise to prominence occurred along with regular associations with Afro-Cuban music. Gillespie's incorporation of Bauza's influence into his music was "instinctive," since "I've always had that Latin feeling.... Maybe I'm one of those 'African survivals' that hung on after slavery."[82] But even more crucial was percussionist Chano Pozo, who floored Gillespie with his singing, dancing, and drumming in three separate rhythms.[83] Tom Piazza notes that Pozo drew from "music that people were making for...their religious rituals," themselves derived from African traditions.[84] Pozo was a Santéro who had been "initiated into the Abakua secret society, whose origins can be traced back to the Calabar region of southern Nigeria."[85] Pozo was featured prominently in Gillespie's 1947 big band debut, not least on the feature "Cubana Bop." Despite its enthusiastic reception, its musical synthesis scrambled expectations. Some listeners found Pozo especially unnerving. *Life* reported that the "[f]renzied drummer...whips beboppers into a fever with Congo beat" and "[s]houting incoherently, drummer goes into a bop transport"; *Downbeat* said "Manteca" "was done almost as a tribal rite, becoming downright primitive."[86] Even bassist Al McKibbon was flummoxed by "this guy beating this god damn drum with his hands."[87]

Pozo did more than this. In the middle of "Manteca," he improvised religion as well: grooving hard, Pozo "delivers a Lucumi chant" transforming the piece into a petition to the *Orishas*.[88] For Gillespie, Pozo's chants and exclamations mid-tune announced not just Cuba's distinctive religious history but a shared diasporic identity. Indeed, these very collaborations and blendings were possible because, as Gillespie put it, "we both speak African."[89] Gillespie's fascination with Cuban music continued after Pozo's violent death in 1948, and its emphasis on hybridity shaped his tweaking of American religious identity in tunes like 1959's "Swing Low, Sweet Cadillac," whose mix of modern jazz, Cuban rhythm, and satire exemplified Gillespie's knowing disdain for cultural pieties. This sonic excess was facilitated by twinned religiosities, allowing Gillespie to expose what George Lipsitz identifies as "the connections between the secular and the sacred in the history of slavery and segregation in the United States."[90]

Afro-Cuban jazz has become quite commonplace, but while its ritual elements are infrequently discussed they remain essential to players.[91] Percussionist Chief Bey was introduced to Yoruban religions by Olatunji in the 1960s and says, "[T]he music drew me to the religion in the first place."[92] After his first exposure to Yoruba music, Bey made his own log drum out of a tree trunk. Bey, now a Yoruban priest who performs as often in house ceremonies as with jazz bands, explains, "We use the music to placate the deities. The music *is* healing, and the drum *is* magic...I stay close to home and play for the *Orishas*."[93] The very presence of sacred Bata drums in the United States, and in jazz, serves a sonic-consecrational purpose: since each drum is associated with a rhythm, which is a prayer or petition to one of "the forces that rule the universe" (elements or *Orishas*), playing them purposively transforms sound and environment.[94] Many musicians, like Steve Berrios or Babatunde Lea, have been initiated into these techniques, the *toques de santo* (sometimes called "the secret hand") and understand that "[a]ny percussion instrument has a spiritual vibe to it," whether used for a religious ceremony like a *tambor* or played in a club to "lift up their spirit."[95] Lea believes that "polyrhythms are a metaphor for universal culture," so African understandings of the integrity of "mind, body, and spirit" can be taught through the drum in ways that resonate beyond their particular contexts.[96]

Indeed, performers like Bebo Valdes or Omar Sosa not only play instruments that have been blessed but often understand the performance space as a kind of container or conduit for *ashe*, or spiritual power. For a performance, Sosa "drapes a red cloth out from the inside of the piano" and lights candles on stage to create a ritual space where the voice of the *Orishas* might be heard more clearly: "If you don't listen to the Elders, you're never going to come out with something new and fresh."[97] The instruments contain something of the power they also seek to invoke; they are both medium and substance of the *Orishas*, present in the playing, improvisation the embodied knowledge of communication with spirits. When Sosa plays for them in the right rhythms, it "feels like prayer to me" and enables him to "translate the message."[98] Mela practices neither Santéria nor Catholicism, but these traditions nonetheless shape his drumming: "[w]hen you come from a place with such a strong tradition and a strong background, of course that helps you to combine with anything else."[99] Mela plays with a sometimes searching quality detectable in his exuberant drumming. He told me that jazz is a model for the way we live, and it is fundamentally religious, "because you are trying to connect your own thing with something that you never heard before."[100] Jazz is all about chasing down this "never heard," and just like jazz, Mela rejects the idea that religion can even be contained: "I pray every day, and I *never* go to church!"[101] He plays for the love ("God gave me a gift to play music"), for the rent, and because it is a "very strong thing to play jazz...for me, man, it's very spiritual."[102] But again we find ourselves in the flow of time, unable to fast-forward to insight; one can only make a ritual of each moment. This is why, Mela says, "I'm meditating with my drums, you know?"

Play the Mountain: Steve Coleman

Steve Coleman grew up on Chicago's South Side and followed a different route to these traditions. The young altoist learned from Chicago heavies Von Freeman and Bunky Green the importance of musical freedom and developing your own sound. Landing in New York at the tail end of the loft jazz scene, Coleman worked actively in a wide range of bands while crafting his voice. He played with a dry, occasionally hard-edged tone that fit perfectly with his rhythmically sculpted phrases; and he absorbed collective sounds far from what he learned in big band section work, poring over records of West African kora music and then-new rap when he wasn't reading ancient wisdom literature.

Jazz lived on the stretch in the early 1980s. Musicians like Coleman and cornetist Graham Haynes woodshedded in streets and in cramped, after-hours venues, experimenting with repeating, hip-hop–influenced phrases that some saw as anathema to "America's classical music." The two developed close associations with sympathetic musicians like Greg Osby, Cassandra Wilson, and David Gilmore, forming the collective M-BASE (Macro-Basic Array of Structured Extemporizations) to catalyze "growth through creativity."[103] They asserted that "[i]t is the spiritual component that is most often misunderstood" about jazz and other "creative music of the Afrikan diaspora."[104] This conviction fueled the new sound, filled with craggy rhythms winding over multiple measures, too quick and complex to count. There was jittery electronic funk, hot flashes of bop syntax, sometimes ethereal vocals.

Coleman developed an interest in symbolic communication and explored the possibility that music could evoke the power of nature's four elements, or even the fifth: spirit. He heard rhythm everywhere: "[t]he cadence of the language...basketball" and even in the sidereal rhythms of planetary motion, sunrises, galaxies wheeling through space.[105] He began to calibrate his music to these realities, emulating the universal forms, playing what was in nature. In time this led him into rigorous study of African and diasporic musics, whose rituals Coleman found similarly linked to the sonic-sacred cosmos. In 1993, following a path jazz musicians from Randy Weston to Don Cherry had traveled, he studied Dagomba drum music in Ghana, linking his rhythmic obsessions to African traditions of the talking drum. The rhythmic and melodic shapes of his group Five Elements were "just like church...call and response, which has been going on since Africa."[106] Music was about language circulating, energy and information flowing from one element, place, or time into another. Its very rhythmic density could establish a context for democratic cooperation, extending beyond self and form in the realization of higher principles, as musicians play different rhythmic cycles or follow written lines that seem to pull against the gravity of pulse.

In the mid-1990s, Coleman began an exhaustive study of Yoruba culture and traveled to Cuba to study Santéria and Candomblé.[107] At 1996's Havana Jazz Festival, he collaborated with dancers and Cubano musicians like AfroCuba de Matanzas, inaugurating a transitional phase in his music. Now preoccupied with the ritual qualities of structured improvisation, Coleman focused on musical collaborations as the realization of spiritual growth. His big band The Council of Balance released *Genesis/The Opening of the Way*, which Coleman says was inspired by Kabbalah and biblical accounts of creation. He sought to gather information from these disparate sources, harvesting from them commonalities and inferences about spiritual insight and energy.[108]

While still insistent that his ideas were rooted in the African diaspora, and seeing himself as a kind of griot, Coleman's conceptual framework was fluid. He began to consolidate his research into a musical system that theorized natural cycles, color relations, and numerology alongside harmony, tone, and rhythm. Compelled by "the relationship of language to music," Coleman thought it possible for improvised musical performance to become a kind of sonic ritual that could not just enact the talking drum tradition but facilitate "the transmission of information" *from* past eras and other cultures into the postmodern now (if that sounds like the kind of trans-historical connectivity imagined by Theosophy, it is perhaps worth noting that Coleman once led a band called The Secret Doctrine).[109]

In seeking to balance and harmonize so many interlocking parts, Coleman imagines polyphonic music as a medium for reckoning with the challenges of temporality and dynamic change. With no settled answers, no cessation of movement, all human expression deals in coordinating rhythms across time, in the always precarious attempt to maintain form amid an ongoing flow. These very efforts at coordination are rituals, Coleman avows, and he finds evidence of this across cultures (which he refers to with titles like "Li Bai Astrology" or "Ritual Septet [Fire]"). Coleman explains the symbolic and conceptual implications by recalling that he and a friend were observing a mountain, and Coleman said, "Man, it would be great if I could play that mountain." His friend asked, "You mean, pick up your horn, be inspired by the mountain, and play the feeling?" "No," Coleman responded, "actually play the mountain." His friend told him that was impossible, but Coleman insisted, "[W]hat I want to do is look at the mountain and have it represent something to me in symbolic form, just like the notes on the paper do and just play it."[110]

Here the problem of language's limits confronts the improviser not as impasse but as the possibility of enacting what ostensive reference cannot. If one learns how to listen to "who you are vibrationally and in spirit," one encounters the self as a network of "coded information" that connects emotion and contemplation with natural forces.[111] In omnipresent cycles (breath, rhythms, seasons) one discovers that "certain numerical patterns that are present in music are also present in astronomy, sun spots, and the cycles of eclipses."[112] To compose is effectively "to plan a musical ritual" that coordinates these patterns as intervals, rhythms, and bodily relations, simultaneously expressing and facilitating spirituality.[113] Improvisation itself thus reenacts cosmogony. Beginning in 2007, Coleman performed "musical rituals" focused primarily on "the Soli-Lunar Cycle," where cycles of the moon express the ceaseless movement between Yin and Yang.[114] These modes focus the organization of rhythm and intersubjectivity and capture the modulation and improvisational flux of the universe. So if ritual is sonically tethered to "concepts of dynamic equilibrium that exist in Nature," you can play the mountain.[115] Coleman's system links these ideas through symbols denoting esoteric realities reflected in nature, which in turn may be notated. Resonating with ancient conceptions of a *musica universalis*, Coleman describes his music as "analogous to a dynamic sacred geography projected through sound."[116]

The arrangement and performance of these elements depends on determining and realizing favorable conditions for their co-resonance and merging. This is another familiar aspect of ritual, and Coleman situates his ideas in a continuum of divination practices across cultures, from Tarot to "geomancy, sociomancy, chiromancy or necromancy."[117] Whether using color, signs and cards, or numbers, "it is the intervals and their combinations, as well as the relationship between pitches and their movement (space and time relationships)" that facilitate change (or "modulation") through sound.[118] He recently described these as "temporal impressions" aimed at "the gathering, through musical symbolism, of the energy of particular moments."[119] Recent recordings commence with what he calls "a sonic ritual that opens the way" for pieces shaped by natural elements and the rhythms associated with specific *Orishas*, though their sound is a long way from "Night in Tunisia."

Proper ritual articulation of music's "vibratory power" holds opens the possibility that "music projects not only the quality of the time in which the creator of the music lives, but also qualities of periods of time in the future."[120] The music can thus be inspiring: in the colloquial sense, in that it connotes the in-breathing of spirit (and its release through instrumental vessels), and in the sense that it can shape a utopic sensibility, even fostering the unification of humans and between humans and the universe (an alignment that promotes healing, and which Coleman has likened to acupuncture through performance). Structure is both catalyst and context. It disciplines, focuses, facilitates, and summons. Tapping into something perennial through form yields no certainty, but "there is a kind of energy that is a part of all of us, and it gets expressed in an individual way in each of us."[121]

Coleman's aesthetic links musically to the staccato precision of ritual music, the combinative ceremonialism that increasingly characterizes certain American spiritualities, and to the diasporic translocation of ritual forms from their original context into new performance spaces. His current music continues to be informed by Yoruba devotional music, numerology and rhythm, and astrological principles. Playing becomes a divination ritual itself, where the vibrational properties of a sonic universe are activated through instruments, including the membrane of the ear. A song, a rhythm, a hot solo all amplify these constants, and remake them in the flow of time. Ritual freezes and distills so that we can experience these transitory, vibratory realities. Music connects levels of reality that a disenchanted world holds apart, its sonic language reaching inward and outward "all the way to spiritual vibration."[122] Performance itself is understood as a form of collective learning; simply by sounding out esoteric principles and connectedness, reality as touched by sound becomes informed *by* precisely what is being modeled *in* sound. So Coleman plays on, his intensely held lines and urgent tone suspended over a continual flow that sounds like watching blood flow under a microscope. He plays on because music "plants the seed to start moving on to a higher realization of who we are."[123] So who is Steve Coleman, he who plays the mountain? "I am, period. I am that I am."[124]

The Machine Contracts: The Art Ensemble of Chicago

Such assertions of identity were never simple for the Art Ensemble of Chicago (AEC). African percussion, street refuse, innumerable horns, and assorted toy noisemakers crowded their stage as surely as genre significations crowded their sound. There was Roscoe Mitchell, stone-faced, his street clothes standing out as perhaps the deepest of ruses. There was Lester Bowie in his lab coat and hard hat, up for the grind of tone science. There were the robed and face-painted Joseph Jarman (later a Buddhist priest and martial arts expert), Malachi Favors Maghostut, and Famodou Don Moye. They whirred and clicked like a Partch composition, played the dozens, groaned as one. Young, gifted, and black covers it to a certain extent but this music was miles away from Aretha. Except when it wasn't.

Favors, Mitchell, and Bowie had come up in the AACM and decided to start their own band based on their shared commitment to experimentalism and multi-instrumentalism. They got plenty of gigs, but almost always got fired when they finished playing. Their set-long suites stitched together heated free improvisations with mutated versions of standards. They got deeper into the "little instruments" as a way of conveying their Africanism, but also contended that "African" was a lineage vast enough to encompass any music that was expressed in the proper spirit. And when Jarman joined, their theatrical performance grew into ritual or ceremonial music. With face painting, chanting and recitation, the pacing of the suites, and percussion circles, the group performed what George Lewis calls "multiple mode expression," incorporating "extramusicality."[125] Their transgressive performance crashed the barriers separating "high" music from "low," vernacular culture from "art." Mitchell's *Sound* and Jarman's *Song for* appeared in 1966, the latter noted for its "magic feel for theater, martial airs and the spoken-word 'Non-Cognitive Aspects of the City'."[126] They rehearsed daily but, after a promising start, it was "impossible for us in the States."[127]

Hearing that Europe was more open to new music, they relocated to Paris in 1969. Soon joined by percussionist Moye, the AEC became known for their combination of sonic maelstroms, unexpected humor, and "ritualistic percussion jams."[128] They crafted an elaborate, theatrical blend of melody and non-idiomatic sound, hot solos and collective improvisation, song-form and sheer splenetic mess. And in them they blended biting humor with commentary: on jazz, on blackness, on social conditions. For example, "People in Sorrow" has an ominous, nearly spectral feel that is punctuated by a childlike voice crying, "Mommy, there's a rat scratchin' in the walls," followed by a police siren. *Certain Blacks* ("certain blacks . . . do what they wanna!") is poised, Philippe Carles notes, "between political slogan and hymn."[129]

The group began to signify on religion too. On "Old Time Religion," Favors sawed away on a pedal point, while Bowie spoke as a holiness

preacher. Half drawl, half old-man mutter, the performance is spectacu-
larly piss-taking and sincere all at once: "And God said unto Jacob (yes he
did), a-*rise*... and go up to Bethel, and lay up there, and make there an
altar.... That's what he told him!" The sermon—and the responses of the
"congregation"—came untethered in under a minute, with barely intelli-
gible syllables, growls, ragged cries, all signifying on centuries-old misrepresentations of black sound and religion. "*Yes he did!*" "Mm-hmmm."
"Gwa'head." "*Save me, Jesus!*" And then to the rocking motion of the bass,
a rolling "mm-hmmm," "a-men," as the group intoned, "Give me that old-
time religion." Or consider Jarman's poem tucked inside *Reese and the Smooth
Ones*, which writes of the "return to history" on "a nigger/slave/ship" from
out of "godless seasons" in Europe's "hollow cities." Jarman instructed, "as
the master (ONEGOD) watches," the true struggle is not to forget "ALL
that is beautiful in this universe and the next."

Upon returning stateside, their polyphonic performance emerged as a
kind of sonic distillation of African American culture and religion. White
counterculture freaks loved the AEC, as they lurched and stalked the stage,
making guttural noises, eructations, vomiting out pure sound, and goading
participation from an audience who may not have known they were participating in self-mockery, recycling the stereotypical reception of the "savage"
musician's sweating brow. Amid sincere, tuneful moaning, a bicycle horn or

FIGURE 5.2. Roscoe Mitchell, Lester Bowie, and Joseph Jarman performing in
the 1970s. Photograph copyright William E. (Bill) Smith.

gong might pull the rug out. Jarman bellowed verse: "The sun done got maaaaad. The moon is sad. The flowers, they cry aaaaaaaallll daaay. *Drums!*" Thwack! Horns, whirrs, and clicks. Alongside shrieking/sobbing confessions as if from a madman in the corner, another voice shucks, "You know I love you baby." These contrasts were central to the AEC's aesthetic, as dulcet sustained tones, unison vocal weeping, or declamatory notes over small percussion articulated their riotous commitment to "Great Black Music" and also their resistance to settling or codification.

Such performances were jumbled enough to take you out of your comfort zone, but they were always formalized. Performances might open with a solemn, solitary gong and proceed from there into what the AEC called an "ancestral meditation" (which could mean anything from a drum circle to a meditation on a powerful ancestor like Bob Marley).[130] A 1979 Washington, D.C., concert opened with all members standing "in silent prayer, facing the east."[131] Bowie's mad-eyed mischief compelled visually, bedecked as he was in not just his lab coat but sometimes garish suits and gold-rimmed glasses (Bowie, when leading his Brass Fantasy, sometimes playfully referred to himself as Niggerace). Stoic Mitchell and rapt Favors and Moye (both in face paint, the latter often wearing a coolie hat) listened to Jarman's invocation to "the spirit of the heavens and the earth working inside your body."[132] As they exposed audiences to the range of Great Black Music, the AEC's ritual would also keep listeners on their toes. Indeed, part of their purpose in performing exclusively in the theatrical, processional, ceremonial mode was to hold together contrasts and apparent tensions in the sort of sonic space anthropologists once referred to as liminal. What could account for the simultaneous use of megaphones and djembes? What were audiences to make of the "theatrical mix of shamanistic ritual and funny noises, African face paint and weird space bop"?[133] The AEC reveled in such code-scrambling, making long hushed passages as integral to the performance as the free jazz freak-outs.[134]

Some called it "Dadaist theatre," dressed up with a ritualized tour through "jazz's history and pre-history—music from the sanctified churches, minstrel shows and bawdy houses of late nineteenth and early twentieth century America."[135] Others described it as "an odd mixture of sacrament and blasphemy…ritual and riot."[136] And of course, there was an undeniable, in-your-face pranksterism to their carefully constructed performances: at the most solemn moments, Jarman's hands stretched skyward, one member might mug at the audience or let loose a mighty raspberry.[137] Bowie once strode menacingly across the stage with a shotgun in his hands, followed by a sequence where another member "danced with an oversized Raggedy Ann doll, accompanied by Malachi Favors's banjo."[138] The group romped through "Hail to the Chief" while an actor dressed as a four-star general in an LBJ mask gesticulated on a podium until "one of the musicians hurled a cream pie in his face."[139] Later, Jarman read the Gettysburg Address and, when he reached the passage insisting "all men are created equal," "disgustedly threw away the script."[140] Yet another performance featured a backdrop of posters depicting Klansmen and Southern sheriffs, and a playacted murder onstage, ending with a body dragged off.[141]

Into the 1970s and 1980s, the AEC fine-tuned these juxtapositions sonic, ritual, and instrumental. They collaborated with the South African choir Amabutho and began to explore more thoroughly non-American expressions of Great Black Music. Bowie traveled considerably during this period, drinking deep of reggae and ska in Jamaica, and jamming with Fela Kuti on one of his multiple trips to Africa.[142] It was Favors who most carefully articulated the ritual, ceremonial properties of their music. Deeply informed by his study of African music and culture, Favors insisted that when you "go back in our history as black Americans...you will pick up the sound of African ceremonial music."[143] They romped playfully through reggae on "Ja," or rocketed through an "Old Time South Side Street Song," always insisting that the music had an experiential quality that, as Bowie insisted, "you just can't explain" precisely *because* it was "heavily spiritual."[144] The inescapable, uncatchable, ineffable qualities of "religion" remained a subject of ritual play, as the AEC "set up situations" (though refused to resolve them) highlighting this wordlessness.[145] The whole of their performance was designed to stage—through improvisation, reference, jarring combinations—a context wherein the very problematic nature of these key terms like "black" and "religion" could be explored, if only in tweaking the audience's expectations.

The whole shebang, Bowie agreed, "is a ritual...we are there for that moment only, and we try to spiritually condition ourselves to be open to receive whatever conflicts may happen, and shoot our way that particular evening."[146] For Jarman, the performance "space is TRANSFORMED into... a beautiful shining sound object waiting to tone the infinite sound."[147] Rituals aim to bring about "[s]alvation through music," and when it works "[t]he machine contracts. We remember only the infinite experience of the joy, the sound, the music."[148] While AEC performance signifies continually on religion, there is also the clear sense that they believe their music also *constitutes* it. Moye believed that the sheer otherness of this spiritual music might foment "a good, old-fashioned revolution" or at least cut through "[t]he bullshit."[149] Jarman "went off and became a Buddhist priest" who runs a Brooklyn dojo, until "the voice needed me back."[150] Even when back, Jarman made sure that his improvisational activities both with and without the AEC included opportunities for him to perform as a Buddhist (he often recited or chanted Buddhist sutras where he once read his own incantatory verse).

More than simply what happens onstage, the sound itself constitutes a ritual connection between time and idiom. Playing sets up a space where the very presence of history and culture enables a move outside of culture, elaborating codes beyond the codes. Many have likened the AEC's "mythic ritual elements" to those performed by West African griots: "a revision (as opposed to a repetition) of traditional African *oral* poetry in a distinctive and contemporary *aural* narrative instrumentalism."[151] According to Bruce Tucker, their use of contrast, juxtaposition, humorous play, and multi-instrumentalism generates "an epic myth of identity in a diasporic context of profound discontinuities."[152] Robin Kelley hears in their riotous avant-garde stew "a self-conscious sonic memory of the Middle Passage, the overthrow of slavery, dance halls in the age of Jim Crow, migration and city life, rebellion against brutality, and black love."[153]

But of course and as always, the AEC also delighted in improvising on the very idea of Africanism, too, confronting audiences with expectations about essential blackness and spirituality, the reality of the sweating brow here evoked and disassembled ritually. While there was an undeniable pedagogical element to their performances, it is perhaps more fruitful to see ritual as winking furiously when it posits any essence to identity. This, after all, was a group whose early (and, to most, obvious) parodies of minstrelsy led to the musicians being accused of—what else?—minstrelsy.[154] They teased audiences with the veneer of authenticity, with the real, with truth itself. Here, they insisted, was a pipeline to the past. See this face paint? Authentic. Hear these drums? Traditional. But while they really meant it, they also didn't mean *only* it. The masks they often wore should be understood not just as traditional ceremonial garb but as metaphors for the group's disposition. Nothing was out of place in their ritualism, each horn-honk, leer, or chant a moment in a temporal flow that cannot be reduced to mere continuity but constantly regenerates the hot, dense, multitudinous moment of creation itself.

Any point in the history of "jazz" could emerge at any moment, perhaps even any point in history itself; so performance became a sonic staging *of* these histories, not with the intention of framing or fixing them but instead enacting a simultaneous engagement with and distance from its modern origins. As Norman Weinstein wrote, these efforts were integral to the music and meant to "invok[e] spiritual powers."[155] Through the imaginative linkages with Africa the Art Ensemble plays with impossibility, not just trying to shoehorn all music into a single expressive tradition but the impossibility of categories themselves when faced with the surpassing energy of the spirit. The experience of being an African American creative musician, dislocating and often cruel, is addressed through what Tucker calls "a living ritual rather than a simple ceremony" (referring here to Victor Turner's well-known distinction: "Ceremony *indicates*, ritual *transforms*.")[156] And transformation cannot occur with over-planning, strict limits, or any attempt to confine sound and spirit. Once immersed in the totality of performance, players could then respond at will, since, for Jarman, "they are free, [and] there's no separation between these forms."[157] Or as Bowie put it, "You rehearse, practice just to enable you to be able to receive the spirit and you just kind of follow the spirit."[158]

Weinstein traces such practices all the way back to "the peacock pageantry of the cakewalk, that signifying on European country airs, and before that, the African village royal procession," and notes, too, the precedent of "the Garveyite parades of 1920s Harlem as a multimedia art event."[159] But he also cautions that the griot was traditionally no mere repository of cultural memory but, significantly, "offers the spiritual entertainment that gives the illusion that all has been woven together."[160] Cultural critics might be tempted to locate in such crosscutting interpretative performances, subversive as they are, something like the revenge of the subaltern. But as Lewis points out, the AEC more accurately expresses Zora Neale Hurston's "will to adorn."[161] Equally rooted in African American signifying practices, Hurston's playful acknowledgment of the literary, imaginative quality of all human experiences captures the AEC's Africanism (and their desire to extend it) alongside their discomfort with essentialism and reductionism. And as Lewis aptly points out, the AEC's use of "traditional" instruments hardly links the group to Africa alone: their "expressions of auditory and visual iconography" might conjure up gamelan processions or Hindu sacred epics as surely as the idioms of the African diaspora.[162]

The AEC takes "religion" to the stage, placing it in the center, in everyone's view, and unpacks its multitudes. Their ritual allows for confession, theater-cum-history lesson, and perhaps even a sacrifice of "authenticity" itself in the name of a more fluid, improvisatory form of identity, one that encompasses the beauty of ugliness, the scars inevitable on the face of even the most carefully crafted art, the sublime coherence of chaos, and the entropic in the most careful composition. Life itself is a stage, perhaps, and even the audience becomes a kind of instrument in helping the AEC establish frames allowing them and us to color outside their lines, and to see where categories break down. In establishing ritual contexts for "blurring…the edges between music and environmental sounds," they also blur the lines separating entertainment from history, satire from spirituality.[163] These evocations effectively write the group into American religious history, not simply because of their associations with AACM communitarianism or their participation in post-1950s Pan-African spirituality.[164] They also give voice, as Robin Kelley notes, to W. E. B. DuBois's identification of a persistent "new song" sung by successive generations of African Americans, each remaking culture and history and religion in ways that are "improvised and born anew out of an age long past."[165] That they use these same materials to call attention to their limits simply reminds us that this is all as slippery as "religion" itself. An AEC ritual may go back thousands of years, but it also slips into the future, always receding, erased like a sand painting, evaporating like water. For Bowie this was the point: "Some things work, some things don't." And Favors concurred: "Just like life."[166]

One on One: Milford Graves

Think about those moments when, in solitary concentration or unbidden during activity, you become aware of your heart's thudding in your chest, the flow of your blood, the rhythm of your breath. In those brief experiences of intensely aware embodiment, do you try to imagine the moment of cessation, that abrupt punctuation awaiting us all? Do you try to calm yourself, willing the moment to pass? Or do you, somehow, get into it? What if, in fact, you got so into it that you imagined you could dominate Shaquille O'Neal one-on-one? That you could transform your body into a living conduit of cosmic energy? That you could play a drum kit in four different meters simultaneously, one per limb, each synched up to your pulse, itself articulating in different meters, one per limb? If you thought these things, you might be Milford Graves.

Graves grew up fascinated by cinematic depictions of Vodou and Native Americans practicing herbalism. Some of his earliest musical experiences were playing Afro-Cuban music, which exposed him to Santéria via Bata drummers. Graves insists, "The music that I play is directly linked to African music and Afro-Cuban music that is used in Santéria."[167] Obsessed with percussion, Graves wanted to play timbales like Tito Puente. But after seeing the classic Coltrane quartet, with the unstoppable Elvin Jones, Graves switched to traps. By the mid-1960s he was obsessed with playing along with the tablas on Ravi Shankar records. He experienced a lightbulb moment seeing Charlie Parker playing drums in "rhythms...identical to many rhythms that are found in West Africa and the Caribbean."[168] He came to believe that improvisers, from whatever musical or religious tradition, "are naturally practicing a form of Zen: so much has been stripped away that they have been forced to go deep inside their inner selves and totally open themselves up to new levels of consciousness."[169] With Graves's plunge into consciousness, we move from Ellington's and Williams's church ritual and Coleman's or the AEC's self-conscious ritualism to the ritual coordination of body and sound to induce new experience.

Whitney Balliett wrote that Graves, one of the most celebrated percussion innovators of the 1960s, "never sounded a regular beat...repeatedly developing a welter of booms and rifle shots and clicks and tinklings."[170] He played ferocious solo concerts in city streets, his whirlwind limbs making a blur of his dashiki. He wanted to resuscitate the drum's centrality to African and African American culture. Audiences were bowled over not just by Graves's percussive inventions but by the physicality of his performances, thudding urgently but with a compelling grace and technical fluidity. He rested his foot atop a tom-tom to achieve timbral variety, a scuffed sole facing the audience as the kit shook. He surrounded his body with a vast array of gongs, woodblocks, rattles, and gourds. He sang, yodeled, moaned as if in possession, and lectured the audience (mostly, though not always, between pieces). And he played his own body with as much technique and imagination as his drums.

To Graves, performance expressed musicians' "traditional functions as healers of the spirit and transmitters of psychic energy and enlightenment."[171] Graves associates each rhythm with particular feelings, so that playing polyrhythms leads to an irreducibility of emotion, culture, and performance that he identifies as African: "[y]ou pick up the drum and you think of the Black man."[172] Graves insists that, though the drum was banned among slaves, rhythm cannot be co-opted: "[a]s long as you've got the [Graves performs on his body]—boom, chik, back-a-doo-kick—then you've got the drum. Don't think it's no jazz music or new music or avant-garde, revolutionary; it's been around a looong time. It went underground here."[173]

This outlook on African self-expression and resistance drove Graves's insistence on musicians' self-organization, leading to his ostracism by promoters and labels fearing he was "too political."[174]

While Graves certainly explored Black Nationalism during the 1960s, he distinguished cultural pride from narrow sectarianism or exclusivism, both of which he saw as partly responsible for African Americans' alienation from their own spiritual traditions.[175] Seeing inflexibility as an impediment to musical and spiritual development, in the 1970s Graves began to study self-discipline through plant biology, pulmonary science, and martial arts. He linked them to an African cultural continuum that, as with the AEC, contained a flexibility that carried it beyond historical limits, which Graves believed enabled it to undo negativity in one's life. And he was neck-deep in negativity in the 1970s, when he acidly summed up the improviser's life in America: "the positive aspect is when I survive."[176] Musical and spiritual survival required escape from binding references and identifications, relying instead on creative perception at the intersection of past and present.

In the mid-1970s, Graves stumbled upon the LP *Normal and Abnormal Heart Beats*. Graves recalls that it was "a record for cardiologists. It blew my mind. Everyone says the heart is the drum and the drum is the heart, but here were *the secret rhythms, man*."[177] He was gravitating to the idea that tone, not rhythm, was at the heart of drumming. With the advent of the drum, he claimed, humanity's "indwelling spirit" manifests in religious experience where "the body goes through various types of emotional changes."[178] With the proper context, "your whole body's vibrating."[179] To understand these experiences, Graves studied biorhythms and root doctoring together: "if you're to be a master drummer you have to know about herbs."[180]

Graves worked daytimes "as a medical technologist running a veterinary laboratory."[181] His study of music took him beyond conventional history, to the conclusion that "any sound-machine played by a Black person automatically takes on a different meaning."[182] The vibratory powers of sound, when coordinated properly, could not help being transformative. And the combination of musical intentionality with improvisation's temporal immediacy creates an even richer opportunity for reflection on embodment. Graves was convinced that music healed emotionally and biologically, because in performance "[y]ou reach a point where your body is so energized that physically you have to slow your metabolism down."[183] This is precisely one of those vibratory experiences—at the intersection of

timbre, frequency, and flesh—that Graves knew was conducive to spirituality, like those moments in "the Baptist Church when the preacher used to
shake and use a particular tone of voice."[184] He recalls seeing women in his
church "fall out" when in need of healing, and his own sympathetic trem-
bling convinced him that "a divine type of belief can heal."[185] Graves believes
that humans are at a crossroads, "where the Yoruban deity Elegba rules,"
and are prepared to understand the intersection of vibration, science, and
healing.[186] Specific rhythms "are so similar to cardiac rhythms that it is un-
believable."[187] And synching these rhythms transforms both mental and
physical states, yielding divine insight and bodily wellness. The key to this
is an immersion in rhythm that facilitates ritual coordination of one's relation to time. If all life is rhythmic at its core—sidereal, tidal, corpuscular—
then appropriating ritual traditions coordinated to these realities helps
articulate these truths in your bloodstream. Graves began conducting
workshops exploring the relation between music and biology and grew
convinced that their effects could be assessed scientifically.

These notions echo loudly in American religious history, replete with
traditions—stretching from Spiritualism's belief in the scientific veracity
of universal fluid to Transcendental Meditation's conviction that mantras
produced lactic acids that altered brainwaves (not to mention with composer Alvin Lucier's use of brainwaves in some of his musical experiments)—positing the integration of mind, body, and spirit in healing.
Whether consciously or not, Graves improvises with these traditions when
contending that "music can be used in a medical way to actually stimulate
different parts of the body and even to heal."[188] He cofounded the Institute
of Bio-Creative Intuitive Development to study how "music can be used as
a therapeutic means of assisting with psychological problems."[189] It all
starts with the heartbeat, after all. Understanding this means that humans
can be prepared for any situation: one trains one's body for peak physical
performance (in martial arts or behind the kit), according to the flow patterns of the circulatory system; or one tends one's own garden according
to the natural rhythms of seasons. This is the key to the experience of true
freedom, then. Just as "free jazz" is a misleading description for music
deeply shaped by African culture, so improvisation cannot involve just
playing whatever you want, whenever you want: it can only work when the
musician understands "it's like being controlled by your sub-conscious
self, deeper things of which you're not aware."[190]

The juxtapositions in Graves's holism flow from his sense that there are
"fractals in basic drum rhythms and in the structures of African dance."[191]

So there is no sense in locating scarification rites or acupuncture on one side of a human cultural continuum and technological networks and "sophisticated" jazz on another; as Graves put it, "the three-piece-suit guy has got to meet the guy with the feathers and beads on."[192] Graves's assemblage of skeletons, Ziploc bags filled with herbs, painted drums, and computers might puzzle some, but he manipulates these reception dynamics in ritualized confrontations with expectations not unlike the AEC's. He may stalk the stage like a wrestler, his body draped in robes and bells but moving as quickly as the NBA point guards he admires. Audiences may not understand "all my vocal stuff" or the painted drums (half Fillmore poster, half African mask).[193] But it all connects with the greater purpose of "play[ing] for a higher force... [so] you can go into a state where you do not operate according to earthly laws."[194] So the most divine music is unearthly, yet rooted in a particular place, accessible to those in tune with their own heartbeat, as Thoreau once mused about drummers.

Jazz is the music that most embraces the provisional, and in which freedom can lead quickly to indecision, botched experiment, or failed communication. But Graves sees these very possibilities as conducive to states of non-attachment or even nothingness. In the gap between plan and execution, known and unknown, there is only the pulse and tone of that most basic human rhythm. He continues his measurement of it in his cramped basement lab, filled with drums, herbs, and medical equipment.[195] Graves notes that "I'm getting sound from an electrical event and... a muscular event."[196] He describes the "four-part harmony" from the heart's chambers, which he emulates when articulating his own pulse differently in each limb. Harvard's Baruch Kraus, who insists that Graves's work parallels emergent academic research, concurs that "when you listen to the heart at full frequency, it's like a jazz ensemble."[197] Graves asserts that cardiac arrhythmias replicate some of the most important ritual rhythms in Bata music and describes how playing this music correlates with experiences of "hysteria, anxiety, even anemic conditions": "When you go into possession [Graves extends his arms, rolls his eyes back, and chants] ay-zay-zi-do, ay-DOOOO, eh-eh, ay-DOOO, ay-day-day. I say, record that and we'll see what goes on. We'll see all these kind of arrhythmias happening. But they're good arrhythmias," like those produced in Yoruba ritual.[198]

There is personal and social benefit in coordinating the heart's rhythms with what is heard. While culture and constraint still matter, Graves finds it foolish to live as if race was a relevant biological or spiritual reality. This would be living and musicking based on "what's on the outside," not on those universals that we all have "on the inside."[199] Once players hear "the real grand fundamental tone that comes from the people," they can improvise to rewire the heart.[200] Graves obsessively records the pitch of human heartbeats in order to create tones and rhythms for just this purpose. He runs the recordings through computer programs displaying "the numeric values for the frequencies of sound."[201] Graves also mixes musicians' heartbeats using his computer, talking all the while about how "to augment the 'prima materia' of the heartbeat with the 'ancient mathematics' of the Golden Ratio."[202] He has recently taken to calling music Cosmo-Mystical-Spiritual (CMS).[203] Exciting the sound, and thus the body, helps "decipher the concealed and hidden energies within and beyond the universe."[204] Activating "the total body" is the gateway into a mystical system, where one drinks up the sun's energy, consumes what good earth gives, and becomes a sonic-cosmic being who does not so much chant mantras as become the breath of the universe when properly receptive, one's own blood the messenger of divine information.[205] The body's expansion into the universe has scientific, musical, and religious resonance. Graves gives it a Kabbalistic or Gnostic spin at times: "The SPIRITUAL allows one to perceive concealed wisdom (MYSTICISM) and how to transmute (ALCHEMY) and germinate (MAGIC) their receivings to the unexposed to produce innovative-creative music."[206] At times he even waxes yogic, when talking about the conduction and reception of energy in the tuned body. But what draws together the biological, scientific, sonic, and mystical is the arrangement and disposition of components in the ritual of performance.

How like a modern Helena Blavatsky this sounds, as Graves plumbs various cultural and religious traditions to isolate their common heartbeat—a Golden Ratio, a ventricular rhythm—and express them through sound in order to heal. This is more than just jazz; in "an evolving period of collision vibrations" it is necessary to reinvestigate the "responsibilities and task of the musician."[207] Sound itself, as distilled vibratory energy, can connect to quantum physics, conduct solar energy through the body, reveal the bio-resonance of pitch changes, and link contemporary science with "Dogon philosophy."[208] Graves connects revived ancient wisdom with quantum information because "[t]he present situation in the universe requires that a musician be totally aware of what is taking place on the greater cosmic environment of Vibration."[209]

This use of varied techniques (acupuncture or biofeedback) to incorporate sound into the body is seen by some as a clear extension of Shamanic traditions.[210] We might also situate Graves's exploration of healing practices within a long lineage of evangelical healing practices he likely learned about in those same religious communities where he first encountered sonic healing: God's power to heal physically and spiritually; the laying on of hands by healing evangelists or in Pentecostal traditions; or the healing energies experienced in gatherings like the Toronto Blessing. Graves is clearly, however, far more interested in the efficacy of non-Western sources, and his investigations reflect a broader interest in natural medicine in contemporary America. Indeed, his understandings of sonic resonance and energy bear some resemblance to the category *qi* in Chinese traditional medicine or *prana* in Ayurvedic healing (his practice of acupuncture and herbal remedy underscores such links). Even less formal traditions of "alternative medicine"—like homeopathy, Therapeutic Touch, aromatherapy, or chiropractics—trade in notions like "vital force" or "Innate Intelligence." The common denominator among these various approaches is, according to Candy Gunther Brown, the conviction that "[b]lockages or imbalances in the flow of energy are believed to cause illness."[211]

Many jazz players share this belief in healing sound. Paul Hewitt used music "as a healing tool for those with degenerative neurological conditions."[212] Rashied Ali believed that music "has a kind of a power...maybe even a healing force there somewhere."[213] Travis Laplante, who once suffered from debilitating vertigo, practices Qi Gong medicine that he considers integral to his solo saxophone performance. He views performance as "a treatment whose aim is to break down energetic blockages in the listener...to help people realize their function in the universe."[214] And pianist Horace Silver practiced Transcendental Meditation, interested in the integrity of physical, conceptual, and religious in his playing. For a time he was affiliated with a prayer group exploring self-help, holistic medicine, and metaphysical music.[215]

The conduction of energies across, between, and inside bodies grounds these musical practices. The improviser's intersubjectivity, here refracted in that most basic experience of knowing your heart, is a means of rejecting the control of technology and form, not in the name of sterile self-mastery but in the name of flow, provisionality, and openness to experience. All meters occupy, and demand a reckoning with, the flow of time, recognition of which Graves finds liberating: from a mechanical conception of the self, or from the commodification of art. Graves performs mostly solo and speaks regularly of the continued need to investigate selfhood primarily. Perhaps this is why Professor Graves—basketball obsessive and one-time amateur boxing league champion—insists that he could take Shaq in a one-on-one fight: "Anytime. You hurt him where he's not used to being hurt. Then teach him to heal himself, get him in tune with his natural frequencies."[216] Sweet science, indeed.

Becometh Fissional Construct: Cecil Taylor[217]

Before I ever heard Cecil Taylor I had read about him and seen photographs of him playing piano. A small, light-skinned African American with graying dreadlocks and colorful clothing, Taylor sometimes wore shades and headwear. His head was often thrown back, his cupped hands poised above the keys, as if he were in thrall to his music. What I recall most about Taylor, though, was the blur in almost every photo I saw. Who was this fury, I wondered, who seemed to move at a speed beyond the shutter's eye? There were reports about bandmates wilting from the exertion, as Taylor played with such force and intensity—his continual movement in cascading thirty-second notes or an elbow slam-dunking a chord—that shards of ivory flew from the keyboard like bullets. Would instrument or self submit first?

And then I heard him, a roar of otherness and sheer velocity that seemed too fierce, too forbidding. Aside from the deluge, there were spiky bagatelles and unexpected lyric flourishes. The music's logic eluded me, as did Taylor's poetry: "Corolla! Corolla! LUUUU-BAAAAY!!!" But in time I was hooked by the glorious solo records, filled with sheer protean energy and bookended by little rhapsodies; by the catharsis and agonies of the 1970s Unit, which simply hammered away at sound itself for hours at a time, as if each swell could help them move further into the heart of the cosmos; and by Taylor's collaborations with European free improvisers in the late 1980s. And the first time I saw Taylor dance, I was unsure if he was performing some unknown martial art (at one point he seemed to strike the crane pose), taking the mickey out of the audience, or calling on spirits. After prancing in his dancer's pants and slippers to the piano bench, he sat with uncanny stillness, his head bowed and face deep in concentration, until the air seemed to crack in half with the force of his music.

The Juilliard-trained Taylor has since the 1950s been reinventing jazz piano, bringing to it the dissonances and polytonality of new music along with the galvanic energies of free jazz. The astonishing technique and energy of Taylor's language has influenced so many generations of players that it is now impossible to play cluster chords without the association.

There is a flow and lasting intensity to his playing that seems to demand submission, insisting that you enter its atmosphere entirely or not at all. There is total speed and perfect stillness, as notes hang limpidly in air while also barreling through it. But while at first the weight and density of sound overwhelms you—a release, an orgasm—it becomes apparent over time that there is organization to it, not merely in the formalist sense (compositional kernels alive in the torrent) but a context and direction that give the notes a solemnity of purpose, as if each exhilarating glissando or thunderous mashed chord in the lower register were part of an invocation, some rite from a tradition hitherto unknown to the listening adept.

What meanings are located in this assemblage of coordinated activity, ritualized motion, and free sound? Taylor once said, "There is no music without order—if that music comes from a man's innards. But that order is not necessarily related to any single criterion of what order should be as imposed from the outside."[218] The creation and expression of order within the flow of time, using sound to sculpt that temporal experience, has been explicitly linked by musicians to ritual, to that "temple of invention." Taylor is sometimes compared to a shaman or to different natural forces, and has been described as the most powerful piano innovator since Monk, since Tatum. Yet he has been not just overlooked but often maligned in the United States since, in the mid-1950s, he began his "Excursions on a Wobbly Rail," to cite an early title. A student of jazz's piano masters and classical composers, Taylor also insisted on the Africanism of his approach, comparing his playing to dancing and reminding listeners that the piano is a percussion instrument, made up of "eighty-eight tuned drums." He fused blues, church music, and a fascination with Indian and Balian music on his early sides, binding them in an insistence on music's "physicality."[219]

Frequently sipping on champagne and smoking, Taylor describes his influences in a languorous, often halting cadence. He "grew up listening to his father singing shouts and hollers."[220] He is influenced by history and the natural world, claiming, "[T]he Aztecs knew about zero at least five hundred years before the Europeans. What is new? New is none! New is the primordial organization of what existence is. It is waaaater. We come from the sea."[221] As Taylor discovered jazz, he became compelled by the self-creation of its avatars. But he is just as quick to effuse about Judy Garland or James Brown's emphasis on the one. These things hang together—champagne, Marvin Gaye, Aztec history, and poetry—because for Taylor "[m]usic is an attitude, a group of symbols of a way of life."[222] In this

marvelous echo of Clifford Geertz's theory of religion, what draws disparate experiences together into music is preparation to enter the ritual of
spontaneous composition itself: "[t]he joy of practice leads you to the celebration of creation. And now when I practice—and Mommy, hear me!—I
know how to *do* it."[223]

Faced with serious economic hardship and unable to land many gigs,
Taylor concluded early on that "[w]hen the hosannas of democracy blare the
loudest, it's when personal options…become the narrowest. It's at that
point that the poet really sees the dimension of the work that is possible."[224]
He refused to compromise his aesthetic and insisted that his music was
continuous with tradition: "[m]usic to me was a way of holding on to Negro
culture, because there wasn't very much of it around."[225] Freed from ideolog-
ically limited understandings of "swing" or "the blues," jazz is really about
"the energy that moves the music" and "the physicality of the musician."[226]
Taylor aimed in his self-defining performances "to imitate on the piano the
leaps in space a dancer makes."[227] By the late 1960s, Taylor formed his
long-standing trio with drummer Andrew Cyrille and alto saxophonist
Jimmy Lyons, who described the group's ascension beyond technique,
saying: "[i]t's not about any cycle of fifths, it's about *sound*."[228] Cyrille and
Taylor were said to exchange in "neo-African hollers and chants" during performance.[229] Taylor embraces this to some extent, likening his music to
Yoruba ritual; but it is always more than this, he and his musicians insist: "a
living organism" or street music with new energy.[230] For the creative musician, this was the only route to playing something spiritually pure according
to Taylor, since "this is a materialistic society and no one ever asked you to
be involved in spiritual values."[231] And this is why Taylor has insisted that
"[j]ust to permit a real feeling seems revolutionary in our society."[232]

One can almost hear in Taylor's contemptuous statement that America
has "no fucking blood!" an echo of C. Wright Mills's disdain for "cheerful
robots," of Holden Caulfield's railing against the phonies.[233] To express his
multitudinous self, Taylor dove deep not only into sound but into African
cultural history in order to blast past the very confines of identification. It
is simply the movement of the spirit—as broad as the universe, as intimate as the heart—that he follows: "You've got the will, so the spirits will
do it."[234] Taylor hears the flourishing self in concert with spirits as a reconfiguration of time, fusing chance and form, player and audience, in an
immersive, embodied, ecstatic now, with "[r]hythm-sound energy found
in the amplitude of each time unit."[235] Drummer Jerome Cooper says
this approach "was very religious to me, so I just called it North American

ritualistic drumming, 'cause I'm not from Africa."[236] Cooper heard in Taylor's example griots and shamans who could "manipulate physical phenomena."[237] To enter a state of receptivity to transformation, though, the music had to take you to "areas which are magical rather than logical."[238]

If America has "no fucking blood," Taylor's music is the sheer circulatory rush of existence, in which "[r]hythm is life the space of time danced thru."[239] As pianist Matthew Goodheart puts it in his superb study, Taylor here is commending a total practice wherein "the world itself is altered."[240] This notion is expressed in Taylor's poetic invocations, which Nathaniel Mackey describes as "the things...that he makes up his world with."[241] Aldon Lynn Nielsen locates Taylor in "a signifying genealogy that includes the writings of Marcus Garvey *and* W.E.B. DuBois, as well as the prophetic oral traditions of the African-American sermon."[242] Nat Hentoff describes the force of the music as "spirit-probing," hearing "the deep, exploding sense of natural forces" in its "elemental energy."[243] Taylor concurs: "Part of what this music is about is not to be delineated exactly. It's about magic, and capturing spirits."[244] He describes the musician's "self divination" as equal parts introspection and plunge into cultural memory.[245] To pursue the spirit is to "attempt to hear the calling of those great black minds that have preceded one," where new creation depends on ancient languages that Taylor describes suggestively as "Yoruba memoir other mesh in voices mother tongue at bridge scattering Black."[246]

To improvise is to speak the languages of the spirits, of ancestors' memories: "a set ritual song cycle in tongues the heat Harlem long ages past rested glory from."[247] Yet what the body puts back out in sound—in the "anacrusis" of pitched, notated materials, described by Goodheart as "small cells or aggregates of tones"—is always swept up into the flow of experience.[248] More than just capturing Taylor's multimedia improvisation, "anacrusis" is the co-operation of language and ritual (and performance and time) in what Taylor calls a "Unit flow," "an orbit in which players, amalgamations of known *material* and experiential energy, move."[249] Technique and form still matter, but because "the establishment has problems dealing with the rituals involved" improvisation "realize[s] the beauty of all the other things that those traditional concepts have attempted to hammer out."[250] To Taylor this effort is, like those forces shaping "jazz" itself, a religious one. But, he cautions in a way that shapes this book, "I don't know what religious means you know...I think that it has to do with recognizing the greater creative forces and understanding that every living thing is a part of that garden of nature's activities."[251]

Taylor's own *Garden 1 & 2* marked the point where he finally committed
to recitation and dance at the beginning of concerts, inspired largely by his
longtime study of Noh, kabuki, and gagaku. About these ritual prepara-
tions, Taylor said, "Jazz isn't supposed to have methodological constructs,
but dance is set movements, and moving is a kind of religion."[252] In eras-
ing any difference between bodily movement, music, and identity, Art
Lange sees Taylor realizing a quasi-Emersonian "continual quest for form
via activity."[253] This is correct so far as it goes; but to see Taylor's hands
poised to crash on ivories, his mouth agape and rapturous, intensified
visage framed by a spotlight, this is to see the *telos* of the activity too, in
what Taylor wrote in verse as a "[c]omplete submission to the spirits."[254]
Taylor builds through the body and the concreteness of experience, dismissing the values of "the whole materialist world" that insists that "things
of the spirit are not thought to be important, because they can't be *seen*."[255]
The trick for the improviser, then, is to elude the fixity of critical summa-
tion, to make of one's self a "fissional construct" to explode linguistic convention and use the shards to remake the world according to one's own
conception of the beautiful. As part of the process of this "whole search in
life" (which is "to find out who one is"), it is natural that "an investigation
of one's religion... [uses] poems, ritualised chants, references to American
Indians, to voodoo... because American culture, as I perceive it, is *that*."[256]

This ritual unfolds in sound and rhythm, and in Taylor's cosmos Aretha
and Ali are powerful spirits too. Taylor's integration of dance, poetry, and
pianism proved polarizing too. Some wanted the volcano right away, not the
grace of a dancer in space. Beslippered, he might shake bells or carry candles as he stakes out ritual space and recites verse, perhaps the Aztec rhapsody "Chinampas" or the ecstatic invitation to the loas, "Erzulie Maketh
Scent." In each case, the ritual proceeds similarly: thematic material is
announced in a tense hush, tentative probing interaction begins, the rise
and fall of improvisational energy like a jetliner climbing, that unique crashing momentum that feels like surf, and the long denouement that concludes in a series of Taylor miniatures, brilliantine fragments that close
his concerts like parting benedictions.

Ritual here is a "progression of course" that commutes concepts into
sound and contrasts "the defacement of all that is spiritual" with new
sonic bodies and languages.[257] Like the ritual parameters that exist to be
surpassed, language exists to call attention to its own limits, to allow the
self to escape the self and in so doing become realized. But what is fundamental to each summoned moment is an acknowledgment of "[t]he

FIGURE 5.3. Cecil Taylor, in full flow. Photograph copyright William E. (Bill) Smith.

spirits—they're the ones that have changed my life....[T]hey're here, and it would not have been that way had they not lived. So I always genuflect."[258] Taylor is aware of the otherness he projects: "I come out and I'm gonna chant and wooooo" and the audience "are all, 'Oh no, wait a minute, what the fuck is this.'...Well of course. But here I go."[259]

Taylor seeks "to create *forms* that govern the energy."[260] Spirits and sources collide, where obvious meaning is less important than realizing that "word-sound is power," which Steve Vickery likens to "the beguiling by the shaman in the initiation."[261] For all that the trope of self-expression is recognizably American, Taylor's self-enactment announces and then obscures itself in "a mystery realm of invocation, a haunting and healing root magic."[262] So we are reminded again of that ineffability, that evanescence at the heart of jazz's spirits rejoicing. This resistance to fixity is part of jazz's evasion of its own identity, of spirit's ability to animate jazz and jazz up religion itself, that dusty singularity. If the "spirits have been kind enough to endow you" with more time, then you owe it to the spirits not to play aimlessly but to focus ever more acutely on playing for them properly: "the concept of ritual...takes the effervescence out of the stomach" so you can get outside of the self and get the job done.[263]

A piano is a drum, its rhythm mediating between humans and spirits. Each improvisation has its own language, just as each spirit has its own "mysteries" that the improviser must divine in order to locate himself or herself in the saturated cosmos. The study of the forms is the study of motion, the complex weave of spirits and humans, earth and sky, that gives sound its spiritual, even magical properties; for "[s]ound, once it begins, goes occult."[264] Taylor embraces this, practicing incessantly as "preparation to enter the realm of the spirits," with the chastening knowledge that we cannot know or determine what happens there.[265] And that entrance into the temple of creation involves "the harnessing of power and authority through ritual and magical means," the figurative and even literal creation of worlds out of music, incantation, and dance.[266]

History as self-invention, sound as poesy, dance as natural composition; all are part of what Taylor calls "the celebratory essence of the spirit as it passes through us."[267] In his orbit form may be elusive, its scattered fragments gathered up in real-time reassemblage. Meter or blueprint may be obscured in the onrush of experience: yes, "[s]ometimes you just get lost, but you always try to reach that level of transcendence."[268] So who cares about categories? The spirits are everywhere, literally pouring out of all that is. It is our only task, Taylor reminds, to celebrate their uproarious multitude. For "[w]e are the transitory poems. The mountains will be here, and perhaps we will be part of the mountain. You know there are certain West African tribes that believe that life is just a part of death, and when the chemical composition changes—some of them believe that they may become a mountain stream, star, whatever."[269] Only become.

JAZZ HAS WRITTEN rituals for church, staged rituals as history, constructed sonic-spatial orientations to the cosmos, played for the *Orishas*, coordinated the pulse, and poured forth in sound that races ahead of itself toward self-actualization. Through chant, liturgy, musical mappings of seasons and stars, sound is drawn from the cosmos into jazz and sent from it back to the source. While we cannot say exactly by what processes a drum becomes sanctified or a spirit made materially present, for example, these ritualists make clear what it means to listen and play from the presumption that this is meaningful, that this is true. They play with the conviction that music demarcates a particular kind of space and time, and that coordinated activity through these dimensions brings those attuned to the sound in contact with things we call "religious." Yet unlike myriad sociological or anthropological accounts of religious ritual, even those that focus on liminality, one of the most powerful registers of the sacred here is not simply that which is clarified or distinct, but that which is amorphous, spilling beyond all formulations. As Tim Hodgkinson writes, "Real music happens when ideas are outrun by events."[270]

What does ritual accomplish? How do we know its purposes if they are mostly sonic, only occasionally gestural, but almost never verbal? Do they do more than "signify" and do they in fact transform perception, being in the world? What established orders of otherness (from the world, or from other states of being) do they bring into existence, even if temporarily? We see above how religio-musical ritual moves from the real to the imaginary and back in a kind of sonic-sacred isomorphism, which pianist Marilyn Crispell likens to "a ceremonial ritual, almost akin to a kind of Shamanism."[271] So the ritualists herein, and those I could have addressed (e.g., Jeanne Lee's Earthforms Rituals or Kahil El'Zabar's Ritual Trio), use ritual to rewire the body, against the jazz system, against race, and into the realm of the spirits and healing resonance, the loas, the divine breath.[272] Amiri Baraka observed that "[m]usic and its rituals can be used to create a model whereby identity can be understood as something other than a fixed essence."[273] But beyond the identitarian and representational, in ritual's tactile, sonic, expressive milieu, the contextual and institutional factors that mark something as recognizably "religious" are largely absent; and oftentimes, jazz's ritual performances are detached from religious cultures and communities as they are commonly understood. They subsist, instead, in repetition, invocation, and attention to mood, setting, or structure. With ritual, that form one thought one knew, we begin to drift from the known into something emotionally resonant but beyond the self, something expressive but formless. Jazz's resistance to closure, that hallmark of spirits rejoicing, opens wider still.

6

The Tao of Mad Phat

JAZZ MEDITATION AND MYSTICISM[1]

MANY PEOPLE READING this have memories of listening to records on turntables, an experience inevitably accompanied by the crackle of dust on needle, the occasional warp on the black platter, and the warmth of analog sound. Some also have memories of playing along with records, tapping out a drumbeat on your thighs on the edge of your bed or backing the needle up repeatedly, trying to figure out that tricky solo. We establish relationships with sound in this way, ones not reducible to mere entertainment. The late soprano saxophonist Steve Lacy consistently explored such relationality through multiple media, performance, and self-cultivated spirituality. On his 1974 solo recording *Lapis*, Lacy recorded himself playing along with a solo performance by Sidney Bechet. This gorgeous piece illustrates the continuity between early jazz and post-1960s experimentalism, relating to inspiration and a future made possible by a past. Amid the doubled crackle and pop of vinyl—from Lacy's Paris apartment and on our own stereos—we cannot help thinking about relationship: between self and other, performer and audience, presence and absence. These relations are inscrutable, unknowable, floating away into the past along with each decaying note.

For me, such questions are deeply ingrained in music-making, particularly in improvisational music, which depends on generous, engaged listening, and receptivity. Most of the questioning happens in performance itself, usually while trying to assess what works in the moment but occasionally dealing with off-stage experience too. In 2001 my band Unstable Ensemble was booked in the sublimely resonant space of Pittsburgh's First Presbyterian Church. I walked the grounds and the interior alone, thinking of my father and other loved ones passed on, and decided I wanted to open our set with something beautiful just for them. We chose Jimmy Giuffre's "Jesus Maria," and our set that evening was glorious. Later I remembered this as I woke from a dream one night with an album title in my head: *The Liturgy of Ghosts*. Instead of just a typical 3:00 A.M. scrawl on the notepad by the bed, I woke with a fully formed understanding of this phrase and its importance to me. It is said that it pains ghosts to haunt the living, so my thought was that perhaps playing ghost music—improvisational music that is always absent as soon as it is present—is a kind of intercession, a musical liturgy that reduces the ghosts' pain, and thereby our own as it helps us become less haunted.

Gods and spirits and presences. Vessels and sources. These mystical tropes recur not only in recognizable religious discourses but regularly among jazz musicians, compelled by relation, sound, and spirit. What accounts for this and what does it mean, in terms of musical practice and in thinking about religions? We saw above how ritualized modes of embodiment in music have both obvious and elusive religious dimensions. Yet an equally abiding religious preoccupation is the desire, if not to escape or transcend the body then at least to empty it of ego in the name of connecting to the universal, the cosmic, or the fundamental energy of reality itself. Significant to many musicians' understanding of jazz's religiosity or spirituality is the experience of transformed perceptual or emotional states. This chapter explores these from the perspective of religious experience in three separate fashions. First is an examination of the disciplines musicians pursue in cultivating these states: some musicians practice various forms of meditation, while others seek transformation by establishing relations with spirits. Second is a survey of the actual experiences of these states as musicians describe them (regularly recurring language posits that the improviser becomes a vessel for divine sound or an instrument of the Creator). Last is an exploration of the resonances these experiences are said to have with known, predominantly mystical, religious traditions.

Musicians' accounts of meditational practices, peak experiences, relations with spirits, and mysticism focus on the modalities of selflessness and absorption in the sonic *nous*; they lean away from singularities and thus locate jazz in a wide range of American religious improvisations on the relation between spirits and humans. This is a way of thinking about inspiration, musicians' sense of receiving sonic gifts, becoming transformed by sacred sound, and musical relationality as a religious category. Unlike others, this chapter mostly traces themes in the aggregate, pointing to resonances that echo in both jazz and religion, even if they appear as if without source or antecedent; I improvise on them with an ear for these resonances, not to stitch them together in a falsely cohesive composition.

This represents a vivid opportunity to examine these transformed sound experiences and selves as imagined "data" for religion. Certainly these themes are consonant with those of American metaphysicals or those who identify as "spiritual but not religious." Ostensibly defined against the gravities of institutional and traditional history, "spirituality" as defined by interpreters like Catherine Albanese, Courtney Bender, and Robert Fuller is distinct from "religion" in its focus on purportedly universal, non-institutional, "awareness and recognition of the intangible connection between all things."[2] Personal and combinative, such spirituality seeks "understanding of a higher essence of oneself," "heightened inner awareness," and personal transformation.[3] Robert Ellwood notes that since the mid-twentieth century artists especially have appropriated the languages and images of perennial philosophy, the mystical sub-traditions of mainline religions, or abstractions of Zen Buddhism, outside of their contextual specifics.[4] "Spirituality" subsequently became the byproduct of three interlocking impulses identified by Albanese: "a newly arrived Asian presence, the theosophical legacy, and the New Thought tradition."[5] Yet to adduce these sonic experiences of becoming vessels simply to an expression of contemporary interest in "spirituality" seems limiting, even if their combinative impulses co-resonate. Aside from the interest in the experiential as such, particulars matter in "spirits rejoicing" insofar as the experiences—not just actual performances but awareness of their transformational significance—can only occur through the recognition of particular others, as we see below. Musicians avow that through meditational focus on objects or texts, through ways of knowing or transformations catalyzed by saints or spirits, or through the mystic traditions' "sense of being grasped and taken over by an Other Power" the self can be integrated, the hidden made manifest, or the audient made aware of the creative energies of existence itself.[6] These descriptions recur among musicians in themes that, from meditation to mystic awareness, are like different angles of hearing the same experience. Real sound in jazz functions analogously to real knowledge, where the inner realm is the focus of intense religious scrutiny: what are its limits or possibilities, what mysteries can it unlock, to what realms can it travel under proper circumstances? Answers lie in personal transformation and a deeper understanding of the cosmos itself, which is the focus of the next chapter.

Let the Thing Happen: Meditation

What are these states of receptivity, and how does one achieve them? Meditation is commonly used among jazz musicians, and while it could be thought of as a kind of ritual, musicians focus less on its preparatory aspects than on its results. As a practice of selflessness, it takes musicians to some interesting places. Mental training has considerable implications for cognition, agency, and perception, all focused on the acute responsiveness improvisation requires. Some meditation aims directly at emptiness, impermanence, the attainment of no-self. It is also used as a kind of mental cultivation or visualization training, a technique for focus and concentration. Guitarist John McLaughlin recalled that Miles Davis heard sounds that could only be realized if his band abandoned conventional techniques for states of mind closer to Taoist conceptions of *wu wei*, or receptivity to the flow of things rather than deliberate agency.[7] In the immediacy of the process, it is difficult to distinguish between experience and attributions of meaning without positing the very ordering of the senses that meditation aims to recalibrate. The body remains central, but like an instrument can be reconfigured as a vehicle for transcending limits or imagining alternatives to the din of the world.

Some meditative traditions focus on the transformative properties of sound itself: peyote songs or sung mantras are understood to tap into "a deep vibration of Consciousness."[8] Other meditational practices are more seamlessly integrated with everyday life, as with the "Jazz Mindfulness" programs one finds occasionally in American cities. Many improvisers come to these practices through the influence of composer John Cage, who said often that music's purpose was to "quiet the mind, thus rendering it susceptible to divine influences."[9] Influenced by D. T. Suzuki's lectures on Zen, Cage turned away from the modernist obsession with self-expression to explore chance operations and repetition, saying "music is continuous, it is only we who turn away."[10] Terry Riley and La Monte Young wrote long-form trance music whose vibration might induce hypnogogic states, often imagining that in so doing they were tuning the listener's vibrations in a kind of yogic union. Pauline Oliveros used tape music and drone-makers as "ways of listening and ways of responding" that she considers meditational or ceremonial.[11]

These preoccupations are everywhere among spirits rejoicing. Percussionist Marc Edwards practiced Transcendental Meditation for years, "to reach the awaken state," and now combines meditation with Reiki and yoga.[12] Woody Shaw practiced Qi Gong, which fellow trumpeter Ingrid Jensen relates to "energy you get from within when you're in tune with not only the music, but with the physical, spiritual, emotional, and mental parts."[13] For Jensen, meditation "connects the instrument with my body."[14] During a crisis of faith, Bennie Wallace had "an encounter with a power that is inexplainable" and "was taken totally out of my physical mind," reaching a clarity he seeks to regain with regular meditation.[15] This "state of energy" also "takes you away from the conscious mind that seems to inhibit the intuitive process of playing."[16] Vocalist Theo Bleckmann has "developed a list of internal steps to get myself out of my ego, or false, self and back into my musical, or true, self."[17] Bassist Gary Peacock studied Zen and macrobiotics in Japan, writing occasionally for the influential *East-West Journal*. He has practiced *zazen* meditation since the 1970s, studies at New York's Zen Mountain Monastery, and leads prison meditation workshops. He believes that music actually prepared him for Zen, rather than the inverse. After years of approaching his instrument with the goal of mastery and self-expression, Peacock claims his playing improved by regaining his "beginner's mind" and focusing on sonic awareness: "the attention is on the sensory-emotional aspect...then I let it go."[18] For Peacock, this meditational focus on impermanence is realized continually in the already impermanent sonic medium; *zazen* is, like jazz, "a heightened sense of awareness."[19]

Percussionist Brian Adler pursues similar states using different foci. His first musical experience was "playing an Indian drum as an accompaniment to Sanskrit chants."[20] Adler, who "grew up in and around a meditation retreat center," was convinced that there was "more to life than meets the eye."[21] He and vocalist Sunny Kim provide improvisational accompaniment to sacred texts (e.g., the Sufi poet Rumi), seeing their work as part ritual and part meditational pursuit of what Adler calls "higher consciousness."[22] Attentiveness to texts facilitates a receptivity to sound that mirrors the conceptual surrender one seeks in meditation. Adler recalls that once he began to focus his music in this way, it "seemed to manifest from nowhere," in a musical flow that paralleled the flow of existence.[23] Openness to "that voice" behind the music "has to do with Freedom...a release from the suffering of one's own human limitations towards experiencing a greater union with a higher consciousness."[24] Jazz is a music "of the present moment," and Adler feels he plays his best when "I am not the one doing the playing," no longer "attached to the notes" but instead "a vessel to channel a greater unifying energy."[25]

Reedist Mark Whitecage was turned onto Zen by Eric Dolphy in the early 1960s, and for decades has incorporated meditational practices into his music with partner and fellow reedist Rozanne Levine. Levine is a lifelong student of religions, and with The Performance Group in 1970s Manhattan she explored "Buddhism, spirituality, anthroposophy, astrology,

American Indian lore."[26] Her involvement with yoga and improvisation developed alongside her use of "meditation and exercise" to facilitate "joining one's breath and mind to one's movement."[27] Levine told me she sees "life as a giant mandala," a perception she tries to convey through music ("a pathway to transcendence") and through chakra tuning.[28] With Whitecage she has built crystal structures for "tuning" vibrations, seeing them as "meditation tool[s] to widen our view of ourselves and to accept the multiplicity of life."[29] Musical meditation helps Levine "leave my thinking mind" to focus on "feeling and expressing the universal energy."[30] Percussionist Dan Weiss pursues such experience through the Indian method of *chilla*, "where the musician is left alone...[to] become one with the music."[31] Undergoing physical deprivation with only one's instrument, the demanding process is a different kind of attunement, one that "enhances awareness levels."[32]

Pianist Myra Melford once asked the Wisconsin River to heal her. The young Melford would later pursue the idea that "music is an attempt to recreate this internal, divine music, the primordial om, that is itself the same energy that creates all forms...and which is also the source of supreme bliss."[33] She became transfixed with the idea that when sound "vibrates at the right frequency to harmonize or create a resonance with the physical world," it enlightens and heals.[34] She told me that these beliefs made musical labels misleading since all that mattered was beauty and receptiveness to growth.[35] This sense of art surpassing limits has propelled her to perform with sacred texts and to become a rigorous "student of yoga and meditation" and martial arts, all processes aimed at dissolving perceptual boundaries as she does in her pan-stylistic improvisations (which reflect her interest in music ranging from gamelan to African percussion).[36] She links "being in a meditative state of focus"—where the self experiences bliss as perceptual boundaries dissolve—with "the aural space I want to build through music."[37]

Melford's yoga teacher directed her to Hindustani music, which prompted her use of harmonium drones and chant. After studying raga and meditation in India, Melford became interested in the intersection of Sufi poetry, pre-Socratic philosophy, and Buddhist meditation. She began to incorporate different modes and scales into her playing to reflect her aesthetic conviction that "all things flow...from all, one and from one, all."[38] Other musicians pursue such combinations as well. Pianist Marilyn Crispell has studied ley lines, astrology, and Gaia traditions and focuses especially on "[m]editation...going inside myself."[39] She feels this allows her music to connect "with your energy or with the primal energy that exists in the universe."[40]

Lacy brought the idea of focus and medium to the center of his multimedia explorations. He looked to Thelonious Monk, Cage, poets, and performance artists to understand how one line, one note could possess the gravity of a star. He was a patient player, allowing silence to speak, constructing spare improvisations that many likened to Japanese brush painting. In performance, Lacy seemed wholly deliberate but also intent on abandoning himself to something beyond his tune. Indeed, his music focused on emptying and musical conduits. He worried the boundary between improvisation and composition, and between genres, exploring aesthetics, politics, and spirituality. His instantly recognizable sound seemed to match his interest in the possibility of a wholly distinct identity that could merge, improvisationally, with the space and silence conditioning it.

During his formative years, he experienced several musical awakenings. First there was Bechet: "a certain *life force*, a *sound* rising up, a sublime shock."[41] Then, after a period in the Dixieland revival scene in 1950s Manhattan, Lacy collaborated with Cecil Taylor and experienced something like musical metanoia. It was Monk's music that was definitive, and Lacy compared it to Alice's looking glass: "[i]f we can get through the mirror, there's another country on the other side."[42] As Monk's bandmate for a time, Lacy heard the music like a strange altar call. He began to lead his own bands under Ezra Pound's modernist dictum "Make it new."[43] But for Lacy, innovation could come through renewed engagement with tradition, tilling and watering old earth rather than simply scorching it.

He spent time touring Europe and dived into the emerging free music scene there, compelled by the possibility and challenges of playing unconditioned by genre, instrument, or expectation. To Lacy, this was not just musically fresh; it also jibed with his catholic aesthetic and his growing sense of contemplation through sound, which he called "being on the brink of the unknown and being prepared for the leap."[44] After settling in Paris in 1970 with partner Irene Aëbi, Lacy grew convinced that this unknown could be most readily approached through a medium of focus and concentration, rather than simply free improvisation. He began composing settings for texts. Though he had begun working on his *Tao te Ching* suite by 1967, one of his first text choices was Buckminster Fuller's "The Sun," part of Lacy's long-standing effort to think through broader issues of cosmology, purpose, meditation, and meaning. Lacy said of this piece, "We set it like a priest's litany."[45]

Lacy was reared Jewish, but considered himself a "Jewgitive," refusing "to be bound by ethnic, racial, or cultural preconceptions."[46] For Lacy, artistic and spiritual development would come not so much through the erasure of the ego as the transformation of subjectivity, opened and permeated by the very processes it sought to facilitate. The uncluttered aesthetic he'd begun forging in 1950s New York—when "Zen was in the air, everyone was reading John Cage and thinking about sound and silence"—became central to Lacy's musical investigation of the edges of self and genre.[47] He could sound querulous and avian, unafraid to let a single note resound or to rework the same small kernel of a phrase, rather than fill all available space. Though interested in multiple media, Lacy's soprano seemed to tell stories about paring away, the discarding of experience as a mode of openness to surprise where music becomes "a device for inducing reverie…an articulation of time and/or space."[48] What was important was to play with appropriate focus and presence, a sense of music's simultaneous permanence and immateriality in "musicians' encounter with the spirit, in space and time."[49]

Lacy saw his six-part *Tao* suite as an experiment with temporality and selfhood. Lacy's broad interest in Asian religions and aesthetics led to *Traces* (which explored the texts of Ryokan), a long-standing collaboration with Japanese dancer Shiro Daimon, and a song-cycle rooted in Buddhist sacred texts. While he was "interested in many religions, spiritual matters," the *Tao te Ching* specifically compelled him as an orientation that might be beyond system, even beyond "religion."[50] He said, "I believe in what's good and right. I really think it's the same thing, God and good. I'm very religious, but I have my own religion. I read Lao Tzu."[51] Taoism kept Lacy focused on mystery and the unknown, on the meaning to be gleaned from the always-renewing process where the disciplined, receptive musician might encounter "magic." His music chased down such encounters with the unexpected and uncontrollable, as "phenomen[a] beyond technique. It's when the gods are smiling."[52] The improviser cannot get in the music's way, and should seek only to be open to what these smiling gods demand.

Jazz might then be a kind of language for expressing the ineffable, or the sound accompanying the silence that might otherwise fill this palpable unknown. It is perhaps sound that is the only real response available, since words fall flat and fail to embrace the provisionality of their "truths," already evaporating. Who made that sound, me or someone else? How did that perfect moment coalesce only to fade so quickly? Did you mean to do

FIGURE 6.1. Steve Lacy and Maarten Altena in concert. Photograph copyright William E. (Bill) Smith.

that or was it a mistake? Lacy describes this fragmentary, unresolving, un-stable creativity as "[n]ot exactly a blank—more like a blink...let the thing happen. It's not you that does it—it's IT that wants to be done."[53] Music's most powerful values are affective, not notational: it induces reflection ("life on its way...life on its way..."), suspends conventional time (a piercing, held tone that seems to float away from pulse), communicates in ways familiar (poetry and recitation) or unfamiliar (Lacy's lifelong fondness for duck calls).

Likening it to sculptors working from uncarved stone, Lacy insisted that "[m]usic always tells you what to do next."[54] In following it, the improviser serves as part of an intercession, an opening on listeners' behalf to the sound of the moment. Music cannot be constrained by form, expectation, or ego (especially not the ego of the audacious player who instructs listeners how to hear). It might use tradition (a text, or perhaps a brief resonance of *gagaku* or plainsong) but only to move beyond tradition's constraints to a place where aspirants (picking up on a widespread impulse in religions) use art and beauty as the vehicle for meditation, identity, and change. But is it "religion"? Perhaps this religiosity—this heightened being in the world, this lit awareness—has something to do with keeping things alive, with sustaining a certain vitality, a spirit even. Like the very idea of jazz, or form, different media were for Lacy vessels for thinking about vessels that can be used by other vessels, musicians. They are worlds made up of crystallized relationality, of always-gone improvised moments hung like stars in our memory. Vessels, then, are the way to focus the vessel of the self. Like the "little mystical texts" he returned to, improvising was "about life and death, and faith and hope and prayer, and communication."[55] Like Walter Benjamin's angel announcing the redemption of the past, music announces the meaning of what is always already passing away from the moment the note escapes the instrument, each idea another exhalation bringing us forward in time. In this, improvising recalls Ralph Ellison's reflections on losing and finding identity simultaneously. There is your reed, your mouthpiece, your lead sheet, your poem, and here is your moment, your friends, your audience, and your life. What is it all for? What do you believe in its presence, in its wake? Filled with a kind of faith, but perhaps a stronger resistance to formulae, Lacy sidestepped such questions to his end, saying only, "We don't determine music, the music determines us; we only follow it to the end of our life: then it goes on without us."[56]

The Next Pregnant Second: Indeterminate Relations

With Lacy we see that meditational focus brings musicians to a kind of limit experience, in terms of perception, ability, and even the body. But for the many players who do not use forms/vessels as Lacy did, perhaps do not even use meditation, how might jazz shape the relation between self, sound, and spirits? The late saxophonist Thomas Chapin also read his dog-eared copy of the *Tao te Ching* every day, thinking of Gil Barretto's sense that "[t]he inner calling acts as third force, making the art into the vehicle of transcendence."[57] Just before his death from leukemia, Chapin noted that "it is best to be in both worlds, Music as the bridge."[58] This notion of music as a bridge between worlds, state of awareness, or modes of being is central to yogic traditions that posit union as vibratory, or to ecstatic Christian or Islamic traditions in which sonic immanence is performed bodily. Saxophonist David Murray has noted the similarity between jazz performances and "spirit possession": "the feeling that I've felt so many times in the church of people just going completely off."[59] Control and abandon in moments of peak experience, transforming how you occupy the cosmos. These are the terms of religion, and they are heard everywhere in jazz, here in the experience of losing yourself to sound in order to establish particular relations through it.

Gilbert Rouget once wrote about sound's ability to induce states of "ecstatic contemplation" or states of "possession."[60] In spirits rejoicing, both states converge through the avowed co-presence of players and spirits, made possible because sound is "intrinsically and unignorably relational," with knowledge and experience possible only through interactivity.[61] This is what happens when the music simply overwhelms and reorients you. Saxophonist Darius Jones, another child of Pentecostalism, notes, "I'm searching for the Holy Ghost." And in this quest "music can touch you… it's literally alive and it's touching you. That's what spirituality is."[62] Percussionist Joe Stone believes that many musicians are attracted to free improvisation because they want to get out of technique, "even get out of themselves."[63] French horn specialist Tom Varner likens jazz to "heightened reality," an evocation of feeling that aims both to deepen and lessen mystery, to generate compassion and openness.[64] Dave Brubeck speaks of moments "when you can be beyond yourself," while fellow pianist Vijay Iyer avers that musicians can experience autoscopy in performance.[65] Keith Jarrett acknowledges "a surrender that overcomes us as players… and leads us on to the next pregnant second."[66] This is a condition that leads nearly to trance states, which Jarrett calls "a sacred thing."[67] Percussionist William Hooker insists that when receiving energy from such experiences, he must "offer up all of my energy… to a higher source."[68] This sound-energy is, to percussionist Paul Murphy, a way to "find my relationship to both the physical and metaphysical universe and the creator"; he finds these peak experiences and heightened states "similar to meditation but meditation is not felt by others."[69] Bassist Adam Lane exults in the indefinability of such experiences, praising them as "connections to the universe...sweet slaps in the face that make you 'jump for joy'...[and] obliterate reality."[70]

IT IS THIS non-referentiality of experience that is most compelling to some improvisers, echoing the disdain for category heard so regularly in these stories. Is it jazz? Is it religion? Does it matter? These were the questions tenor saxophonist Ellery Eskelin and I kept coming back to over a long afternoon in his apartment, sipping lemon water. Eskelin once told me that he was influenced by almost every sound the tenor could produce, a statement that reveals his desire to live and play beyond distinctions.[71] What is salient about improvising for Eskelin is "[t]aking what you know into the unknown," something he described as having "heavy overlap with how spirituality is talked about."[72] His mother played organ in Pentecostal churches and his father, musical eccentric Rodd Keith, once was associated with the PTL ministries, a family gravitation to intensity and the ecstatic not lost on Eskelin. While the intensity of playing tenor surpassed the intensity of the Baptist Church for him, Eskelin is still drawn to such experiences and refuses to distinguish between religiosity, physicality, and music, saying, "I crave an integrated experience."[73] While he practices meditation and yoga—striving to be "one-minded, committed to what you're doing in the moment"—Eskelin returns consistently to the inability of language and categorization to capture the experience he is nonetheless tempted to call spiritual. The language of "another force...guiding" the music, or of egolessness, seems to belie the physicality and rationality improvisation requires. He told me subsequently that "I've come to recognize that much of what I had been grappling with is addressed in Zen... [which] helps get beyond some of the mental traps that come up when trying to parse out the 'big questions'."[74] But somehow, despite the limitations of language and self, Eskelin says, "[M]y inability to put things in spiritual and religious terms goes into the horn."[75] And what comes out might be beyond language too.

Pianist Connie Crothers is fascinated by indeterminacy too, but unlike Eskelin embraces the terms "religion" and "jazz" for the possibilities they contain. A student of Lennie Tristano, Crothers insists that art can overcome pessimism and ignorance, "because to me the story's not over until it's *over*. And there's a creative possibility up until that final moment."[76]

Creativity for her is "all *about*" the moment one recognizes "you didn't know you could feel or experience *that*."[77] These experiences awaken something within the self, leaving the experiencer with "a much deeper grasp of not only the thing itself but what it refers to, you know, the moment you're in and what it means."[78] Music plunges you into "the creative mystery" that human beings share; in fact, this is why Crothers agrees with Sheila Jordan's testimony "jazz is my religion," since musical collaboration exemplifies what Crothers believes is "the real content of spirituality": "[i]t's not like something that exists external to you that you adapt your own consciousness to...it lives within us," and we give shape to it and relate to it through forms, externals that resonate with what is "deep within...I think that's what the soul means."[79]

Trumpeter Dennis Gonzalez once advised me, "Bivins, breed your own rhythm section."[80] We had just performed together when Gonzalez was on tour with sons Aaron and Stefan in their trio Yells at Eels. This sense of connectivity and relation is intimately bound up with Gonzalez's sense of religiosity, where what Crothers calls the "deep within" is made real through contact with realms and figures outside of us. Reared a conservative Baptist in South Texas, Gonzalez recalls stern hellfire sermons blended with "beautiful and heartfelt" ritual and music, feelings he explicitly seeks to realize in his intense, jubilant writing and improvising.[81] Musically active from age five, Gonzalez says, "My life is a constant search," a notion reflected in music that draws from classical, South African township, spirituals, free jazz, and punk rock. Gonzalez's experience with the largely African American music of his tradition led to regular collaborations with African American jazz players in the South, where he established particularly strong connections with New Orleans musicians Kidd Jordan and Alvin Fielder. He also sometimes attended his neighborhood's Catholic church and recalls the "mysterious symphony" of the mass and his awakening desire "to understand those things that I could not see...a hidden universe existed somewhere."[82] In relation to these other places and other spirits, Gonzalez believes that artists strive "to invent one's own universes," spaces and/or sounds of connection with hidden things.[83]

After the demise of the DAAGNIM (Dallas Association for Avant-Garde and Neo-Impressionist Music), an organization he cofounded, Gonzalez recorded his early "Hymn Series." Gonzalez, who regularly plays his horn in church, dedicates his hymns to "the ones who have given me the courage to keep...expressing the deepest part of my Spirit."[84] These hymns to figures like Don Cherry, Bob Marley, and Julius Hemphill (whom he refers to as "witnesses" and "Elders") reflect the music of their dedicatee, and incorporate idioms including Persian classical music, Malian griot songs, or the spirituals that still compel Gonzalez.[85] They race exuberantly, or dwell in a contemplative atmosphere. In adapting traditional music or composing his own religious pieces, playing jazz itself becomes a religious action for Gonzalez, with all the provisionality and ephemerality involved in that formulation: each trumpet line part of a catechism, each rim shot an amen, the whole comprising what he calls "beautiful sounds of prayer and hope."[86] Jazz is music of the unknown, and playing it can bring people into what Gonzalez calls "the Mystical Spiritual, the undefined region between religious practices from the world of people and Spirit."[87] He hears his music as "a meeting place where [audiences] and I connect and communicate, where the energy of that life force crosses over into me…[a] lucid dream they can use to reshape their spirits."[88] The spirits within and without can travel as rapidly and mysteriously as sound itself, connecting what Gonzalez calls "the Infinite" within us and a material world that "hides many planes of existence."[89]

The notion of spirits being present in the music is widespread, often attributed to the peak experiences so many players chase. Horace Silver used to talk to relatives "in my head," as a way of preparing to "pass over into that other dimension" while he played.[90] Jemeel Moondoc noted that once "the music got so intense that spirits came into the room…we were calling the ancestors, and they came."[91] These things beyond us, within us, seem made really present in notes, pulses, timbres, and lines, their sounds like gateways into those hidden realms Gonzalez notes or, once gone, memories stamping us with the transformative experience language cannot grasp. The very fluidity of sound may be analogous to those numinous experiences of overwhelming presence and being; something must be responsible for this heightened clarity of space-time. Perhaps the world itself is sound, as in the Hatha yoga tradition, and these experiences are of resonant beings listening to themselves, and thus to God.[92] It may be what guitarist Tisziji Munoz calls "sublime Isness," a manifestation of "pure Spirit" that the improviser "can communicate…by the creative fire of unconsciousness or super-conscious mind alone," seeking not to understand but simply to play with tongues and hands of fire.[93] The prison house of language may be inescapable; but if you can hear or even nearly see the air itself, as I recall from a Brooklyn performance with percussionist Tatsuya Nakatani, those "pregnant moments" lend themselves to poetry, whose very authorial possibility turns back to reflect the experience's power. Jazz is thus the medium of spirit communication and spirit-stuff itself. As percussionist Adam Rudolph puts it, musicians "arrange these overtones as they move through time...like a radio signal from the cosmos."[94] The simultaneous inward and outward voyage that sound enables means, as Narada Burton Greene told me, "we're all instruments" that "connect to the inner Spirit."[95] Or as Art Blakey said, inversely, jazz is "like something moving from the Creator to the artist to the audience."[96]

Small Little Gods: Overwhelmed by Presence

No less a skeptic than Friedrich Nietzsche once wrote, "[O]ne could hardly reject altogether the idea that one is merely incarnation, merely mouthpiece, merely a medium of overpowering forces."[97] Far from Nietzsche's idiom, jazz musicians have consistently announced the existence of similar states when seeking to facilitate the movement Blakey noted. That these experiences are sacred is usually considered a given, whether shorn of traditional reference altogether or inclusive of particulars. In expressions of gratitude, submission, and exultation, musicians describe themselves as recipients of divinely bestowed creative energy, where improvisation is seen as a way of establishing one's place in a sonically sacred cosmos. So in playing the sound of the cosmos in jazz, the impetus is either to remove the self altogether (so as to get out of sound's way) or to transform the body into an instrument or vessel of the divine.

For Arthur Blythe, the musician blows life into the horn: "I'm a receiver of the musical spirit....I just opened up, Jack, and became a receptacle for the shit."[98] Vocalist Carmen Lundy notes, "I feel like something is just singing through me. That's what I mean by the spiritual thing."[99] Drummer Shannon Jackson expands, saying, "It's a cleansing experience which in a religion they would say...'It's a feeling of being able to communicate with all living things.'"[100] Leroy Williams likens this to "oneness with the music...like you're in tune with the universe."[101] Billy Higgins says, "[A] musician is just a transformer....I receive the music from somewhere else."[102] Keith Jarrett speaks about abandonment, and trust in the sound, so that improvisation "is a 'blazing forth' of a 'Divine Will.'"[103] Adam Rudolph modifies this description, characterizing performance as a matter of "humbly trying to be prepared to let things flow out," channeling one's inner voice and a cosmic creative power through an instrument.[104] Quincy Jones has always "trusted the divinity part....I'm just a terminal, a conduit for the music...that melody has to come straight from

God."[105] The famously self-critical Sonny Rollins admits, "I let the music play me... that's my best work."[106] And fellow tenorist Charles Lloyd talks about playing as a "chance to try to tell the truth" since "music goes to states that are so much deeper" than language.[107] Some musicians have even avowed the reality of such experiences while critical of religions. Hampton Hawes once spat, "Fuck a cross, a church and all that... man-made shit"; "I play for the Creator... and let everything come out of me, like my body is a tool."[108] And Nina Simone once said, with acid humor, "I am very aware that I am an instrument. I have fights with God every day."[109]

What unites all these expressions is the conviction that sound is energy, living through you, coming through hands and lungs. To experience it in these registers, with this intensity, is thought to be a kind of contact with the divine itself. Jane Ira Bloom experiences an "alpha state" where everything becomes sound; Joanne Brackeen senses energy surrounding her piano and strives to "play from that form"; and Cassandra Wilson describes the "trance-type thing that I go into" when "surrendering, or being a vessel."[110] This opening of consciousness allows the improviser to, as India Cooke notes, "channel psychic energy."[111] The subtle body can see itself when this openness and flow is achieved: Jackie Pickett reports that "[w]hen the group enters an 'out of body' space... [you can] see the group playing."[112] This is not so much meditation or relation as a modulation of those states into an experience of co-presence, player and spirit. LaDonna Smith describes improvisation as "a vehicle for connection of my Spirit with the Great Mystery and Cosmic Creator. As an improviser, I am thankful to be a listener and a player in the direct flow of the Universe."[113] Multi-instrumentalist Daniel Carter also believes that improvising is a mode of connection with the divine. Becoming attuned to the possibility of being the divine's instrument, and cultivating states of "openness," is as important as any technique.[114] Carter calls this "a process of dismantling old connections and building new ones... trusting the flash."[115] Don Cherry once said, "[P]laying music to reflect God is a whole reality that holds the truth. That's it."[116] And Darius Jones concluded, "It's the life-force, you know what I'm saying? I don't have a choice anymore."[117]

These storms of energy and inspiration, the awareness of sound-spirit moving through the atmosphere into and out of you, are linked with processes like automatic writing, spirit mediumship, and consorting with angels. For bassist Stephan Crump, the pursuit of such moments is somewhat more modest in what it can attain: "[w]e're dealing with fundamental aspects of our humanity, and you can't let yourself be paralyzed by how dark it is" in society.[118] Finding "spiritual fulfillment through work," Memphis-born Crump plays with a limberness and full-toned assurance that seem perfectly responsive to the music. In some sense this flows from his pre-performance ritual, in which he "meditate[s]" and "spend[s] time focusing on getting into the zone, connecting to the music."[119] Playing is, for Crump, not just about technique but "what information is chosen from the universe"; "you're not really creating the music so much as you are a conduit . . . letting the universe flow through you."[120] Music involves "traveling to another dimension" constituted by different perspectives that, if "arrived at in a harmonious manner," can make some kind of "truth": "this is why the arts are so important to our humanity, because the act of creating demands a heightening of your sense of empathy."[121]

Fellow bassist David Friesen, who plays in a fantastically expressive manner often as lithe as a cello, identifies these experiences with a very robust form of Christianity. Reared Jewish, Friesen converted at fourteen and came to accept that "you're able to discern truth by the power of the Holy Spirit," something he feels translates directly into music-making.[122] Friesen attended Multnomah School of the Bible and started playing jazz in coffeehouses. The intimacy and sincerity of the coffeehouse scene, combined with jazz's emotional purity, convinced Friesen that music was a divine gift: "the Lord filled the note that I played, and the substance was love. . . . [I]t has nothing to do with me, it has everything to do with the Lord."[123]

One of Friesen's chief concerns was to practice focusing, giving your all, in order to "take my eyes off myself so I can listen and be able to respond creatively to what I hear."[124] A sandaled Friesen played soft hymns to open up passionate, effusive solo coffeehouse concerts, where he became known as a "resident guru."[125] Following a regimen where he would "seek the Lord and pray . . . and practice," Friesen experienced a vision of a pool filled with colors never seen before.[126] He claims the Lord appeared, saying, "This is a pool I've given to you, and it will fulfill the note."[127] The pool *was* a note, its multitudes flowing into the world through sound. More than this, Friesen says the Lord told him that the substance of the notes "is my love," which "will splash and cover" the audiences who hear them.[128]

Playing is thus a kind of ministry, showing through commitment, passion, and humility that sound announces God's kingdom. Friesen has continued having visions reminding him that he plays to give glory to God. The musician, God's instrument, must only "be still in the Spirit and listen," must "follow the note" instead of the ego.[129] This total concentration might be thought of as the improviser becoming a vessel of trust, striving to hear God's voice and do only what the music requires, to "see the light of God's love—and that's how the music was going to be *used*."[130] So, as Friesen put it, "[M]usic has its own power, and it's the Lord that gives it its own power or not."[131] The music "is coming through me; it's not coming from me."[132] The musician must simply "walk by faith," get the self out of the way, keep following God's notes, and "He'll take care of the rest."[133]

Tenor saxophonist Ivo Perelman occupies a differently populated cosmos, one equally committed to spiritually driven improvisation. His style can be incendiary, yet is also possessed of an emotional woundedness; from the effusiveness of Gato Barbieri to the lyrical howl of Albert Ayler, Perelman synthesizes saxophonics as surely as practitioners in his native Brazil combine religiosities. He had, by his own account, "a Brazilian-Jewish upbringing."[134] He went to a Jewish school, studied the Bible, but he also had "one foot in the Afro-Brazilian *Candomblé*, religion."[135] He was attracted to the latter's ritual and expressivity, where "entities come down and they take over people's bodies."[136] For Perelman, spirits are present whenever jazz is really played. Indeed, he suggested to me that "you can't play this music without at least having an access to the spiritual world."[137] While some would hear in this statement Perelman's debt to a Kabbalistic "sense of union with the Divine," Perelman—who has performed Jewish liturgical music—senses spirits operating on a more general, vibrational level.[138] He notes that "the moment I put my hand on the horn and it starts vibrating, I turn into a different being."[139]

Two things are at work here. First, Perelman believes jazz is "the only art form that allows one to mimic the Creator" since "you are mirroring the creative forces of the universe."[140] But because "the dramatic forces are so strong, you become a meditator while you do this, you become deeply spiritual."[141] In this sense, jazz reminds Perelman of "those Afro-Brazilian rituals...where one person is embodying the spiritual entities, and a lot more is being affected by the strong process...[s]o people are benefiting from every single creative music that takes place."[142] Self becomes sound, becomes multitude, as the distance between beings is collapsed in the urgent sonic now. To Perelman, this is music's basic nature and also its promise, if played well. "You have to be there without being there," he says, in a state that is equally rational and abandoned, "a subject of stronger forces but at the same time mirroring those forces that are godly, we are small little gods each of us."[143] For Perelman, jazz's very spontaneity makes it "the ultimate continuous religion," its cathartic flow and irresolvability opening up fundamental questions that "deepen your sense of humanity," showing that beauty is possible despite (even because of) the elusiveness of answers.[144] He calls jazz "an open wound of society, and religion" since it exposes the fragility of our certainties; but jazz is also "a *sangria*" that teaches us "acceptance and surrender."[145]

Fire Being Sound: Mysticism

Having come this far with spirits rejoicing, the improviser now stands outside of traditions, communities, narratives, and rituals to become a body transformed in its urgent, quickened relation to a sonically alive cosmos. From this vessel pours sonic star-stuff. This cosmos will be explored in the next chapter, but the transformed self—through meditation, non-referential peak experiences, and becoming vessels—opens into a consideration of mystical dissolution, too.[146] While this theme has been prominent in jazz since Coltrane, few musicians have articulated it as consistently and publicly as contrabassist William Parker. The Bronx native has since the 1970s crafted his unique sense of rhythmic momentum, a burbling, almost incessant pizzicato that is at home in free space as it is in pulse-driven contexts. Just as compelling is his arco work, where his bowing creates an eldritch sound that seems to emerge from the astral plane. For Parker, these are just some of the infinite sounds of the Creator, in whose service improvisers seek to convey openness, generosity, ecstasy, and gratitude through music.

An avid reader of mystical literature, Parker was absorbed by South Asian sacred texts as a young player and named many of his tones and techniques based on concepts he studied. He meditated and prayed regularly before performance, hoping that "[b]y emptying himself of extraneous and mundane thoughts, he could evoke the 'spirit.'"[147] He claims to have received most of his musical ideas in visions and dreams (including several vivid ones involving Native American figures like Geronimo and Quanah Parker). Parker saw free improvisation as the means by which musicians become "vehicles through which the Creator sends vibrations."[148] Through a kind of religio-musical intonation, Parker reported experiencing new emotional states, going into trances while playing, feeling his bass levitate off the stage, and receiving images "of heaven or ... of a world that is at peace."[149] He contends that while playing, "you go into this corridor of light and if you play the right tones, there's a door at the end and inside are all the secrets of life."[150] Parker calls this "an awakened trance state," a kind of dilated perception that "opens you up to the other, other worlds."[151]

The language Parker uses to describe this sound invokes the mystical Godhead, the God-beyond-God. Others, however, hear it as an expression of post-1960s combinative spirituality, of the sort often dismissed as banal or as less concerned with traditional particulars than with self-fashioning (although it should be noted that the elements being combined, such as dream contact with spirits, have deep roots in American metaphysical religions). Parker believes, however, that the very abstraction of the language enables listeners to "contrast the awareness of joy with the lack of such experiences" in society, giving them a way of articulating alternate forms of knowing and experiencing.[152] While he believes that music teaches one how to live well, he looks gimlet-eyed at American injustice and pronounces: "we were doomed from jump street."[153] Music can at least temporarily relieve the experience of these blasted landscapes: "one note can make flowers grow."[154] Through contemplation and realization in sound, music can become coextensive with the divine. Parker traces this insight to his early perception of music "as a religious experience some want like a miracle of a burning bush with the fire being sound."[155] When lit by this sound, the improvising self expands compassionately "to allow the music to flow through us ... to give birth to itself."[156]

Parker's longtime colleague, the late saxophonist David S. Ware, was also deeply invested in jazz as mystical awareness. Reared Baptist, Ware grew up listening to gospel and jazz tenors like Illinois Jacquet. After hearing the call of Coltrane and spending time with Cecil Taylor in the 1970s, Ware came to associate music with "the search for what man is about ... the expansion of consciousness."[157] But though Ware's huge tenor sound, with its fierce upper-register flights and melodic innovations, was linked to avant-garde jazz, he was a close associate of Sonny Rollins, whom Ware idolized and whose investigations of yoga and meditation Ware emulated. Rollins later taught Ware how to circular breathe, a practice Rollins insisted had many "spiritual ramifications" and which was instrumental in cementing the musical and the religious for Ware.[158] When Ware dropped out in the 1980s, he practiced obsessively and meditated on the *Bhagavad Gita*, whose teachings were relevant not simply because they brought him into the fold of a particular tradition but because they pointed beyond all modes of human classification to "that cosmic reality that makes all related."[159]

Ware saw music as "the secret ingredient" for realizing "the larger cosmic Self."[160] The tones themselves bring forth particular modes of knowledge and embodiment that Ware claimed led to "Pure Consciousness or God."[161] The often tempestuous nature of his music was to him a reflection of the ceaseless change of existence, but also a plea to be led to the One. Music both expresses and catalyzes openness to this change, leading to an immersive, expansive mindset in which Ware says people can learn to "let the river flow."[162] To this end, Ware sought to open what he called the "third ear" when improvising. And indeed, his music possessed an incredible sense of flow, his heavy, sometimes caustic tone shaping one urgent idea after another, headlong on the torrent of sound. Whether finding the cosmos through an old standard, or verging into ecstasies on his own compositions, Ware believed he was striving for "aware[ness] of our source . . . because that's where peace is."[163]

Ware approached these ideas from several different vantage points, almost all non-Christian. After emerging from retirement in the 1990s, he sought to achieve through sound an awareness of the Tao, about which he said: "if you see things from that level, everything makes sense."[164] This was a totality he sought to express through his horn, feeling that it enabled him to see existence not so much from outside the self, but from "within your higher self," which is the stuff of life, the stuff of God.[165] Ware insisted on "using that saxophone as a pathway to God," but sought ultimately not only the removal or disciplining of the ego but a kind of mystical absorption.[166] He said, "I want to merge into the absolute . . . go to the perfect state and stay there."[167] Improvising was for Ware a way of understanding a Creator who also improvises and also to accept that "[t]here are forces that we have no control over."[168] During his last decade, suffering from complications from kidney failure, Ware began a rigorous study of Vedic literature, compelled by its conviction that "all subjects are related . . . all subjects come from God."[169] Ware heard each note as a fragment of creation, emerging from and returning to its creator.

He abandoned entirely the idea of playing music for himself and gave "my music over to a force of nature called Ganesh."[170] Ware revered Ganesh's relation with "arts and science and wisdom."[171] He wrote poems and performed dedications to the unity of Shiva and Shakti, to the Maharishi Mahesh Yogi and the power of mantras to create bliss, and to the divine creativity and mystery he saw embodied in Ganesh, who he described as "intimately connected to this world. . . . He is one of us and we are of him."[172] And of his last solo performances before his death in 2012, Ware noted that each one "express[es] different orders of Being. When you listen, learn to open your third ear. . . . It will expand who you think you are."[173]

FIGURE 6.2. David S. Ware, performing solo in Italy. Photograph by Luciano Rossetti © Phocus Agency.

And listening to these last improvisations, their cries and long spooling lines and rough punctuations all bound together in the mutable movement of being alive, you could almost hear Ware's desire to be brought in "to the subtle astral planes...out of this tormented world into a world of light and pureness."[174]

Pianist Matthew Shipp explicitly identifies with mystical traditions and conceives of his music as a mode of relation to the flow of time, one that problematizes the body, language, and assumptions about religion. Shipp's style is urgent but pensive, his pianism billowing up in dark clouds that create their own sonic atmosphere. He told me his musical sensibility is shaped by "my whole kind of gnostic philosophy of what language is," describing the improviser as a "logos generator" who "partakes of the metaphysical quest of generating a musical universe."[175] Shipp once trained for the Episcopal priesthood and remains fascinated by ritual and "the process of alchemy in as far as we translate that to the alchemy of musical language."[176] Shipp claims he has "always been into music for religious reasons," since "religion has to do with the generation of the word," the latter term analogous to a musical note.[177] But if music is a sonic language, and the improviser seeks to deconstruct it, what happens to "religion"?

Depending on his mood, Shipp might describe music "as a way to silence the mind" or refer to "the science of placing notes as a kind of Kabbalah."[178] Yet he is just as likely to profess that he is chasing down cosmic energy and vibrations, dismissing religions altogether as naming and reducing things improperly. Perhaps this is simply a function of Shipp's abiding interest in language, for—like many musicians in this book—he openly embraces the term "spirituality" and revels in its synthetic possibilities: "[s]pirituality is, for me, the understanding of frequency and energy and how a universe or a coherent language is generated from said energy."[179] But while religions seek to understand the processes and patterns of the universe, Shipp believes they fail to tap into the links between intelligence, spontaneous creation, language, and sonic order. So, he concludes, "[W]hy deal with the religions? Just approach the generating force of super intelligence in and of itself."[180]

Yet in one of the same switchbacks you hear in his music, Shipp also embraces specific religious figures and traditions nonetheless. He claims to "operate out of a whole Christian mystic tradition like people like William Blake, St. John of the Cross or Meister Eckhart."[181] He speaks frequently of mystics and renunciants, stating his desire to "retire the world" like a *sannyasin*.[182] And while there is, despite his music's abstraction, a profound materiality and physicality to Shipp's playing (as well as a sometimes stirring, hymnal quality), his thinking is rooted equally in Emersonian speculation, mystical reckonings with the limits of ostensive reference, and highly esoteric readings of Christian kenosis, creation, and resurrection. God, he explains, is a verb rather than a static noun, and "Christ in the middle is the pineal gland, the third eye, which looks inward and brings us life."[183] He describes the New Testament as a "solar myth" and notes that it was Christ's revolutionary genius to understand "the original energy that generated the universe," and of which we all partake on the vibrational level.[184]

This is precisely what mainline traditions have lost, for Shipp, and what musical creativity might restore. The very meaning of the virgin birth, he suggests, is that "the energies of the universe are always being born anew and language continually regenerates itself."[185] The ossification of jazz tradition also overlooks the eternally regenerating vibratory order: "I mean who gives a fuck about Duke Ellington? He's worm meat."[186] What is eternal is the change that improvisers tap into when playing, insight into which is common across the mystical traditions that inspire Shipp and also of increasing interest to American practitioners who would fuse alternative spiritualities with popular cosmology. Contemplation and sound invention take one into "the higher room, which is going up for the Last Supper" or "that unity that is the Godhead."[187] The Cross is "a metaphor for the Tree of Life" connecting all existence through vibration; Adam and Eve symbolize divinity as the unity and synthesis of opposites; and what results is cosmic consciousness, "the transubstantiation of notes" into "the pure electricity of the universe."[188]

Shipp improvises beyond Christianity too. He ranges in conversation between references to Helena Blavatsky and Annie Besant, William Reich's orgone accumulator and Jacob Boehme's *urgrund*. He invokes perennial philosophy, saying, "[I]f you're Walt Whitman or a Zen Buddhist there is no difference," only the mathematical frequencies of music that turn the "body electric" into a "circular temple."[189] To Shipp, the cosmos was generated in an *illo tempore* of pure sound, whose magnetic frequencies still resonate like background radiation, a big bang giving way to eternal pulse, awaiting the improviser attuned to the song of heaven like J. S. Bach, Hildegard von Bingen, and Emanuel Swedenborg. At the edge of consciousness, and in the molecules of fingers pressed to ivory, "you're aligning yourself with the cosmic rhythm" by becoming a self through the connection to frequencies, and the flow within them.[190] What happens, Shipp says, is the state of "Flow X," where through the exchange of intentional music and cosmic receptivity, infinite possibility exists in a charged musical moment. He prefers to use the bass register to explore this modality, likening it to Emerson's phrase, "I and the abyss."[191]

Beyond "jazz" and beyond "religion," the improviser finds the silence of the void and the sheer infinity of harmonics, singing in blood and interstellar dust beyond "the cultural assumptions to the pure electricity of the universe."[192] The improviser is also grounded, as when Shipp claims, "I believe in an America as exemplified by Whitman and Emerson but America has never reached its own poetic nature, therefore it has become a seething cauldron of materialism and greed."[193] Perhaps he is actually more like Melville's Bartleby, then, preferring not to accept sociological or conceptual givens. Or perhaps the endless openness of improvisation echoes another Emersonian assertion, "I become a transparent eye-ball," where building the cosmos repeatedly *ab novo* shows how "atoms hook and un-hook, move in dream-life sequences, ejaculate themselves from the deepest recesses of the subconscious and become spirit turning into a piece of nature."[194] The sheer range of Shipp's reference surpasses the conceptual limits of "religion." All that matters is the ascent in sound: "if you were able to really delve into that pure pool of electricity, you would transcend being a human being and become an angel, and therefore disappear."[195]

FROM MEDITATION TO relation, selflessness to mysticism, we see here a range of improvised (and improvising) subjectivities constituted through "religion," all means of rejecting the control of form and social constraint in the name of openness to divine experience. John Corbett notes that musicians who confront technology and instrumental limits inevitably do so using the very modernist categories—"self," "expression," and "voice"—that partly form their constraints.[196] But in the relational spirituality, med-itational media, self-emptying, and mysticism embraced by these musicians, we see the simultaneous fragmentation of the unitary subject—leading to a desire to disappear completely—and its reconstitution in sound, alongside spirits. Spirits rejoicing may seem initially to exemplify the modernist self's scorn for particularity. But these musicians seek to break down the boundary separating them from their instrument, and from the universe, leading to images of disembodied instruments and bodies everywhere, near ghosts of self and machine chasing spirit with a butterfly net. We hear from these players that sounds must be made to flow only as themselves; but they must also, as we must, work in the service of the spirits they also strive to acknowledge by their very articula-tion. Music speaks through the player, who must get outside of the self in order for the real music to arrive; but this sound, which is understood as religious in its essence, can also only emerge through the individual's distinctive expressive powers, the practice of which is an additional religiosity.

Sound, that gift of the gods, is also the medium of self-invention and self-abnegation, each activity tethered to an intention and conviction that it is religious. Suspended in moments of time pregnant with meaning, sonic potentials realized become indices of other worlds into which the abandoned self is transported, each struck note dulling the ego, each vibration removing another blinder to perception. Music heralds worlds, made equally of relation and of the sheer flow of immediate experience. While musicians disagree about the survival of the will in these enhanced moments, the absorption through music into something larger is what resonates consistently across these encounters where music lifts off and spirits rejoice.

These musical suspensions of the self occur in the condensation of time and aesthetic abundance said to be beyond ego, drawn by the imperative to cease theorizing selfhood and simply play. These experiences are wholly real to those who have them. But what portrait of the religious can be fashioned from what is said and unsaid? There are echoes, in these descriptions of vessel-states, of religions speculating about the subtle body ascending beyond the flesh, into a realm of electromagnetism, vibration, conscious energy endowed with purpose. Improvisation actualizes consciousness of these realities as religious ones, and also transforms this consciousness through involvement in creative action: energy sits, waiting to be tapped, but also exists through the processes in which jazz participates, processes understood as connections with the real rather than the perfection of the self.

These explorations also present us with an opportunity for thinking about and hearing differently how musicians become conscious of their own religiousness, even if that term is scorned. In this one could certainly connect these musicians not just with a broad realm of esoteric traditions but to aesthetic theorizing, including various formulations of ineffability at the intersection of the aesthetic and the religious. These are, however, not just debates about cognition and attributions, since the sounds and languages herein situate these reckonings with subjectivity (and the limits of scholarly analysis of them) in musical settings that collapse any distinction between aesthetic and spirit.[197] Improvising is understood as a mode of directing consciousness and intention in ways avowed as "spiritual" or "religious"; and in these ascriptions, and their dissolution in improvised sound, something about the musicians' experience of their world, of music, of spirits, is changed phenomenologically, whether or not observers can see or notate it.[198]

Making music is thus about fittingness and submission to those powers that bestow the gifts of sound and those patterns of tonal relation in-
herent in the religious fabric of things. But it is also, precisely in the
degree to which the states of awakening and receptivity discussed in this
chapter are possible, about not fitting into any a priori models of music
or religion, relationships or time. As William James once wrote, "[I]t
is . . . the inner dispositions of man himself which form the center of interest."[199] The Jamesian sense that aesthetics can strengthen conviction,
or that "unseen powers" have sway (a "sphere of influence") over our
actions in (and dispositions toward) the world, looms large in jazz's
senses of religiosity.[200] And these intuitions of the infinite, the experiences
of intimate spirits, also signal a mode of creative nonparticipation in mainstream American culture going back to at least the Transcendentalists. If
change occurs through the cultivation of these states—which edify, expand the self, and make the listener aware of religious presence—then
we can hear spirits rejoicing as a sonic current through traditions of
American self-fashioning and reflection that link nineteenth-century
metaphysicals and contemporary meditation practitioners, channeling
communities, and ecstatic chanters.

Improvisation that aims to rejoice with the spirits thus, as Courtney
Bender writes of metaphysical experiences, "live[s] within bodies that are
always attuned to the immanent divine."[201] The belief in vessel experiences, musical mental transformations, and relations with spirits are both
the substance of what many jazz musicians call spirituality and the vehicles through which they name and give shape to it. The music itself seems
often, in Parker's thrumming bass or Lacy's incisive lines, to evoke the
merging and intensification that it pursues. This suggestive parallel—
where descriptions of vessel-states are understood as mere descriptive vessels themselves—shows the unity of what Bender calls "an experience and
its account."[202] Post hoc accounts of spirits rejoicing in jazz thus translate
what is largely regarded as untranslatable—that smoke Ned Rothenberg
warned me I was chasing—but they are also experienced doubly in the
context of wordless, often free-form sound. These are experiences both of
and beyond the body, resonating in a long history of American metaphysical practices and imaginings, rooted in the physical disciplines of music-
making that seeks to play the heart of the world or nature's vibratory
essence against a tone-deaf culture. Among these ineffabilities and noetic
states moves musical presence, which musicians claim simply to know,
insisting that the spirit is working. If they confront us once more with the

problem of language, we find for the players in this chapter specifically that this very fleetingness is the substance of a beauty that can change your life, that music is sacred precisely in its experiential reach beyond the naming conventions of a culture that marks them as deviant, shiftless, inefficient, or even naive. The lid of language lifted, the music moves beyond the circulation of blood or exchange of bodies into its own atmosphere, and others beyond.

7

Other Planes of There

THE TRUMPET'S NOTES just seem to hang there, as if with each plosive they create a gauzy thickness suspending them in air as they move across rhythms, resounding endlessly. Somewhere between cooing breaths and bright fanfares, the billowing sounds of Wadada Leo Smith's ensemble New Delta Ahkri take their cues from those brass notes, drifting like a Calder mobile. The space the musicians inhabit, though, is not simply the soundscape but a conceptual one, shaped by Smith's system of metaphysics and musical notation known as Ankhrasmation. Such fusions of improvisation and cosmological speculation are also found in Ornette Coleman's Harmolodics, George Russell's Lydian Chromatic Concept, and Anthony Braxton's Tri-Axium system, among others, imaginings of sound, humanity, spirituality, and the universe. Yet aside from the compelling languages and concepts within these systems, this lineage of sonic metaphysics in jazz resonates further within an American tradition of cosmic imaginauts that encompasses Emanuel Swedenborg, Noble Drew Ali, Heaven's Gate, and Theosophy's universal chord.

It is a tradition known for its defiance of traditionalism, at times burrowing deep into subcultural soil while also brimming with universalism. It celebrates the mystical yet insists on its scientificity. It uses the imagery and rhetoric of cosmic otherness to situate humanity in a creative universe, rejecting custom for dreams of a cosmos tuned precisely and alive with vibratory possibility. To these composers, the starry beyond resembled not at all the cold, silent void depicted in Stanley Kubrick's *2001*; it was, rather, an inviting expanse, a universe still coming to know itself, still pushing outward, and, as cosmologists had begun to assert by mid-century, limitless. And it was noisy.

In a world of the "sweating brow," belonging to this vast, humming beyond rather than the gloomy earth held great appeal. And yet it was not simply the dream of a celestial utopia that compelled; it was spirits at play in a divine architecture as sonic as it was spatial. The awakened musician could compose a way into that structure, become part of it, but also contribute to it creatively. This required systems: study of non-conventional sources (both musical and esoteric), new modes of transcription and notation, symbolism, and an eye to synthesizing genres, experiences, and even gods. One thinks most obviously of Sun Ra's fascination with space imagery, as he shuttled from corner to corner on Chicago's South Side in the 1950s, decked out in a robe of fake leopard skin and hatted with a fez, while carrying tomes of secret lore. As we saw earlier, Ra's understanding of the sacred past connected the dots between space travel, astrology, ancient technologies, biblical numerology, and cosmic sound.

But he was not alone among American religious practitioners or among jazz musicians in speculating about the beyond. This is no surprise, given the human propensity to contemplate the starry heavens above, to see in the wheeling firmament an order giving shape to our own drifting, a pattern of meaning beyond the flesh, an ethereal harmony of the fragments of life that seem to swirl—unbidden, chaotic—in confusion around us. The moon and the tides, the sidereal shapes traced in recurring axes or constellations, and the great interlocking vastness of which we are so infinitesimal a part, all these have preoccupied jazz musicians in America, as this music bloomed during the Space Age. The imagery of Ike-age rockets and crew-cutted astronauts dotted many a 1950s LP, the unmistakable grapheme of the atom superimposed over that of the martini. Those modernist dreams fusing lifestyle consumption and sleek technology crescendoed in space exploration, another frontier to settle and another reservoir of kitsch to celebrate, with little green men and their flying saucers.

Jazz musicians smitten with similar dreamings also sought to harness something of the expanding universe in their very sounds. This was popular especially among amplified jazz musicians in those years immediately following the moon landing. Chick Corea's Return to Forever became a vehicle not just for high-octane fusion but for L. Ron Hubbard's sci-fi imaginings. The Mahavishnu Orchestra exuded the serenity of Hindu contemplatives as well as the choppy futurism of "Celestial Terrestrial Commuters." And even outside the United States, Finnish percussionist-composer Edward Vesala told his erstwhile guitarist, Raoul Björkenheim, that he should play less guitar and more "shooting stars." Space was not just a fancy or a possibility though. For other musicians, space travel was a rebuke, a slap to the face. Gil Scott-Heron sang acidly, "[A] rat done bit my sister Nell, but whitey's on the moon."

But beyond the merely dreamy or the dismissive, other possibilities abounded. And these possibilities put the improviser in a relationship with the cosmos itself, realizing some kind of harmony with existence through the construction of a metaphysic. Jason Kao Hwang strives to enter a vibrational field in which "[i]mprovisation discovers and reveals another universe."[2] Matthew Shipp sees his piano as "a rocket ship, that can take sound and generate frequencies upwards in a funnel."[3] Percussionist William Hooker contends that "the real music is the song of the heavens...the eternal symphony of the highest realm."[4] Referring to Emerson's oversoul, Narada Burton Greene says, "The collective unconscious is coming through us, we are just a medium for some deeper levels of expression."[5] Prince Lasha believes "we are guided by the unseen angelic force of the creator."[6] Jazz reaches for "the universal song...the essence of existence," to James Finn.[7] Faruq Bey believes that when music is made, "[t]here's a sphere of vibration, a wave that surrounds you" and the improviser is "trying to make a rational order of it."[8]

Flautist Nicole Mitchell engages science fiction narratives as modes of sense-making, order-bestowing. Improvisation, she says, recapitulates the "silence before creating," a sonic cosmogony that Mitchell explores through compositions inspired by Octavia Butler's *Xenogenesis* trilogy.[9] Narratives like Butler's allow Mitchell not just to articulate, through Butler's social criticism, her own musical motivations but to explore further "the relationship between the 'real' and the 'unreal'" and to "be in the timeless space of the intuitive."[10] Sam Rivers also found jazz to be "like the universe: the more you see, the more there is."[11] But if sound itself is some kind of alternate world, the cosmic truth brought vibrating into a world of false appearances, what meanings are derived from or ascribed to it? What religious disciplines can ensure contact with this cosmo-sonic divine? Far from the traditional housings of this book's beginnings, we have reached the vastness of space. Below I describe jazz's systems of meaning reaching into the unknown, hearing there a divine presence that is channeled through their own sonic and conceptual architecture.[12]

"Space Church": Ornette Coleman and Harmolodics

There will never, ever be another musician like Ornette Coleman. He changed jazz and American music, broadly speaking. He has received a

Grammy, a Pulitzer, and a MacArthur "genius" grant. And he is the only person ever to perform with the Grateful Dead, the Master Musicians of Joujouka, and Jacques Derrida. One hears his singular name before the actual music, whose speed and unpredictability rattled listeners decades ago. His was a musical revolution that was as regularly mocked as it was reviled: when he wasn't being accused of assailing the standards of musical decency or being a talentless hack, Coleman was associated with gags about not wanting to pay for "free jazz." But the sweet, soft-spoken Coleman's explanations of his musical system (Harmolodics) and his general beliefs revolve around his changing understanding of "love," which he often equates with God or music. Listen to "Science Fiction," where over a frantic free pulse and darting multidirectional horns, Coleman's echo-drenched voices announces, "The. Art. Of. Living. Is. Written. In. The Bible." Why did Coleman intone these words? What was the sound of his living, and how was it to be played?

The Colemans of Fort Worth were "a religious family," and the saxophonist remembers "going from one church to the other listening to gospel music."[13] Coleman picked up the alto at fourteen, teaching himself scales as he heard them and doggedly playing his own thing, even in church. He developed an organic, soulful sound on the horn and began touring with gospel and R 'n' B bands. But Coleman almost gave up playing after he faced racial discrimination and general disregard for music, since "I thought that I was only adding to all that suffering."[14] His mother challenged him, "[Y]ou want somebody to pay you for your soul?"[15] And Coleman felt "re-baptized."[16] He began to pursue music he hoped was morally and spiritually pure, starting by cultivating his own authenticity in comportment and musical style.

Making a typically suggestive association, Coleman claimed that "being an individual and not in anyone's way" was akin to being "more religious."[17] For a time, Coleman joined Silas Green's New Orleans minstrel show but was fired for "trying to make the band too modern."[18] He picked up a gig at a sanctified church, where he could play music "without feeling guilty," and played bebop dates when he could.[19] But he grew restless with the "modern" music's conventions and started to follow the melodies beyond their chordal restrictions. After relocating to Los Angeles in 1951, Coleman met poet and cellist Jayne Cortez at a Jehovah's Witness Bible study group. They married in 1954, and Coleman converted. He wrote furiously, sketching out ideas for what he would later call "Harmolodics." Most players, however, were repelled by Coleman's ideas and his sound: that tart tone, the odd gaps in his phrasing that sometimes floated above implied rhythm, those unpredictable note choices that seemed to belong to un-heard chords. Charlie Haden was an exception, and he wanted to jam with Coleman. When he arrived at Coleman's crib, the bassist felt as if he was entering some kind of laboratory, one overrun with staff paper, LPs, reeds, and other musical paraphernalia. Coleman instructed Haden to "[j]ust play what you hear," and Haden found the spontaneity revelatory: "Each note was a universe. Each note was your life."[20] That freedom and vast-ness, along with musicians' individuality, is the bedrock of Harmolodics, whose chief dictum was "play the music, not the background." The ideas were not simply musicological; rather, through improvising certain higher principles and states of being could be realized in "[f]reedom from con-ventional modes of thought and conclusions about every aspect of life."[21]

In Harmolodics, emotionality should guide both the feel of a composi-tion and its mechanics: rhythms should follow "natural breathing pat-terns" and "[t]here are some intervals that carry that *human* quality if you play them at the right pitch."[22] It was Coleman's intention to loosen up harmony and free up melody to catalyze democratic group expression. Combined with his experiments in tone (he wanted his crying sound to recall the church bands he had played in), his music polarized, leading many to conclude that he was either a "messiah or charlatan."[23] On his 1958 debut *Something Else*, Coleman's melodies were still steeped in the blues, and the band swung like mad. But they also sounded like bop tunes on basement meth, shuttling forward at crazed velocity with notes pulled apart like taffy until the pure tones and pulses stood nakedly revealed, bracing and alien. With Don Cherry, Haden, and Billy Higgins, Coleman landed a multi-record deal with Atlantic and made way for New York upon the release of *The Shape of Jazz to Come*, which opens with the jaw-dropping dirge "Lonely Woman." The rhythm spoke in the language of triplets but felt like free verse. Haden's emotional double-stops acted gravitationally but in several different orbits at once, while the horns soared high above, untethered and unnervingly free. Reactions proliferated rapidly as Coleman's quartet settled in for a months-long residency at the Five Spot Café. While vibraphonist Lionel Hampton loved the sound, trumpeter Roy Eldridge confessed, "I listened to him high and I listened to him cold sober. . . . I think he's jiving baby." Leonard Bernstein called Coleman a genius, but Miles Davis snorted, "[P]sychologically, the man is all screwed up."[24] Fights occasionally broke out among audience members.[25] And bassist Jimmy Garrison once sat in and quickly freaked out, exclaiming,

"Stop this goddamn music, ain't a fucking thing happening, what do you Negroes think you're doing?"[26]

The quartet worked regularly, and theirs was called the music of rebellion: Francis Newton described Coleman's generation of musicians as "alienated, the internal emigrants of America."[27] But Coleman, who had left the Jehovah's Witnesses, saw himself as playing a kind of folk music that would enlighten the open-eared. The saxophonist continued his spiritual inquiries, but insisted on love and inclusivity: when attending a 1960 Nation of Islam convention, he "could hardly play for all the hate around me."[28] Frustrated by social animosity and inadequate compensation following his triumphant early records, Coleman changed his music. With bassist David Izenzon and drummer Charles Moffett, he played defiantly abstract sound, elongated and melancholy. Dropping out of the scene occasionally, Coleman pursued this sawing, often melismatic music as "his heartcry."[29] In playing ever more independently of form, Coleman believed that he was pursuing more directly his own spirituality and/as self-expression. He referred to his relationship to sound itself as one of love, which is also how he described his relation to the human species.[30]

During the late 1960s and early 1970s, Coleman began to think on a broader scale. He wrote a score for the film *Chautauqua Suite*, works for theater and dance troupes, the opera *The Visitation*, and two orchestral works: "Inventions of Symphonic Poems" (1967) and "Sun Suite of San Francisco" (1968). Disgruntled with the limits of "jazz," Coleman contemplated writing a symphony to underscore the democratic and spiritual implications of Harmolodics. Coleman spent a night on the Crow Reservation in Montana and came up with the piece's title, *Skies of America*: "let me see if I could describe the beauty, and not have it be racial or any territory. In other words, the sky has no territory."[31] He hired the London Symphony Orchestra, hoping "to express the sky" itself. In the piece, Coleman's thematic statements move briskly like clouds to the horizonless drift of those endlessly bending notes.[32] Still swinging, it invokes the perambulations of a Charles Ives composition, supplemented by free-bop and serialism. Coleman described the piece as primarily "about difference, but also a certain way of rebalancing."[33]

Coleman has always insisted that "all notes should be equal."[34] This was, to Coleman, the heart of his music's accessibility and its democratic potential to fuse self-creation with collectivity. These commitments were revivified on a trip to Nigeria, where Coleman was knocked out by the "willingness to give your soul to total strangers through the music."[35]

What he found in Africa, then, was universalism itself: "[t]he only creden-
tials you need are human form and planetary citizenship."[36] The point of
playing, then, is for Coleman to produce "an everyday sound that communicates the raw experience of unstructured cosmic consciousness."[37] That
this consciousness is so basic to humanity makes transcultural communication possible, and its ideal form is sound. If nobody tries to push sound
around, it can free you: "no one player has the lead. Anyone can come out
with it at any time."[38]

Coleman traveled to Morocco in 1973, along with Robert Palmer and
writers Brion Gysin and William S. Burroughs, to seek out the Master
Musicians of Joujouka. They were fascinated by the lore surrounding this
village where music was said to be played continually. It was Coleman's
vision of a perfect society, where sonic angels best our selfish devils. Coleman raved that these musicians could play "in a key that hasn't been
developed in other keys, like in America"; in other words, their improvisatory freedom was not shackled by harmony like earlier forms of "jazz."[39]
Humans may speak in different languages, wear different clothing, or
worship different gods; but to Coleman, these are just different ways of
expressing fundamentally similar concerns or energies, different notes in
the same song.

So music that insistently speaks a single language is, to Coleman, disconnected from human emotion and spirituality. Though all communication can generate beautiful music, Coleman believes it is through the
specific—jamming with the Dead, composing for David Cronenberg's
Naked Lunch, or in a Joujouka ritual—that one reaches the universal.
Gysin recalls that it wasn't just Coleman trying to fit in with the Joujouka
musicians; they also "matched his themes with ritual music."[40] Listening
to the recordings of the encounter, his ragged cry and quavering tone
sound perfectly apposite to the churning, droning sound of the local musicians. Was it a "religious" experience for Coleman? He certainly found it
analogous to his early experiences "play[ing] for a country evangelist,
healing people."[41] It was like church insofar as it was "music that is totally
created for an emotional experience."[42] To Coleman, this puts you in touch
with the source of creation; yet "the closest we've come to the thing that
created life is a word called 'God,' and that spells 'Dog' backwards. So that
puts us in the dark."[43] Being in the dark, though, may be partly the point.
This is not to suggest that Coleman is invested in apophatic theology; but
the "meaning" in improvisation is momentary, emergent in our relational
response to others and to the temporal flow we experience as beings

situated in a cosmos of change. The appropriate response to this "darkness," then, is to cultivate beauty and joy.

The free and polymorphous relation of notes in Harmolodics, where the melody is liberated from chords, is not just the music on the chart; it is one's own life as composition, an act of Emersonian self-creation through jazz. This is what Coleman believes spirituality connotes: the realization of one's own authenticity ("the thing I can be is the best human I try to attempt to be") as part of "the eternity of human beings," absorbed into a sea of feeling.[44] The collaboration proved to Coleman the real possibility of different cultures and spiritualities merging for a time through sound, even as they preserved their distinctiveness. He sought to realize these ideas in his new electric outfit Prime Time. With snaking, repeating lines, Prime Time was Coleman's groove maker, a trance improv music inspired by the Joujouka musicians who "changed together, as if they all had the same idea."[45] But the structure and syntax were Coleman's own: "everyone is playing a separate melody or a unison but...everyone's playing, like, an independent lead."[46]

This was Harmolodics in its pomp, with pulse, harmony, and melody circulating as one in the bloodstream of the species, crashing riotously against the world's tympanum. To Coleman, it was literally inhuman to buy into what he calls the "caste system of sound," which promotes hierarchical

FIGURE 7.1. Percussionist Edward Blackwell, Ornette Coleman, and Charlie Haden in performance. Photograph copyright William E. (Bill) Smith.

thinking that isolates us from our own feelings and consequently from each other.[47] Harmolodics, by contrast, connects human feelings and relationships to those higher things some call God, others math, and still others the relation between notes and intervals in the heavens: "the mathematical part of how we address sound is different than how the sound addresses what we call harmony."[48] It is that on which his music improvises, and in which it rejoices. If the music is happening, "it sounds like it's going out. Which means it's coming from [your] soul."[49] This is the only way, he believed, you could possibly find out the kind of person you are.

The attempt to superimpose limited human frameworks on the purity of divine sound—which is love, humanity's purpose—is to become further alienated from the emotional core of our reason for existence. The fundamental Harmolodic imperative, by contrast, suggests that "if you apply your feelings to sound...you'll probably make good music."[50] To Coleman, this is effectively a religious aspiration: "[b]eing a human, you're required to be in unison: upright."[51] To attempt mastery of such situations would not only be to overstep the limits of human knowledge in obvious ways, or to attempt to manipulate other humans; it would also be to close down the flow of experience, to cut off the dialogic nature of existence, to play God. Coleman is emphatic about this quasi-idolatrous feature of codification, systematization: "I would like to have the same concept of ideas as how people believe in God. To me, an idea doesn't have any master."[52] Seeking out the limits of perception and language, and realizing that all naming and classifying are flawed, improvisers thus learn to accept the provisionality of experience and thus get closer to what Coleman thinks of as divine.

It was with the purpose of gathering like-minded dreamers, and facilitating spiritual explorations, that Coleman established the arts space Caravan of Dreams in Fort Worth, in 1983. The space had once housed a "commune" described as "a 'Jonestown-like' cult."[53] Coleman was differently inspired. He had been very affected by meeting Buckminster Fuller, whose belief that human creativity can prevent the extinction of the species resonated with Coleman.[54] He sought to unite Harmolodic utopianism with Fuller's beliefs in the piece "The Oldest Language," which would have 130 musicians from across the world living together for six months in order to "reconcile their cultural and linguistic differences before learning Coleman's score."[55] If music was sacred, as Coleman thought, it would transform isolated humans into "unisons," in temporal and experiential flows they could experience freshly. Harmolodics resists formulation even to the point of denying the relevance of scientific theory: when one inter-viewer invoked Heisenberg's "uncertainty principle," Coleman responded curtly that he was "no longer talking chemistry but alchemy."[56] It is sweeter than science, Coleman says, and deeper too. He even improvises on the Bible: "It says in the Bible that in the beginning God created light, it doesn't say God created the sun, right? Maybe human beings are the real true light."[57] Harmolodics refracts this light, showing people it is inside them (though not necessarily like the Quaker "inner light"; perhaps more like the light of eternity wearing one of Coleman's vinyl suits) and in-herent in the flow of life itself. He also considers this to be at root a salvific notion: "I don't try to please when I play. I try to cure."[58]

For Coleman, these are not matters for a distant heaven but for the real-ization of the fully human in the earthly present. Tomorrow may have been the question in his futuristic youth, but for Coleman the realization of au-thentic feeling in the moment is "what God meant by putting breath in human beings."[59] Human beings exist, in fact, to realize their own eternity. There is no genealogy or classificatory system that can contain feelings, whose sonic manifestation makes it possible for us to become uncon-ditioned beings. One simply awakens to the universe singing its song through you by becoming aware of sound's physiological effects, the way its color unlocks emotion, perception, and reverence. In this present, we are made to become sound; and this free sound is "not about race, it's not about sex, it's about the quality of human beings living in an eternity be-cause God don't kill."[60]

Although it writes tunes you can hum and play again, Harmolodics establishes no creeds. Coleman addresses this, unconsciously attuned to the apophatic, wondering, "Is there a God outside of church? I hope so. But how should I know?"[61] It is the not knowing that counts, the uncer-tainty and risk in life itself, which is the ultimate improvisation. And if a musician "tries to do the best he can his own way...he's just showing [that] God exists."[62] Some have heard in such postulations an echo of "Sartre's existentialism (with its emphasis on trusting the instincts as a guide to existentialist action) and German romantic ideas of genius—that intuitive originality for which no rational rule can be given."[63] Yet the de-sire to translate concepts into sounds, and sounds into experience, also recalls Emerson, who wrote, "The ancients, struck with this irreducible-ness of the elements of human life to calculation, exalted Chance into a divinity...the universe is warm with the latency of the same fire."[64] As Coleman expounds on it, sound is limitless and can unlock the imagination, expanding the self thereby in "an 'eternal cycle' of 'improvisation and pre-composition.'"[65] We jam forever on these democratic vistas, since music "has some democracy in it; it's just the styles that get in the way."[66] Coleman's "Space Church" is thus continually being born, then theorizing itself, and holding services in sound. Is it *really* "religion," though? Sure, if musicians just reveal the existence of God, as Coleman contends. His utopian aspirations positing self-creation within the collective resonate with traditions like the Oneida perfectionists or Brook Farm, here pulsing in the lineage of American maverick composers. But as Cherry observed of Coleman's influence and ideas, "Spiritually, he is an example.... Ornette or anybody who has something that they're reflecting from the spirit—either in their creativity or just their daily life—to me that's a religion. And that's reflected in the music."[67]

The Horizontal Man: George Russell and the Lydian Chromatic Concept

If you invent a musical system bringing together Greek philosophical ideas about the sidereal relationship between tones and the intuition that chordal freedom can lead to spiritual growth, you might be forgiven for thinking you are owed some acclaim. Cincinnati-born George Russell developed from his strong church upbringing an early interest in music, gravitating initially to drums and the music he heard in "those holy roller churches" whose parishioners would "rock—and I do mean *rock*—the earth as they sang."[68] Russell had "a number of religious experiences as a child" and, while he initially felt no personal connection with African American Christianity, its music "opened a door to a life...that was exploratory and that was an open door to the universe."[69]

Russell began to write and perform jazz. During a 1941 hospitalization for tuberculosis, he "began musical theoretical investigations that later culminated in the *Lydian Chromatic Concept of Tonal Organization* (LCC)."[70] Russell wanted to learn every chord, scale, and progression in existence. Echoing the Greek sense that studying intervals and tones revealed astronomical principles, Russell "felt there was a system begging to be brought into the world. And that system was based on chord scale unity."[71] A healthy Russell got a gig drumming in Benny Carter's Chicago band, but ultimately "decided that writing was my field."[72] Hospitalized again, he dove into music theory with the single-minded intention to build his own musical system. Like Coleman, Russell's sound construct entailed both self-creation and dialogue with the cosmos. He was compelled primarily by what he called the "gravitational pull" that tonal centers exerted on performances (especially "the ability of linear tetrachords to imply a tonic").[73]

In the late 1940s, Russell became instrumental in the transition from bebop into modal jazz, seeking "to give musicians more freedom...[by] replacing chords with scales as the primary basis for improvisation."[74] The freedom from chordal stasis, or excess "gravity," unlocked the use of a vast range of influences, large expanses of color and timbre, without precluding vigorous rhythm. These were the root sensibilities of the LCC, in whose creative freedoms Russell saw crystallized cosmological principles of discipline and humility. He described the LCC as "a more serious, less egotistical pursuit" of improvisation than the conventional path of "hot" solos.[75] Ranging over genres from classical music to American vernacular, Russell was in demand as a composer and arranger (as with so many others in this book, he collaborated with Dizzy Gillespie's Afro-Cuban band). And in 1953 he published *The Lydian Chromatic Concept of Tonal Organization*, codifying his methods for moving beyond conventional Euro-American tonality. Rooted in the non-standard Lydian mode, Russell's idea was to decenter, and thereby democratize, tonality so that musicians could "improvise in any key, on any chord."[76]

Russell was fond of saying that in his system, musicians could not play any "wrong notes," only more or less compelling ones.[77] Superficially this might sound similar to Coleman's emphasis on emotionality; but for Russell these note choices were less about self-expression than assembling the elements that would allow the music to pour outward, upward, into the universe from which it simultaneously emerged. Russell thus tapped into a compositional tradition broadly associated with Ives, combining themes, overlapping scales, and elaborate structures held together by a single tonal center.[78] From one, many. As Russell began to write more ambitious compositions and lead his own recordings, the LCC was described as "the first profound theoretical contribution to come from jazz."[79] On dazzling small-group records like *Stratusphunk* and *Ezz-Thetic*, the music rocketed forward with rhythmic authority, impossibly precise counterpoint and polyvocality, and the harmonic and textural range of a big band realized in the open world of Russell's concept. Yet the jazz system wore him down, and Russell retreated to Europe in the mid-1960s. Revivified there, Russell composed "a mass, a score for *Othello* as a ballet, and the orchestral suite with tapes and jazz soloing called *Electronic Sonata for Souls Loved by Nature*."[80] The results were often overstuffed with so many different ideas that it was like listening to the moment of creation, energy exploding into the universe in manifold forms, each element of Russell's music with a toehold in some recognizable genre or idea but sounding collectively like some sort of cosmic hymn brought to us by celestials. Through long-form explorations like "Uncommon Ground," "Time Line," and "The African Game," Russell created music (and often multimedia experiments) that extended his LCC to its limits. The "nine events" of "The African Game" documented the cradle of civilization throughout history (chronicling humanity's fragmentation into what Russell calls the "Cartesian Man"), returning to "the image of Africa as a game board in which the Divine intervened to open the game of humanity with a dice throw."[81]

It was after returning to America that he began, in the 1970s and 1980s, to describe what he saw as the LCC's conceptual and spiritual implications, his conversations now brimming with "asides to cosmology, archeology, and the psychology of consciousness."[82] Against the idea of music as entertainment, Russell insisted that music exists "to educate, to learn about the stars, or how to live your life."[83] Music should not "lull and put you to sleep or coddle you"; its purpose is "to fuck you up and to shock you to come awake 'cause most of us are asleep."[84] Russell saw the LCC as a source of spiritual, not just artistic, sustenance; it was a vehicle for higher levels of shock. He now described the LCC as "the 'all and everything of tonality' and the 'all and everything of music.'"[85] Russell began to correlate his ideas with those of Georges Gurdjieff, P. D. Ouspensky, and pre-Socratic philosophy of music.[86] He was taken with Gurdjieff's synthesis of traditions, and the mystic's links between "gravity, harmoniousness, [and] space travel."[87]

The best way to express these ideas in sound was not simply to "apply" texts to musical compositions or vice versa; as always, the trick was in playing, experimenting, throwing oneself into the unpredictable momentariness of sound itself. What mattered to Russell was music's vibrancy, not its genre. He insisted that true musicians had to reject sham materialism in order to pursue music's higher possibilities, including social reform. Russell had something grander in mind, then, than simply sonic freedom. For Russell, the prejudices that hamper social growth manifest in music too.[88] Part of this has to do with misunderstandings of the capaciousness of "jazz," which Russell claims obscures genuine spirituality with "the art/soul dichotomy of jazz valuation."[89] Against such dualisms, the LCC reconfigured the known with its own language for describing the flux and possibility of musical existence: "the Concept also embodies a philosophical critique of goal-oriented Western civilization."[90]

Russell embraced the ancient theory of correspondences and harmony by which the person becomes attuned to the resonant structure of the cosmos ("mathematics"), and in so doing becomes situated within a larger process of spiritual development ("history"). He spoke of realizing "supra-vertical tonal gravity" in sonic terms, and "identified his investigations with the musical soul-searching of the medieval monasteries," especially early music's focus "on vital resolving tones, nucleus-notes around which everything else elegantly orbited."[91] These syntheses should not, Russell insisted, be described as abstract "freedom" (a category he disdained). Rather, "[e]verything is under a law....I believe in levels. The thing called freedom is one of the higher objective laws of tonality."[92] As Russell explained, the LCC "crystallized two objective forces of the way jazz music manifests: horizontal, state of tonal quality and vertical, state of tonal gravity.... [Y]ou come closer to that individuality by having a fuller awareness of tonal, rhythm, psychological laws."[93] For Russell's "horizontal man" music can sound an infinite number of ways as long as it focused on "putting the question to your intuitive center and having faith, you know, that your intuitive center will answer."[94]

Russell did not mean to collapse art and spirituality into mere subjectivism (for this would be to concede another debatable duality), but to insist that music *as such*, when realized "on an objective level," can "evoke in the listener something beyond music; some state or some law beyond music."[95] Development—personal, cultural, musical, spiritual—proceeds inevitably along multiple axes, and the LCC sought to capture that multiplicity and enable the focused musician to direct her own development meaningfully within a cosmos already meaning-soaked. Russell's own invocations of pre-Socratic philosophy, quasi-Swedenborgian renderings of a universe in sound, and the languages of science and democracy constituted a multiplicity as evident as that of his music. At the heart of his concept he posited a "spiritual essence" that could transcend the rational components of music theory, or embrace subverted doctrines against the very idea of doctrine. We also see a reckoning with the ubiquity of language and category as a step on the way to their realization and dissolution, part Hegelian *aufhebung*, part Derridean surplus. But its purpose is not just to make mischief with our settled ways of hearing and living. No, the LCC is about the beauty that comes through reorganizing key elements. And for Russell, "If America has a future, jazz has a future: the two are inseparable."[96] Yes, the chromatic America—like the chromatic universe—contains an infinity of pasts that bloom like an impossible chord into an infinity of futures.

A *Super Highway to the Cosmics: Anthony Braxton's Tri-Axium System*

As a South Side Chicagoan in the 1960s, Anthony Braxton was a vora-cious, catholic listener and reader. Chicago—the city of Moody, the Progres-sives, and the Nation—is recognized for its powerful religious lineages, but it has just as indelibly shaped jazz, often in concert with religions.[97] Braxton's neighborhood was populated by churches, mosques, and temples, and he was exposed to both traditional music and a powerful Africanist sensibility. The young choirboy Braxton's mother ensured he diligently did his homework and attended their Baptist church, where he absorbed its musical repertoire along with "pieces of the cultural puzzle that shaped an image of his people."[98] But Braxton was also obsessed with pulp sci-fi, comics, and space movies.[99] Add to that omnivorous musical tastes shaped, as Ronald Radano notes, by the South Side's sonic ferment, where mu-sical evangelists, raw blues, and doo-wop quartets rubbed elbows just as surely as street-corner preachers did.[100] Braxton's affinities ran to extremes that his peers sometimes found challenging. The young alto saxophonist swooned for the "square" sounds of Sammy Nestico or Stan Kenton as well as Ayler or Mingus and loved alto saxophonists Paul Desmond and Eric Dolphy equally. It was here that Braxton first bristled against the notions of "blackness" and "whiteness" that held apart musical worlds he wanted to mash together. Seeking music that could span these gaps, Braxton fell in with the AACM, whose focus on the production of sound rather than con-formity to genre helped him develop musical concepts beyond technique or style.

Braxton began to develop his compositional and improvisational aes-thetic and started "to read intensively in philosophy and religion," poring over "cult books on mysticism and Daisetz Suzuki's and Alan Watts's studies of Zen" at Roosevelt University.[101] He began constructing a system that could function as a resource for ideas, languages, and symbols, fusing traditions of Afrocentricity, the spiritual ethos of experimental jazz in the 1960s, and progressive understandings of American culture. This "restruc-turalism" in/of "jazz" involved reimagining religion in America's past and future too. The ultimate result was Braxton's Tri-Axium system, designed to articulate links between mystery religions, hieroglyphics, the cosmos, and democratic sound. Having early on codified twelve basic "language types" as the foundation of his music, Braxton studied religions more rigorously in the late 1960s, cribbing from John Cage and Karlheinz Stockhausen while reading Alice Bailey, the *Bardo Thödol*, the *Book of Oahspe*, and more. He contended that reality is vibratory, and that inventing his own systemic/theoretical languages could realize "musical challenges to conventional perceptions [and] would naturally lead society to a higher level of knowledge."[102]

As Graham Lock notes, Braxton's graphic titles, initially used to give structural or thematic indicators for improvisation, began to assume symbolic significance in terms of his own musings on his music's cosmological resonance: his "dimensional drawing" drew from Braxton's "research into astrology, numerology, and systems of correspondence that he traced back to 'the ancients' and in particular ancient Egypt."[103] More than simply the kind of "automatic writing" one witnesses in, say, channeling circles or Shaker drawings, Braxton used them to locate his system "in a parallel network of mystical and religious symbolism."[104] Where Ra invoked such languages and histories to point out religious ignorance and racial "insanity," Braxton's system links the utopian imagination with the unlimited possibilities of sound and interplanetary vibration (even including a piece for orchestras performing on different planets or solar systems simultaneously). Mathematics, the cosmos, self-discovery, and God are all aspects of a singularly resonating reality that is accessed musically. Braxton believes, with Russell and the pre-Socratics, that there are "cosmic and concrete laws that govern what this existence really is."[105] He attributes this insight to "something much greater than me—God or the Creator or the Cosmics."[106] But this would be "a restructured God" or "a new concept of love" that emerged in sound.[107] If music can vibrate freely while tethered to principle and purpose, then it becomes "a super-highway, to the Cosmics."[108]

For Braxton, musical and spiritual self-creation depended on the possibility of restructuralism in aesthetics and culture. The experience of the "reality of the sweating brow" prompted his obsessive investigations into democratic possibility, one component of which was his investigation of Pan-Africanism and Egyptology. A key influence in these explorations was Yosef ben-Jochannan's *African Origins of Major "Western" Religions* and *Africa: The Mother of Civilization*.[109] To study the past was to look futureward and Braxton wrung from these materials an expansive universe of sonic multitudes. Anticipating his life's preoccupations, Braxton insisted by the mid-1970s that "[t]he challenge of the next cycle of creative music will call for both new and traditional solutions...[and] the widest possible informational and vibrational stance."[110] He shared with his contemporaries a sense of enthusiasm about self-determination, but his buoyant optimism changed to disappointment as he lamented those cultural forces or institutions that tried "to separate the music from its meta-reality implications."[111] So he sought to "*extend* traditional African-American associations of art and the sacred," not contravene or merely preserve them.[112]

In his growing compositional system, he used instrumentations and musical idioms that often specifically signified against "jazz" and its reception dynamics. While "creative music" eschewed curatorial approaches to genre, Braxton continued working out some of his most fundamental ideas in relation to past innovators. Bebop, for example, was praised not just for its rhythmic and harmonic creativity but its detachment "from the Baptist Church continuum."[113] He used the categories "vibrational reality" and "affinity insight" to underscore the spiritual example of creative musicians. He described tenorist Warne Marsh as part of the "European mystic lineage."[114] He insisted, "Sun Ra is not a joke!...This is a man who understands the world of abstract consciousness and the mystical dynamics of music."[115] Ornette Coleman was a prophet who "delivered his vision of the world."[116]

Like other religionists of the era who turned from a purportedly disenchanted modern period to a pre-industrial or pre-Christian past, Braxton became compelled by mystery religions, Gnosticism, hermetic teachings, and "suppressed Western history" as well as African history.[117] Braxton saw in such awakenings to "real" information the expansion of specific intel-

FIGURE 7.2. Anthony Braxton, digging in on contrabass clarinet. Photograph copyright William E. (Bill) Smith.

lectual, spiritual, and musical lineages beyond their originary contexts into a dialogic relation with other traditions and "affinity wavelengths" (just as surely as he felt he was dialing into the "true information" about creative music masters). Rosicrucians, Hermes Trismegistus, or Ra were alike in underscoring the historic sources of what he understood as his "mystical and composite world purpose": "to create a positive music that will be helpful to humanity."[118] The "sacred potential of musical expression" connected griots and shamans with jazz restructuralists. Against staid understandings of the jazz modern, Braxton believed the spirituality of the West had been occluded and that jazz had to go back in order to go forward. To realize American democratic potentialities, the creative musician had to know Egypt and Mars. Braxton shuffled between temporal references, spatial imaginaries, and favorite records as frequently as he changed instruments while playing, noting, "I've come to see the beauty in all differences, and I've also come to see that there are no differences."[119] His music drew together apparently incompatible approaches, instrumentations, and thought systems so as to "exceed the boundaries between artist and audience, between art and life."[120]

But these fundaments of Braxton's emerging system were lost in his critical reception, condescendingly celebrating his "eccentricities" (his pipe smoking and fascination with chess, for example) while ignoring the historic and conceptual grounds of his experimentalism. Signed to Arista for a hot minute in the 1970s, Braxton used his major label funding to sponsor his most elaborately dreamed projects as reflections of what he and Max Roach described as "a continuum that links the present with the past" through "well defined principles basic to African American culture."[121] Befuddled audiences and critics had trouble locating "jazz" in his compositions for four orchestras or his through-composed pieces for tuba ensembles. As Braxton's Arista deal fizzled and he entered a dark 1980s, he described his treatment by mainstream jazz media as "gangsterism."[122] Jazz remained "a little box" that could not contain creative, spiritual music; "swing" was a kind of aesthetic tyranny.[123] To Braxton, "'[j]azz' is the name of the political system that controls and dictates African-American information dynamics."[124] Braxton's music during this period sought to balance the universal and the particular; and in music's very fluidity he heard both religion and democracy as possibilities of creative freedom in the context of constraint. "[T]he challenge of American musics," Braxton observed, "has been how those projections have sought to fulfill the concept of democracy that the early fathers put together."[125]

Braxton's performances housed both collective and individual expression, a nearly Deweyan realization of potential through "dynamic participation." In this it established what Lock, paraphrasing bassist Mark Dresser, called "a paradigm of how to live."[126] It is not just that this musical sociality is also spiritual; the process also depends on engaging the totality of human wisdom traditions and interrogating opposites: order/chaos, composition/improvisation, Europe/Africa, and individual/collective. He drew on older, scorned vehicles like marches to embody the transformational possibilities of the past, calling his rousing "Composition 58" (dedicated to John Philip Sousa) "a positive spirit indicator that has the power to motivate involvement" (Braxton is well known for his love of college marching bands and takes subversive pleasure in turning such materials into experimental media).[127] This assemblage of a "personal language" built from the past is Braxton's vehicle for combining influences from Frankie Lymon to Stockhausen, but is also a recognizably American form of self-fashioning through eclecticism and modification of historic inheritance. As Lock writes, Braxton's improvisations on Africanisms recall the "trope of limping" in Legba's presence in non-canonical rhythms.[128] To link black identity to something as narrow as "jazz," then, is to distort the music's real legacy. Defining your terms is defining your history, whose multiplicity is realized in Braxton's long-standing use of collage compositions (which he likens to multiple individuals in different practice rooms simultaneously, each leaving the others alone) and pulse tracks (where rhythmic principles can stitch together or sunder different interpolated compositions, much as Braxton does with history).[129] Like different strands of history, group members are "working towards a feeling of *one*," representing their mutual accountability within the social or compositional frame and the dialogic respect that is the planet's best hope.[130] In Braxton's world, the past is a kind of accelerant to musical and cultural possibility as "we're moving towards the world of spirituality."[131]

The Tri-Axium system represents Braxton's attempts to "encod[e] [the] mystical implications" of music in ways that look beyond Western/European culture dominance.[132] He describes himself as "not much in agreement with the religious particulars of the last two thousand five hundred years," and thus hopes his system facilitates "a reexamination of our relationship with the spiritual aspects of existence but also the formulation of 'new gods.'"[133] From his solo pieces built on his twelve "language" areas to the collage and pulse-track work of his small groups or the multimedia pieces or "ritual and ceremonial musics" of recent decades, Braxton notes that "[i]n my music system, every composition connects together."[134] A piece's "primary identity" is its compositional structure; its "secondary identity" refers to its adaptability to other instrumentation, media, or contexts (one of his favorite examples is the possibility that an army of "400 tubas" can play any piece); and its "genetic identity" refers to cellular components that can be moved and recombined with those of other compositions, like an "erector set."[135]

This dense weave elaborated over decades is heard in every area of Tri-Axium music: a piano player plots the craggy course of "Composition 96" while bassist and drummer nail an additive pulse track from the Kelvin series, while Braxton rockets outward, part Warne Marsh reserve, part acetylene torch. The music's in(ter)dependence reflects Braxton's contention that the cosmos is "an inseparable network of energies or degrees of vibration," linked to the scientific "move to create a 'unified state' which demonstrates a vibrational synthesis of forces" in existence.[136] The links between numerology and pictograms both represent and facilitate these goals, according to Braxton's Tri-Axium writings; in this, Braxton not only draws together folk art traditions of the African diaspora but recalls Humbert de Superville's *gesamtkunstwerk*, an effort at "scoring" buildings using mythical systems and symbols that are spatial, temporal, and sonic.[137] Braxton believes that if humans become attuned to these dimensions of existence, music can literally open galaxies of possibility, perceptual awakening, social reform, and travel beyond Earth.

Conceiving of his early works as "planet level musics," Braxton went on to note that as he grew more preoccupied with religious matters his musical scope expanded: pulse tracks were now "like a solar system," the system's "environment structures" were "like a galaxy," the whole calibrated to realize "cosmic matters about which we know nothing."[138] The "solar logic" of musical information allows individuals to inhabit the Tri-Axium system creatively. Braxton sometimes links these possibilities to astrological signs, assigning each planet a series of phraseological signatures to serve as springboards for improvisation.[139] At each level—planetary, solar, galactic—these structural principles make possible certain parameters of growth, provided they are calibrated to what Braxton calls the three degrees of "affinity insight" grounding all music: self-realization, relation to the group, and relation to God.[140]

In time, Braxton's interest in the performative qualities of these ideas led him to focus on "form" and "the forces it sets into motion."[141] His "ritual and ceremonial musics" allow for "participation with meaning" and for the imaginative projection of utopic or fantasy spaces in performance.[142]

After a period of studying Native American and Indonesian ritual music, Braxton inaugurated his Ghost Trance Music, with compositions rooted in "a melody that doesn't end."[143] The music is carefully constructed—across thirteen categories, including Hieroglyphic, Ritual, and Imaginary State Models—so as to explore "a form of meditation that establishes ritual and symbolic connections [that] go beyond time parameters and become a state of being in the same way as the trance musics of ancient West Africa and Persia."[144] Braxton saw the GTM as facilitating "the hope of dynamic positive celebration and trans-global 'actuality.'"[145] This means something like the establishment of aesthetic-spiritual solidarity through enhanced experience of "the churning radiance of cosmic ether (that we call reality)" and its "phenomenon of 'sound wonder and vibrational instigation.'"[146]

The GTM is sort of a "theme park" mapping out domains of "vibrational presence," a notion that relates to the Trillium opera series Braxton considers his crowning spiritual achievement. Many of his compositions since the 1980s have been represented by graphemes and drawings of characters populating the operas, all taking place in the Tri-Axium system Braxton now describes as "a fantasy world comprising twelve 'city-state' regions."[147] Each region is linked to characters like Shala or Bubba John Jack, themselves associated with one of Braxton's twelve original "language types," the whole comprising what Lock calls "an interactive virtual reality."[148] These twelve different musical areas, characters, city-states, "points of identity," or "mythologies" link together like some alternate Hegelian synthesis realized in sonic, sub-atomic vibratory power.[149] More than an idiosyncratic expression of postwar religious syncretism, Braxton's system aims to construct alternate universes, equal parts sci-fi and esoterica, its sounds busily overlapping like multiple time streams in the newly discovered vastness of God's imagination.

We are beyond science and into poetry, theater, and ceremony. Braxton envisions celebrating his system's possibilities for representation and interaction at a "twelve day festival for world dynamics."[150] He dreams of having all twelve of his operas performed simultaneously by ensembles on different planets, in far-flung galaxies. Braxton, who avows, "I believe very much in God," is thus thinking transcendentally in the conventional and in the Kantian sense of establishing the conditions for sonic experiences of wonder and edification.[151] Music is a vehicle for what Braxton calls "the higher forces" leading us to "cosmic zones" where the innovators are those "who initiate new worlds...[or] their own universe."[152] This system points up, up, and away. After all, Braxton exults, "[T]he challenge of a next thousand years would be the new super-spaces which are now opening up in physics...and what these could pose for better understanding relationships, better understanding spiritual dynamics and intention."[153] And, with a wink, he adds: "[t]his is another context, outside the concept of 'blow, baby, blow,' if I could say it like that."[154]

Another Dimension in Music: Wadada Leo Smith's Ankhrasmation

I admit that I bought my first two Wadada Leo Smith albums (*Divine Love* and *Kulture Jazz*) because of their titles. That quickly became an afterthought as I bathed in his wholly affecting sound. Smith's music was no torrent of expressionism, nor was it anything one might customarily associate with "jazz," since its textures, harmonic language, and instrumentation seemed superficially more apposite to new music. Expectations dissolved in the sheer spaciousness of the billowing timbres, the exquisite held tones, the attention to those granular elements where instrumental voices blended. There was too much tension and energy to call it meditative; it was too purposeful, considered, and deftly wrought in its restraint. Smith's composition titles suggested ritual, jazz tradition, and cosmic speculation. Were these concepts "audible" in his warm, singing trumpet that seemed so unhurried, so unconcerned with leaving a technical impression and instead were intent on what might basically be sound recognizing itself?

Born in 1941, deep in the Mississippi Delta, Smith describes his religious upbringing as "[e]ssentially Christian."[155] He immersed himself in church music and, in time, jazz and trumpets. Playing in blues and R 'n' B bands, Smith honed his chops and in the mid-1960s traveled up that mighty river to Chicago, where he joined the AACM in 1967.[156] Smith was even then developing ideas that he would eventually assemble into first a notational system, then an aesthetic, and later both a metaphysic and a history. During "the Christian part of my journey," Smith investigated theoretical "models," symbols and languages, for those things "I began to discover."[157] He "found out that notes have gravity" that "could be accentuated into other areas" like religion.[158] Smith meant gravity here in the literal sense, as in the influence a note could have on notes and timbres and pulses surrounding it, but he also had in mind the gravitational pull sound could have on one's life: "[i]f you ever discover anything you can never lose it."[159] Musical matters, then, are essentially spiritual since they

contribute to human development. While Smith acknowledges the beauty
of the Christian tradition in which he was reared, through music he came
to realize that "spirituality really is not about the fact that you have to go
to church; it has something to do with realigning oneself with the
Creator."[160]

Compelled by the possibility of wholeness and connection, Smith
wanted to play music "to influence physical, spiritual, and psychic changes."[161]
In the AACM, Smith's varied activities were held together by the idea of
religious self-cultivation.[162] Noting of religion that "the word itself means to
realign," Smith champions the unity of activity: "[y]ou realign because the
process of living somehow forces a process of disconnect."[163] Yet as Piero
Scaruffi notes, unlike "the 'scientists' of the AACM," Smith "viewed music
as a vehicle, not as a goal."[164] Smith explored Rosicrucianism as a philosophical accompaniment to his musical explorations, contending that his
first recorded piece was animated by Rosicrucian concepts.[165] Smith told
me he appreciated Rosicrucianism's engagement with "ritualistic and mystical realities brought on in ancient Egypt."[166] Its emphasis on gnosis and
the transfiguration of base elements (knowledge, spirit, sound) compelled
Smith, who said Rosicrucianism "liberated me to have no fear about notes . . .
or to be able to dream and have visions."[167]

Throughout the 1970s, while studying ethnomusicology at Wesleyan
University, Smith's Kabell label documented his "multi-improvisations"
using horns, homemade percussion devices, and what he called "mobile
sounds" in atmospheric, at times nearly laminal, music that explored the
implications of a single note's gravity and reverberations. Smith "began to
design a notation system for scoring sound, rhythm and silence, or for
scoring improvisation, a technique I term *ahkreanvention*," or, increasingly, Ankhrasmation.[168] He told me that Akhreanvention "means to
create and invent at once."[169] It was constituted by a language of symbols
and graphemes indicating "rhythm units" through which he could "calibrate
the relationship between sound and silence."[170] In this system, "the value
given to an audible unit is followed by the relative equivalence of silence."[171]
Smith's shift to the term "Ankhrasmation" captures how he sought to articulate these values, their relative musical and relational gravity. He came
up with the term by combining words from different languages, including
Egyptian ("ankh" means "vital life force"), Amharic (in it, the word "ras"
means "head" or "father"), and "a universal word for mother: Ma."[172]
Explaining his inspiration in the Egyptian cross, which is used to touch
various body parts, Smith prefers the term "Ankhrasmation" because "it

means divine life force connecting father and mother" and hence denotes the multiple sources informing his playing.[173]

Since Smith believes music "affects your life whether you like it or not," it must realize modes of intersubjectivity that contribute to human betterment and spiritual development.[174] With *Songs of Humanity*, Smith began more explicitly to extend his interest in various religious systems (especially Japanese Buddhist aesthetics). Smith grouped together these ideas in "research on different kinds of philosophical and spiritual thinking."[175] His emphasis on relationality in music—between people, between notes, between whole systems of thinking—reflected Smith's growing "interest in multiculturalism and social justice."[176] The music had a quiet intensity, blooming in expectation and attentiveness compelled by dramas left unresolved, effusions held in check. It moved in spare, flowing gestures that allowed a single line or struck note to resonate. In the sheer openness of the musical space, the interaction of musicians demanded focus and clarity over technique or expressive freak-outs. For Smith, this musical being in the world created intensities that spanned the spiritual and the mundane, situating improvisers and listeners in space/time in a way that led to heightened awareness of duration, color, silence, and interactivity.

Smith says Ankhrasmation "reconstrues the hierarchy of Western harmony, motion and melody as well as processes of composition and improvisation."[177] The symbols designate velocities, durations, relationships, and occasionally timbres, its symbolic content largely directional and contemplative. Ankhrasmation's graphic scores at times resemble Klee or Kandinsky drawings (whereas Braxton's look more like architectural plans for newly colonized planets), with swooping lines, broad shapes, and bold dashes of color that imply "velocity units," durations, or moods/modes of interaction. They thus rely heavily on the improviser's creative imagination, not just her technical prowess. As turntablist Ikue Mori puts it, Ankhrasmation is "like following the map of the cosmic journey."[178] And Smith agreed wholeheartedly with me when I observed that his system was not merely notational but was spiritual. So as a piece cycles through panels/ drawings, the open dynamic field and seemingly limitless possibilities for interaction are held to be registers of spirituality: the appreciation for discrete objects moving in the void of silence and space, the always emergent but elusive possibility of creation/destruction, the coordinated activity of ritual. They are designed to stimulate the kind of reverence and wonder Smith believes is a basic characteristic of the human's relation to the cosmos, each of us a note in the universe's chord.

This potential of relational matrices is another metonym for the human condition, in Smith's estimation. Stepping into the unknown is what allows spirits to rejoice, where the "inspiration that arises" rushes in "like a tsunami, when the ensemble is in tune and connected with each other."[179] Together, musicians might even proceed through "the door that opens to the 'other side'…[a] space or an artistic dimension…common to mystical experience."[180] In emphasizing relationality, Smith reasserted that jazz was "a religious form of art with the power to uplift frustrated people."[181] Fundamental is individual liberty, something Ankhrasmation acknowledges by considering "each performer as a complete unity."[182] The realization of selfhood only occurs contextually, whether alongside other performers, relating to the natural environment, or even through self-conscious co-presence with sound itself. In each case, Smith "seek[s] another dimension in music" where the self is realized in relation to a sound-saturated cosmos, where each note's unique potential and transitory nature resemble our own.[183]

This sensibility, Smith emphasizes, enables one to express in sound "the wonder and gorgeousness of nature" and other contexts or traditions sustaining creativity.[184] It resonates further in what Smith calls "American music," an experimental compositional legacy flowing from Ives and Scott Joplin through Harry Partch and Cage. This lineage is expressed most powerfully among African Americans who "made new discoveries in performing techniques and established new systems to retain improvisations," one of which is "jazz."[185] Smith listens to the land sing of "jazz," transcribing it in tones that recall Whitman and Thoreau: "this improvisational music that I see, that I feel, that bursts all about us in this world, that's conveyed to us from the many different other worlds and that's held intact through our minds from the universe."[186] Nature, tradition, and the cosmos have their rhythms, and creative music must for Smith be attuned to these as "the universal principles of all when created through the cosmic powers of the all."[187] Like Andrew Jackson Davis's "republic of spirit," the universe is overrun with sound-spirit waiting to be fashioned in music "that prompt[s] the newness, right-nowness of totality."[188] Each note opens into a world saturated by divine energy, and if improvisations are animated by universal principles—levels of harmony, cycles and return, tension and resolution—the "wholeness of sound-rhythm" is "created cosmically" anew via "the speaking of the spirits" from specific cultural locations.[189]

With these ideas in mind, Smith began in the 1980s to explore different religions. He felt that, as integral as his explorations of space and silence were to his growing self-understandings and awareness, there needed to be other ways to "communicate his spiritual message more clearly."[190] On *Human Rights* and *Procession of the Great Ancestry*, Smith articulated his growing interest in vernacular song form (including blues and reggae, and later some very deep funk) and in Rastafarianism, whose themes of life force, vibrations, and manifestations of divinity Smith filtered through his cosmology of sound. Smith adopted the name Wadada (which means "love" in Amharic) as part of his embrace of Rastafarianism, which he told me occurred following "[m]y basic discovery... through Bob Marley."[191] He "went on a pilgrimage to Jamaica, and I went to all of the sites in his songs... quite a spiritual uplifting."[192] He saw this not as a rejection of Christianity so much as an extension of long-held ideas: "one of the decrees of the Christian religion is its waiting for the Messiah... [s]o it wasn't really very hard [to embrace Rastafari] when those natural mystics came out and started talking about a spiritual force that connected the soul level connection with the spirituality and the social captivity."[193] Much of Smith's music of the 1980s focused on Rasta themes, which to him were also universal in their focus on identity, nature, and spiritual-social resonance. Moving from this particular tradition to what is shared, Smith also began to think about the power of musical protest and bearing witness to truths that political power denies. Music was not simply entertainment but "a forum to create this undeniable quest to achieve the ultimate goal for freedom and liberty."[194]

Between the mid-1980s and mid-1990s, Smith focused on his academic career (he has been a professor at Cal Arts for many years) but since then has documented his music in projects of considerable range. On *Tao-Njia* and *Light upon Light* he realized his system's principles using traditional music from various cultures. He composed hymns for the environment, dedications to master musicians, and played consistently intense free improvisation. But the biggest transformation in Smith's life came with his conversion to Islam in 1995. Smith told me, "I had kind of [seen] what Rastafari could do in terms of my spiritual journey, and what was lacking was the notion of organization."[195] He began to "look for a more ritualistic involvement."[196] Reading the Qur'an and the Hadith avidly, Smith felt that he "had found home for the first time."[197] Accepting the totality of his religious journey, Smith made a number of practical changes, including adding Ishmael to his name in order to signify his participation in Islam's genealogy.

Smith has since structured his life and music around Islamic practice. Before composing, practicing, and teaching each day, Smith says, "I usually do prayer and read the *Koran*. This takes about one hour. Then I drive to the Mosque...[where] I do prayer."[198] His embrace of Islam was consistent with his religious inclinations since childhood, framing experiences from the mundane to the cosmological, including his musical system, since "religion plays a big part in helping people realign themselves and bring them to their Creator."[199] Just as his pilgrimage to Jamaica was essential for Smith to realize such ideas during his Rasta phase, so too was taking the Hajj of paramount importance for his self-actualization as a Muslim.

Smith believes that Islam helps him realize his musical principles at their fullest. But he does not think that audiences need to embrace the specificity of his religion to experience joy or fulfillment. He believes that if his music is embraced on its own terms—its stillness, spaciousness, and (thinking of one of his oft-used titles) "reflectativity"—listeners "can be changed by a musical event."[200] And if this is possible, larger change is—through the refracted power of transformed perception and consciousness—achievable through sound too. Without art, Smith insists, "[S]ociety would've collapsed a long time ago."[201] Smith notes that, like his beloved Thoreau, he does "not expect or demand anything in return" for his art, remaining confident in the effects of sincere engagement with music.[202] Smith agreed enthusiastically with my suggestion that people exposed to creative music might become better people because of the music's role in their lives: "[t]hat's a true fact, you know. And people...understand and have a better relationship with other people, if they hear music in the context that we talk about," rather than simply "feel[ing] good for the moment."[203]

The prophet or the artist can bring about a different way of being in the world. Smith described this capacity as practically hierophanic: "it *is* very powerful....You have to really step out and it's a moment of real engagement."[204] Smith's projects are designed to direct and embody such perceptual transformations. In a general sense, then, he thinks of his music as a whole as a kind of "spiritual music. And if I went a little bit deeper, I call it Islamic music. And if I'm going a little bit deeper, I call it Sufi music."[205] Each orientation realizes Ankhrasmation's goal of "allow[ing] the person a moment to reflect minus the distraction of living."[206] He describes this experience of creativity as very much a kind of Turnerian liminality: the listener has "the same problems, but they have experienced a few moments of liberation to give them enough energy to carry on until the next challenge comes."[207] The experience is mutual when musicians and audiences experience this welling up of emotion and its sustaining power: "You set up this kind of invisible wave that ties you into your audience. The connection is non-verbal and has all to do with a special tuning that takes place" between knowledge and emotion.[208]

Sharing space-time together, it is the immediate bloom of sound and rhythm that transforms encounters into opportunities, since "[e]very ensemble is like a planet in the cosmos and every leader of an ensemble has a master plan about creation."[209] Even when combining various aesthetics with his system—as he does with music inspired by Noh plays or with the furious electric music of Miles Davis—Smith avows that "[t]he purpose of music is to quiet man's soul so he can hear what the higher self inside is talking about."[210] This very contrast with worldly perception amplifies the sociopolitical implications of Smith's recent projects, Cosmic Music (focused on "the issues of borders, refugees, and immigrants") and Tabligh (which "deals with the issue of the way people look at Islamic ideas and people in Islam").[211] He wants Ankhrasmation to establish new ethical worlds for audiences, focusing on "creative images that cause people to think in a provocative way" about these and other issues.[212]

It may be, then, that the openness and engagement demanded by Ankhrasmation represent Smith's understanding of radical democratic politics (and the necessity of spirituality therein). As Joyce Feigenbaum of Cuneiform Records put it to me, "ALL of Wadada's work is very spiritual... tapping into the *other* through improv."[213] During the first decade of the new millennium, Smith became increasingly compelled by the historical inheritance of his ideas. He began composing his masterpiece to date, the five-hour suite *Ten Freedom Summers*, a chronicle of the civil rights movement. His reckoning with this seminal moment in American history—when musical, religious, and political forces coalesced in a great, if partly unrealized, opportunity—was also fueled by a sense of urgency and concern about what he regards as the "spiritual violence" visible in contemporary America, which he attributes to a shared religio-political condition that requires transformation or healing. "If a person's leg has gangrene," he explained, "you've got to amputate it.... [O]ur society has changed and it is changing, but that change has caused a lot of injury among people who thought they had all the power."[214] This is a trauma created by disconnectedness, in Smith's reckoning, which music can address by awakening us to the need for reconnection. Smith calls the civil rights movement the "most transformative" moment in American history, whose story provides a unique opportunity to realize the potential of creative music to further those transformations. Focusing on key persons and events, Smith marries

FIGURE 7.3. Wadada Leo Smith in performance. Photograph by Scott Groller, copyright Cuneiform Records.

history with music as part of his conviction that creative music did more than just accompany the civil rights movement. He explained to me that if Malcolm X, Martin Luther King Jr., Thurgood Marshall, and other freedom fighters had taken as their soundtrack the music of the Aylers, John Coltrane, Don Cherry, and others who played "spiritual music," things might have gone even further in the direction of political and spiritual liberation: "[n]o one thinks that the music can liberate them directly... but really, that free music coming out the early Fifties and Sixties, that's what that meant."[215]

Ten Freedom Summers realizes Ankhrasmation principles using a variety of ensembles, to reckon with episodes in African American religious history. While frequent Smith collaborator Vijay Iyer has warned of jazz that purports to be a history lesson, Smith said of this work, "I've always thought about the meaning of my music, how I would like for it to find its meaning in society."[216] The music is not merely didactic but aims to distill and edify at once. As ever, Smith interpolates multiple American musics, conjuring moods of disorientation, anger in the face of injustice, resolution through slow-burn funk, and defiant optimism. The music moves in a burnished bronze reflective space, which could almost be heard as deliberative, with individual instruments goading the collective into possibility. Smith's own playing is stirring, as he holds long tones that seem to create their own context, finding some new space after the tragedy captured in portraits of Emmett Till, the Little Rock Nine, and Medgar Evers. At times the ensembles seem to reach beyond themselves, fulfilling Smith's particular vision of democratic sound and spirituality while also capturing long traditions of American musical experimentalism. As dark as *Ten Freedom Summers* gets, its music is ultimately uncontainable, inexorable, overflowing with energies yet always tethered to an overarching sense of purpose, knowing it inhabits that moral universe whose arc bends toward justice.

"Democracy" barrels forward, hesitant to commit to one direction, thematically exemplary as multiple voices coexist in a piece made up of successive moments, never a finalized coherence. And the epic concludes with the haunting, chastened "Martin Luther King, Jr.: Memphis, the Prophecy." Smith, who witnessed and participated in this history, is playing to us our better and lesser angels, defiantly refusing to pin a smiley face on a history that, like his music, is ongoing and aimed at the possibility of freedom summers to come. For Smith, engaging history is part of his investigations of interaction and communication in the idioms of jazz and spirituality.

That the laws and traditions of U.S. democratic culture have not been perfectly fulfilled is no indictment of them; rather, Smith insists that "there is still a mechanism for one day having success."[217] Like music, like one's own interpretation of spirituality, these things "have to undergo constant revision to become what they were dreamed about."[218] More than simply a method, Ankhrasmation seeks to draw together traditions and seekers in joyful noise whose sameness and multiplicity can realize new spaces, new worlds of sound. Smith's movement through traditions is in some sense parallel to the story of American religions writ large, the sound of his musical system mirroring the reflection and prayerfulness it also enjoins.

"One Organ of Total Comprehension"

Cornetist Lawrence D. "Butch" Morris, a veteran of New York's loft jazz scene in the 1970s, devised a flexible system of conducted improvisation that he called Conduction. With an elaborate range of hand signs, Morris was able to coax from ensembles around the world a startling array of colors and instrumental possibilities. He insisted that each player took responsibility for the music while also surrendering to its demands, a twinned disposition that he told me developed and transformed mind and spirit through sound.[219] Morris said that the goal of Conduction was not only to eliminate oppressive form by embracing abstraction, but to realize among musicians "[o]ne organ of total comprehension."[220] Conduction aimed at what he called an "Extra Dimension" "that thrives in a real-time transmission of relationships and meaning."[221] Most heard Morris's music as seriously avant-garde, but he told me that all of his music was "based on/in Spirituals (Gospel), Blues, R&B, Jazz and the inner-self. All of these musics...are about devotion and understanding."[222] He saw his methods as simply "tools to reach new goals of expression" since "[i]t is the PRIMUS OF THE SPIRIT (of self and community) that allows anyone to give as they do.... The spiritual is in the giving and devotion."[223]

So while Morris did not construct elaborate metaphysical systems like Braxton, reconfigure harmony like Russell or Coleman, or find the sustaining silence in Smith's Ankhrasmation, his Conduction captured—even in single, elegant hand gestures—the spiritual investments in the very idea of shaping music, using form to bring certain ideas and aspirations into being, including religious ones. This notion of building systems of meaning is deep in the American grain, from the architecture of the apocalyptic to the multiple worlds of Mormon cosmology to the enchanted universe of Scientology, where clear humans roam free of MEST (matter, energy, space, and time). Americans construct their own languages for reckoning with the void, consciously or not sitting in with a historical ensemble playing Walt Whitman's heart music beneath stars shining with meaning. They also talk to these skies, in dreams of ancestors, maps of heaven, or deep inquiries into the folds of time. All of this is recognizable to "religion," it should be clear. But when it comes through horns and drums and strings, is it less so? And if it lacks words that tell you it is religious, do we then rule it out of this already nebulous category?

Coleman, Braxton, and others are not simply composing their lives or their worlds in and through sound; they are giving shape to and improvising on "religion" itself by locating it in new systematic housings. Far from the relatively familiar shapes of traditions, narratives, and communities (even if these are less stable locations than one might imagine), and beyond even the practices of ritual or selflessness, jazz's self-authorship in the space of its own sheer openness represents perhaps its most "religious" of gestures. It is easily indexed to religious history, pregnant with themes resonating with spirits rejoicing. The ancient Greek understanding of music was indebted to an overall conception of the relation of the human to the natural world (in which chords were understood relationally, with particular note arrangements capturing varied dispositions), and Roman thinkers like Boethius alleged that a composer "'put together' his vision of the cosmic order of these physics ... [in] *musica mundana*, or 'music of the world.'"[224] Marsilio Ficino wrote, following Plotinus's *De Rebus Philosophicus* and al-Kindi's medieval treatise *De Radiis*, that "all realities emit vibrating rays which together compose the harmonious chorus of the universe."[225] For Socrates, music was a model for justice; Ptolemy organized time and space according to musical scales; Kepler used intervals to measure planetary motion; and Newton believed the "soul of the world" was "musicotheological."[226] Traces of the originary sound of creation vibrate in dust and stars and motion, their changing oscillation and manifestation forming patterns that humans can divine, imitate, summon, and join for a range of benefits and insights. The harmonic whole gives shape to things in their thingness, which can be construed as overtones, resonances, and modes by which we might become attuned to a fundamentally sonic existence.

Sound is a means by which we might analyze and understand mystery; it is also the substance of that which begs understanding. It is the stuff of enchantment and spirits, but also the form that summons those spirits to rejoice with us. Sound is something to absorb, consume, let permeate our vibratory selves, so that we might intuit the universe as a map (or better, a score) of sonic "scriptures" showing that the space between us and the divine is both vast and non-existent at once.[227] Is this, then, what these systems seek to do: score the cosmos, bridge the gap between the Monad of creation and our fleshy vehicles? Is improvisation thus a form of automatic writing, or the kind of channeling that Helena Blavatsky addressed in *The Secret Doctrine*?[228]

These jazz metaphysicians—inheritors of the traditions named above, co-dwellers in the America of Elijah Muhammad and the Mother Plane—surely number among the most powerful visionaries in American religion. Throughout this book we have seen how "jazz" inevitably, from traditions to the mind coming to know itself, "lifts the bandstand." Here, spirits come to rejoice in liftoff itself, the whole family of musical traditions grabbing hold of Sun Ra's "Rocket No. 9" as it takes off for the planet Venus, and beyond. The very imagination of "religion" itself takes place on planes vibratory, Gnostic, sidereal. These systems are built for sound to transform bodies, and music is understood in terms of their specifics: the sonic surplus of improvisation is felt, by those who consciously inhabit these systems, as the current of sonic transformation orchestrating fingers and lungs to produce the right sounds; in the whirling possibility of an LCC composition the musician senses correspondences with the infinity of the Creator, each carefully wrought decision forming horizontal bodies; the forward tug of Coleman's unleashed Harmolodic sound frames music-making as the link between democratic sound and divine love; Braxton's vast system aims to make it possible for each human to become a "friendly experiencer" of sound, numbers, discovery, and the universe; and Smith's Ankhrasmation stills and settles, with its insistent silences and spaces, recoloring the atmosphere reflective. Music is neither ontologically nor temporally prior to the systems, but their momentary recognition, transportation device, or index to read the stars.

It is customary in religious traditions, particularly in mystical or metaphysical sub-traditions, to posit human bodies as manifestations of cosmic energies, the body electric at times transformed into pure consciousness. Could we then see improvising, perhaps especially as practiced in and through these metaphysics, as a kind of yogic form of becoming immense, of unleashing energies and potentials, practicing and sensing a mode of selfhood that is beyond the limits of selfhood? These different architectures of meaning, then, provide the sonic, interactive cues by which participants become responsive to the religiosity that the systems themselves posit was there all along, was the only thing that could possibly bring such

music into being, could summon—instrumentally, spiritually—such altered states of energy from the vastness of the all.

The self becomes part of the sound, which is a part of these metaphysics, which are part of divine creation itself, however improvised, however understood. The entire universe is electrified, magnified, ascended in
vibratory flux. As with Spiritualism's engagement with cosmic frequencies,
the yogic attention to the *kundalini* energy opening the "portal of cosmic
being," or even the Emersonian fascination with electromagnetism, jazz
cosmologies posit that reality itself is a sonic medium.[229] Jazz is realized in
time, is *of* time, its sequential momentariness like an eternal genesis whose
raw components and originary cosmic fluid give way to structure, mystic
chords assembled and dissolved like seasons, life cycles, stars dying to be
born anew. The energies that come alive in music surpass the limits of the
material, even considering the absolute, exacting physicality of music-
making. Indeed, awareness of this play of limits and vastness is, to these
theorists among others, precisely what leads to transformation, the simultaneous expansion and dissolution of the self; and the aspiration to create
music of pure possibility—in these various "cosmic" musics, like other
idioms outside of "jazz" (*gagaku* court music, La Monte Young's "dream
chord," Tuvan throat singing, Olivier Messiaen's celestial symphonies, or
P-Funk landing the Mothership in Constitution Hall)—is the desire to
create new worlds, new galaxies, as Braxton enthuses.[230] Jazz's connection
between musical and spiritual innovation dwells in and relies on the very
provisional and protean qualities of existence that inspire the heavenward
dreaming to start. The interlocking of parts in metaphysical wholes, and
the reach beyond genre, seem apposite to the music made through these
idiosyncratic architectures, embodying and resounding with their own
sonic thematics: silence, self-reference, harmonic freedom.

What is at stake here for improvising musicians is not so much an
aesthetic appreciation of the stars, a musical astrology, a preoccupation
with extraterrestrial life, or a sonic creation story. What underwrites these
systems is theorization of sound as transformative. While the experiential
has been a concern throughout this book, the subjects of this chapter theorize the human experience—positioned before the source of mystery,
awakening, or enlargement beyond the limits of personhood itself—as
both sonic and religious. The construction of systems here facilitates not
simply a new level of creative music-making, but religious insight that is
historical and futuristic, individual and social.

From Kant to Niebuhr, religious thinkers have found significance in humanity's smallness before the universe's vastness. For the musicians discussed here, it is possible that the void itself, the very dark expanse of as-yet unrealized art, is what constitutes "religion." If so, then these systems are assemblages of names given to the inexorable flow of life, to paraphrase Gilles Deleuze and Félix Guattari. In jazz this starry heaven is made sound, its basic mutability a confirmation that improvisation is truth, the real. Religion is thus the substance, the vector, the medium, the name. As sound reaches beyond limits, the long fetch of the cosmic imagination deposits a "religion" knowable in its sheer awestruckness, its affective gravity. As William James once wrote, "If religion is to mean anything definite for us, it seems to me that we ought to take it as meaning this added dimension of emotions, this enthusiastic temper of espousal...the keynote of the universe sounding in our ears."[231] Listen.

8

"Spirits Rejoice!"

BEYOND "RELIGION"[1]

For poetry was all written before time was, and whenever we
are so finely organized that we can penetrate into that
region where the air is music, we hear those primal war-
blings and attempt to write them down, but we lose ever and
anon a word or a verse and substitute something of our own,
and thus miswrite the poem.

—RALPH WALDO EMERSON[2]

"ONE." THAT'S WHAT Thelonious Monk said onstage when Ben Riley and
the other Young Turks in his 1960s band went too far out and, having lost
their way, needed a lighthouse in the fog. After long, patient minutes,
Monk reminded his bandmates where the one was, where the tune was.[3]
So where are we now? We left off in a state of pure vibration, having begun
chapters ago in the familiar location of a structure, a lineage. Has the journey
been a continuous or a fragmentary one, amenable to narrative or merely
grouped together in false assemblage? And what might the significance or
meaning of these chapters be—for "jazz," for "religion," for scholarship?

My goals in bringing these stories together in this shifting constellation of ear trumpets have been twofold: suggesting that we can think
about both jazz and American religions in fresh ways, and also raising
questions about the study of "religions" themselves. This may be a single
goal bifurcated; for in complicating what we can know about jazz and
religion separately, their inevitable togetherness emerges. I have tried not
to indulge in the academic overdetermination of the material with shoe-
horned theory, and instead let the cases and frames emerge *as* theoretical
orientations to spirits rejoicing. These "arrangements" also resonate with
those in the study of religion in recent decades: musical explorations in

Islam or Scientology facilitate understanding of the creative adaptations Americans have made to traditions, especially since the 1960s; spirits rejoicing's religio-musical chronicles are woven into new understandings of the religious past to emerge in the last half-century; the religio-sonic pedagogy of the UGMAA or BAG resounds in a long history of religious communitarianism; new focus on the intentionality of bodies and the pliability of ritual makes room for the improvised settings of spirits rejoicing; practices of egolessness and talk of vessels resonate with scholarly conversations about affect and cognition in religion; and jazz's cosmologic systems emerge from the atmosphere of American maverick composition and from broader histories of sonic metaphysics. So this music fits with reconfigurations of "religion" among scholars as well as practitioners, and in "jazz" these conversations take shape and can be heard. I have written with the sensorium of religions in mind, striving to flesh out the sound and practice of jazz and its religiosities in descriptions of playing, practicing, gigging, and communicating that, I hope, have made more of this subject than simply the acknowledgment that jazz belongs to music, music to sound, and sound to senses. About power and the limits of "religion" more will be said below. But I bring these considerations up here to trouble them with another blast of music.

The first spacious, exploratory lines of Anthony Braxton's alto solo on "Composition 40F/23J," from 1976, are like hand gestures in space. They float, buoyed by brisk swing, until Braxton's tone becomes more heated, as he seemingly huffs and howls through the bell of the horn, his phrases more dense and rapid. The music races at such velocity that it sounds like it may fall apart completely, reaching a point of such intensity that Braxton finally issues three staccato yawps that elicit a massive roar from the audience. What "meaning" can we hear in Braxton's changing tone, or in his quartet's herky-jerky rhythmic language? We saw previously that in the mid-1970s Braxton briefly enjoyed major label support and was identified as jazz's next standard-bearer of authenticity, a designation of considerable complication and burden. The conceptual omnivore Braxton found himself saddled with the expectation that his innovations would be bound by the conventions of swing, shouting horn solos, and running the changes.

For Braxton, these unspoken assumptions were the product of "the reality of the sweating brow" (RSB) discussed throughout this book: the palpable field of racialized expectations audiences have when engaging "jazz," often understood to be music played by sweating, cathartic, emotionally exuberant black performers who, as critic Gene Santoro writes, "aren't supposed to think, just sort of squirt out carefree improvised noises with a Sambo grin: that's their natural talent as well as their preordained upper limit of cultural achievement."[4] The RSB lurks behind musicians' investments in tradition, counter-memory, and community, and shapes their practices and system-building. But the "jazz" that supports and institutionally transmits presumptions about the limits of black creativity is also linked to powerful historical idioms of religio-racial control. Braxton laments the "spectacle diversion syndrome" by which "Western media subvert the spiritual dimensions of non-Western cultures by focusing on their surface particulars."[5] Against "the stereotype 'jazz' musician who swings, blows and gets down all night long . . . not so far removed from the stereotype black stud or 'sex man,'" Braxton used performance to kick dirt on this racial habitus.[6] Sometimes his thrilling saxophone solos like the one discussed above were through-composed, a scandal to the presumption of the "intuitive" improviser.

Remember Lester Bowie: it all depends on what we know about jazz. Much work in jazz studies has, following George Lipsitz's example, focused on "serious play" and the importance of counter-representation. Jazz's improvisations on religion constitute such challenges to prevailing racial representations and their surrounding social conditions. These dynamics were shaped broadly by a mid-twentieth-century American modernity, an unconscious cosmopolitan secular in which pluralism, technology, and abundance seemed to entail to critics an existence defined by habituation to a placid, routine life of pleasures emptied of meaning. Public imagination held that jazz had morphed from an exoticized, urban, eruptive, and polymorphous source of panic to a lifestyle choice or soundtrack to safe sophistication; this fantasy mirrored those positing the domestication of postwar politics in the institutional balance of polyarchy and of religion in a kind of liberal interiorization.

Regardless of the narratives we could spin about the co-optation of cool, and the religion and politics of this era, we know the truths that these lies conceal: the mutual imbrication of modernism and its others, secularism and religion, improvisation and composition, a polysemy and coarticulation that render fluid all that seeks stability. Religion did not play nice, politics never enjoyed full legitimacy, and jazz remained illegible.[7] Still freighted by that other modernism, the notion of an authentic self-creation made possible through overcoming one's cultural inheritance, jazz's refusal to be limited by genre is, as Art Lange notes, "an obvious enough metaphor for an individual overcoming the immensity of America."[8] Such overcoming, however, is never complete, particularly as the very intellectual habitus generating dreams of self-authoring is shaped by and births the RSB, which smuggles in a conception of "religion" with a deep racial history that musicians are acutely aware of and actively resist with religiosities both emphatic and inscrutable.

The expanded "knowings" about religion in this book complicate those older presumptions above, but I argue that they also point beyond standard academic formats. There is always more music to play, even of scholarly songs, but below I offer some conclusions by exploring how spirits rejoicing's resistance to closure serves to counter the RSB; drawing together the book's two keywords and arguing that the fuzziness of "jazz" and "religion" as stable signifiers resonates with contemporary debates about "religion" and the "secular," leading scholars to realize the ineluctably poetic qualities of their craft; and proposing that the scholarly engagement with spirits rejoicing—and its terminological limits—constitutes no closure of descriptive and analytic possibility but a fresh way to think about religious experience, since it is the fleeting experience of presence and absence conjoined that is so powerful to those who avow the music is sacred.

The Reality of the Sweating Brow

We know now that jazz has been experienced religiously (by both players and audiences), but in response to the RSB these religiosities take shape in protest, satire, and counter-representations. These performances are improvised exchanges between players and audiences, and in their restless motion, a fluid creativity that does not settle, jazz is established as a flow rather than a genre; its religiosity is ever incomplete, continually changing and resounding even out of earshot. As notes blend with prayer, rhythm with ritual, the sound of spirits rejoicing emerges through an agency simultaneously constrained and polymorphous. Gary Peters calls improvisation a "rethinking of freedom in terms of memory," starting points that far exceed modernist conceptions of the self focused merely on autonomy or which "reduce improvisation to a glorified love-in dressed up as art."[9] These are, after all, creative musical and religious practices focused on the agon of alterity and representation, and crafted in often bleak circumstances.

Trumpeter Roy Campbell described to me how an improvising musician navigates the RSB. In post-Giuliani New York, each year seems further to diminish the creative arts that have long drawn people to what some musicians call "Monster Island." While tourists flock to the expensive Blue Note and Iridium—where scant evidence exists of jazz as a younger, developmental music—venues change (the Knitting Factory is now a pop club), close (Tonic, Sweet Basil, CBGB's Down Under, and too many more to name), or migrate from loft to loft, borough to borough. With fewer and fewer working opportunities for bands, and little support from city sources, most players either move or scrape together a living giving lessons and playing "door gigs." Campbell explained with mordant humor, "[T]hese are what I call McDonald's Happy Meal gigs. You know, you only get enough to pay for a Happy Meal."[10] This fascinating reference invokes not only the corporatism of American cities but an empty sustenance that contrasts with the intentions and aspirations of most musicians. Can jazz sustain in McWorld, transforming and ennobling those who fall under its spell? The question certainly resounds in the particular spaces of neoliberalism, but it also links back to the long tradition of racialized misrepresentation that, flourishing unconsciously even among benevolent hipsters, constrains black subjectivity, creativity, and religiosity.

Drummer Andrew Cyrille answers the question by calling the music "a kind of spiritual moat providing a means of self-identification and happiness for those who will listen and understand."[11] Certainly the moat is meant to keep out false representations. But there is something much larger here, evident in analysis and central to musicians' self-understandings and aspirations. Sound does more than simply stir up "religion." As Campbell told me, "[M]y music *is* my religion.... I play what I live and have experienced, and it's about history, about spirit, it's all connected."[12] These are the connections often obscured by a racial habitus whose long history echoes in parallel interpretations of jazz and religion. Though this field of expectation and constraint directly impacts African American musicians, who stand in the center of this history, its effects are felt by all performers, even if unconsciously. Curtis Evans documents changes occurring to the "racial habitus" between the nineteenth and twentieth centuries, in categorical shifts from "savage" to "emotive savant," from degraded "animism" to "civilized religion."[13] "Race" came to depend on "religion" as one of its fundaments, and the racial taxonomies central to American public life took shape in part via a discourse that posited black religion's innateness, emotionality, primitivism, and irreducibility. Both attraction and revulsion turned on these imagined traits, their wildness, their excess, their merging in spectacle. Jazz was born amid and took shape in these very conversations linking racial imaginaries with religious naturalism and its sociopolitical implications. So too have jazz audiences persistently recapitulated these tropes, theorizing black creativity for the creators.

While cultured despisers may once have lamented black religion's "heathenish observances," "insane yellings," and "violent contortions," these very "unhallowed performances" and enthusiasms have long titillated white jazzbos who make of black vernacular music a cultural accessory.[14] It was through the noisy embodiment of black religion that critics fashioned their understanding of black culture, proximity to which they warned could endanger one of falling under the spell of those sounds, lusty and immediate. As Laurie Maffly-Kipp notes, this religio-racial imagination denigrates cultural particulars—for example, Henry McNeal Turner once overheard fellow sea passengers who "reasoned the negro out as fit for nothing but to play, drink whisky, and steal from the white race"—while valorizing abstract primitivism.[15] Such sensory expression has also been the vehicle through which jazz's reception dynamics reinforced key features of the racial habitus. Archie Shepp called jazz "the product of the whites—the ofays—too often my enemy," but also "the progeny of the blacks—my kinsmen."[16]

American civic identity has always been bound up with, even dependent on, such representations of dark-skinned others. The extremism and abandonment associated with black expression have persistently been associated with threats to social stability or moral rectitude, even as their apparent exoticism proved alluring to audiences and observers. Musical performance, ostensibly a "natural" outlet for black expressivism, has been cited as evidence of the sorts of ontological enthusiasms rendering African Americans unfit for other kinds of public discourse or participation. Yet from vaudeville to the Art Ensemble of Chicago stretches a tradition of performances employing these same objectifications in order to suspend social and religious disciplines, to satire and skewer convention, and to transform orientations to and experiences of one's social world. As George Lewis writes, evoking racial typologies in performative settings serves not just to ratify them but to place "emphasis upon resistance, and its excavations of subaltern and marginalized histories of sound."[17]

In this tradition, religions have frequently served as both objects of and vehicles for subversion—mocking religious reductionism or seizing hold of it in order to control its direction in history or music. Through shifting use of the languages and practices of "religion," musicians have confronted or evaded or jazzed the languages and practices of authenticity that have often functioned as constraints on creativity and agency. This has not taken place through "religion" exclusively, or always even obviously; and as I wrote in chapter 1, many religious communities were deeply nervous about jazz in its early decades, complicating any easy association with jazz and the "amen cadence" just as it is deceptive to name it the sound-track to modernity. But religions, in all their unstable formations, have been "critical levers" in performance, community, and devotions; in relations of power between musicians and spirits, in meditation or trance states, in musical cosmologies that point beyond the social order. Religions are not simply countersigns for players; rather, in these improvisations toward gods and spirits, drums are struck differently, breath becomes quickened by spirits, and ears awaken to the edifying possibilities of music that makes it possible to live differently in the world.

Yet Albert Ayler's dreams of universal sound were dismissed by review-ers who sneered, "Sincerity, alas, has never yet sufficed to make notable art."[18] Coltrane's innovations were denounced as "anti-jazz."[19] "Jazz" again emerges as a discourse of commercial, aesthetic, and hence cultural limi-tation, even as its democratic freedoms are trumpeted. Attempts to move beyond its well-heeled expectations (gentlemanly swing, soul patches, Debussy-like chordal substitutions) are often met with questions about its authenticity. Braxton describes his endeavors as "creative music" since, "if I write an opera, then of course it's a jazz opera. If I go have a hamburger, it's a jazz hamburger."[20] Pianist/composer Anthony Davis has said, "If somebody uses tradition as a way of limiting your choices, in a way that's as racist as saying you have to sit at the back of the bus."[21] Clarinetist and composer Don Byron links such cultural and political limitations not only to slavery and Jim Crow but to the Tuskegee experiments conducted on African American sharecroppers beginning in 1932, which he describes as "metaphors for African American life."[22] It is easy to understand the urgency of these contentions considering that jazz criticism and "recep-tion dynamics" have often appropriated the fantastical languages described by Evans, Maffly-Kipp, and Ronald Radano. In the 1930s, purportedly rep-utable jazz criticism was published with titles like "Shout, Coon, Shout!"[23] Louis Armstrong was called a "noble savage," whose playing exuded "in-tensity" and "intuition."[24] Of course, Armstrong was also accused of "race betrayal" while Charlie Parker was dismissed as "too intellectual."[25]

By the mid-1950s, these representations of jazz had been disseminated broadly, yielding a kind of jazz orientalism whereby African Americans "naturally" channeled the exoticism audiences craved, even as musicians could only rarely be anything other than a heated, sexualized other or a smil-ing ingratiate.[26] Narratives of jazz's naturalism and exoticism thus recapitu-late arguments about black religion and culture, upon whose expressions

American cultural, religious, and musical truths have depended. If spirits rejoicing rarely settles in one place, and resists conventional demonstrations of its own salient qualities, how can constraint be overcome more than provisionally? The performances considered in this book are aware of their transitory nature, but also of their power. While their religiosity cannot easily be detached from the social location of the performers, or the musical from the religious, the performance as improvised event with multiple meanings cannot avoid signifying and resonating in ways resistant to conventional talk about jazz, religion, and subjectivity. This is of course not to overlook the manifold constraints shaping these performances; but here sound and subjectivity are coproduced in moments both subject to the presence of the spirit and liberated by its distance from the mundane.[27] So performance in/of the tensional spaces of identity is always both voluntary (in the mode of "play") and coerced (in the inevitability of "codes"), ineluctably wrapped up with that which it seeks to elude, merely by the power of ostensive reference.

At work here is the cultivation and preservation of alternate black histories and religiosities against the leveling critical gaze of a history with American roots in the seventeenth century. Musicians' engagement with this inheritance, with or without overt irreverence like the AEC's or discursivity like John Carter's, has consciously lived and performed religiosity in efforts to recapture language and symbolism, inverting expectations by playing into them. This is something more than simply taking ownership of the languages of denial, and more than just satire; it is also an index of Zora Neale Hurston's "lying up," which Radano reminds is central to American understandings of race. This is embodied in expressive styles seeming to exult in the older associations of the term "jazz," which Yusef Lateef once enumerated "nonsense, balderdash, bilge, blather, bunkum."[28] To these add an improvisational tendency to mockery and satire: the AEC's mugging preacher, Duke Ellington's proffered pork chop, or Monk's assertion that "[s]ometimes it's to your advantage for people to think you're crazy."[29]

Yet such strategic anti-essentialism resonates differently in consideration of spirits rejoicing. If, as Nathaniel Mackey says, expressive arts are "reaching toward an alternate reality, [and] music is the would-be limb whereby that reaching is done," religions are like mutagens transforming already unstable identities into vehicles of new experience or change.[30] So in the world of Happy Meal gigs and the RSB, there is an ineluctably political element even to the unpredictable play of elements that we seek to render distinct and recognizable with the terms "music" and "religion."

Even if jazz has not always communicated the structural constraints of its condition explicitly, it has regularly articulated what Paul Gilroy calls "opportunities for democratic, oppositional agency" through sound.[31] Careful attention to the local, particular forms of this agency has revealed a consistently religious (or "spiritual") emphasis posited by the musicians: "religion" as a mode of expression and performance; "religion" as a code-scrambler undermining routinization and co-optation; or improvisation as a kind of evasion, supplemented by religious "mystery," discursive "incoherence," *jouissance*, or polysemy.[32]

But somehow this focus on codes and play still somehow relies too heavily on the politics of language. Even if we think of horns and strings and drums as constituting a "speech" of some kind, we must look to how bodily practice yields practical reason, and how comportment, intersubjectivity, and movement shape our experience of our world, whether as musicians or listeners. Jason Stanyek refers to such "intercorporeality" as "a body-based, face-to-face exchange of ideas and sounds."[33] In other words, as opposed to mystifications of "sound itself," attending to situatedness and embodiment can help not only foreground race and similar protean categories but can help attend to difference, ambiguity, and provisionalism. Focus on the religious performances of resistance to constraints gives new resonance to these sounds—their echoes traveling from listener to listener—even as it eludes fixation, phrase after phrase, possibility after possibility. More than simply pointing out the limitations of old aesthetics, performance has served as the vehicle by which new aesthetics and religiosities are tried out and recalibrated.

Even here, though, I risk reducing, settling on a single conceptual orientation without recognizing the depths it conceals. My goal all along has been to ask what we are missing in our stories of American religion, what we are failing to hear. By writing these spirits rejoicing into the narratives of American religions, and linking them to anthropologically recognizable practices like ritual or meditation, this book has affirmed the legitimacy of experiences too often overlooked. Yet if enshrining memory and identity in song, in musical playfulness, is one way of eluding the grasp of alien representations, the academic tendency to focus on anti-essentialist "performance" seems slightly too boilerplate for a music so restless for change; its self-satisfied conclusion that agency as such is a form of "resistance" fails—despite Cecil Taylor's admonition that genuine feeling in America is revolutionary—to match its subject in liveliness.

Jazz, with its wordplay and stylistic signifying, and its religious intensities, has been a vehicle for musicians to establish themselves as "creative

non-participants in mainstream culture."[34] Critique and mordant humor
are classic survival strategies employed by outsiders, and so the playfulness with identity and theatrical "staging" of conventions to expose their
limits are subversions often mistaken for "mere" entertainment.[35] But language is never merely communicative or utilitarian; it is itself a show, a
performance, in its abundance, its otherness, its secrecy and mystifications. More than that, the enormity of spirits rejoicing is also a claim for
religious experience resonating emphatically in the study of religions.

Something Clean, Sparkling, Elusive

Resistance to naming and representation is a register of jazz's volatility,
but it is one that is also a *part* of American religions. The problems of classifying something as "religious" or not bedevils Americans in each historical phase, wrestling with the distinction between "religion" and "cult," or
meditating on the collective effervescence linking revivals and tailgate
parties. The capaciousness and abstraction by which jazz is named *as* religious is no evasion of the particulars of history—communities established
or rituals undertaken—but a means by which religion's surplus and volatility are announced, which serves also as the means by which listeners
might understand their immersion *in* it. Duke Ellington once said that
"[j]azz is tied to many stories... none of which could be true."[36] While resistance to codification resonates importantly with traditions of African
American religious practice that avoids the critical gaze, musicians have
continually announced that spirits rejoicing is not merely a vector of
self-determination but the vehicle of transformation of consciousness and
community. The music resonates within a critical tradition established by
W. E. B. DuBois, "emphasizing the realm of spirit as a site of black achievement," where music is understood as a singular gift of the gods to culture.[37] But spirits rejoicing constitutes its own traditions of American
religious innovation, too, scrambling identities by inscribing its difference
across the face of the known with swing or shrieks, from *ppp* or *fff* to be
heard above culture's din.

   To think about music largely devoid of ostensive reference, of canonical
text or ritual, invites not just historical linkages like the above but the
problem of language as such. Does jazz thus demand to be heard in parallel
with the "religion as *sui generis*" tradition, notably cultivated by those who
hear it as the sound of America's uniqueness, a "natural language" distilling
its cooperative, democratic spirit?[38] In this, would Duke Ellington's famous

dictum that music is "beyond category" become a category itself? Other languages beckon, both opportunity and transgression. Jason Kao Hwang told me that any consideration of jazz and religion took one necessarily into the "post-linguistic."[39] So when Hart Crane urged, as early as 1922, "Let us invent an idiom for the proper transposition of jazz into words! Something clean, sparkling, elusive," we now hear perhaps only that final word in our continually failing efforts.[40] If music points, then, it points to non-pointing, refers to non-reference, gestures at no gesture. Jazz embraces ritual and mystery, and complicates givens in the name of a larger, generative process of self-cultivation that resists the world's efforts to, as T. S. Eliot wrote, "fix you in a formulated phrase."[41] When language so demonstrably cannot denote that which it seeks to be about, we are tempted to conclude that its architecture is not habitable but only tentative, teetering: when language breaks down, then, we regenerate it in "translations," laminations, unsatisfying or false projections, even knowing excess and decentering. So I have known, in constructing this archive, that I am still chasing that smoke. Yet a different poet, Paul Celan, wrote that "[l]anguage remains unlost, in spite of everything."[42] The elusiveness of spirits rejoicing is no analytic or authorial problem, at least not one that puts an end to things; its wispiness does not vex, nor do its changing shapes and densities force me to call in question what I have written about the ephemera of the moment before. No, it is this very mobile quality that compels, like that certain something in the sound of a voice, the indescribable grain and texture, that evocative noise that we can describe but never pin down. And though there is surely no false finality that can or should be announced, with so fluid a subject and so reverberant a music, the names and narratives and categories proposed here sound out the place of spirits rejoicing in American religions.

The very traditions of improvised play documented in this book invite the embrace of the *ars poetica* of American religious studies itself, our own inevitably improvisatory complicity in fabrication and the celebration of its possibilities. I have put no words in anyone's mouth or horn that were not there, but these chapters—as sure as they are that "religion" is central to jazz's histories and that "jazz" moves through American religions—remind us continually of the switchbacks, momentary convergences, lipstick traces, and harmonies that wink at you, appearing and receding in your earholes and your stories. Think: it was at the very moment when Russell started constructing the LCC that Sun Ra saw in Fletcher Henderson's charts the template for cosmic self-knowledge, that Coltrane heard in Bird the flight to infinity, that Lacy heard new monastic possibility in the spare logic of

the onliest Thelonious Monk, and that more and more musicians began
to sense that, though there was really no such thing as "jazz," in making
fuzzy this genre they might make clearer—or at least more powerful—the
category "religion" or "spirituality."

To evoke this, I have sought a writing that "occup[ies] corresponding
frequencies" with the music.[43] As these themes and histories and methods
jam together in the ongoing surplus of sound and spirit, "religion" emerges
in multiple and changing shapes through the same exuberant play and
rejoicing *poesis* that also leads to its dissolution. Having described the fluid,
improvisatory qualities of ritual, community, and other religious themes
and practices, my claim is that this constant motion, in and out of attributions, is *itself* a part of the music's history, and of American religion's. The
problem of language does not stand watch, keeping us from understanding
religious experience; it is at least part of the substance of that experience.

It has historically been through the voices, movements, and senses of
religions that the RSB has been located and denounced. These efforts are
recognizable in the history of American religions, even though "religion"
is as elusive as "jazz." But if a theatrical ritual confronts us with our analytical limits, if a new story about religion alters our understandings, if
meditational practices or cosmologies frame the occasion of performance,
what then do we learn more broadly about American religions through the
sounds of jazz? Faithful to complexity and contradiction, we see that while
jazz is an object or expression of religion, religion also gets jazzed. This is
not merely descriptive, but is made material in the sounds, the practices
required to make the sounds, and the experience of musical spirits. More
than a series of subversive practices, these expressions spill expansively
over their limits the moment they are pointed out, sounded out, a phrase
stretched past the breath, a pulse beyond meter. Rather than linking up to
long-standing interpretive traditions seeking to explain religions via some
antecedent form of determination, my evocations of spirits rejoicing have
sought to lay bare the timbres and densities of each religious theme,
describing contextually how spirits rejoicing is lived and practiced: in
pleasure, tactility, sound, and space, as well as modes of perception or cognition. Just as music-making is an ongoing process of relating rhythms
and notes to space, of engendering feelings through performance and
embodied interactions, religion is similarly intersubjective and protean
rather than simply dialogic (self and other, matter and mind).

These practitioners show that their music simply cannot be separated
from the investments in and interrogations of religion that suffuses it. Many

of jazz's most enduring expressions (Ellington, Coltrane, Mingus, and more) would not be what they are without religions, and this entails more than simply an airy acknowledgment of "spirituality" (even though that formulation itself is a part of this history, just as its discursive formation is so enduringly a part of the American religious firmament). So despite the difference these performances can be heard as announcing, and beyond their links to communitarianism or cosmology, they also constitute what Lipsitz calls "the alternative archives of history," enacted in the doing as well as the word.[44] A field that celebrates each new journal unearthed from an antebellum home or every newly discovered collectivity (no matter how small) gathering to channel a divine being or peruse a sacred text should surely affirm the existence of so expansive an archive, documenting not simply self-determination and resistance through sound but an entire compendium of religious practices, ways of knowing, and sonic documents that have been understood by those performing and hearing as sacred presence. Over the last century, in many different elsewheres, sounds out of your earshot have been made in ways flowing directly into and out of their context's most obvious and continual religious engagements: the improvisations on ritual format and the limits of tradition, the cultivation of practices of the self, the foregrounding of relational practices and sonic intercessions between human and divine, the formation of intentional communities, or the telling of new information about the past, the cosmos, and the future. The sounds express, contain, provoke, endorse, and *are* these engagements.

To see how jazz has been a part of the changing religious habitus of the United States in the last century is to understand with new vibrancy the elusiveness of the category "religion" itself, since it makes possible such combination and fluidity. We thus see that not only are these (predominantly African American) musicians among the century's notable religious visionaries, their sounds themselves enact what practice and text make visible elsewhere: these omnivorous readers and questioners and experiencers announce a powerful refusal of boundaries that is increasingly a hallmark of American religions themselves. As surely as the sounds of the church were once heard spilling into the streets, into ostensibly "secular" music, so too does this sonic archive show the movement between "spiritual" and "aesthetic," putatively "alternative" religious figures like Father Divine and some alleged "mainstream," or the tropes of modernism and a cosmic-astral vision of human emancipation. Musicians, in their openness to improvisation and combination, gather up the dualities that usually guide analysis and render from them new forms, the whole entanglement like a large ensemble jam, showing how powerful a current of American religious experience spirits rejoicing is. In this we hear another lesson from Eric Dolphy: we may not be able to recapture sound, but sound doesn't disappear.

Repeat This Mystery

Pause. And begin again. Spirits rejoicing proposes new ways of listening to American religions and jazz, in counter-melodies and overtone series I have argued are more central to the performance than previously imagined. The relative absence of what one usually expects from an "archive" or from "evidence"—jazz's audibility on a recording, or as central in a narrative of religion—is precisely why spirits rejoicing demands more than the standard scholarly tropes of recovering marginalized agency from the past, or retelling narratives newly garlanded with the latest scholarly fashion. So in this book I have *made up*—that is, improvised or poetically elaborated rather than falsified—ways of hearing, proposing categories that are fully and obviously there while also resistant to settled interpretation. By making up/imagining, I have in mind a deliberate practice of trying to think and play beyond the written notes of cultural and academic convention; to fabricate new positions from which to engage and encounter. This multiplicity and playfulness seem appropriate, since there is no straight line to draw between nineteenth-century vernacular music and free jazz, much less between African American Protestant song form and Sun Ra. The connections are, rather, multiple and errant, even as they help establish American religions as fundamentally sonic and expressive. As soon as one identifies historical antecedents, which make possible a certain kind of narrative about jazz and religion, there is a Lester Bowie raspberry coming along to disrupt things.

Because there is no continuous narrative, no musical/racial/religious essence, no single practice or community to privilege, soundings and themes have helped "to draw out in sound" what a horn, drum, or double-stop conjure as "religious" or "spiritual."[45] It has been my hope that these themes better capture jazz's sonic religious, too, as well as articulate more crisply its materiality and sociality: the musical structure and networks of religious selves both made possible by and resistant to these conditions. But music's and religion's felt qualities inevitably flow beyond our frames—in immediacy, experience, and awakening—and thus always improvise on and subvert convention. This dissipation makes possible "flash moments" of recognition, where earlier categories or commitments musicians and listeners might have (Christian, Buddhist, metaphysical) serve as opportunities to rebuild in cognitive, aesthetic, or communal terms, all ascribed as religious. This is not to deny that players and listeners contend fervently that the links and relations (to gods and spirits and the universe) exist *prior* to language; indeed, it is because of the importance of these self-understandings that I have been able to situate these musicians in particular orbits and histories of religio-sonic visionaries.

These maps reveal their own limitations, of course, since the resistance to boundaries shared by "jazz" and "religion" may also be a condition of *writing* about these subjects, language's inability to cling to the very things alleged as certain. Their movement between abstraction and particularity, and our own frustrated hopes for resolution, are part of what Radano identifies as music's propensity to create "generative, constitutive effects" that we rename, knowing our own artifice as we do so.[46] The experience of our own cognitive, interpretive limits might, however, be the very quality of thinking that opens us more fully to the receptivity necessary to study something like spirits rejoicing. The thematic focuses of this book, then, might also be thought of as contributions to debates about the very utility of the category "religion," whose fluidity and boundary-crossing does not so much vex analysis as present a suggestive parallel with improvisation itself. So perhaps new ways of knowing or interpreting religions are possible not in spite of but because of these smoky realities. As trumpeter Dave Douglas suggestively observed, "[T]he mystical, fleeting aspects of music are what unite it with our everyday experience, what permit it to be understood."[47] Precisely by discovering spirits rejoicing's resistance to containment we encounter language's opening to possibility, through incantation, evocation, and *poesis*.

Jazz and religion are continually becoming, even becoming each other, in a shared constellation of play, intensities, and sustained experiential attunement to what the Transcendentalists once thought of as "a world in which each person makes his own truth from what works for him."[48] In some cases, as with Matthew Shipp, it is "spirituality" that makes this possible, with the presumption that this term denotes something non-institutional, dwelling in feeling primarily, and thus distinct from "religion"; in other cases, as with Wadada Leo Smith, it is the very solidity of tradition and lineage that is said to enable the particularities and depths of experience. Yet regardless of the formation we give to the experience—the religious conditions for sound, the sonic conditions for religion—we find that music is understood as a vehicle for the deity's or the spirits' appearance, and for the cultivation of the sensibilities (joyful, reverent, solemn) attendant to such presence.[49] Jazz is a summoning, a bringing forth of the very thing it purports to be *about* and to describe.

As John Milbank wrote in a different context, "[W]e can respond to the ungraspable mystery of incarnation only indirectly—through our own bodily, imagined performances, which seek, however faintly, nonidentically to *repeat this mystery*."[50] This is what the performer does with the unknown results continually spooling futureward; this is what the religious practitioner does in the pregnant space between presence and absence; this is what the scholar does, knowing that I cannot escape the framework of a language that is too limiting, hoping only that I might occupy a more malleable frame as befits my subject. Both "jazz" and "religion" are formed and embodied in multiple ways to become what Courtney Bender calls "practices through which religious experiences become things that people can talk about, and that they can interpret and ponder"—or that they can sound out in new performances.[51] We may not have "data" in Jonathan Z. Smith's sense, or a way of making something solid of smoke. But we have an archive of sound and words *improvising on* the condition of smokiness, a compendium I have heard and transcribed. The more we listen, the more we hear jazz's challenge to representation and its withdrawal from scrutiny alike, each of these concluding themes resounding in each of the case studies preceding it. However, faced with the enormity of these concerns and practices over a century, and the unruly nature of both religion and jazz, it seems almost too pat to conclude with Smith that "religion" is the scholar's creation, too. In leaning on lying up and poetic complicity, I clearly am calling attention to the improvisational relation between scholar and subject (in my focus on linguistic drift and minds of winter). But the music has been played, forcefully, committedly, passionately, devoutly, and to conclude only that jazz itself conjures a fog of religious attributions that link to history would foolishly undermine how centrally and palpably these properties of the sonic sacred have been *experienced* and *practiced*.

To pick up a guitar, chant a sutra beside a piano, paint one's face, or feel oneself merging with the "holy la" is precisely to experience the confinement of format and its suspension in free sound, free spirit. Spirits rejoicing reveals the cracks of the world and of our languages, but before it we might feel transported in and by sound's very elusiveness, like what Herman Melville called the "ungraspable phantom of life."[52] Sound reminds us that the world itself is in continual flux, vibration, and transmutation; and as Ajay Heble writes, jazz engages this world in its own sonic medium of change and evolution.[53] Sound races ahead of and lags behind its own beat, and its beyondness can only be felt and responded to like spirits themselves, which to David Toop makes listening itself "a specimen of mediumship, a question of discerning and engaging with what lies beyond the world of forms."[54] We hope words will bring the self and the world into tune, but it fades as surely as it emerges, shimmering into and out of sound and vision, leaving us with inferences and possibilities rather than a line connecting all dots.

Yet is this not the very substance of the experience of the spirits, rather than the impossibility of holding onto it? On one level, such polymorphousness marks all traditions in their oscillation between frozen moments of memory and practice, and the surplus of experience beyond traditional bounds. But, more than this, the complex entanglements of "religion" and the "secular," along with the hyperdrive multiplication of American religiosities, show that the story of the last American half-century is *about* the blurring of the category "religion" itself, along with aggressive attempts to reassert its clarity in public life. Spirits rejoicing can be seen as an antidote to these violent reassertions, even as it constitutes another, equally deep vein in American religion.

Spirits rejoicing grab you with abstraction and teach you about the religious particular, recapitulating a dynamic central to "religion" itself, whose barely audible limits we seek in the outer reaches of our hearing. I do not mean to posit through these observations simply a different kind of essentialism, the *via negativa* of non-description. This would be to fall back on a prototypically modern formulation of the religious, one that privileges the autonomous experience of non-referentiality. More than just positing a singularity in a book that elsewhere undermines such efforts, to conclude that we must only describe the condition of linguistic frustration would overlook the intense groundedness of the music, its insistence on particularity, and its embodied, experiential articulation. So I have tried, in the conceptual to and fro I have written from throughout this book, to propose in language the conceptual balance of writing simultaneously about language's limits *and* writing about bodies working and experiencing in sound. In this, I find that spirits rejoicing confronts us with what we do in the study of religion, striving audaciously to propose in writing an experience we know eludes us. Scholarly openness and receptivity do not entail that we adopt the simplistic sympathy of the chronicler but urges us to recognize that we share with our subjects the condition that drives our inquiry. In other words, to write about religion is possibly to experience something that religious people themselves experience: the absence of language and the attempt to restore it. This is not normative for spirits rejoicing, much less for religions as such, but it is a fruitful orientation to sound and presence.

In this I follow the recent writing of Robert Orsi, who urges us to take the realness of this presence, and this in-betweenness, seriously.[55] Against a long-gestating disciplinary bias against the "primitive" or "enthusiastic" or embodied, Orsi reminds us that if the study of religion is about anything, it may in fact be about precisely these presences. Yet my focus on spirits rejoicing foregrounds the category *absence* too, not in the sense of the sacred's withdrawal so much as the thoroughgoing suspension of the taken-for-granted bifurcations of the modern (inner and outer, self and other, embodied and epistemological), leaving a bothness or wholeness that confront thinkers about religion with the partiality of our categories and assumptions. Even if we acknowledge the realness of presence we cannot see or experience ourselves, even as we rethink the vitality and urgency of sonic prayers, the receding horizon of language reminds us of the ineluctability of absence to these experiences of religion. So to ask "what is the power of prayer, or music?" is to ask "what is the power of *being heard*?" Even if we swap out the aurality of my formulation, and substitute for it "acknowledged" or "felt," spirits rejoicing is about not simply improvising in a relational network of sacred beings but also the practitioner's sense that to experience this cosmos is to be overwhelmed, lost, alone just as sure as it is to experience communion and presence.

These sacred worlds are not simply fragile in any conventional sense. The always-ongoing music is animated and inspired by the very possibilities of slipping and drifting away, bidding the spirits to return precisely when they are experienced as absent: a heightened experience gone too fast, a leaf skittering across your backyard on a night when you desperately miss someone, the keen sense that the unseen strides in your midst. And if this language of overwhelmedness and lostness is suggestive, it is to say that one of presence's textures might usefully be captured by this language evoking the slipping away of things (from Dolphy to descriptions, from leaves to memories).

To "pray" and "believe" and "experience" through sound, along with sound, drenched in sound, then, means more than that we lack words (a notion common in the study of religion, from those theorists of the numinous in the disciplinary past to constructivists of the present who focus on the fabricated quality of the category "religion" itself). Spirits rejoicing reminds us that we can never notate experience fully, because in the act of writing it we keep experiencing, and all the while those doubled experiences change and change again. As Orsi writes, religion can only be thought about and questioned and studied in particular constellations of meaning and activity; this, he says, is why we keep turning over terminological and methodological issues, because the comparative enterprise continually reminds us that our acts of recognition are partial, that the resemblances we posit may be imagined or serve some other agenda, that our language excludes.[56] But as above, think not of impossibility as a frustration or finale. Let us not forget that the sounds are produced and heard on the ground of culture, as musicians and listeners try and fail to tune the world for just one more pregnant second. The music comes from ideas had by people in exchange with one another, rooted in and responding to communities and histories. They are made by bodies (yes, even sweating ones) hoping and struggling to give shape to the protean air itself.

Spirits rejoicing plays the unexpected to us. It forces us to break from scholarly format and entertain a religious studies that cannot resort to pat licks. Like improvisers, we learn to place value in the doing, the continual generation of possibility from the registers of language and absence and sheer sonic power, in all its dimensions of duration and time, emotion and affect, memory and the momentary body. These bid us once more to reconsider and make possible refreshed relations with those we chose to write about. These sounds, these musicians, these religions elude and exceed whatever formulations we can give to them, even as they are situated in the textures of everyday life and of American history. They take shape briefly sometimes, mutably, configured differently: religion on the rimshot, or the spirit's melody. In them, what Flaubert called "the littleness of life that art exaggerates" is commuted into music itself, played anew continually but always drifting away from us in time.[57] And religion, that dazzling fabrication, is our own art form, which we use to make art of our selves.

So "religion," too, has its own sweating brow, in its own blunt limits. But while we sense outside our tracings of spirits rejoicing the mistaken assumptions that prevent us from hearing, the beyondness signaled by the limit itself is a fresh start; it proposes another beginning possible following each pause. Amid these emergences and erasures we sense unseen networks of uncanny sound, paradoxes, and aporiae of knowing. As we chase the impossibility of writing about sound and religion, of thinking about something while simultaneously trying to understand how we can experience it, the abundance and everywhereness of this subject creates a kind of discursive overdrive, a distortion of the signal and the referent that under-scores the means by which we amplify our subject, creating feedback and ghost tones that we imagine exist independently of our doing, exulting in their release while at the same time craving their capture in the drive of a lone medium (sound or image or word). The spiritual aspirant and the striv-ing author alike become no-input mixing boards, resonating wires, struck membranes through which such questions project. How drab it would be to attempt to explain away the mystery, to locate finally that language that "fits" the non-ascribable experiences music can conjure in us, seemingly unbidden, that sudden transformation in us itself like a possession.

We ultimately learn something about the fate of these words in America, and the growing choruses of religion's haziness. This is more than the increase of the "nones" documented by the Pew Research Center or an artistic withdrawal from the roil of the polis; we see here how steadily a certain strain of musical creativity, fully modernist and wholly non-modern, has sounded out shared conditions in our secular, just as surely as it has fed and responded to known historical patterns. Can we not imagine these horn players calling from American rooftops a summons to witness to the glory of the smoke? Hear these drummers sound the thrum of the for-ward drive that bears us onward, relentless and sustaining at once. The condition of "religion" does not depend on these sounds any more than they can hope to define one another. But *that* is also the story of religion today: mad like Ayler on the edge of the bridge, ready to abandon its origins only to return like the Art Ensemble of Chicago, rapt like the supplicant before the transporting power of Coltrane's sound, furious and weeping like Mingus. In the sheer unrivaled manyness of American religion we seek out and sense the limit, no theorist's parlor game but weirdly the sur-est index of the real in a world smoldering away in fast forward. To embrace the likelihood of failure, and the certainty of finitude, is to momentarily experience the glorious, bittersweet transitoriness of being alive. This music has been an index of these feelings and has prophesied these changes in certitude; but it also *is* what we say it is *about*: the sense, the reach, the ac-ceptance of falling short, and the holy conviction to move forward, head turned up to the heavens.

These speculations of course are themselves analogical and rhetorical, and hence part of what I aim to question. But playing with that is partly the point and possibility; for when these spirits rejoice, they jar the senses and scramble convention, evoking in the process their own sources and limits. But these limits, these limits, there's something to them. Charles

Ives knew this: "[m]any sounds that we are used to do not bother us, and for that reason are we not too easily inclined to call them beautiful?" "Spirituality" or "religion" or "jazz" may be categories unable to escape their overdetermination or evanescence, no matter the beauty or sizzle an author intends. But in the very "ugliness" of their inevitable frames we might find the questions that bother us and open us up too. So open wide, skies. Open wide, ears. In failure we find fresh beauty and possibility. Abbey Lincoln knew this:

> I said to Max, "You know, Thelonious said to me, 'don't be so perfect.' What does he mean?" And Roach said, "He means make a mistake." Well I didn't know what either one of them were talking about. But I do know. Ha ha. You take a chance and you reach for something. And if you didn't make it, you reach for it anyway. Whew. They call it jazz.[58]

They call it "religion" too. Amen . . .

Notes

CHAPTER I

1. This chapter's title comes from John Coltrane's 1965 recording.
2. See Paul Gilroy, *The Black Atlantic: Modernity and Double Consciousness* (Cambridge, Mass.: Harvard University Press, 1995).
3. Ronald Radano, *Lying Up a Nation: Race and Black Music* (Chicago: University of Chicago Press, 2003), xiv.
4. George Lipsitz, *Footsteps in the Dark: The Hidden Histories of Popular Music* (Minneapolis: University of Minnesota Press, 2007), viii.
5. Ludwig Wittgenstein, *Philosophical Investigations* (Saddle River, N.J.: Prentice Hall, 1973), 126.
6. See Constance Classen, *Worlds of Sense: Exploring the Senses in History and Across Cultures* (New York: Routledge, 1993); John Corrigan, ed., *Religion and Emotion: Approaches and Interpretations* (New York: Oxford University Press, 2004); and Leigh Eric Schmidt, *Hearing Things: Religion, Illusion, and the American Enlightenment* (Cambridge, Mass.: Harvard University Press, 2002).
7. Stephen Marini, "Hymnody and History: Early American Evangelical Hymns as Sacred Music," in *Music in American Religious Experience*, ed. Philip V. Bohlman, Edith L. Blumhofer, and Maria M. Chow (New York: Oxford University Press, 2006), 123.
8. Ibid., 124.
9. Philip Bohlman, "Introduction: Music in American Religious Experience," in ibid., 9.
10. Marini, "Hymnody and History," 149, 151.
11. Cited in Roland Barthes, "The Grain of the Voice," in *The Sound Studies Reader*, ed. Jonathan Sterne (New York: Routledge, 2012), 504–5.
12. Quoted in Daniel J. Levitin, *This Is Your Brain on Music: The Science of a Human Obsession* (New York: Plume, 2006), 17.

13. Robert Walser, preface to Walser, ed., *Keeping Time: Readings in Jazz History* (New York: Oxford University Press, 1999), vii.

14. Michael Whiticker, "Morton Feldman: Conversation Without Cage," *Ossia: A Journal of Contemporary Music* 1 (Winter 1989): 6.

15. Mark C. Taylor, *About Religion: Economies of Faith in Virtual Culture* (Chicago: University of Chicago Press, 1999).

16. David W. Stowe, *How Sweet the Sound: Music in the Spiritual Lives of Americans* (Cambridge, Mass.: Harvard University Press, 2004), 3.

17. See Jonathan Z. Smith, *Imagining Religion: From Babylon to Jonestown* (Chicago: University of Chicago Press, 1982).

18. Quoted in Robert O'Meally, ed., *Living with Music: Ralph Ellison's Jazz Writings* (New York: Modern Library, 2001), xxxii.

19. Personal conversation, May 2004. This book focuses on American musicians, who often themselves meditate on questions of "American-ness." Obviously jazz's development in America has reflected its surroundings, the experiences and aspirations of American players, and turned in on itself reflexively in a way that is peculiar to American self-consciousness. Yet it is important to note the historic importance of Europeans, Africans, and Latin Americans from jazz's earliest decades to the present.

20. See Howard Reich, "Michelle Obama Subject of Jazz Ode," *Chicago Tribune*, September 3, 2009.

21. Stanley Crouch, "Jazz Writer Crouch, 'Considering Genius' of Jazz," National Public Radio, *News and Notes*, July 14, 2006, http://www.npr.org/templates/ story/story.php?storyId=5557551.

22. See, for example, William Dean, *American Spiritual Culture: And the Invention of Jazz, Football, and the Movies* (New York: Continuum, 2006); Shane Lee and Philip Luke Sinitiere, eds., *Holy Mavericks: Evangelical Innovators and the Spiritual Marketplace* (New York: New York University Press, 2009), which compares improvisatory sermon styles to jazz; Sharon Welch, *Sweet Dreams in America: Making Ethics and Spirituality Work* (New York: Routledge, 1998); and George Yancy, ed., *Cornel West: A Critical Reader* (Cambridge: Wiley-Blackwell, 2001).

23. For analysis of such classificatory difficulty, see David Ake, Charles Hiroshi Garrett, and Daniel Goldmark, eds., *Jazz/Not Jazz: The Music and Its Boundaries* (Berkeley: University of California Press, 2012).

24. Daniel Fischlin, Ajay Heble, and George Lipsitz, *The Fierce Urgency of Now: Improvisation, Rights, and the Ethics of Cocreation* (Durham, N.C.: Duke University Press, 2013), xix.

25. Quoted in Amiri Baraka, "The 'Blues Aesthetic' and the 'Black Aesthetic': Aesthetics as the Continuing Political History of a Culture," *Black Music Research Journal* 11, no. 2 (Autumn 1991): 109.

26. Quoted in *Miles Electric: A Different Kind of Blue* (BBC, 2004).

27. See Ronald Schleifer, *Modernism and Popular Music* (Cambridge: Cambridge University Press, 2011).

28. Roger A. Bruns, *Preacher: Billy Sunday and Big-Time American Evangelism* (New York: Norton, 1992), 283.

29. Alex Ross, *Listen to This* (New York: Farrar, Straus and Giroux, 2010), 16.

30. Neil Leonard, *Jazz: Myth and Religion* (New York: Oxford University Press, 1987), 4.

31. Ibid.

32. Jon Michael Spencer, "An Overview of American Popular Music in a Theological Perspective," in *Theomusicology: A Special Issue of Black Sacred Music*, ed. Jon Michael Spencer (Durham, N.C.: Duke University Press, 1994), 208–9.

33. Lawrence Levine, *Black Culture and Black Consciousness: Afro-American Thought from Slavery to Freedom* (New York: Oxford University Press, 2007), 293–94.

34. Alex Ross, *The Rest Is Noise* (New York: Farrar, Straus and Giroux, 2007), 153.

35. See George McKay, *Circular Breathing: The Cultural Politics of Jazz in Britain* (Durham, N.C.: Duke University Press), 24–31; and John Corbett, *Extended Play: Sounding Off from John Cage to Dr. Funkenstein* (Durham, N.C.: Duke University Press, 1994), 232. Jacques Attali, *Noise: The Political Economy of Music* (Minneapolis: University of Minnesota Press, 1985) is a more recent example of such economistic interpretation.

36. Quoted in Walser, *Keeping Time*, 6.

37. Ibid., 8. Pianist Tatum was, of course, an early exemplar of jazz's capacious and innovative harmonic possibilities.

38. Ibid., 32.

39. Ibid., 34.

40. See Ann Taves, *Fits, Trances, and Visions: Experiencing Religion and Explaining Experience from Wesley to James* (Princeton, N.J.: Princeton University Press, 1999).

41. Walser, *Keeping Time*, 16.

42. Bunny Crumpacker and Chick Crumpacker, *Jazz Legends* (Layton, Utah: Gibbs Smith, 1995), 40.

43. Ibid.

44. Quoted in Valerie Wilmer, *As Serious as Your Life: The Story of the New Jazz* (New York: Serpent's Tail, 1992), 26.

45. Ibid., 133.

46. Crumpacker and Crumpacker, *Jazz Legends*, 46–47.

47. Mimi Clar, "The Negro Church: Its Influence on Modern Jazz," *The Jazz Review* 1, no. 1 (November 1958): 16.

48. Ray Allen, *Singing in the Spirit: African-American Sacred Quartets in New York City* (Philadelphia: University of Pennsylvania Press, 1991), 24.

49. Guthrie P. Ramsey Jr., *Race Music: Black Cultures from Bebop to Hip-Hop* (Berkeley: University of California Press, 2003), 52.

50. This injunction comes from Rahsaan Roland Kirk's 1968 recording *Left and Right*.

51. See, among others, Scott DeVeaux, *The Birth of Bebop: A Social and Musical History* (Berkeley: University of California Press, 1999); Samuel A. Floyd, *The Power of Black Music: Interpreting Its History from Africa to the United States*

(New York: Oxford University Press, 1996); Krin Gabbard, ed., *Jazz among the Discourses* (Durham, N.C.: Duke University Press, 1995); Ajay Heble, *Landing on the Wrong Note: Jazz, Dissonance, and Critical Practice* (New York: Routledge, 2000); Graham Lock, *Blutopia: Visions of the Future and Revisions of the Past in the Work of Sun Ra, Duke Ellington, and Anthony Braxton* (Durham, N.C.: Duke University Press, 1999); Ingrid Monson, Daniel Fischlin, and Ajay Heble, eds., *The Other Side of Nowhere: Jazz, Improvisation, and Communities in Dialogue* (Middletown, Conn.: Wesleyan University Press, 2004); Robert O'Meally, Brent Hayes Edwards, and Farah Jasmine Griffin, eds., *Uptown Conversation: The New Jazz Studies* (New York: Columbia University Press, 2004); Ramsey, *Race Music*; and Stowe, *How Sweet the Sound*.

52. See Franya J. Berkman, *Monument Eternal: The Music of Alice Coltrane* (Middletown, Conn.: Wesleyan University Press, 2010); Leonard L. Brown, ed., *John Coltrane and Black America's Quest for Freedom: Spirituality and the Music* (New York: Oxford University Press, 2010); Harvey G. Cohen, *Duke Ellington's America* (Chicago: University of Chicago Press, 2010); Robin D. G. Kelley, *Thelonious Monk: The Life and Times of an American Original* (New York: Free Press, 2009); and Tammy Kernodle, *Soul on Soul: The Life of Mary Lou Williams* (Boston: Northeastern University Press, 2004).

53. Floyd, *The Power of Black Music*; Albert Murray, *Stomping the Blues* (New York: Da Capo, 1989); and David Rosenthal, *Hard Bop and Black Music, 1955–1965* (New York: Oxford University Press, 1992).

54. Robin Sylvan, *Traces of the Spirit: The Religious Dimensions of Popular Music* (New York: New York University Press, 2002).

55. Leonard, *Jazz*, ix.

56. Eric Porter, *What Is This Thing Called Jazz? African American Musicians as Artists, Critics, and Activists* (Berkeley: University of California Press, 2002), 241. See also Ingrid Monson, *Freedom Sounds: Civil Rights Call Out to Jazz and Africa* (New York: Oxford University Press, 2007).

57. Scott Saul, *Freedom Is, Freedom Ain't: Jazz and the Making of the Sixties* (Cambridge, Mass: Harvard University Press, 2003), 25.

58. Amiri Baraka, "Jazz and the White Critic: A Provocative Essay on the Situation of Jazz Criticism," *Downbeat* 30, no. 23 (August 15, 1963): 16–17, 34.

59. David Stowe, "Both American and Global: Jazz and World Religions in the United States," *Religion Compass* 4, no. 5 (May 2010): 312–23.

60. Ralph Ellison, *Shadow and Act* (New York: Vintage, 1995), 212.

61. Throughout the book, all discussions of the music itself are based on my own notes and transcriptions, unless otherwise indicated.

62. See John Szwed, "Antiquity of the Avant Garde," in *People Get Ready: The Future of Jazz Is Now!* ed. Ajay Heble and Rob Wallace (Durham, N.C.: Duke University Press, 2013), 44–58.

63. See Catherine L. Albanese, ed., *American Spiritualities: A Reader* (Bloomington: Indiana University Press, 2001); and Leigh Eric Schmidt, *Restless Souls: The*

Making of American Spirituality (Berkeley: University of California Press, 2012).

64. Robert A. Orsi, "When 2 + 2 = 5," *The American Scholar* (Spring 2007): 34–43.

65. See Jason C. Bivins, "'Only One Repertory': American Religious Studies," *Religion* 42, no. 3 (2012): 395–407.

66. Ann Taves, *Religious Experience Reconsidered: A Building-Block Approach to the Study of Religion and Other Special Things* (Princeton, N.J.: Princeton University Press, 2009).

67. See Ronald Radano's discussion of this point in *Lying Up a Nation: Race and Black Music* (Chicago: University of Chicago Press, 2003), xiv.

68. Wallace Stevens, *The Collected Poems of Wallace Stevens* (New York: Vintage, 1990), 9.

69. Robert Rusch, "Interview with George Russell," in *Cadence* 3, nos. 7 and 8 (December 1977): 16.

70. Mark C. Taylor, *About Religion: Economies of Faith in Virtual Culture* (Chicago: University of Chicago Press, 1999), 1.

71. Quoted in Ross, *The Rest Is Noise*, 133.

72. Quoted in ibid., 168.

73. Quoted in ibid., 164.

74. Interview in Hamilton College Archives, July 27, 1995.

75. Harry Gilonis, notes to AMM/MEV, *Apogee* (Matchless Recordings, 2005).

76. Quoted in Mary Russo and Daniel Warner, in *Audio Culture: Readings in Modern Music*, ed. Christoph Cox and Daniel Warner (New York: Continuum, 2004), 52.

77. Personal conversation, May 2011.

78. Christopher Small, *Music of the Common Tongue: Survival and Celebration in Afro-American Music* (New York: Riverrun, 1987), 212.

79. George McKay, *Circular Breathing*, 23.

80. Quoted in Steve Lake, liner notes to Edward Vesala, *Ode to the Death of Jazz* (ECM, 1986).

81. Kenneth Patchen, "What Is the Beautiful?" in *Collected Poems* (New York: New Directions, 1968), 310–13. There may be a very few readers who note that there is a wink buried in this reference. The marvelous drummer/composer John Hollenbeck released an album by this title, containing a dazzling recitation of this poem by Kurt Elling.

CHAPTER 2

1. The title is from Wadada Leo Smith's 1983 recording.

2. See Robert Fuller, *Spiritual but Not Religious: Understanding Unchurched America* (New York: Oxford University Press, 2001); and Wade Clark Roof, *Generation of Seekers: The Spiritual Journeys of the Baby Boom Generation* (New York: Harper Collins, 1993).

3. See Eddie Glaude Jr., "The Black Church Is Dead," http://www.huffingtonpost .com/eddie-glaude-jr-phd/the-black-church-is-dead_b_473815.html.

4. See Eddie S. Glaude Jr., "Updated with Response: The Black Church Is Dead—Long Live the Black Church," http://www.religiondispatches.org/archive/atheologies/2331/updated_with_response%3A_the_black_church_is_dead%E2%80%94long_live_the_black_church.

5. Jose Pedro, "James Polk: Recipes from the Doctor," http://www.allaboutjazz.com/james-polk-recipes-from-the-doctor-dr-james-polk-by-josep-pedro.php.

6. Interview in *Cadence* 7, no. 10 (October 1981): 10.

7. Louis Armstrong, "Satchmo and Me," *American Music* 25, no. 1 (Spring 2007): 108.

8. Valerie Wilmer, *As Serious as Your Life: The Story of the New Jazz* (New York: Serpent's Tail, 1992), 134.

9. Richard Iton, *In Search of the Black Fantastic: Politics and Popular Culture in the Post–Civil Rights Era* (New York: Oxford University Press, 2008), 161.

10. Ben Ratliff, *The Jazz Ear: Conversations over Music* (New York: Times, 2010), 116.

11. Ibid., 118.

12. Valerie Wilmer, *Jazz People* (New York: Da Capo, 1970), 45.

13. Gary Giddins, *Weather Bird: Jazz at the Dawn of Its Second Century* (New York: Oxford University Press, 2004), 23.

14. Hamilton College Archives, September 18, 2003.

15. Ibid.

16. Elliot Simon, "Odean Pope: A Singular Voice in the Choir," http://www.allaboutjazz.com/odean-pope-a-singular-voice-in-the-choir-odean-pope-by-elliott-simon.php.

17. Jay Cocks and David E. Thigpen, "That Old Time Religion," *Time*, July 17, 1995, 61.

18. Personal communication, January 2010.

19. Marc Minsker, "Sam Rivers: A Giant Among Us," http://www.allaboutjazz.com/sam-rivers-a-giant-among-us-sam-rivers-by-marc-minsker.php?pg=4&width=1024?page=1.

20. Personal conversation, July 2010.

21. Howard Mandel, notes to *Wildflowers: The New York Loft Jazz Sessions* (Knit Classics, 1999).

22. "Sam Rivers' Musical 'FireStorm,'" National Public Radio, *The Tavis Smiley Show*, July 2, 2004.

23. Ibid.

24. Rivers, liner notes to Sam Rivers, *Portrait* (FMP Records, 1997).

25. Personal conversation, July 2010.

26. National Public Radio, July 2, 2004.

27. Personal conversation, July 2010.

28. Quoted in Wilmer, *As Serious as Your Life*, 95.

29. Ekkehard Jost, *Free Jazz* (New York: Da Capo, 1974), 121.

30. Quoted in John Kruth, "The Healing Force of the Universe," in *Signal to Noise* 36 (Winter 2005): 21.

31. Frank Kofsky, liner notes to *Love Cry* (Impulse Records, 1968).

32. Peter Niklas Wilson, notes to *Lörrach, Paris 1966* (Hatology Records, 2002).

33. Wilmer, *As Serious as Your Life*, 96.

34. Kruth, "The Healing Force of the Universe," 17.

35. Ibid.

36. Giddins, *Weather Bird*, 475.

37. Ibid., 18.

38. Robert Palmer, notes to Albert Ayler, *Live at the Village Vanguard* (Impulse Records, 1998).

39. Wilmer, *As Serious as Your Life*, 100.

40. John Litweiler, *The Freedom Principle: Jazz After 1958* (New York: Da Capo, 1984), 159.

41. Ibid., 161.

42. Ibid., 163.

43. Hans Schreiber, notes to Ayler, *Spiritual Unity* (ESP Records, 1964).

44. Quoted in "Don Cherry on Albert Ayler, Part One," http://www.youtube.com/watch?v=fK0BBz1Sbzg&feature=related.

45. Kasper Collin, director, *My Name Is Albert Ayler*, 2005. On the Elmo Hope anecdote, see Jason Weiss, *Always in Trouble: An Oral History of ESP-Disk', The Most Outrageous Record Label in America* (Middletown, Conn.: Wesleyan University Press, 2012), 21.

46. Kruth, "The Healing Force of the Universe," 19.

47. Wilmer, *As Serious as Your Life*, 106.

48. Kruth, "The Healing Force of the Universe," 21.

49. Ayler, liner notes to Albert Ayler, *Bells—Prophecy* (ESP Records, 1964).

50. Kruth, "The Healing Force of the Universe," 17.

51. Ibid., 110.

52. Albert Ayler, "To Mr. Jones—I Had a Vision," in *The Cricket: Black Music in Evolution!!!* ed. Amiri Baraka (Jihad Productions, 1969): 27–30.

53. Wilmer, *As Serious as Your Life*, 110.

54. Collin, *My Name Is Albert Ayler*.

55. Joe Gross, "Albert Ayler's Peaks and Valleys," *Austin American-Statesman*, October 10, 2004. See also, Brian Morton, "Flowers for Albert," *The Nation* 279, no. 17 (November 11, 2004): 32–34.

56. Quoted in Peter Brotzmann, notes to Brotzmann, *Die Like a Dog* (FMP Records, 1994); and Wilmer, *As Serious as Your Life*, 111.

57. Collin, *My Name Is Albert Ayler*.

58. The term "psalm-swinging" is from Hal Russell, *The Hal Russell Story* (ECM Records, 1993).

59. Wilmer, *As Serious as Your Life*, 111.

60. Interview with Robert Rusch, in *Cadence* 5, no. 2 (February 1979): 16.

61. Ayler, liner notes to *Live at the Village Vanguard*.

62. Quoted in Tim Hodgkinson, "Holy Ghost," in *Arcana V: Music, Magic and Mysticism*, ed. John Zorn (New York: Hips Road, 2010), 211.

63. Todd Margasak interview with Charles Gayle, *Butt Rag*, no. 9 (Spring 1994): 7.

64. Interview in *Cadence* 27, no. 4 (April 2001): 16–17.

65. Quoted in Russ Musto, notes to Charles Gayle, *Look Up* (ESP Records, 2012).

66. Joseph Chonto, notes to Charles Gayle, *Touchin' on Trane* (FMP Records, 1993).

67. Phil Freeman, *New York Is Now! The New Wave of Free Jazz* (Brooklyn, N.Y.: Telegraph Company, 2001), 78.

68. Margasak, interview with Charles Gayle, 10.

69. Ibid.

70. "Q&A: Charles Gayle on Homelessness, Streets the Clown, and His Faith," http://blogs.villagevoice.com/music/2012/02/charles_gayle_interview_streets_the_clown.php.

71. "Charles Gayle: Interview by James Lindbloom (March 2000)," http://www.furious.com/perfect/charlesgayle.html.

72. Ibid.

73. Interview in *Cadence* 27, no. 4 (April 2001): 19.

74. Author transcription of performance from Gayle, *Look Up* (ESP Records, 2012).

75. Ibid.

76. Ibid.

77. "Charles Gayle: Interview by James Lindbloom (March 2000)."

78. Interview in *Cadence* 27, no. 4 (April 2001): 19.

79. "Charles Gayle: Interview by James Lindbloom (March 2000)."

80. Interview in *Cadence*, 19.

81. Ibid., 18.

82. Christopher Chase, "Prophetics in the Key of Allah: Towards an Understanding of Islam in Jazz," *Jazz Perspectives* 4, no. 2 (August 2010): 157.

83. Ibid.

84. Robin D. G. Kelley, *Thelonious Monk: The Life and Times of an American Original* (New York: Free Press, 2009), 126. See also "Moslem Musicians," *Ebony*, April 1953, 104–11.

85. Kelley, *Thelonious Monk*, 126.

86. David Rosenthal, *Hard Bop and Black Music, 1955–1965* (New York: Oxford University Press, 1992), 277.

87. Kelley, *Thelonious Monk*, 127.

88. Chase, "Prophetics in the Key of Allah," 165.

89. Francis Davis, *Outcats: Jazz Composers, Instrumentalists, and Singers* (New York: Oxford University Press, 1990), 47.

90. Ibid., 49.

91. Kelley, *Thelonious Monk*, 143.

92. Graham Lock, *Chasing the Vibration: Meetings with Creative Musicians* (Exeter: Stride, 1994), 45.

93. Chase, "Prophetics in the Key of Allah," 160–61.

94. Andre Henkin, "Abdullah Ibrahim: African Magic," http://www.allaboutjazz .com/abdullah-ibrahim-african-magic-abdullah-ibrahim-by-andrey-henkin.php.

95. Lock, *Chasing the Vibration*, 54.

96. Ibid.

97. Ibid.

98. Interview in *Cadence* 10, no. 1 (January 1984): 6.

99. Wilmer, *As Serious as Your Life*, 44. Another Coltrane bandmate, saxophonist Pharaoh Sanders, became Muslim during this period and recorded a string of albums praising the Creator.

100. Nat Hentoff, notes to McCoy Tyner, *The Real McCoy* (Blue Note Records, 1967).

101. Quoted in ibid.

102. Quoted in Thornton Smith, notes to McCoy Tyner, *Expansions* (Blue Note Records, 1969).

103. Quoted in Bob Palmer, notes to McCoy Tyner, *Sahara* (Milestone Records, 1972).

104. Quoted in Chase, "Prophetics in the Key of Allah," 172.

105. Ezra Gale, "Stretching the Canvas," *Jazziz* 16, no. 2 (February 1999): 54–55.

106. Yusef Lateef with Herb Boyd, *The Gentle Giant: The Autobiography of Yusef Lateef* (Irvington, N.J.: Morton, 2006), 56.

107. "Yusef Lateef: A Composer Who's Hard to Categorize," National Public Radio, *All Things Considered*, March 3, 2005.

108. Interview with Marc Myers, http://www.jazzwax.com/2008/02/yusef-lateef-pa.html. See also Andrew Gilbert, "Curiosity Made the Cat: Yusef Lateef's Musical Journey Resists Categorization," *The San Diego Union-Tribune*, October 27, 2005.

109. Interview with Marc Myers.

110. Quoted in Doug Fischer, "Lateef Has Based His Career on Innovation," *The Ottawa Citizen*, June 29, 2006.

111. See Chase, "Prophetics in the Key of Allah," 167.

112. Lateef with Boyd, *Gentle Giant*, 107.

113. Ibid., 111.

114. Ibid., 133.

115. Gale, "Stretching the Canvas," 55.

116. Lateef with Boyd, *Gentle Giant*, 145.

117. Lateef with Boyd, "In the Name of God the Gracious the Merciful," in *Arcana V: Music, Magic and Mysticism*, ed. John Zorn (New York: Hips Road), 245–46.

118. Ibid., 250.

119. Eric Porter, *What Is This Thing Called Jazz? African American Musicians as Artists, Critics, and Activists* (Berkeley: University of California Press, 2002), 243.

120. Interview with J. R. Mitchell, in *Cadence* 8, no. 1 (January 1982): 20–21.

121. Personal conversation, January 2010.

122. Ibid.

123. Hamilton College Archives.

124. Wayne Enstice and Janis Stockhouse, *Jazzwomen: Conversations with Twenty-One Musicians* (Bloomington: Indiana University Press, 2004), 57.

125. Ibid., 82.

126. Ibid., 85.

127. Ibid., 86.

128. Victor L. Schermer, "Bobby Zankel: Peaceful Jazz Warrior," http://www.allaboutjazz .com/bobby-zankel-peaceful-jazz-warrior-bobby-zankel-by-victor-l-schermer .php&page=1.

129. Ibid.

130. Harvey Siders, "Harold Land," *Jazz Times* (May 2001): http://jazztimes.com/ articles/20245-harold-land.

131. Ibid.

132. Quoted in *Cadence* 9, no. 3 (March 1983): 16.

133. Victor L. Schermer, "Sonny Rollins: Hardy Perennial," http://www.allaboutjazz .com/sonny-rollins-hardy-perennial-sonny-rollins-by-victor-l-schermer.php.

134. Ibid.

135. David Stowe, "Both American and Global: Jazz and World Religions in the United States," *Religion Compass* 4, no. 5 (May 2010): 312–23.

136. Quoted in Arthur Taylor, *Notes and Tones: Musician-to-Musician Interviews* (New York: Da Capo, 1993), 170.

137. Valerie Reiss, "Herbie, Fully Buddhist," http://www.beliefnet.com/Faiths/ Buddhism/2007/10/Herbie-Fully-Buddhist.aspx.

138. Ibid.

139. Mike Bradley, "Hancock Half-Hour," *The Times* (London), July 4, 1998.

140. R. J. DeLuke, "Herbie Hancock: Inspired by the Written Word of a Friend," http://www.allaboutjazz.com/herbie-hancock-inspired-by-the-written-word-of-a-friend-herbie-hancock-by-rj-deluke.php.

141. "Herbie Hancock," National Public Radio, *All Things Considered*, October 21, 2001.

142. Ratliff, *The Jazz Ear*, 1.

143. Michelle Mercer, *Footprints: The Life and Music of Wayne Shorter* (New York: Tarcher, 2004), 14.

144. Quoted in Ratliff, *The Jazz Ear*, 8.

145. Martin Wisckol, "The Spiritual Shorter," *The Orange County Register*, October 6, 2006.

146. Philip Booth, "Saxophonist Shorter Blows on Life, Creation," *Tampa Herald-Tribune*, October 27, 2002.

147. Mercer, *Footprints*, 205.

148. The above account is informed by Dizzy Gillespie and Al Fraser, *To Be or Not…to Bop* (New York: Da Capo, 1985).

149. E. Taylor Atkins, "Sacred Swing: The Sacralization of Jazz in the American Bahá'í Community," *American Music* 24, no. 4 (Winter 2006): 394–96.

150. Ibid.

151. "Dizzy Gillespie Video Interviews," http://bahairants.com/dizzy-gillespie-video-interviews-315.html.

152. Ibid.

153. Taylor, *Notes and Tones*, 123.

154. Josephine R. B. Wright, "Conversation with John Birks 'Dizzy' Gillespie," *Black Music Research Journal* 4, no. 1 (Spring 1976): 82.

155. Ibid., 87.

156. Atkins, "Sacred Swing," 386; and Taylor, *Notes and Tones*, 135.

157. Atkins, 402.

158. Ibid., 404.

159. Terrell Kent Holmes, "James Moody: Timeless," http://www.allaboutjazz.com/james-moody-timeless-james-moody-by-terrell-kent-holmes.php.

160. http://www.bahaiviews.net/2009/10/07/on-how-flora-purim-became-a-bahai-i-challenged-dizzy-again-he-recited-the-prayer-perfectly/.

161. Ashante Infantry, "Cindy Blackman's Got the Beat," *The Toronto Star*, June 7, 2008.

162. Todd Gordon, "Tierney Sutton: In Union There Is Strength," http://www.allaboutjazz.com/tierney-sutton-in-union-there-is-strength-tierney-sutton-by-todd-gordon.php.

163. Ibid.

164. Carl L. Sager, "Tierney Sutton: Not a Material Girl," http://www.allaboutjazz.com/tierney-sutton-not-a-material-girl-tierney-sutton-by-carl-l-hager.php.

165. "Oluyemi Thomas: Positive Knowledge," http://www.allaboutjazz.com/php/article.php?id=29936.

166. Personal conversation, April 2011.

167. Ibid.

168. Ibid.

169. All quotations in this paragraph from ibid.

170. Interview in *Cadence* 3, no. 9 (January 1978): 16.

171. http://www.sptimes.com/2006/04/20/Weekend/Corea_continues_to_fi.shtml.

172. "What Are Some of the Results from the Application of Scientology Technology? Here Are but a Few...," *New York Times*, May 12, 1985.

173. Janet Reitman, *Inside Scientology: The Story of America's Most Secretive Religion* (New York: Mariner, 2013), 71.

174. "What Are Some of the Results from the Application of Scientology Technology? Here Are but a Few...," *New York Times*, May 12, 1985: SC12.

175. Ibid.

176. Corea, notes to Circle, *Paris Concert* (ECM Records, 1972).

177. Graham Lock, *Forces in Motion: The Music and Thoughts of Anthony Braxton* (New York: Da Capo, 1988), 286.

178. Quoted in an interview with Frankie Nemko, *Guitar Player*, October 1974.

179. Doug Fisher, "Forever Grateful," *The Ottawa Citizen*, April 24, 2006.

180. Ty Cumbie, "Chick Corea," http://www.allaboutjazz.com/chick-corea-chick-corea-by-ty-cumbie.php.

181. Richard Behar, "The Thriving Cult of Greed and Power," *Time*, May 6, 1991.

182. Stephen A. Kent, "Hollywood's Celebrity Lobbyists and the Clinton Administration's American Foreign Policy Towards German Scientology," *Journal of Religion and Popular Culture* 1 (Spring 2002), http://utpjournals.metapress.com/content/l2x3840780572mq7/fulltext.pdf.

183. Fisher, "Forever Grateful."

184. Esther Berlanga-Ryan, "Chick Corea: Creative Giant," http://www.allaboutjazz.com/chick-corea-creative-giant-chick-corea-by-esther-berlanga-ryan.php.

185. Joshua Cohen, "Last Man Standing: The Acquisitive Music of John Zorn," *Harper's Magazine*, May 2009, 75.

186. Ibid., 52.

187. David W. Stowe, *How Sweet the Sound: Music in the Spiritual Lives of Americans* (Cambridge, Mass.: Harvard University Press, 2004), 184.

188. Josh Kun, *Audiotopia: Music, Race, and America* (Berkeley: University of California Press, 2005), 50.

189. Lester Koenig, notes to Shelly Manne, *Steps to the Desert* (Contemporary Records, 1963).

190. Neil Tesser, "Traditions: In Jazz We Trust," *Jazziz* 23, no. 6 (June 2006): 24–25.

191. Kun, liner notes to Katz, *Folk Songs for Far Out Folks* (Reboot Stereophonic, 2007).

192. Ibid.

193. Byron, notes to *Plays the Music of Mickey Katz* (Nonesuch, 1993).

194. Francis Davis, *Bebop and Nothingness: Jazz and Pop at the End of the Century* (New York: Schirmer, 1996), 172, 182.

195. Cohen, "Last Man Standing," 74.

196. Ibid., 73.

197. See Jeffrey Matthew Janeczko, "'Beyond Klezmer': Redefining Jewish Music for the Twenty-first Century" (PhD diss., University of California, Los Angeles, 2009).

198. Quoted in Seth Rogovoy, *The Essential Klezmer* (New York: Algonquin, 2000), 154–55.

199. Janeczko, "Beyond Klezmer," 6.

200. Jeremy Eichler, "But Is It Jewish?" *The Jerusalem Report* (November 13, 1997).

201. Janeczko, "Beyond Klezmer," 6.

202. Joel Lewis, "Heavy Shtetl: The New In-Your-Face Jewish Music," *Moment* 20, no. 4 (August 31, 1995): 46.

203. Tamar Barzel, "An Interrogation of Language: 'Radical Jewish Culture' on New York City's Downtown Music Scene," *Journal of the Society for American Music* 4, no. 2 (May 2010): 217–18.

204. Lewis, "Heavy Shtetl," 46.

205. Ron Nachmann, "Radical Jewish Culture: John Zorn's Tzadik Label," *Tikkun* 20, no. 1 (January/February 2005): 78–79.

206. Ajay Heble, *Landing on the Wrong Note: Jazz, Dissonance and Critical Practice* (New York: Routledge, 2000), 180.

207. "Masada Songbook: Zorn Redefines Jewish Music," National Public Radio, *Weekend Edition*, November 13, 2005.

208. www.tzadik.com. The link to the "RJC" section of the label's website brings up Zorn's statement on these matters.

209. Larry Blumenfeld, "John Zorn," *Jazziz* 16, no. 8 (August 1999): 42–48, 80.

210. http://www.thecjm.org/on-view/in-the-past/john-zorn-presents-the-aleph-bet-sound-project.

211. See Ben Ratliff, "A Most Prolific Composer Opens His Book of Angels," *New York Times*, September 12, 2006.

212. John Brackett, *John Zorn: Tradition and Transgression* (Bloomington: Indiana University Press, 2008).

213. Janeczko, "Beyond Klezmer," 55.

214. George Robinson, "Toward a 'Radical Jewish' Aesthetic," *The New York Jewish Week*, September 27, 1996, 29.

215. Barzel, "An Interrogation of Language," 239.

216. Steve Smith, "Sephardic Tinge," *Signal to Noise* 41 (Spring 2006): 29.

217. Eyal Hareuveni, "Frank London: The Jew with the Horn," http://www.allaboutjazz.com/frank-london-the-jew-with-the-horn-frank-london-by-eyal-hareuveni.php.

218. Ibid.

219. Saby Reyes-Kulkarni, "Ben Goldberg: A Clarinetist's Journey into 'Radical Jewish Culture'," http://alarm-magazine.com/2010/ben-goldberg/.

220. Seth Rogovoy, "Digging into Jewish Liturgy for Musical Inspiration," *Forward* (September 3, 2004): 15.

221. Greg Wall, "Horn O' Plenty," in *Arcana V: Music, Magic and Mysticism*, ed. John Zorn (New York: Hips Road), 398.

222. Janeczko, "Beyond Klezmer," 255.

223. Eyal Hareuveni, "Paul Shapiro: Swinging the Mundane with the Holy," http://www.allaboutjazz.com/paul-shapiro-swinging-the-mundane-with-the-holy-paul-shapiro-by-eyal-hareuveni.php.

224. Ibid.

225. "Jazz Gets a Jewish Twist," National Public Radio, *All Things Considered*, September 29, 2003.

226. Marion S. Jacobson, "New Jewish Music and Radical Jewish Culture," http://www.shma.com/2010/11/new-jewish-music-radical-jewish-culture/.

227. Seth Rogovoy, "Radical Music for the New Global Shtetl; New Recordings Combine Dizzying Cosmopolitanism with Distinctly Jewish Melodies," *Forward* (April 29, 2005): 10.

228. Ned Rothenberg, liner notes to Rothenberg, *The Lumina Recordings* (Tzadik, 2006).

229. Personal conversation, May 2011.

230. "Ned Rothenberg's 'Inner Diaspora,'" National Public Radio, *Fresh Air*, March 27, 2007.

231. Personal conversation, May 2011.

232. Hafez Modirzadeh, "Aural Archetypes and Cyclic Perspectives in the Work of John Coltrane and Ancient Chinese Music Theory," *Black Music Research Journal* 21, no. 1 (Spring 2001): 75–106.

233. See Wilmer, *As Serious as Your Life*, 167.

234. See Kirk Silsbee, "Don Cherry Interview," *Cadence* 9, no. 4 (April 1984): 5–11; and Steve Voce, "Obituary: Don Cherry," *The Independent*, October 21, 1995.

235. Nat Hentoff, liner notes to Don Cherry, *Complete Communion* (Blue Note Records, 1965).

236. Jost, *Free Jazz*, 149, 152.

237. Francis Davis, *In the Moment: Jazz in the 1980s* (New York: Da Capo, 1996), 148.

238. Thomas Millroth, notes to Don Cherry, *Live in Stockholm* (Caprice, 2013).

239. Davis, *In the Moment*, 149.

240. Ibid., 153. See also Don Pullen's border-crossing investigations of the links between African American musical traditions and those of Cubans and Native Americans.

241. Mike Heffley, *Northern Sun, Southern Moon: Europe's Reinvention of Jazz* (New Haven, Conn.: Yale University Press, 2005), 13.

242. Ibid.

243. Will Hermes, *Love Goes to Buildings on Fire: Five Years in New York That Changed Music Forever* (New York: Faber & Faber, 2011), 174.

244. Ibid.

245. These are notions recently popularized by figures like Eckhart Tolle, J. Z. Knight, and others.

246. Quoted in liner notes to Don Cherry, *Hear & Now* (Atlantic Records, 1977).

247. Davis, *In the Moment*, 154.

248. Robert Rusch, review in *Cadence* 4, nos. 2 and 3 (May 1978): 39.

249. Chuck Berg, "The Fox Is Big on Bop," *Jazz Education Journal* 39, no. 2 (October 2006): 63.

250. Interview in *Cadence* 35, nos. 10–12 (October–December 2009): 41–42.

251. Interview in *Cadence* 33, no. 5 (May 2007): 5, 14, and 16.

252. Ken Weiss, in *Cadence* 30, no. 9 (September 2004): 39.

253. Dave Holland, notes to Holland, *The Razor's Edge* (ECM Records, 1987).

254. "Bansuri Master Deepak Ram Tackles Jazz," National Public Radio, *Morning Edition*, July 8, 2008.

255. Prana Trio, *The Singing Image of Fire*, author's copy of one-sheet from mail distribution.

256. Personal conversation, January 2010.

257. *Wikipedia*, "Hamid Drake," http://en.wikipedia.org/wiki/Hamid_Drake.

258. Interview in *Cadence* 30, no. 3 (March 2004): 3.

259. Lloyd Peterson, *Music and the Creative Spirit* (Lanham, Md.: Scarecrow, 2006), 89.

260. *Cadence* (March 2004), 6.

261. Ibid., 6.

262. Ibid., 7.

263. Ibid.

264. Steve Lake, notes to Peter Brotzmann, *Little Birds Have Fast Hearts, Volume 1* (FMP Records, 1998).

265. Ken Vandermark, interview with Hamid Drake. Archived at http://home.earthlink.net/~quinnah/hamidint.html.

266. Ibid.

267. Ibid.

268. Ibid.

269. Ibid.

270. Ibid.

271. Ibid.

272. Personal conversation, February 2010.

273. Alexandre Pierrepont, notes to Hamid Drake and Bindu, *Reggaeology* (Rogue Art Records, 2010).

274. Ibid.

CHAPTER 3

1. The title is from John Carter's 1989 recording.

2. Brian Lonergan, "George Lewis: AACM Veteran," http://www.allaboutjazz.com/george-lewis-aacm-veteran-george-lewis-by-brian-p-lonergan.php.

3. Jed Rasula, "The Media of Memory: The Seductive Menace of Records in Jazz History," in *Jazz among the Discourses*, ed. Krin Gabbard (Durham, N.C.: Duke University Press, 1995), 156.

4. George Lipsitz, *Footsteps in the Dark: The Hidden Histories of Popular Music* (Minneapolis: University of Minnesota Press, 2007), xi, 91.

5. Laurie Maffly-Kipp, *Setting Down the Sacred Past: African-American Race Histories* (Cambridge, Mass.: Harvard University Press, 2010), 3.

6. Ibid., 3.

7. Eddie Glaude Jr., ed., *Is It Nation Time? Contemporary Essays on Black Power and Black Nationalism* (Chicago: University of Chicago Press, 2002).

8. Maffly-Kipp, *Setting Down the Sacred Past*, 23.

9. Charles Mingus, *Presents Charles Mingus* (Candid, 1960).

10. Charles Mingus, *Music Written for Monterey* (Sunnyside, 2006).

11. Mingus, quoted in Nat Hentoff, *Jazz Is* (Montclair, N.J.: Limelight, 1984), 34–35.

12. Ibid.

13. Eric Porter, *What Is This Thing Called Jazz? African American Musicians as Artists, Critics, and Activists* (Berkeley: University of California Press, 2002), 103.

14. Ibid., 105.

15. Ibid., 141.

16. Ekkehard Jost, *Free Jazz* (New York: Da Capo, 1974), 36.

17. John F. Goodman, *Mingus Speaks* (Berkeley: University of California Press, 2013), xiv, 139.

18. Horace J. Maxile, "Churchy Blues, Bluesy Church: Vernacular Tropes, Expression, and Structure in Charles Mingus's 'Ecclusiastics,'" *The Annual Review of Jazz Studies* 14 (2009): 66.

19. Ibid., 71, 75.

20. David Schiff, "The Many Faces of Ives," *The Atlantic*, January 1997, 87.

21. Goodman, *Mingus Speaks*, 25.

22. Ibid., 11.

23. Quoted in Jennifer Griffith, "Mingus in the Act: Confronting the Legacies of Vaudeville and Minstrelsy," *Jazz Perspectives* 4, no. 3 (2010): 348.

24. Goodman, *Mingus Speaks*, 11, 104, 17.

25. Scott Saul, *Freedom Is, Freedom Ain't: Jazz and the Making of the Sixties* (Cambridge, Mass.: Harvard University Press, 2003), 152.

26. Charles Mingus and Edmund Pollock, notes to Charles Mingus, *The Black Saint and the Sinner Lady* (Impulse, 1963).

27. From Thomas Reichman documentary, http://vimeo.com/10769018.

28. Charles Mingus, *Beneath the Underdog: His World as Composed by Mingus* (New York: Knopf, 1970), 3, 11, 45.

29. Ibid., 225.

30. Ibid., 53.

31. Porter, *What Is This Thing Called Jazz?* 146.

32. Ibid., 34–35.

33. Ibid., 254.

34. Ibid.

35. Ibid., 146.

36. Goodman, *Mingus Speaks*, 201.

37. Quoted in George McKay, *Circular Breathing: The Cultural Politics of Jazz in Britain* (Durham, N.C.: Duke University Press, 2005), 22.

38. Mingus, *Beneath the Underdog*, 291.

39. Porter, *What Is This Thing Called Jazz?* 147.

40. http://sonic.net/~goblin/8mingus.html; and personal communication, May 2014.

41. https://docs.google.com/presentation/d/1F8-6TblWKBFIHgZ351w-qQ8y8urGMHBdgt9YuhB8_HI/embed?hl=en&size=l#slide=id.p.

42. Mingus, *Beneath the Underdog*, 1.

43. Monson interview with Simon Rentner, "Reimagining Africa: From Popular Swing to the Jazz Avant-Garde," http://www.afropop.org/wp/2513/ingrid-monson/.

44. "Abbey Lincoln: Development of a Jazz Singer," National Public Radio, *Fresh Air*, March 25, 1986.

45. Playthell Benjamin, "The Death of Sister Soul," http://commentariesonthetimes .wordpress.com/2010/08/16/the-death-of-sister-soul/.

46. Ingrid Monson, *Freedom Sounds: Civil Rights Call Out to Jazz and Africa* (New York: Oxford University Press, 2007), 173.

47. Ibid., 174.

48. Malcolm X, "I Don't Mean Bananas," in *The New Left Reader*, ed. Carl Oglesby (New York: Grove, 1969), 207–22.

49. Margo Guryan notes to Roach, *Percussion Bitter Sweet* (Impulse Records, 1961).

50. Porter, *What Is This Thing Called Jazz?* 173.

51. Peniel Joseph, *Waiting 'Til the Midnight Hour: A Narrative History of Black Power in America* (New York: Henry Holt, 2007), 39–40.

52. Farah Jasmine Griffin, "When Malindy Sings: A Meditation on Black Women's Vocality," in *Uptown Conversation: The New Jazz Studies*, ed. Robert O'Meally, Brent Hayes Edwards, and Farah Jasmine Griffin (New York: Columbia University Press, 2004), 113. See also Jacqueline Castledine, "Gender, Jazz, and Justice in Cold War Freedom Movements," in *Freedom Rights: New Perspectives on the Civil Rights Movement*, ed. Danielle L. McGuire and John Dittmer (Lexington: University of Kentucky Press, 2011), 223–46.

53. Quoted in Graham Lock, *Chasing the Vibration: Meetings with Creative Musicians* (Exeter: Stride, 1994), 85.

54. Review in *Cadence* 7, no. 6 (June 1981): 47.

55. Wayne Enstice and Janis Stockhouse, *Jazzwomen: Conversations with Twenty-One Musicians* (Bloomington: Indiana University Press, 2004), 350.

56. "Abbey Lincoln's Letter Home," National Public Radio, *All Things Considered*, March 20, 1993.

57. "Abbey Lincoln: Development of a Jazz Singer."

58. "Jazz Singer and Activist Abbey Lincoln," National Public Radio, *The Tavis Smiley Show*, April 15, 2003.

59. Lock, *Chasing the Vibration*, 86.

60. "Dusted Reviews: ROVA & The Nels Cline Singers—The Celestial Septet," http://www.dustedmagazine.com/reviews/5691.

61. Benjamin Looker, *"Point from Which Creation Begins": The Black Artists' Group of St. Louis* (St. Louis: Missouri Historical Society Press, 2004), 157. Such themes of community, rights, and self-determination are explored vividly in Daniel Fischlin, Ajay Heble, and George Lipsitz, *The Fierce Urgency of Now: Improvisation, Rights, and the Ethics of Cocreation* (Durham, N.C.: Duke University Press, 2013).

62. Looker, *"Point from Which Creation Begins,"* 157.

63. Valerie Wilmer, *As Serious as Your Life: The Story of the New Jazz* (New York: Serpent's Tail, 1992), 23.

64. Ibid.

65. Looker, *"Point from Which Creation Begins,"* 158.

66. Amiri Baraka, notes to Archie Shepp, *Four for Trane* (Impulse Records, 1964).

67. Kevin Whitehead, *Why Jazz? A Concise Guide* (New York: Oxford University Press, 2010), 80. See also Denise Sullivan, *Keep on Pushing: Black Power Music from Blues to Hip-Hop* (Chicago: Chicago Review Press, 2011), which situates the New Thing alongside other expressions of early 1960s "freedom music," from Sister Odetta to Miriam Makeba.

68. Beaver Harris, interview with Robert Rusch, in *Cadence* 9, no. 4 (April 1983): 20.

69. Manning Marable, *Malcolm X: A Life of Reinvention* (New York: Viking, 2011), 465.

70. Interview in *Cadence* 5, no. 3 (March 1979): 4.

71. Wilmer, *As Serious as Your Life,* 156.

72. Ibid., 161.

73. Archie Shepp, liner notes to Shepp, *Mama Too Tight* (Impulse Records, 1966).

74. Ibid.

75. Clifford Allen, "Archie Shepp: I Know About the Life," http://www.allaboutjazz .com/archie-shepp-knowing-the-life-archie-shepp-by-clifford-allen.php?&pg=3.

76. Ibid.

77. Ibid.

78. Wilmer, *As Serious as Your Life,* 33.

79. Norman Weinstein, *A Night in Tunisia: Imaginings of Africa in Jazz* (Montclair, N.J.: Limelight, 2004), 136.

80. John Litweiler, *The Freedom Principle: Jazz After 1958* (New York: Da Capo, 1984), 135.

81. Clifford Allen, "Archie Shepp: I Know About the Life," http://www.allaboutjazz .com/archie-shepp-knowing-the-life-archie-shepp-by-clifford-allen.php?&pg=3.

82. Daniel Walden, "Black Music and Cultural Nationalism: The Maturation of Archie Shepp," *Negro American Literature Forum* 5, no. 4 (Winter 1971): 153.

83. Ajay Heble, *Landing on the Wrong Note: Jazz, Dissonance, and Critical Practice* (New York: Routledge, 2000), 15.

84. George Lipsitz, *Dangerous Crossroads: Popular Music, Postmodernism, and the Poetics of Place* (New York: Verso, 1994), 179.

85. David Kastin, "Fred Ho and the Evolution of Afro-Asian New American Multicultural Music," *Popular Music and Society* 33, no. 12. Quote from Kat Chow, "Iconoclastic Musician Takes Measure of His Life: 'I Became a Fighter,'" *Code Switch* (February 22, 2014).

86. Fred Ho in *Wicked Theory, Wicked Practice: A Fred Ho Reader,* ed. Diane C. Fujino (Minneapolis: University of Minnesota Press, 2009), 48.

87. Ibid., 23, 55.

88. Ibid., 150.

89. Robin Kelley, quoted in Kastin, "Fred Ho and the Evolution of Afro-Asian New American Multicultural Music," 4.

90. Ho in Fujino, *Wicked Theory, Wicked Practice*, 59, 74.

91. Kastin, in "Fred Ho and the Evolution of Afro-Asian New American Multicultural Music," 3, 5.

92. Ibid., 5.

93. Ho in Fujino, *Wicked Theory, Wicked Practice*, 94.

94. "Social Activism Underpins Asian American Jazz, National Public Radio, *Weekend Edition*, June 10, 2001.

95. Bill Shoemaker, "East Meets Left: Politics, Culture and Asian-American Jazz," *Jazz Times* (September 2003): 82–87.

96. Personal conversation, January 2010.

97. Ibid.

98. Ibid.

99. Larry Kelp, notes to Jon Jang, *Tiananmen!* (Soul Note Records, 1993).

100. Deborah Wong, notes to Jon Jang, *Paper Son, Paper Songs* (Soul Note Records, 2000).

101. Shoemaker, "East Meets Left," 84.

102. Hamilton College Archives interview, September 17, 2003.

103. Ibid.

104. Michael Dessen, "Improvising in a Different Clave: Steve Coleman and AfroCuba de Matanzas," in *The Other Side of Nowhere: Jazz, Improvisation, and Communities in Dialogue*, ed. Daniel Fischlin and Ajay Heble (Middletown, Conn.: Wesleyan University Press, 2004), 176.

105. John Szwed, *Space Is the Place: The Lives and Times of Sun Ra* (New York: Pantheon, 1997), 29.

106. Ibid.

107. Francis Davis, *Bebop and Nothingness: Jazz and Pop at the End of the Century* (New York: Schirmer, 1996), 158.

108. Szwed, *Space Is the Place*, 31.

109. Interview in *Cadence* 4, no. 4 (June 1978): 6.

110. Pete Gershon, "21st Century Music," *Signal to Noise* 55 (Fall 2009): 15.

111. Wilmer, *As Serious as Your Life*, 81.

112. Rusch, *Jazztalk: The Cadence Interviews* (Fort Lee, N.J.: Lyle Stuart, 1984), 64–65.

113. Wilmer, *As Serious as Your Life*, 89.

114. Ibid.

115. John Corbett, *Extended Play: Sounding Off from John Cage to Doctor Funkenstein* (Durham, N.C.: Duke University Press, 1994), 221.

116. Szwed, *Space Is the Place*, 65–67.

117. Ibid., 68–69.

118. Davis, *Bebop and Nothingness*, 159.

119. John Corbett, "One of Everything: Blount Hermeneutics and the Wisdom of Ra," in *The Wisdom of Sun Ra: Sun Ra's Polemical Broadsheets and Streetcorner Leaflets*, ed. John Corbett (Chicago: WhiteWalls, 2006), 5.

120. Sun Ra, "Jesus Said, 'Let the Negro Bury the Negro,'" in Corbett, *The Wisdom of Sun Ra*, 71.

121. Ibid., 115.

122. Ibid., 96.

123. Szwed, *Space Is the Place*, 7.

124. John Corbett, Anthony Elms, and Terri Kapsalis, eds., *Pathways to Unknown Worlds: Sun Ra, El Saturn, and Chicago's Afro-Futurist Underground 1954–68* (Chicago: Whitewalls, 2006), 119.

125. Gershon, "21st Century Music," 16.

126. See Corbett, *Extended Play*; and Graham Lock, *Blutopia: Visions of the Future and Revisions of the Past in the Work of Sun Ra, Duke Ellington, and Anthony Braxton* (Durham, N.C.: Duke University Press, 2000).

127. Lock, *Chasing the Vibration*, 148.

128. Ibid., 154; and Corbett, *The Wisdom of Sun Ra*, 87.

129. John Litweiler, *The Freedom Principle: Jazz After 1958* (New York: Da Capo, 1984), 144.

130. Szwed, *Space Is the Place*, 109.

131. Ibid., 137.

132. Ibid., 259.

133. Francis Davis, *Outcats: Jazz Composers, Instrumentalists, and Singers* (New York: Oxford University Press, 1990), 24.

134. Ajay Heble, *Landing on the Wrong Note: Jazz, Dissonance and Critical Practice* (New York: Routledge, 2000), 131.

135. Sun Ra, *Soundtrack to the Film* Space Is the Place (Evidence Records, 1993).

136. Author transcription, Ra, *The Creator of the Universe, Lost Reel 1* (Transparency Records, 2009).

137. Szwed, *Space Is the Place*, 309.

138. Ibid., 310.

139. Lock, *Chasing the Vibration*.

140. Litweiler, *The Freedom Principle*, 144.

141. See David Brent Johnson, "Suite History: Jazz Composers and the African-American Odyssey," http://indianapublicmedia.org/nightlights/suite-history-jazz-composers-africanamerican-odyssey/.

142. Yusef Lateef with Herb Boyd, *The Gentle Giant: The Autobiography of Yusef Lateef* (Irvington, N.J.: Morton, 2006), 154.

143. Jerry Schwartz, "Epic Suite Follows 400 Years of History," *The Atlanta Journal and Constitution*, July 15, 1998.

144. Ibid.

145. "A Talk with Dave Brubeck," National Public Radio, *The Tavis Smiley Show*, August 20, 2003.

146. Francis Davis, *In the Moment: Jazz in the 1980s* (New York: Da Capo, 1996), 18.

147. Ibid., 12.

148. Ken Weiss, Philadelphia scene report in *Cadence* 33, no. 5 (May 2007): 136.

149. Harvey G. Cohen, *Duke Ellington's America* (Chicago: University of Chicago Press, 2010), 29.

150. Ibid., 59.

151. Ibid., 93.

152. Ibid., 194.

153. Ibid., 206.

154. See David Metzer, "Shadow Play: The Spiritual in Duke Ellington's 'Black and Tan Fantasy,'" *Black Music Research Journal* 17, no. 2 (Autumn 1987): 137–58.

155. Quoted in Bruce Tucker, "Narrative, Extramusical Form, and the Metamodernism of the Art Ensemble of Chicago," *Lenox Avenue* 3 (1997): 30.

156. Cohen, *Duke Ellington's America*, 215.

157. Ibid., 216.

158. Lock, *Blutopia*, 109.

159. Cohen, *Duke Ellington's America*, 222.

160. Lock, *Blutopia*, 109.

161. Cohen, *Duke Ellington's America*, 228.

162. Lock, *Blutopia*, 97.

163. Ibid., 98.

164. Cohen, *Ellington's America*, 260.

165. Ibid., 301.

166. Ibid., 330.

167. Ibid., 339, 383.

168. Ibid., 392.

169. Ibid., 402.

170. Sanders, notes to Duke Ellington, *Black, Brown & Beige* (Columbia Records, 1999).

171. Bret Sjerven, "Neglected Treasures—John Carter and Bobby Bradford on Flying Dutchman," http://bphresh.blogspot.com/2012/06/neglected-treasures-john-carter-bobby.html.

172. John William Hardy, liner notes in John Carter and Bobby Bradford, *The Complete Revelation Sessions* (Mosaic Records, 2010).

173. Charles Sharp, "Seeking John Carter and Bobby Bradford: Free Music and Community in Los Angeles," *The Black Music Research Journal* 31, no. 1 (Spring 2011): 65–83.

174. Hardy, liner notes in Carter and Bradford, *The Complete Revelation Sessions*.

175. Ibid.

176. Larry Kart, quoted in Sjerven, "Neglected Treasures."

177. Robert Levin, quoted in ibid.

178. Transcribed from author copy of November 24, 1979, Tübingen performance.

179. Interview in *Cadence* 6, no. 2 (February 1980): 12.

180. David P. Brown, *Noise Orders: Jazz, Improvisation, and Architecture* (Minneapolis: University of Minnesota Press, 2006), 46.

181. Don Snowden, "John Carter Obituary," *Los Angeles Times*, April 14, 1991.

182. Ibid.

183. Joachim-Ernst Berendt, notes to *Dauwhe* (Black Saint Records, 1982).

184. Carter, notes to *Dance of the Love Ghosts* (Gramavision Records, 1987).

185. Ibid.

186. John Carter, liner notes to *Fields* (Gramavision Records, 1988).

187. Ibid.

188. John Carter, notes to *Shadows on a Wall* (Gramavision Records, 1989).

189. Ibid.

190. Weinstein, *A Night in Tunisia*, 93.

191. Paul Gilroy, *Small Acts: Thoughts on the Politics of Black Culture* (New York: Serpent's Tail, 1994), 37.

192. Art Lange, notes to Francois Houle, *In the Vernacular* (Songlines Records, 1998).

193. Ibid.

194. Quoted in Robert Walser, *Keeping Time: Readings in Jazz History* (New York: Oxford University Press, 1999), 336.

195. Wynton Marsalis, quoted in Davis, *In the Moment*, 29.

196. Gene Lees, *Cats of Any Color: Jazz, Black and White* (New York: Da Capo, 1995), 195.

197. Stanley Crouch, "Whose Blood? Whose Fields?" notes to Marsalis, *Blood on the Fields* (Columbia, 1997).

198. Ben Ratliff, "An Oratorio of History with History of Its Own," *New York Times*, February 25, 2013.

199. It is worth noting that many of the characters central to the historical imaginings in this chapter, like Juba and Gabriel, feature in Arna Bontemps's 1936 novel *Black Thunder*, which Allen Dwight Callahan describes as "a fictional account of the biblical interpretation" undergirding slave revolts. See Callahan, *Talking Book: African Americans and the Bible* (New Haven, Conn.: Yale University Press, 2006), 134–35.

200. Crouch, "Whose Blood? Whose Fields?"

201. "Marsalis' Sharp Social Critiques Come with Cool Riffs," National Public Radio, *All Things Considered*, March 12, 2007.

202. Porter, *What Is This Thing Called Jazz?* 305.

203. Lock, *Blutopia*, 2.

204. Weinstein, *A Night in Tunisia*, 75.

205. Lock, *Blutopia*, 61.

CHAPTER 4

1. The title is from the Art Ensemble of Chicago's 2003 album.

2. Norman Weinstein, *A Night in Tunisia: Imaginings of Africa in Jazz* (Montclair, N.J.: Limelight, 2004), 116.

3. Jeffrey C. Isaac, "Oases in the Desert: Hannah Arendt on Democratic Politics," *American Political Science Review* 8, no. 1 (March 1994): 156–68.

4. See John Patrick Diggins, *The Lost Soul of American Politics: Virtue, Self-Interest, and the Foundations of Liberalism* (Chicago: University of Chicago Press, 1986); Frances Fitzgerald, *Cities on a Hill: A Brilliant Exploration of Visionary Communities Remaking the American Dream* (New York: Simon & Schuster, 1987); and Donald E. Pitzer, *America's Communal Utopias* (Chapel Hill: University of North Carolina Press, 1997).

5. George Lipsitz, *Dangerous Crossroads: Popular Music, Postmodernism, and the Poetics of Place* (New York: Verso, 1994), 3.

6. Ibid., 35.

7. This term is from Benjamin Barber, *Jihad vs. McWorld: How Globalism and Tribalism Are Reshaping the World* (New York: Ballantine, 1996). I use it to refer to the neoliberal cultural and economic environment in which jazz struggles to be heard.

8. Graham Lock, ed., *Mixtery: A Festschrift for Anthony Braxton* (Exeter: Stride, 1995), 9.

9. Ray Pratt, *Rhythm and Resistance: The Political Uses of American Popular Music* (Washington, D.C.: Smithsonian Institution Press, 1990), 23.

10. Benjamin Piekut, *Experimentalism Otherwise: The New York Avant-Garde and Its Limits* (Berkeley: University of California Press, 2011), 108.

11. Ibid., 130.

12. Interview in *Cadence* 8, no. 3 (March 1982): 12.

13. Francis Gooding, notes to *Spiritual Jazz: Esoteric, Modal + Deep Jazz from the Underground, 1968–77* (Now Again Records, 2009).

14. See David G. Such, *Avant-Garde Musicians Performing "Out There"* (Iowa City: University of Iowa Press, 1993), 84; and George E. Lewis, "Teaching Improvised Music: An Ethnographic Memoir," in *Arcana: Musicians on Music*, ed. John Zorn (New York: Hips Road, 2000), 83. CMS line from Will Hermes, *Love Goes to Buildings on Fire: Five Years in New York That Changed Music Forever* (New York: Faber & Faber, 2011), 174.

15. Billy Bang, liner notes to Bang, *Sweet Space* (Anima Productions, 1979). See Hermes, *Love Goes to Buildings on Fire*, 172.

16. Ronald M. Radano, "Jazzin' the Classics: The AACM's Challenge to Mainstream Aesthetics," *Black Music Research Journal* 12, no. 1 (Spring 1992): 81.

17. George E. Lewis, *A Power Stronger Than Itself: The AACM and American Experimental Music* (Chicago: University of Chicago Press, 2008), ix–xi.

18. Ibid., 57.

19. Ibid.

20. Ibid., 68.

21. Ibid., 62, 75, 413.

22. Ibid., 82–97.

23. Ibid., 99.

24. Ibid., 110.

25. Ibid., 116.

26. Ibid., 122.

27. Ibid., 148.

28. Ingrid Monson, *Freedom Sounds: Civil Rights Call Out to Jazz and Africa* (New York: Oxford University Press, 2007), 307. Second quote from Radano, *New Musical Figurations: Anthony Braxton's Cultural Critique* (Chicago: University of Chicago Press, 1993), 105.

29. Radano, "Jazzin' the Classics," 81.

30. Lewis, *A Power Stronger Than Itself*, 192.

31. Robert Rusch interview in *Cadence* 8, no. 10 (October 1982): 7.

32. Gene Santoro, *Dancing in Your Head: Jazz, Blues, Rock, and Beyond* (New York: Oxford University Press, 2004), 251; and Francis Davis, *Outcats: Jazz Composers, Instrumentalists, and Singers* (New York: Oxford University Press, 1990), 59.

33. See "Interview: The Multi-faceted Douglas Ewart," http://www.openskyjazz.com /2009/12/interview-the-multi-faceted-douglas-ewart/.

34. Valerie Wilmer, *As Serious as Your Life: The Story of the New Jazz* (New York: Serpent's Tail, 1992), 117.

35. Lewis, *A Power Stronger Than Itself*, 407.

36. Interview in *Cadence* 34, nos. 10–12 (October–December 2008): 41.

37. "A Fireside Chat with Muhal Richard Abrams," http://www.jazzweekly.com/ interviews/abrams.htm.

38. Lewis, *A Power Stronger Than Itself*, 108.

39. Central to early AACM administration was John Shenoy Jackson, child of Arkansas Garveyites. See Daniel Fischlin, Ajay Heble, and George Lipsitz, *The Fierce Urgency of Now: Improvisation, Rights, and the Ethics of Cocreation* (Durham, N.C.: Duke University Press, 2013), xvii.

40. Wilmer, *As Serious as Your Life*, 113.

41. John Corbett, *Extended Play: Sounding Off from John Cage to Doctor Funkenstein* (Durham, N.C.: Duke University Press, 1994), 120.

42. Radano, "Jazzin' the Classics," 88, 99.

43. Ibid., 88.

44. Ibid., 101.

45. John Litweiler, *The Freedom Principle: Jazz After 1958* (New York: Da Capo, 1984), 198.

46. Benjamin Looker, *"Point from Which Creation Begins": The Black Artists' Group of St. Louis* (St. Louis: Missouri Historical Society Press, 2004), 5.

47. Ibid., 38.

48. See Peniel Joseph, *Waiting 'Til the Midnight Hour: A Narrative History of Black Power in America* (New York: Henry Holt, 2007); Manning Marable, *Malcolm X: A Life of Reinvention* (New York: Viking, 2010); and William L. Van DeBurg, *New Day in Babylon: The Black Power Movement in American Culture 1965–1975* (Chicago: University of Chicago Press, 1993).

49. Benjamin Looker, "Poets of Action: The Saint Louis Black Artists Group," http://www.allaboutjazz.com/poets-of-action-the-saint-louis-black-artists-group-1968-1972-part-1-4-by-benjamin-looker.php.

50. Looker, *"Point from Which Creation Begins,"* xvii.

51. Ben Looker, "A City Built to Music," http://www.thecommonspace.org/2004/12/communities.php.

52. Dennis Owsley, *City of Gabriels: The History of Jazz in St. Louis, 1895–1973* (St. Louis: Reedy, 2006), 162.

53. George Lipsitz, *Footsteps in the Dark: The Hidden Histories of Popular Music* (Minneapolis: University of Minnesota Press, 2007), 116.

54. Looker, "Poets of Action," http://www.allaboutjazz.com/poets-of-action-the-saint-louis-black-artists-group-1968-1972-part-1-4-by-benjamin-looker.php.

55. Ibid.

56. J. D. Parran, quoted in ibid.

57. Looker, *"Point from Which Creation Begins,"* 22–25, 41.

58. Ibid., 26. See also Kenneth S. Jolly, *Black Liberation in the Midwest: The Struggle in St. Louis, Missouri, 1964–1970* (New York: Routledge, 2006).

59. Ibid., 74.

60. Ibid., 104.

61. Ibid., 42.

62. Ibid., 109–10.

63. Ibid., 116, 126.

64. Ibid., 134.

65. Ibid.

66. Ibid., 145.

67. Ibid.

68. Ibid., 9.

69. Julius Hemphill, interview with Suzanne McElfresh, http://bombsite.com/issues/46/articles/1744.

70. Ibid.

71. Susan Johnson, "Hemphill Called the Master," *The Philadelphia Tribune* (September 13, 1994).

72. Lee Jeske, notes to Hemphill, *Flat-Out Jump Suite* (Black Saint Records, 1980).

73. Wilmer, *As Serious as Your Life*, 222.

74. Ibid., 249.

75. "Music and Musicians of the Black Artists' Group in St. Louis: Participant Biographies," http://news.wustl.edu/news/Pages/6491.aspx.

76. Looker, *"Point from Which Creation Begins,"* 148.

77. Ibid., 171.

78. Ibid., 175.

79. Lipsitz, *Footsteps in the Dark*, 109.

80. Looker, *"Point from Which Creation Begins,"* xix.

81. Tapscott, quoted in Clora Bryant et al., *Central Avenue Sounds: Jazz in Los Angeles* (Berkeley: University of California Press, 1998), 301.

82. See Daniel Widener, *Black Arts West: Culture and Struggle in Postwar Los Angeles* (Durham, N.C.: Duke University Press, 2010).

83. Bryant et al., *Central Avenue Sounds*, 215.

84. Ibid., 287.

85. Horace Tapscott, *Songs of the Unsung: The Musical and Social Journey of Horace Tapscott* (Durham, N.C.: Duke University Press, 2001), 92.

86. Steven L. Isoardi, *The Dark Tree: Jazz and the Community Arts in Los Angeles* (Berkeley: University of California Press, 2006), 46.

87. Tapscott, *Songs of the Unsung*, 83.

88. Isoardi, *The Dark Tree*, 1.

89. Ibid., 92.

90. Ibid., 95.

91. Ibid., 107.

92. Widener, *Black Arts West*, 119.

93. Isoardi, *The Dark Tree*, 4–5.

94. Ibid., 6.

95. Ibid., 14.

96. Ibid., 53.

97. Ibid., 94.

98. Ibid., 60.

99. Ibid., 86, 89.

100. Tapscott, *Songs of the Unsung*, 114.

101. Isoardi, *The Dark Tree*, 95.

102. Ibid., 94.

103. Ibid., 98.

104. Ibid., 114.

105. Ibid., 113.

106. Tapscott, *Songs of the Unsung*, 136.

107. Ibid., 139.

108. Isoardi, *The Dark Tree*, 122–23.

109. Ibid., 124.

110. Ibid., 130.

111. Ibid., 145, 151.

112. Peter Walton, "Horace Tapscott: 1934–1999," http://www.blackpast.org/?q=aaw/horace-tapscott-1934-1999.

113. "Horace Tapscott—A Brief Biography," http://www.posi-tone.com/tapscott/bio.html.

114. Tapscott, *Songs of the Unsung*, 147.

115. Isoardi, *The Dark Tree*, 162.

116. Tapscott, *Songs of the Unsung*, 165.

117. Ibid., 166.
118. Brian Cross, *It's Not About a Salary . . . : Rap, Race and Resistance in Los Angeles* (New York: Verso, 1993), 97.
119. Isoardi, *The Dark Tree*, 163.
120. Ibid.
121. Ibid., 256.
122. Ibid., 259.
123. Ibid., 261.
124. Lipsitz, *Footsteps in the Dark*, 100.
125. Isoardi, *The Dark Tree*, 289.
126. Ibid.
127. Ibid., 276.
128. Ibid., 274, 288.
129. Ibid., 297.
130. Ibid., 177.
131. Lipsitz, *Footsteps in the Dark*, 100.
132. Tapscott, notes to Pan Afrikan Peoples Arkestra, *Flight 17* (Nimbus West Records, 2006).
133. Interview in *Cadence* 10, no. 7 (July 1984): 18.
134. Graham Lock, *Chasing the Vibration* (Exeter: Stride, 1994), 98.
135. Ben Ratliff, *Coltrane: The Story of a Sound* (New York: Farrar, Straus and Giroux, 2007), xix.
136. J. C. Thomas, *Chasin' the Trane* (New York: Da Capo, 1975), 83.
137. Both quotes from Ratliff, *Coltrane*, 65.
138. See also Leonard L. Brown, ed., *John Coltrane and Black America's Quest for Freedom: Spirituality and the Music* (New York: Oxford University Press, 2010); Eric Nisenson, *Ascension: John Coltrane and His Quest* (New York: Da Capo, 1995); and Lewis Porter, *John Coltrane: His Life and Music* (Ann Arbor: University of Michigan Press, 2000).
139. Lewis Porter, notes to Coltrane, *The Heavyweight Champion* (Atlantic Records, 1995).
140. Ratliff, *Coltrane*, 108–9.
141. See ibid., 71–72.
142. Ibid., 86.
143. Leroi Jones, notes to *Live at Birdland* (Impulse Records, 1963).
144. Ratliff, *Coltrane*, 83.
145. Quoted in Nat Hentoff, notes to *Transition* (Impulse Records, 1965).
146. See Jill Watts, *God, Harlem, U.S.A.: The Father Divine Story* (Berkeley: University of California Press, 1992).
147. Ratliff, *Coltrane*, 106.
148. *The Major Works of John Coltrane* (Impulse Records, 1965).
149. David Wild, notes to ibid.

150. Quoted in ibid.

151. Wild, notes to Coltrane, *Sun Ship* (Impulse Records, 1965).

152. Quoted in Wild, notes to Coltrane, *First Meditations* (Impulse Records, 1977).

153. Quoted in Nat Hentoff, notes to Coltrane, *Expression* (Impulse Records, 1967).

154. Nisenson, *Ascension*, 166.

155. Ibid., 167.

156. Ibid., 187.

157. Ibid., 192–93.

158. Ibid., 193.

159. Quoted in Lewis Porter, notes to Coltrane, *The Heavyweight Champion.*

160. Quoted in Ratliff, *Coltrane*, 92.

161. Quoted in Ashley Kahn, notes to *One Down, One Up* (Impulse Records, 2005).

162. Quoted in ibid.

163. Spencer Weston, in *Cadence* 3, nos. 1 and 2 (August 1977): 29.

164. Leonard Brown, "Conversation with Yusef Lateef," in Brown, *John Coltrane and Black America's Quest for Freedom*, 198.

165. Nisenson, *Ascension*, 213.

166. Ibid., 149.

167. Ramsey, notes to Coltrane, *The Complete Prestige Recordings* (Original Jazz Classics, 1991).

168. http://www.coltranechurch.org/#!about/csgz.

169. See "Interview with Coltrane Icon Painter Mark Dukes and Archbishop Franzo King," http://blog.sfmoma.org/2010/01/interview-with-coltrane-icon-painter-mark-dukes-and-archbishop-franzo-king/.

170. Personal observation, June 2013.

171. Ibid.

172. See Jack Boulware, "The Church of John Coltrane," http://www.jackboulware.com/writing/church-of-john-coltrane.

173. Samuel G. Freedman, "Sunday Religion, Inspired by Saturday Nights," *New York Times*, December 1, 2007.

174. James DeKoven, "It's St. John Coltrane's Church," *New Fillmore* (July 2, 2009).

175. Boulware, "The Church of John Coltrane."

176. Ibid.

177. Ibid.

178. "The Story of 'A Love Supreme'," National Public Radio, *All Things Considered*, March 22, 2000.

179. Boulware, "The Church of John Coltrane."

180. Ibid.

181. Andrew Gumbel, "Saint John Coltrane Church Faces a Supreme Challenge," *The Baltimore Sun*, February 27, 2000.

182. Harvey Cox, *Fire from Heaven: The Rise of Pentecostal Spirituality and the Reshaping of Religion in the Twenty-First Century* (New York: Da Capo, 1995), 153.

183. Boulware, "The Church of John Coltrane."
184. Ibid.
185. Cox, *Fire from Heaven*, 154.
186. Freedman, "Sunday Religion, Inspired by Saturday Nights."
187. Ramsey, notes to Coltrane, *The Complete Prestige Recordings*.
188. Freedman, "Sunday Religion, Inspired by Saturday Nights."
189. http://deacondukes.blogspot.com/; accessed August 2013.
190. Ibid.
191. Ibid.
192. Ibid.
193. Ibid.
194. Tammy L. Kernodle, "Freedom Is a Constant Struggle: Alice Coltrane and the Redefining of the Jazz Avant-Garde," in Brown, *John Coltrane and Black America's Quest for Freedom*, 73.
195. Franya J. Berkman, *Monument Eternal: The Music of Alice Coltrane* (Middletown, Conn.: Wesleyan University Press, 2010), 23–24.
196. Ibid., 41.
197. Ibid., 47.
198. Ibid., 50.
199. Ibid., 76.
200. Ibid., 7.
201. Ibid., 107.
202. Ibid., 80.
203. Ibid., 66.
204. Ibid., 67.
205. Ibid.
206. Alice Coltrane, notes to Coltrane, *Journey to Satchidananda* (Impulse Records, 1970).
207. Berkman, *Monument Eternal*, 8.
208. Ibid., 81–82.
209. Ibid., 84.
210. Ibid., 79.
211. Kernodle, "Freedom Is a Constant Struggle," 92.
212. Alice Coltrane, notes to *Turiya Sings* (Avatar Book Institute, 1982).
213. "Alice Coltrane: 'Translinear Light'," National Public Radio, *Morning Edition*, September 23, 2004.
214. Berkman, "Appropriating Universality: The Coltranes and 1960s Spirituality," *American Studies* 48, no. 1 (Spring 2007): 43.
215. Ibid., 50–51.
216. Berkman, *Monument Eternal*, 96.
217. Ingrid Monson, *Saying Something: Jazz Improvisation and Interaction* (Chicago: University of Chicago Press, 1996), 13.

218. Josh Kun, *Audiotopia: Music, Race, and America* (Berkeley: University of California Press, 2005), 2–3.

219. Personal conversation, February 2003.

220. Sarah Pike, *Earthly Bodies, Magical Selves: Contemporary Pagans and the Search for Community* (Berkeley: University of California Press, 2001), xxii.

221. Ibid., 14.

222. See Christopher Small, *Music of the Common Tongue: Survival and Celebration in Afro-American Music* (New York: Riverrun, 1987).

CHAPTER 5

1. The title is from Archie Shepp's 1967 album.

2. Personal conversation, June 2010.

3. Quoted in Ben Ratliff, *The Jazz Ear: Conversations over Music* (New York: Times, 2010), 164.

4. Victor L. Schirmer, "Bobby Zankel: Peaceful Warrior," http://www.allaboutjazz.com/bobby-zankel-peaceful-jazz-warrior-bobby-zankel-by-victor-l-schermer.php&page=1.

5. Ibid.

6. Catherine Albanese, "Knowing Through the Body: The Path of Ritual," in *American Spiritualities: A Reader*, ed. Catherine Albanese (Bloomington: Indiana University Press, 2001), 21.

7. See Tamar Frankiel, "Ritual Sites in the Narrative of American Religion," in Albanese, *American Spiritualities*, 23–55.

8. Samuel Floyd, *The Power of Black Music* (New York: Oxford University Press, 1995), 20–21.

9. Catherine Bell, "Performance," in *Critical Terms for Religious Studies*, ed. Mark C. Taylor (Chicago: University of Chicago Press, 1998), 205.

10. Ibid., 207.

11. Ibid., 208.

12. Jonathan Z. Smith, *To Take Place: Toward Theory in Ritual* (Chicago: University of Chicago Press, 1987), 103.

13. Judith Butler, *Gender Trouble: Feminism and the Subversion of Identity* (New York: Routledge, 2006), 25.

14. Ben Ratliff, "Bob Brookmeyer: Raging and Composing Against the Jazz Machine," *New York Times*, May 12, 2006.

15. Lisle Ellis, notes to What We Live, *Fo(u)r* (Black Saint, 1996).

16. Richard Brent Turner, *Jazz Religion, the Second Line, and Black New Orleans* (Bloomington: Indiana University Press, 2009).

17. Roger Lewis of the Dirty Dozen Brass Band, "Dirty Dozen Brass Band Keeps Jazz Funeral Alive," National Public Radio, *The Tavis Smiley Show*, August 25, 2004.

18. Harvey Cohen, *Duke Ellington's America* (Chicago: University of Chicago Press, 2010), 460.

19. Ibid.
20. David Brent Johnson, "Sacred Blue: Jazz Goes to Church in the 1960s," http://indianapublicmedia.org/nightlights/sacred-blue-jazz-church-1960s/.
21. Francis Gooding, notes to *Spiritual Jazz: Esoteric, Modal + Deep Jazz from the Underground, 1968–77* (Now Again Records, 2009).
22. See Johnson, "Sacred Blue"; "Liturgy: Cool Creeds," *Time* (July 9, 1965): 52; and "Jazz Goes to Church," *Ebony*, April 1966, 76–80.
23. See Angelo D. Versace, "The Evolution of Sacred Jazz as Reflected in the Music of Mary Lou Williams, Duke Ellington, John Coltrane, and Recognized Contemporary Sacred Jazz Artists" (PhD Dissertation, University of Miami, Coral Gables, 2013).
24. David W. Stowe, *How Sweet the Sound: Music in the Spiritual Lives of Americans* (Cambridge, Mass.: Harvard University Press, 2004), 199.
25. Cohen, *Duke Ellington's America*, 449.
26. Ibid., 450.
27. Ibid., 449.
28. Ibid., 446.
29. Ibid.
30. Ibid., 448.
31. Ibid.
32. Ibid., 461.
33. Ibid., 450.
34. Ibid.
35. Ibid., 462.
36. Ibid., 464.
37. Ibid., 467.
38. Ibid., 468.
39. Ibid., 469–71.
40. Francis Davis, *Outcats: Jazz Composers, Instrumentalists, and Singers* (New York: Oxford University Press, 1990), 10.
41. Cohen, *Duke Ellington's America*, 475.
42. Ibid.
43. Ibid., 476.
44. Ibid., 483.
45. Ibid., 484.
46. Ellington Symposium, in *Cadence* 4, no. 11 (November 1978): 22.
47. Cohen, *Duke Ellington's America*, 567.
48. John S. Wilson, "Mary Lou Williams, a Jazz Great, Dies," *New York Times*, May 30, 1981.
49. Edward Guthmann, "All the Jazz on Mary Lou Williams," *The San Francisco Chronicle*, May 16, 1991.
50. Wilson, "Mary Lou Williams, a Jazz Great, Dies."
51. Guthmann, "All the Jazz on Mary Lou Williams."

52. Wilson, "Mary Lou Williams, a Jazz Great, Dies."

53. Ibid.

54. Gayle Murchison, "Mary Lou Williams' *Black Christ of the Andes (St. Martin de Porres)*: Vatican II, Civil Rights, and Jazz as Sacred Music," *Musical Quarterly* 86, no. 4 (Winter 2003): 594.

55. Ibid.

56. Ibid.

57. Tammy Lynn Kernodle, "This Is My Story, This Is My Song: The Historiography of Vatican II, Black Catholic Identity, Jazz, and the Religious Recompositions of Mary Lou Williams," *U.S. Catholic Historian* 19, no. 2 (Spring 2001): 85.

58. Francine May Fledderus, "The Function of Oral Tradition in 'Mary Lou's Mass' by Mary Lou Williams" (master's thesis, University of North Texas, 1996), 73.

59. Ibid., 46.

60. Father Peter F. O'Brien, S.J., "Jazz for the Soul," notes to Mary Lou Williams, *Black Christ of the Andes* (Smithsonian Folkways Music, 2004).

61. Eddie Meadows, notes to ibid.

62. Ibid.

63. Ibid.

64. Murchison, "Mary Lou Williams' *Black Christ of the Andes (St. Martin de Porres)*," 602.

65. D. Antoinette Handy, "Conversation with Mary Lou Williams: First Lady of the Jazz Keyboard," *Black Perspective in Music* 8, no. 2 (Autumn 1980): 206.

66. Kernodle, "This Is My Story, This Is My Song," 90.

67. Richard Harrington, "The Jazz Player's Choir of Angels; At the National Cathedral, Mary Lou Williams's Mass Is Performed at Last," *The Washington Post*, March 26, 1999.

68. Wilson, "Mary Lou Williams, a Jazz Great, Dies."

69. Ibid.

70. "Mary Lou Williams at Lady of Lourdes," *New York Amsterdam News*, November 4, 1972.

71. "Mary Lou Williams in Jazz Mass," *New York Amsterdam News*, February 15, 1975.

72. Murchison, "Mary Lou Williams' *Black Christ of the Andes (St. Martin de Porres)*," 621–22.

73. See David E. Anderson, "Dave Brubeck's Sacred Music: 'Composition as Prayer,'" *The Huffington Post*, December 7, 2012.

74. "Modern Oratorios and Sacred Texts (Weekly Podcast)," http://www.wnyc.org/shows/newsounds/articles/new-sounds-podcasts/2011/mar/04/modern-oratorios-sacred-texts-weekly-podcast/.

75. Neil Tesser, "Traditions: In Jazz We Trust," *Jazziz* 23, no. 6 (June 2006): 24–25.

76. Ibid.

77. Martin Marty quote from http://www.plymouthlawrence.com/newsletter_files/JulyRock2014.pdf. Witkowski quote from Tesser, "Traditions."

78. Jon Pareles, "Pop/Jazz," *New York Times*, March 14, 1986.

79. Jairo Moreno, "Bauza-Gillespie-Latin/Jazz: Difference, Modernity, and the Black Carribean," in *Afro-Latin@ Reader: History and Culture in the United States*, ed. Miriam Jimenez Roman and Juan Flores (Durham, N.C.: Duke University Press, 2010), 180.

80. Ibid., 182.

81. Pareles, "Pop/Jazz."

82. David F. Garcia, "'We Both Speak African': Gillespie, Pozo, and the Making of Afro-Cuban Jazz," *Institute for Studies in American Music Newsletter* 38, no. 1 (Fall 2007): 2.

83. Alain Tercinet, notes to *Dizzy Gillespie, Volume 11, 1947 Complete Edition* (Masters of Jazz, 2001).

84. Tom Piazza, "Chano Pozo," National Public Radio, *The Tavis Smiley Show*, March 4, 2002.

85. Robin D. G. Kelley, *Africa Speaks, America Answers: Modern Jazz in Revolutionary Times* (Cambridge, Mass.: Harvard University Press, 2012), 16.

86. Ibid., 13.

87. Ibid.

88. Kelley, *Africa Speaks, America Answers*, 16.

89. Moreno, "Bauza-Gillespie-Latin/Jazz," 184.

90. George Lipsitz, *The Possessive Investment in Whiteness: How White People Profit from Identity Politics* (Philadelphia: Temple University Press, 1998), 159.

91. See Timothy Brennan, *Secular Devotion: Afro-Latin Music and Imperial Jazz* (New York: Verso 2008); and Michael Dessen, "Improvising in a Different Clave: Steven Coleman and AfroCuba de Matanzas," in *The Other Side of Nowhere: Jazz, Improvisation, and Communities in Dialogue*, ed. Daniel Fischlin and Ajay Heble (Middletown, Conn.: Wesleyan University Press, 2004).

92. Interview in *Cadence* 28, no. 5 (May 2002): 21.

93. Ibid.

94. "Bill Summers: A Percussionist in His Own Words," National Public Radio, *Morning Edition*, March 22, 2005.

95. Mark Merella, "Steve Berrios: Latin Jazz Innovator," http://www.allaboutjazz.com/steve-berrios-latin-jazz-innovator-steve-berrios-by-mark-merella.php.

96. Javier Aq Ortiz, "Babatunde Lea's Soul Pools," http://www.allaboutjazz.com/babatunde-leas-soul-pools-babatunde-lea-by-javier-aq-ortiz.php.

97. "Omar Sosa: The Afro-Cuban Alchemist of Jazz," National Public Radio, *Tell Me More*, April 9, 2009.

98. Ibid.

99. Personal conversation, June 2010.

100. Ibid.

101. Ibid.

102. Ibid.

103. "What Is M-Base?" http://www.m-base.com/mbase_explanation.html.
104. Ibid.
105. Interview at www.m-base.com.
106. Andrew Gilbert, "Steve Coleman: A Master of Creative Musical Improvisation," *The Seattle Times*, April 3, 2009.
107. http://www.m-base.com/resume_bio.html.
108. Anil Prasad, "Steve Coleman: Digging Deep," http://www.innerviews.org/inner/coleman.html.
109. http://www.m-base.com/resume_bio.html.
110. Prasad, "Steve Coleman."
111. Ibid.
112. Ibid.
113. Steve Coleman, "The Lunation Cycle as a Point of Departure for Musical Ideas," *Arcana II: Musicians on Music*, ed. John Zorn (New York: Hips Road, 2007), 56.
114. Ibid., 57–59.
115. Steve Coleman, "Regarding the Sonic Symbolism of When and Where," in *Arcana V: Music, Magic and Mysticism*, ed. John Zorn (New York: Hips Road, 2010), 33.
116. Ibid., 67.
117. Ibid., 40.
118. Ibid., 61.
119. Steve Coleman, notes to *Harvesting Semblances and Affinities* (Pi Recordings, 2010).
120. Coleman, "Regarding the Sonic Symbolism of When and Where," 69.
121. Johannes Voelz, "Improvisation, Correlation, and Vibration: An Interview with Steve Coleman," *Critical Studies in Improvisation* 2, no. 1 (2006): 8.
122. Ibid., 12.
123. Fred Jung, "My Conversation with Steve Coleman," http://www.allaboutjazz.com/iviews/coleman.htm.
124. Ibid.
125. George Lewis, "Omar's Song: A (Re)construction of Great Black Music," *Lenox Avenue*, 4 (1998): 69.
126. Ibid.
127. Ibid.
128. Chris Forbes, review of *Americans Swinging in Paris*, http://www.cosmik.com/aa-november04/reviews/review_art_ensemble_of_chicago.html.
129. Philippe Carles, liner notes to *Certain Blacks* (America/Universal, 2004).
130. Mike Joyce, "Art Ensemble of Chicago," *The Washington Post*, September 26, 1984.
131. W. Royal Stokes, "Art Ensemble of Chicago," *The Washington Post*, May 5, 1979.
132. Jesse Hamlin, "Art Ensemble's Shtick," *The San Francisco Chronicle*, February 5, 1990.

133. Ibid.

134. See Geoffrey Himes, "Art Ensemble," *The Washington Post*, October 18, 1980. See also John Fordham, "Black Within Blue: The Art Ensemble Play at the Union Chapel," *The Guardian*, July 13, 1993.

135. "Art Ensemble of Chicago: Anti-Jazz: The New Thing Revisited," http://www .arsnovaworkshop.org/events/art-ensemble-chicago-03-06-2010.

136. Paul Davison, "Great Black Music Comes of Age," *The Harvard Crimson*, May 10, 1979.

137. Ibid.

138. George E. Lewis, *A Power Stronger Than Itself: The AACM and American Experimental Music* (Chicago: University of Chicago Press, 2008), 151.

139. Ibid., 151–52.

140. Ibid.

141. Ibid., 153.

142. Interview with Ted Panken, WKCR, http://www.jazzhouse.org/nlib/index.php3? read=panken8, November 22, 1994.

143. Interview with Fred Jung, http://www.allaboutjazz.com/php/article.php?id=621, October 2003.

144. Interview with Ted Panken.

145. Ibid.

146. Ibid.

147. Joseph Jarman, notes to *Urban Bushmen* (ECM Records, 1982).

148. Ibid.

149. Interview with Fred Jung.

150. Ibid.

151. Bruce Tucker, "Narrative, Extramusical Form, and the Metamodernism of the Art Ensemble of Chicago," *Lenox Avenue* 3 (1997): 35.

152. Ibid.

153. Robin D. G. Kelley, "Dig They Freedom: Meditations on History and the Black Avant-Garde," *Lenox Avenue* 3 (1997): 13.

154. Allan M. Gordon, "The AEC as Performance Art," *Lenox Avenue* 3 (1997): 57.

155. Norman Weinstein, "Steps Toward an Integrative Comprehension of the Art Ensemble of Chicago's Music," *Lenox Avenue* 3 (1997): 6. See also, Michael J. Budds, "The Art Ensemble of Chicago in Context," *Lenox Avenue* 3 (1997): 59–72.

156. Tucker, "Narrative, Extramusical Form, and the Metamodernism of the Art Ensemble of Chicago," 40.

157. Paul Steinbeck, "'Area by Area the Machine Unfolds': The Improvisational Performance Practice of the Art Ensemble of Chicago," *Journal of the Society for American Music* 2, no. 3 (2008): 401.

158. Interview in *Cadence* 5, no. 12 (December 1979): 14.

159. Weinstein, "Steps Toward an Integrative Comprehension of the Art Ensemble of Chicago's Music," 9.

160. Ibid., 10.

161. Lewis, "Omar's Song," 77.

162. Ibid., 88.

163. R. Murray Schafer, *The Soundscape: Our Sonic Environment and the Tuning of the World* (Rochester, Vt.: Destiny, 1993), 111.

164. Kelly notes that the AEC paid attention to Kwame Nkruma and the Mau Mau uprising just as surely as Randy Weston and Art Blakey did.

165. Kelly, "Dig They Freedom," 16.

166. Interview with Ted Panken.

167. Paul Austerlitz, *Jazz Consciousness: Music, Race, and Humanity* (Middletown, Conn.: Wesleyan University Press, 2005), 166.

168. Ibid., 166.

169. Ibid.

170. Mark Jacobson, "The Jazz Scientist," http://nymag.com/print/?/nymetro/news/trends/columns/cityside/5380/.

171. "Milford Graves Documentary," http://www.youtube.com/watch?v=9tNqs8hs9p4.

172. Valerie Wilmer, *As Serious as Your Life: The Story of the New Jazz* (New York: Serpent's Tail, 1992), 14–15.

173. "Milford Graves Documentary."

174. "Chapter 4: 1966–1967," http://www.reocities.com/jeff_l_schwartz/chpt4.html.

175. Interview in *Cadence* 10, no. 10 (October 1984): 17–18.

176. Ibid.

177. Jacobson, "The Jazz Scientist."

178. Interview in *Cadence* 6, no. 5 (May 1980): 7.

179. Interview in *Cadence* 6, no. 6 (June 1980): 10.

180. Ibid., 11.

181. Wilmer, *As Serious as Your Life*, 19.

182. Ibid., 175.

183. Ibid., 168.

184. Austerlitz, *Jazz Consciousness*, 174.

185. Ibid.

186. Ibid., 183.

187. Ibid., 175.

188. Wilmer, *As Serious as Your Life*, 249.

189. Ibid.

190. Ibid.

191. Austerlitz, *Jazz Consciousness*, 168.

192. Ibid.

193. Ibid., 178.

194. Ibid., 171–72.

195. Milford Graves, "Music of the Human Heart May Hold Clues to Healing," National Public Radio, *Morning Edition*, February 28, 2005.

196. Ibid.

197. Chris Jozefowicz, "Offbeat," *Current Science* (December 2, 2005): 9.

198. "Episode 228: What You're Exposed To," http://blip.tv/improvlive365/episode-228-what-you-re-exposed-to-6310600.

199. Ibid.

200. "Professor Milford Graves," http://www.furious.com/PERFECT/milfordgraves.html.

201. Jozefowicz, "Offbeat," 9.

202. Jacobson, "The Jazz Scientist."

203. Milford Graves, "Music Extensions of Infinite Dimensions," in *Arcana V* (New York: Hips Road, 2010), 171.

204. Ibid.

205. Ibid., 173.

206. Ibid., 174.

207. Milford Graves, "Book of Tono-Rhythmology," in *Arcana II: Musicians on Music*, ed. John Zorn (New York: Hips Road, 2007), 110.

208. Ibid., 117.

209. Ibid.

210. Ethnomusicologist Gregory Barz, "Music of the Human Heart May Hold Clues to Healing," National Public Radio, *Morning Edition*, February 28, 2005.

211. Candy Gunther Brown, "Touch and American Religions," *Religion Compass* 3, no. 4 (July 2009): 770–83.

212. Gooding, notes to *Spiritual Jazz*.

213. "Rashied Ali: CACP 10 Questions," http://www.onefinalnote.com/features/2005/ali-rashied/.

214. Travis Laplante email to Stephen Buono, personal communication, May 7, 2012.

215. Ben Sidran, *Talking Jazz: An Oral History* (Rhino Records, 2006).

216. Jacobson, "The Jazz Scientist."

217. Cecil Taylor, "Aquoeh R-Oyo," *Air Above Mountains* (Enja, 1973).

218. Cecil Taylor, notes to *Trance* (Black Lion, 1996).

219. Graham Lock, *Chasing the Vibration* (Exeter: Stride, 1994), 31.

220. Valerie Wilmer, *As Serious as Your Life*, 52.

221. Quoted in *All the Notes* documentary, directed by Christopher Felver, 2004.

222. Wilmer, *As Serious as Your Life*, 45.

223. Cecil Taylor, quoted in *All the Notes*.

224. Chris Funkhouser, "Being Matter Ignited...: An Interview with Cecil Taylor," in *Hambone*, no. 12, 5.

225. Wilmer, *As Serious as Your Life*, 49.

226. Ibid., 71.

227. Ibid., 42.

228. Ibid., 48.

229. Ibid., 49.

230. Ibid., 50, 52.

231. Ibid., 58.

232. Quoted in Bert Noglik, notes to Glenn Spearman Double Trio, *Smokehouse* (Black Saint Records, 1993), http://acanthusleaves.blogspot.com/2006_06_01_archive.html.

233. Valerie Wilmer, *Jazz People* (New York: Da Capo, 1970), 24.

234. A. B. Spellman, *Black Music: Four Lives* (New York: Schocken, 1970), 13.

235. Cecil Taylor, notes to *Unit Structures* (Blue Note Records, 1966).

236. "Roulette TV: Jerome Cooper—Extended Interview," video interview at Roulette, http://vimeo.com/11909795.

237. Ibid.

238. Lloyd Peterson, *Music and the Creative Spirit* (Lanham, Md.: Scarecrow, 2006), 5.

239. Cecil Taylor, notes to *Unit Structures* (Blue Note Records, 1966).

240. Matthew Goodheart, "Freedom and Individuality in the Music of Cecil Taylor," http://users.lmi.net/~mgheart/thesis/title.html.

241. Quoted in *All the Notes*.

242. Aldon Lynn Nielsen, *Black Chant: Languages of African-American Postmodernism* (Cambridge: Cambridge University Press, 1997), 260.

243. Quoted in Nat Hentoff, liner notes to Cecil Taylor, *Jazz Advance* (OJC Records, 1956).

244. Ibid.

245. Quoted in *Imagine the Sound*, directed by Ron Mann, 1981.

246. Taylor, notes to *Unit Structures*.

247. Ibid.

248. Goodheart, "Freedom and Individuality in the Music of Cecil Taylor."

249. Andrew W. Bartlett, "Cecil Taylor, Identity Energy, and the Avant-Garde African American Body," *Perspectives of New Music* 33, nos. 1/2 (Winter–Summer 1995): 279.

250. *Imagine the Sound*; and Lock, *Chasing the Vibration*, 33.

251. *Imagine the Sound*.

252. Quoted in Art Lange, liner notes to Cecil Taylor, *Garden 1 & 2* (Hat Art Records, 1990).

253. Ibid.

254. Taylor, liner notes to ibid.

255. Lock, *Chasing the Vibration*, 29–30.

256. Ibid., 30.

257. Bartlett, "Cecil Taylor, Identity Energy, and the Avant-Garde African American Body," 284; and Lock, *Chasing the Vibration*, 8.

258. Lock, *Chasing the Vibration*, 6.

259. Gene Santoro, *Dancing in Your Head: Jazz, Blues, Rock, and Beyond* (New York: Oxford University Press, 2004), 242.

260. Ekkehard Jost, *Free Jazz* (New York: Da Capo, 1974), 75.

261. "Box: Cecil Taylor in Berlin '88," http://www.fmp-label.de/freemusicproduction/labelscatalog/xfmpse1989a_enreview.php.

262. Ibid.

263. Ibid.

264. Ibid.

265. Chris Funkhouser, quoted in a thread about Cecil Taylor at http://forums.allaboutjazz.com/showthread.php?t=42143.

266. Anthony B. Pinn, *Varieties of African American Religious Experience* (Minneapolis: Fortress, 1998), 6. See also Theophus Smith, *Conjuring Culture: Biblical Formations of Black America* (New York: Oxford University Press, 1995).

267. *All the Notes.*

268. *All the Notes.*

269. Funkhouser, "Being Matter Ignited...," 12.

270. Tim Hodgkinson, "Holy Ghost," in *Arcana V*, 445.

271. Peterson, *Music and the Creative Spirit*, 60.

272. See Eric Porter, "Jeanne Lee's Voice," *Critical Studies in Improvisation* 2, no. 1 (2006): 1–14.

273. Amiri Baraka, "The 'Blues Aesthetic' and the 'Black Aesthetic': Aesthetics as the Continuing Political History of a Culture," *Black Music Research Journal* 11, no. 2 (Autumn 1991): 101–9.

CHAPTER 6

1. The title is from Steve Coleman's 1993 recording.

2. Catherine Albanese, introduction to *American Spiritualities: A Reader*, ed. Catherine Albanese (Bloomington: Indiana University Press, 2001), 1.

3. Ibid.

4. Ibid., 2.

5. Ibid., 9.

6. Ibid., 179.

7. Jim Fusilli, "John McLaughlin: From Miles Davis Protégé to "Old Punk," http://online.wsj.com/news/articles/SB10001424052702303779504579463164133136046?KEYWORDS=mclaughlin&mg=reno64-wsj.

8. Dary John Mizelle, "The Sacred Power of Music," in *Arcana V: Music, Magic and Mysticism*, ed. John Zorn (New York: Hips Road, 2010), 260.

9. William Duckworth, *Talking Music: Conversations with John Cage, Philip Glass, Laurie Anderson, and Five Generations of American Experimental Composers* (New York: Da Capo, 1999), 4.

10. Ibid., 14.

11. Ibid., 173.

12. Taran Singh, "Marc Edwards: Free Jazz Drummer and Percussionist," http://www.allaboutjazz.com/marc-edwards-free-jazz-drummer-and-percussionist-marc-edwards-by-taran-singh.php.

13. Wayne Enstice and Janet Stockhouse, *Jazzwomen: Conversations with Twenty-One Musicians* (Bloomington: Indiana University Press, 2004), 149.
14. Ibid., 150.
15. Interview in *Cadence* 9, no. 5 (May 1983): 20.
16. Ibid.
17. Theo Bleckmann, "The Voices of My Voice: Three Working as One," in *Arcana III: Musicians on Music*, ed. John Zorn (New York: Hips Road, 2008), 42.
18. Florence Wetzel, "Gary Peacock: Zen Bass," http://www.allaboutjazz.com/gary-peacock-zen-bass-gary-peacock-by-florence-wetzel.php.
19. Ibid. See also Steven Collins, *Selfless Persons: Imagery and Thought in Theravada Buddhism* (Cambridge: Cambridge University Press, 1990).
20. Personal conversation, February 2010.
21. Ibid.; and Dave Wayne, "Brian Adler: A World of Percussion," http://www.allaboutjazz.com/brian-adler-a-world-of-percussion-brian-adler-by-dave-wayne.php.
22. Personal conversation, February 2010.
23. Ibid.
24. Ibid.
25. Ibid.
26. Personal conversation, January 2010.
27. Ibid.
28. Ibid.
29. Ibid.
30. Ibid.
31. Lloyd Peterson, "Dan Weiss: The Creative Absence of Egotism," http://www.allaboutjazz.com/dan-weiss-the-creative-absence-of-egotism-dan-weiss-by-lloyd-n-peterson-jr.php.
32. Ibid.
33. Myra Melford, "Aural Architecture: The Confluence of Freedom," in *Arcana: Musicians on Music*, ed. John Zorn (New York: Hips Road, 2000), 134.
34. Ibid.
35. Personal conversation, February 2000.
36. Frank Matzner, "Myra Melford: Mystic Manifestations," http://www.allaboutjazz.com/myra-melford-mystic-manifestations-myra-melford-by-franz-a-matzner.php.
37. Melford, "Aural Architecture," 133.
38. Melford, notes to *The Same River Twice* (Gramavision, 1996).
39. Graham Lock, *Forces in Motion: The Music and Thoughts of Anthony Braxton* (New York: Da Capo, 1988), 188.
40. Ibid., 182.
41. Jason Weiss, ed., *Steve Lacy: Conversations* (Durham, N.C.: Duke University Press, 2006), 159.

42. Ibid., 20.
43. Peter Kostakis, notes to Steve Lacy, *School Days* (Hatology, 2003).
44. Derek Bailey, *Improvisation: Its Nature and Practice in Music* (New York: Da Capo, 1993), 57.
45. Ibid., 100.
46. Weiss, *Steve Lacy*, 4.
47. Ibid., 191.
48. Ibid., 14.
49. Ibid., 41.
50. Ibid., 80.
51. Ibid., 35.
52. Interview with Ben Sidran, on Sidran, *Talking Jazz: An Oral History* (Rhino Records, 2006).
53. Weiss, *Steve Lacy*, 88.
54. Quoted in Peter Niklas Wilson, liner notes to Steve Lacy, *Blinks* (Hat Art Records, 1997).
55. Weiss, *Steve Lacy*, 152.
56. Quoted in liner notes to Steve Lacy and Joelle Leandre, *One More Time* (Leo Records, 2005).
57. Thomas Chapin, notes to Chapin, *Alive* (Knitting Factory Records, 1999).
58. Thomas Chapin, notes to Chapin, *Sky Piece* (Knitting Factory Records, 1998).
59. Sidran, *Talking Jazz*.
60. See Michael Veal, "Starship Africa," in *The Sound Studies Reader*, ed. Jonathan Sterne (New York: Routledge, 2012), 457.
61. Brandon LaBelle, "Auditory Relations," in ibid., 468.
62. Simon Jay Harper, "Darius Jones: From Johnny Hodges to Noise Jazz," http://www.allaboutjazz.com/darius-jones-from-johnny-hodges-to-noise-jazz-darius-jones-by-aaj-staff.php?page=1.
63. Personal conversation, July 2013.
64. Kevin Whitehead, notes to Tom Varner, *The Mystery of Compassion* (Soul Note Records, 1993).
65. "Rediscovering Dave Brubeck," *Jazz Education Journal* 34, no. 3 (November 2001): 40–41; and Vijay Iyer, notes to Iyer, *Solo* (ACT Records, 2010).
66. Keith Jarrett, notes to Jarrett and Charlie Haden, *Jasmine* (ECM Records, 2010).
67. Sidran, *Talking Jazz*.
68. Interview in *Cadence* 6, no. 3 (March 1980): 15.
69. Dominic Fragman, "Paul F. Murphy: Playing Universally," http://www.allaboutjazz.com/paul-f-murphy-playing-universally-paul-murphy-by-dominic-fragman.php.
70. Adam Lane, notes to Lane, *Zero Degree Music* (CIMP Records, 2005).
71. Personal correspondence, 1997.
72. Ellery Eskelin, notes to *Vanishing Point* (Hatology, 2001); and personal conversation, May 2011.

73. Personal conversation, May 2011.
74. Personal conversation, October 2014.
75. Personal conversation, May 2011.
76. Personal conversation, June 2010.
77. Ibid.
78. Ibid.
79. Ibid.
80. Personal conversation, October 2002.
81. Personal conversation, July 2008.
82. Interview with *El Intruso* (March 20, 2010), http://elintruso.com/2010/03/20/dennis-gonzalez/.
83. Ibid.
84. Personal conversation, July 2008.
85. Ibid.
86. Ibid.
87. Ibid.
88. Cicily Janus, *The New Face of Jazz* (New York: Billboard, 2010), 95.
89. Personal conversation, July 2008.
90. Gene Lees, *Cats of Any Color: Jazz, Black and White* (New York: Da Capo, 1995), 80.
91. David Borgo, "Negotiating Freedom: Values and Practices in Contemporary Improvised Music," *Black Music Research Journal* 22, no. 2 (Autumn 2002): 175.
92. Sharon Gannon, "Yoga and Music," in *Arcana V*, 133–50.
93. Tisziji Munoz, "Death: The Father of Creation," in *Arcana V*, 270.
94. Adam Rudolph, "Music and Mysticism, Rhythm and Form: A Blues Romance in 12 Parts," in *Arcana V*, 327.
95. Personal conversation, January 2010.
96. David H. Rosenthal, "The Big Beat!" *Black Perspective in Music* 14, no. 3 (Autumn 1986): 273.
97. Quoted in James Miller, *Examined Lives: From Socrates to Nietzsche* (New York: Picador, 2011), 340.
98. Interview in *Cadence* 3, nos. 11 and 12 (March 1978): 7–8.
99. Paul F. Berliner, *Thinking in Jazz: The Infinite Art of Improvisation* (Chicago: University of Chicago Press, 1994), 392.
100. Ibid., 393.
101. Ibid.
102. Valerie Wilmer, *Jazz People* (New York: Da Capo, 1970), 74.
103. John Litweiler, *The Freedom Principle: Jazz After 1958* (New York: Da Capo, 1984), 234.
104. Eric Ianelli, "Adam Rudolph: The Mysteries of Creation," http://www.allaboutjazz.com/adam-rudolph-the-mysteries-of-creation-adam-rudolph-by-eric-j-iannelli.php.

105. George Varga, "Quincy Jones: A Profile," *International Association of Jazz Educators Journal* 34, no. 4 (January 2002): 2–3, 5–6.

106. "Saxophonist Sonny Rollins Still Swinging Strong," National Public Radio, *Weekend Edition*, April 28, 2007.

107. "Saxophone King," National Public Radio, *The Tavis Smiley Show*, May 5, 2003.

108. Arthur Taylor, *Notes and Tones: Musician-to-Musician Interviews* (New York: Da Capo, 1993), 182.

109. Ibid., 151.

110. Enstice and Stockhouse, *Jazzwomen*, 6, 21, 247.

111. Pauline Oliveros, "Harmonic Anatomy: Women in Improvisation," in *The Other Side of Nowhere: Jazz, Improvisation, and Communities in Dialogue*, ed. Daniel Fischlin and Ajay Heble (Middletown, Conn.: Wesleyan University Press, 2004), 60.

112. Ibid.

113. Ibid., 66.

114. David G. Such, *Avant-Garde Jazz Musicians: Performing "Out There"* (Iowa City: University of Iowa Press, 1993), 139.

115. Ibid., 141.

116. Taylor, *Notes and Tones*, 178.

117. "Dusted Reviews: Darius Jones Trio—Big Gurl (Smell My Dream)," http://www.dustedmagazine.com/reviews/6732.

118. Personal conversation, March 2010.

119. Ibid.

120. Ibid.

121. Ibid.

122. Personal conversation, January 2011.

123. Ibid.

124. Ibid.

125. Interview in *Cadence* 31, no. 6 (June 2005): 13.

126. Ibid.

127. Ibid.

128. Ibid., 14.

129. Personal conversation, January 2011.

130. Interview in *Cadence* 31, no. 6 (June 2005): 14.

131. Personal conversation, January 2011.

132. Interview in *Cadence* 31, no. 6 (June 2005): 14.

133. Personal conversation, January 2011.

134. Personal conversation, July 2010.

135. Ibid.

136. Ibid.

137. Ibid.

138. Norman Weinstein, notes to Ivo Perelman, *En Adir* (Music & Arts, 1996).

139. "Ivo Perelman: The Indisputable Truth of Process (An Interview)," http://cliffordallen.blogspot.com/2013/06/ivo-perelman-indisputable-truth-of.html.

140. Personal conversation, July 2011.

141. Ibid.

142. Ibid.

143. Ibid.

144. Ibid.

145. Ibid.

146. See Timothy Fitzgerald, "Experience," in *Guide to the Study of Religion*, ed. Willi Braun and Russell T. McCutcheon (London: Cassell, 2000).

147. Such, *Avant-Garde Jazz Musicians*, 129.

148. Ibid., 131.

149. Ibid., 129.

150. "Roulette TV: Billy Bang/William Parker—Extended Interview," http://vimeo.com/11928440.

151. Eyal Hareuvini, "William Parker: Everything Is Valid," http://www.allaboutjazz.com/william-parker-everything-is-valid-william-parker-by-eyal-hareuveni.php.

152. Such, *Avant-Garde Jazz Musicians*, 129.

153. Hareuvini, "William Parker: Everything Is Valid"; and interview in *Signal to Noise* 35 (Fall 2004): 23.

154. Hareuvini, "William Parker: Everything Is Valid."

155. Joe Morris, *Perpetual Frontier: The Properties of Free Music* (Stony Creek, Conn.: Riti, 2012), 143.

156. Ibid., 145.

157. Interview in *Cadence* 6, no. 1 (January 1980): 16.

158. Franck MeDioni, "Sonny Meets David," http://www.allaboutjazz.com/sonny-rollins-and-david-s-ware-sonny-meets-david-by-franck-medioni.php.

159. Ed Hazell, "Touching on the Transcendental," *Signal to Noise* 37 (Spring 2005): 19.

160. Ibid., 19, 21.

161. Ibid., 21.

162. "WNUR Interview: David S. Ware," http://web.archive.org/web/20110104195808/http://www.wnur.org/jazz/artists/ware.david/interview.html.

163. Ibid.

164. Ibid.

165. Ibid.

166. MeDioni, "Sonny Meets David."

167. Interview with Thomas Stanley (March 30, 1997), http://musicovermind.org/ware.htm.

168. Interview in *Cadence* 25, no. 12 (December 1999): 101.

169. MeDioni, "Sonny Meets David."

170. Hazell, "Touching on the Transcendental," 22.

171. MeDioni, "Sonny Meets David."

172. Hazell, "Touching on the Transcendental," 22.

173. David S. Ware, notes to Ware, *Saturnian* (AUM Fidelity, 2010).

174. Ibid.

175. Personal conversation, June 2010.

176. Ibid.

177. Ben Ratliff, notes to Matthew Shipp, *By the Law of Music* (Hat Art, 1997).

178. Ibid.

179. Morris, *Perpetual Frontier*, 151.

180. Ibid.

181. "Matthew Shipp," http://burningambulance.com/2010/01/29/matthew-shipp/.

182. Steve Dalachinsky and Matthew Shipp, *Logos and Language: A Post-Jazz Metaphorical Dialogue* (Paris: Rogue Art, 2008), 9.

183. Ibid., 22.

184. Ibid., 23.

185. Ibid., 28.

186. Ibid.

187. Ibid., 33.

188. Ibid., 21, 41, 45.

189. Ibid., 20.

190. Ibid., 24.

191. Ibid., 25.

192. "Matthew Shipp."

193. Dalachinsky and Shipp, 43.

194. Ibid., 97.

195. "Matthew Shipp."

196. John Corbett, *Extended Play: Sounding Off from John Cage to Doctor Funkenstein* (Durham, N.C.: Duke University Press, 1994), 80.

197. Ann Taves, *Religious Experience Reconsidered: A Building Block Approach to the Study of Religion and Other Special Things* (Princeton, N.J.: Princeton University Press, 2009).

198. See Jason C. Bivins, "Dwelling amid Absence," http://forums.ssrc.org/ndsp/2013/05/06/dwelling-amid-absence/.

199. William James, *The Varieties of Religious Experience: A Study in Human Nature* (Rockville, Md.: Manor Classics, 2008), 30.

200. Ibid., 338.

201. Courtney Bender, *The New Metaphysicals: Spirituality and the Religious Imagination* (Chicago: University of Chicago Press, 2010), 57.

202. Ibid., 58.

CHAPTER 7

1. The title is from Sun Ra's 1966 album.

2. Quoted in Ed Hazell, notes to Jason Kao Hwang, *Stories Before Within* (Innova Records, 2007).

3. Michael Galinsky, "Exchanging Files," *Signal to Noise* 25 (Spring 2002): 22.

4. Interview in *Cadence* 6, no. 3 (March 1980): 16.

5. Interview in *Cadence* 25, no. 12 (December 1999): 9.

6. Clifford Allen, "Prince Lasha's Inside-Outside Story," http://www.allaboutjazz .com/prince-lashas-inside-outside-story-prince-lasha-by-clifford-allen.php.

7. Interview in *Cadence* 33, no. 4 (April 2007): 9.

8. Interview in *Cadence* 30, no. 8 (August 2004): 19.

9. Joe Morris, *Perpetual Frontier: The Properties of Free Music* (Stony Creek, Conn.: Riti, 2012), 137.

10. Ibid., 138–39.

11. "At 85, Sam Rivers Creates a Scene in Orlando," National Public Radio, *Weekend Edition*, September 20, 2009.

12. It is because he did not build a system in the same way as this chapter's other exemplars, and because of the centrality of his historical thought, that I do not focus again on Ra.

13. John Litweiler, *Ornette Coleman: A Harmolodic Life* (New York: William Morrow, 1992), 24.

14. "The Other's Language: Jacques Derrida Interviews Ornette Coleman, 23 June 1997," http://jazzstudiesonline.org/files/jso/resources/pdf/TheOthersLanguage .pdf, 323.

15. David Grogan, "Profile: Ornette Coleman," *People* (October 13, 1986): 108.

16. "The Other's Language," 323.

17. Litweiler, *Ornette Coleman*, 48–49.

18. Grogan, "Profile: Ornette Coleman," 108.

19. "The Other's Language," 324.

20. Grogan, "Profile: Ornette Coleman," 108.

21. Litweiler, *Ornette Coleman*, 19.

22. Ibid., 57–58.

23. Robert Palmer, liner notes to Ornette Coleman, *Beauty Is a Rare Thing: The Complete Atlantic Recordings* (Atlantic Records, 1993).

24. All reactions in this paragraph from ibid.

25. Grogan, "Profile: Ornette Coleman."

26. Litweiler, *Ornette Coleman*, 103.

27. Ibid., 84.

28. Ibid., 80.

29. Valerie Wilmer, *As Serious as Your Life: The Story of the New Jazz* (New York: Serpent's Tail, 1992), 66.

30. Ibid., 71.

31. Ibid., 143.

32. John Szwed, *Crossovers: Essays on Race, Music, and American Culture* (Philadelphia: University of Pennsylvania Press, 2005), 212.

33. Ibid.

34. Ibid., 212.
35. Robert Palmer, liner notes to Ornette Coleman, *Dancing in Your Head* (Horizon, 1977).
36. Ibid.
37. Ibid.
38. Ibid.
39. Warren Allen, "Ornette Coleman: Music Is a Verb," *All About Jazz* (September 21, 2009).
40. Litweiler, *Ornette Coleman*, 151.
41. Ibid., 152.
42. Ibid.
43. Allen, "Ornette Coleman."
44. Ibid.
45. Litweiler, *Ornette Coleman*, 65.
46. Simon Jay Harper, "Bern Nix: A History in Harmolodics," *All About Jazz* (August 24, 2009).
47. "Ornette Coleman Wins Music Pulitzer," http://www.npr.org/2007/04/16/9607210/ornette-coleman-wins-music-pulitzer.
48. Lazaro Vega, interview with Ornette Coleman, Blue Lake Radio, January 24, 2007.
49. Ben Ratliff, "Listening with Ornette Coleman," *New York Times*, September 22, 2006.
50. Litweiler, *Ornette Coleman*, 168.
51. Ratliff, "Listening with Ornette Coleman."
52. Ibid.
53. Litweiler, *Ornette Coleman*, 193.
54. Ibid., 185.
55. Francis Davis, *In the Moment: Jazz in the 1980s* (New York: Da Capo, 1996), 136.
56. Litweiler, *Ornette Coleman*, 116.
57. Ibid.
58. Mark Warren, "Interview with Ornette Coleman," *Esquire*, January 1, 2010.
59. Litweiler, *Ornette Coleman*, 114.
60. Warren, "Interview with Ornette Coleman."
61. Ibid.
62. Ronald Radano, *New Musical Figurations: Anthony Braxton's Cultural Critique* (Chicago: University of Chicago Press, 1993), 70.
63. Ingrid Monson, *Freedom Sounds: Civil Rights Call Out to Jazz and Africa* (New York: Oxford University Press, 2007), 285.
64. Ralph Waldo Emerson, *The Selected Writings of Ralph Waldo Emerson* (New York: Modern Library, 1940), 355–56.
65. Monson, *Freedom Sounds*, 286.
66. Kory Grow, "Lost in Translation," *Signal to Noise* 44 (Winter 2007): 52.
67. Don Cherry, quoted in notes to Coleman, *Beauty Is a Rare Thing*.

68. Francis Davis, *In the Moment*, 170.
69. Monson, *Freedom Sounds*, 292.
70. Ibid., 287.
71. Ibid., 288.
72. Ben Ratliff, "George Russell, Composer Whose Theories Sent Jazz in a New Direction, Dies at 86," *New York Times*, July 30, 2009.
73. Monson, *Freedom Sounds*, 288.
74. Ratliff, "George Russell."
75. See John Fordham, "George Russell," *The Guardian* (London), July 29, 2009.
76. Ratliff, "George Russell."
77. Ibid.
78. Fordham, "George Russell."
79. Ibid.
80. Ibid.
81. Norman Weinstein, *A Night in Tunisia: Imaginings of Africa in Jazz* (Montclair, N.J.: Limelight, 2004), 79.
82. Ibid., 73.
83. Interview in *Cadence* 3, nos. 7 and 8 (December 1977): 16.
84. Ibid.
85. Monson, *Freedom Sounds*, 293.
86. Olive Jones and George Russell, "A New Theory for Jazz," in *Black Perspective in Music* 2, no. 1 (Spring 1974): 74.
87. Monson, *Freedom Sounds*, 293.
88. Eric Porter, "'Born Out of Jazz…Yet Embracing All Music': Race, Gender, and Technology in George Russell's Lydian Chromatic Concept," in *Big Ears: Listening for Gender in Jazz Studies*, ed. Nichole T. Rustin and Sherrie Tucker (Durham, N.C.: Duke University Press, 2008), 210–34.
89. Ibid., 219.
90. Ibid., 169.
91. Fordham, "George Russell."
92. Interview in *Cadence* 3, nos. 7 and 8, 10.
93. Ibid., 11.
94. Monson, *Freedom Sounds*, 292.
95. Interview in *Cadence* 3, nos. 7 and 8, 11.
96. Porter, "Born Out of Jazz," 211.
97. Radano, *New Musical Figurations*, 29.
98. Ibid., 46.
99. Ibid., 39.
100. Ibid., 45.
101. Ibid., 114.
102. Ibid., 177.

103. Graham Lock, *Blutopia: Visions of the Future and Revisions of the Past in the Work of Sun Ra, Duke Ellington, and Anthony Braxton* (Durham, N.C.: Duke University Press, 2000), 164.

104. Radano, *New Musical Figurations*, 234.

105. Anthony Braxton, notes to Braxton, *Four Compositions (Quartet) 1983* (Black Saint Records, 1983).

106. Graham Lock, ed., *Mixtery: A Festschrift for Anthony Braxton* (Exeter: Stride, 1995), 249.

107. Graham Lock, *Forces in Motion: The Music and Thoughts of Anthony Braxton* (New York: Da Capo, 1988), 211.

108. Lock, *Mixtery*, 249.

109. Lock, *Forces in Motion*, 231.

110. Braxton, quoted in Graham Lock, notes to *Dortmund (Quartet) 1976* (Hat Art Records, 1993).

111. Lock, *Forces in Motion*, 165.

112. Radano, *New Musical Figurations*, 164.

113. Quoted in Lock, *Forces in Motion*, 65.

114. Lock, *Forces in Motion*, 103.

115. Ibid., 154.

116. Ibid., 87.

117. Gene Santoro, *Dancing in Your Head: Jazz, Blues, Rock, and Beyond* (New York: Oxford University Press, 2004), 247.

118. Lock, *Forces in Motion*, 219.

119. Ibid., 224.

120. Radano, *New Musical Figurations*, 162.

121. Max Roach and Anthony Braxton, notes to Roach and Braxton, *Birth and Rebirth* (Black Saint Records, 1978).

122. Lock, *Forces in Motion*, 67.

123. Ibid., 91.

124. Ibid., 92.

125. Interview with John Corbett, in notes to Anthony Braxton, *Quartet (Victoriaville) 1992* (Victo Records, 1993).

126. Lock, *Forces in Motion*, 7, 145.

127. Anthony Braxton, notes to Braxton, *Creative Orchestra (Köln) 1978* (Hat Art Records, 1995).

128. Lock, *Blutopia*, 152.

129. Graham Lock, notes to Braxton, *Performance (Quartet) 1979* (Hat Art, 1990).

130. Lock, notes to Braxton, *Willisau (Quartet) 1991* (Hat Art, 1991).

131. Lock, *Forces in Motion*, 156.

132. Radano, *New Musical Figurations*, 217.

133. Lock, *Blutopia*, 192.

134. Ted Panken, "Interview with Andrew Cyrille," http://www.intaktrec.ch/intercyrille-a.htm.

135. Ibid.

136. Graham Lock, notes to Braxton, *Birmingham (Quartet) 1985* (Leo Records, 1993).

137. My thanks to David Morgan for this association.

138. Lock, *Forces in Motion*, 205.

139. Notes to Braxton, *Quartet (Victoriaville) 1992.*

140. Lock, *Forces in Motion*, 231–32.

141. Ibid., 241.

142. Ibid., 233–34.

143. James Fei, notes to Braxton, *Composition No. 247* (Leo Records, 2000).

144. Braxton, quoted in Jason Bivins, "An Exhaustive Trance," http://www.dustedmagazine.com/reviews/664.

145. Anthony Braxton, notes to Braxton, *Six Compositions (GTM) 2001* (Rastascan, 2002).

146. Ibid.

147. Lock, *Blutopia*, 186.

148. Ibid., 187.

149. "Anthony Braxton, February 5, 1995, WKCR-FM, New York," http://www.jazzhouse.org/library/index.php3?read=panken6.

150. Braxton, notes to *Trillium*, available at http://tricentricfoundation.org/trillium-r-shala-fears-for-the-poor-composition-no-162.

151. Lock, *Forces in Motion*, 280.

152. Wilmer, *As Serious as Your Life*, 124.

153. John Corbett, *Extended Play: Sounding Off from John Cage to Dr. Funkenstein* (Durham, N.C.: Duke University Press, 1994), 211.

154. Ibid.

155. Personal conversation, September 2011.

156. Howard Mandel, "The Elephant's Memory," *Signal to Noise* 29 (Spring 2003): 21.

157. Personal conversation, September 2011.

158. Ibid.

159. Ibid.

160. Ibid.

161. Bob Ness, "Profile: Leo Smith," *Downbeat* (October 7, 1976), reprinted at http://www.wadadaleosmith.com/pages/interviews_eng_3.html#profile.

162. Franz A. Matzner, "Wadada Leo Smith: The Teacher," http://www.allaboutjazz.com/wadada-leo-smith-the-teacher-wadada-leo-smith-by-franz-a-matzner.php.

163. Personal conversation, September 2011.

164. "Leo Smith," http://www.scaruffi.com/jazz/lsmith.html.

165. Personal conversation, September 2011.

166. Ibid.

167. Ibid.

168. Smith, liner notes to Leo Smith, *Divine Love* (ECM Records, 1978).

169. Personal conversation, September 2011.

170. "Leo Smith," http://www.scaruffi.com/jazz/lsmith.html.

171. Personal conversation, September 2011.

172. Bill Beuttler, "Creating Music That's Never the Same Twice," *The Boston Globe*, 2005, reproduced at www.wadadaleosmith.com.

173. Personal conversation, September 2011.

174. Wilmer, *As Serious as Your Life*, 112.

175. Jeff Jackson, "Wadada Leo Smith's American Music," *Jazziz* (January 2009): 20.

176. Ibid., 22.

177. Mandel, "The Elephant's Memory," 23.

178. Lyn Horton, "Wadada Leo Smith: A Vital Life Force," http://www.allaboutjazz .com/wadada-leo-smith-a-vital-life-force-wadada-leo-smith-by-lyn-horton.php.

179. Ibid.

180. Ibid.

181. "Leo Smith," http://www.scaruffi.com/jazz/lsmith.html.

182. Leo Smith, *Notes (8 Pieces) Source a New World Music: Creative Music* (1973), reproduced at http://www.wadadaleosmith.com/pages/philos.html.

183. Ibid.

184. Ibid.

185. Leo Smith, "(M1) American Music," *The Black Perspective in Music* 2, no. 2 (Autumn 1974): 115.

186. Smith, *Notes (8 Pieces)*.

187. Ibid.

188. Ibid.

189. Ibid.

190. Smith, "(M1) American Music," 143.

191. Personal conversation, September 2011.

192. Ibid.

193. Ibid.

194. Matzner, "Wadada Leo Smith."

195. Personal conversation, September 2011.

196. Ibid.

197. Ibid.

198. Horton, "Wadada Leo Smith."

199. Personal conversation, September 2011.

200. Shaun Brady, "Wadada Leo Smith on How Far AACM—and Society—Have Come," *Philadelphia City Paper*, December 1, 2005.

201. Ibid.

202. Andrew Dansby, "Passionate About Jazz," *Houston Chronicle*, November 4, 2006.

203. Personal conversation, September 2011.

204. Ibid.

205. Ibid.

206. Matthew Sumera, "Wadada Leo Smith: The One Final Note Interview," *One Final Note* (April 2005).

207. Ibid.

208. Horton, "Wadada Leo Smith."

209. Marc Medwin, "Wadada Leo Smith," http://www.allaboutjazz.com/wadada-leo-smith-wadada-leo-smith-by-marc-medwin.php.

210. Ibid.

211. Josef Woodard, "Onward and Upward," http://jazztimes.com/articles/20913-wadada-leo-smith-onward-upward.

212. Ibid.

213. Personal communication, Summer 2011.

214. Personal conversation, September 2011.

215. Ibid.

216. Ibid.

217. Woodard, "Onward and Upward."

218. Personal conversation, September 2011.

219. Personal conversation, January 2011. See also David P. Brown, *Noise Orders: Jazz, Improvisation, and Architecture* (Minneapolis: University of Minnesota Press, 2006), 127.

220. Interview in *Cadence* 24, no. 8 (August 1998): 137.

221. John Zorn, ed., *Arcana II: Musicians on Music* (New York: Hips Road, 2007), 171.

222. Personal conversation, January 2011.

223. Ibid. See also Thomas Stanley's portrait of Morris, "Prime Conductor," *Signal to Noise* 30 (Summer 2003).

224. Mike Heffley, *Northern Sun, Southern Moon: Europe's Reinvention of Jazz* (New Haven, Conn.: Yale University Press, 2005), 28–37.

225. Lawrence Sullivan, introduction to *Enchanting Powers: Music in the World's Religions* (Cambridge, Mass.: Harvard University Press, 1997), 2.

226. Ibid., 5–6.

227. See Jeffrey Kripal, *Mutants and Mystics: Science Fiction, Superhero Comics, and the Paranormal* (Chicago: University of Chicago Press, 2011), 9–15.

228. Ibid., 48–49.

229. Ibid., 125–26, 170.

230. This list of idioms is derived partly from David Toop, *Sinister Resonance: The Mediumship of the Listener* (New York: Continuum, 2010), 6.

231. William James, *The Varieties of Religious Experience: A Study in Human Nature* (Rockville, Md.: Manor Classics, 2008), 47.

CHAPTER 8

1. As I was completing this book, I became aware that contrabassist and scholar Peter Niklas Wilson published a German monograph in 2011 titled *Spirits Rejoice! Albert Ayler und Seine Botschaft* (loosely translated: "Albert Ayler and His Message"). I have been using my book's title in public talks since 2000, and this manuscript has been in preparation with this title since 2008. Additionally, the scope and subject of my work is far different from Wilson's. I have long admired Wilson's work, and I am delighted that we share our enthusiasm for the Ayler performance after which we have both named our books.

2. Ralph Waldo Emerson, *The Selected Writings of Ralph Waldo Emerson* (New York: Modern Library, 1940), 322.

3. Quincy Troupe and Ben Riley, "Remembering Thelonious Monk: When the Music Was Happening Then He'd Get Up and Do His Little Dance," in *The Jazz Cadence of American Culture*, ed. Robert G. O'Meally (New York: Columbia University Press, 1998), 105.

4. Gene Santoro, *Dancing in Your Head: Jazz, Blues, Rock, and Beyond* (New York: Oxford University Press, 2004), 246.

5. Ibid., 114.

6. Ibid., 115.

7. Most of my scholarship to date has focused on exploring these claims about religion and politics. See my *Religion of Fear: The Politics of Horror in Conservative Evangelicalism* (New York: Oxford University Press, 2008); and *The Fracture of Good Order: Christian Antiliberalism and the Challenge to American Politics* (Chapel Hill: University of North Carolina Press, 2003).

8. Quoted in Peter Watrous, notes to John Zorn, *News for Lulu* (Hat Art, 1988).

9. Gary Peters, *The Philosophy of Improvisation* (Chicago: University of Chicago Press, 2009), 2–3.

10. Personal conversation, January 2010.

11. Gene Stephenson and Andrew Cyrille, "Dialogue of the Drums," *Black Perspective in Music* 3, no. 1 (Spring 1975): 53–57.

12. Personal conversation, March 2010.

13. Curtis J. Evans, *The Burden of Black Religion* (New York: Oxford University Press, 2008).

14. Ibid., 69.

15. Laurie F. Maffly-Kipp, *Setting Down the Sacred Past: African-American Race Histories* (Cambridge, Mass.: Harvard University Press, 2010), 187.

16. Quoted in Ajay Heble, *Landing on the Wrong Note: Jazz, Dissonance, and Critical Practice* (New York: Routledge, 2000), 235.

17. George E. Lewis, "Gittin' to Know Y'all: Improvised Music, Interculturalism, and the Racial Imagination," *Critical Studies in Improvisation* 1, no. 1 (2004): 1.

18. Peter Niklas Wilson, notes to *Lörrach, Paris 1966* (Hatology Records, 2002).
19. For a discussion of this article, see Frank Kofsky, *Black Nationalism and the Revolution in Music* (New York: Pathfinder, 1970), 235–36.
20. Quoted in Graham Lock, notes to *Composition 98* (Hat Art Records, 1990).
21. Graham Lock, *Forces in Motion: The Music and Thoughts of Anthony Braxton* (New York: Da Capo, 1988), 1.
22. Don Byron, notes to *Tuskegee Experiments* (Elektra Nonesuch, 1992).
23. John J. Niles, "Shout, Coon, Shout!" *Musical Quarterly* 16, no. 4 (October 1930): 516–30.
24. Ted Gioia, "The Black Primitivist Myth," *Musical Quarterly* 73, no. 1 (January 1989): 130.
25. Bailey, quoted in Lock, *Forces in Motion*, 2.
26. Krin Gabbard, *Jammin' at the Margins: Jazz and the American Cinema* (Chicago: University of Chicago Press, 1996), 2.
27. Judith Butler, *Gender Trouble: Feminism and the Subversion of Identity* (New York: Routledge, 2006). See also Brian Hulse and Nick Nesbitt, eds., *Sounding the Virtual: Gilles Deleuze and the Theory and Philosophy of Music* (Farnham: Ashgate, 2010).
28. Yusef Lateef with Herb Boyd, *The Gentle Giant: The Autobiography of Yusef Lateef* (Irvington, N.J.: Morton, 2006), 112.
29. Robin D. G. Kelley, *Thelonious Monk: The Life and Times of an American Original* (New York: Free Press, 2009), xxi.
30. Nathaniel Mackey, "Sound and Sentiment, Sound and Symbol," in *Jazz Cadence*, 606. See also Mackey's *Bedouin Hornbook* (Los Angeles: Sun and Moon Classics, 2000), whose letters from "N.," of the Mystic Horn Society, to the Angel of Dust capture many of these themes of linguistic instability and sound.
31. Paul Gilroy, *Small Acts: Thoughts on the Politics of Black Cultures* (London: Serpent's Tail, 1993), 10.
32. Ibid., 40.
33. Lewis, "Gittin' to Know Y'all," 13.
34. Maria Damon, "Jazz-Jews, Jive, and Gender: The Ethnic Politics of Jazz Argot," in *Jews and Other Differences: The New Jewish Cultural Studies*, ed. Jonathan Boyarin and Daniel Boyarin (Minneapolis: University of Minnesota Press, 1997), 167.
35. Ibid., 155.
36. Quoted in an Ellington 1966 symposium, reprinted in *Cadence* 4, nos. 8 and 9 (September 1978): 13.
37. Eric Porter, *What Is This Thing Called Jazz? African American Musicians as Artists, Critics, and Activists* (Berkeley: University of California Press, 2002), 3.
38. See Wilder Hobson, *American Jazz Music* (New York: Da Capo, 1976).
39. Personal conversation, January 2010.
40. Quoted in Steve Kulak, notes to Evan Parker, *After Appleby* (Leo Records, 2000).
41. Graham Lock, ed., *Mixtery: A Festschrift for Anthony Braxton* (Exeter: Stride, 1995), 19.

42. Paul Celan, quoted in Chetana Nagavajara, "On the Power, Powerlessness and Omnipotence of Language: From Oral Culture Through Written Culture to Media Domination," *Silpakorn University International Journal* 7 (2007): 110.

43. Gilles Deleuze and Félix Guattari, *Mille Plateaux: Capitalism and Schizophrenia* (Minneapolis: University of Minnesota Press, 1987), 331.

44. George Lipsitz, *Footsteps in the Dark: The Hidden Histories of Popular Music* (Minneapolis: University of Minnesota Press, 2007), xi.

45. Ibid., 14.

46. Ronald Radano, *Lying Up a Nation: Race and Black Music* (Chicago: University of Chicago Press, 2003), 4.

47. Quoted in Lloyd Peterson, ed., *Music and the Creative Spirit* (Lanham, Md.: Scarecrow, 2006), 76.

48. Philip F. Gura, *American Transcendentalism: A History* (New York: Hill and Wang, 2007), 306.

49. See Judith Becker in *Enchanting Powers: Music in the World's Religions*, ed. Lawrence E. Sullivan (Cambridge, Mass.: Harvard University Press, 1997).

50. John Milbank, "A Closer Walk on the Wild Side," in *Varieties of Secularism in a Secular Age*, ed. Michael Warner, Jonathan Van Antwerpen, and Craig Calhoun (Cambridge, Mass.: Harvard University Press, 2010), 81. Italics mine.

51. Courtney Bender, *The New Metaphysicals: Spirituality and the Religious Imagination* (Chicago: University of Chicago Press, 2010), 88.

52. David Toop, *Sinister Resonance: The Mediumship of the Listener* (New York: Continuum, 2010), 3.

53. Heble, *Landing on the Wrong Note*, 75.

54. Toop, *Sinister Resonance*, viii.

55. Robert Orsi, *Between Heaven and Earth: The Religious Worlds People Make and the Scholars Who Study Them* (Princeton, N.J.: Princeton University Press, 2005); and "When 2 + 2 = 5," *The American Scholar* (Spring 2007): 34–43.

56. Robert A. Orsi, introduction to *The Cambridge Companion to Religious Studies* (Cambridge: Cambridge University Press, 2012), 11.

57. Quoted in Julian Barnes, *The Sense of an Ending* (New York: Knopf, 2011), 102.

58. "Jazz Singer and Activist Abbey Lincoln," National Public Radio, *The Tavis Smiley Show*, April 15, 2003.

Bibliography

MAGAZINES AND PERIODICALS

The Atlantic
Butt Rag
Cadence
Current Science
Downbeat
Ebony
Esquire
Forward
Guitar Player
Hambone
Harper's
The Jazz Review
Jazz Times
Jazziz
Moment
The Nation
People
Signal to Noise
Time

NEWSPAPERS

Alarm Press
The Atlanta Journal-Constitution
Austin American-Statesman
The Baltimore Sun
The Boston Globe
Chicago Tribune
The Guardian (London)

The Harvard Crimson
Houston Chronicle
The Huffington Post
The Independent (London)
The Jerusalem Report
Los Angeles Times
New Fillmore
New York Amsterdam News
The New York Jewish Week
The New York Times
The Orange County (NJ) *Register*
The Ottawa Citizen
Philadelphia City Paper
The Philadelphia Tribune
The San Diego Union-Tribune
San Francisco Chronicle
The Seattle Times
Tampa Herald-Tribune
The Times (London)
The Toronto Star
The Village Voice
The Washington Post

WEB ARCHIVES

www.allaboutjazz.com
http://www.bluelake.org/radio/index.php
www.burningambulance.com
www.dustedmagazine.com
www.enotes.com
www.furious.com
www.hamilton.edu/jazzarchive/home
www.innerviews.org
www.jazzhouse.org
www.jazzwax.com
www.jazzweekly.com
www.musicovermind.org
www.npr.org
www.onefinalnote.com
www.thecjm.org
www.tzadik.com
www.villagevoice.com

FILMOGRAPHY

All the Notes (directed by Christopher Felver, 2004).

Imagine the Sound (directed by Ron Mann, 1981).

Miles Electric: A Different Kind of Blue (BBC, 2004).

Mingus (directed by Thomas Reichman, 1968).

My Name Is Albert Ayler (directed by Kasper Collin, 2005).

DISCOGRAPHY

Arranged in order of recording date. For fuller discographies and recommended listening, see http://spiritsrejoice.wordpress.com.

Muhal Richard Abrams. *Young at Heart, Wise in Time* (Delmark, 1974).

———. *Afrisong* (Why Not, 1975).

———. *Blues Forever* (Black Saint, 1982).

AMM/MEV. *Apogee* (Matchless, 2005).

Art Ensemble of Chicago. *1967/68* (Nessa, 1993).

———. *Reese and the Smooth Ones* (BYG, 1969).

———. *Bap-Tizum* (Atlantic, 1973).

———. *Certain Blacks* (America, 1974).

———. *Fanfare for the Warriors* (Atlantic, 1974).

———. *Urban Bushmen* (ECM, 1982).

Albert Ayler. *Bells—Prophecy* (ESP, 1964).

———. *Spiritual Unity* (ESP, 1964).

———. *Love Cry* (Impulse, 1968).

———. *Live at the Village Vanguard* (Impulse, 1998).

———. *Lörrach, Paris 1966* (Hatology, 2002).

Steven Bernstein. *Diaspora Soul* (Tzadik, 1999).

Chief Bey. *Children of the House of God* (Mapleshade, 1997).

Art Blakey. *Orgy in Rhythm* (Blue Note, 1957).

———. *The Witch Doctor* (Blue Note, 1967).

———. *Drums Around the Corner* (Blue Note, 1999).

Hamiet Bluiett. *Endangered Species* (India Navigation, 1976).

Lester Bowie. *The Great Pretender* (ECM, 1981).

Anthony Braxton. *3 Compositions of New Jazz* (Delmark, 1968).

———. *For Alto* (Delmark, 1969).

———. *The Complete Arista Recordings* (Mosaic, 2008).

———. *Dortmund (Quartet) 1976* (Hat Art, 1993).

———. *Creative Orchestra (Köln) 1978* (Hat Art, 1995).

———. *Composition 98* (Hat Art, 1990).

———. *Performance (Quartet) 1979* (Hat Art, 1990).

———. *Four Compositions (Quartet) 1983* (Black Saint, 1983).

———. *Birmingham (Quartet) 1985* (Leo, 1993).

———. *Willisau (Quartet) 1991* (Hat Art, 1991).

———. *Quartet (Victoriaville) 1992* (Victo, 1993).

———. *Composition No. 247* (Leo, 2000).

———. *Six Compositions (GTM) 2001* (Rastascan, 2002).

Anthony Braxton and Max Roach. *Birth and Rebirth* (Black Saint, 1978).

Peter Brötzmann. *Die Like a Dog* (FMP, 1994).

———. *Little Birds Have Fast Hearts, Volume 1* (FMP, 1998).

Dave Brubeck. *Truth Is Fallen* (Atlantic, 1972).

———. *La Fiesta de la Posada* (CBS, 1979).

Donald Byrd. *Free Form* (Blue Note, 1962).

Don Byron. *Tuskegee Experiments* (Elektra/Nonesuch, 1992).

———. *Plays the Music of Mickey Katz* (Nonesuch, 1993).

———. *Love, Peace, and Soul* (Savoy, 2012).

Roy Campbell. *Ancestral Homeland* (No More, 1998).

John Carter. *Echoes from Rudolph's* (Ibedon, 1977).

———. *A Suite of Early American Folk Pieces* (Moers, 1979).

———. *Night Fire: An American Folk Suite* (Black Saint, 1981).

———. *Dauwhe* (Black Saint, 1982).

———. *Castles of Ghana* (Gramavision, 1986).

———. *Dance of the Love Ghosts* (Gramavision, 1987).

———. *Fields* (Gramavision, 1988).

———. *Shadows on a Wall* (Gramavision, 1989).

John Carter and Bobby Bradford. *The Complete Revelation Sessions* (Mosaic, 2010).

———. *Self-Determination Music* (Flying Dutchman, 1970).

Thomas Chapin. *Alive* (Knitting Factory, 1999).

———. *Sky Piece* (Knitting Factory, 1998).

Don Cherry. *Complete Communion* (Blue Note, 1965).

———. *Live in Stockholm* (Caprice, 2013).

———. *Relativity Suite* (JCOA, 1973).

———. *Eternal Now* (Sonet, 1974).

———. *Hear & Now* (Atlantic, 1977).

Cyrus Chestnut. *You Are My Sunshine* (Warner Bros., 2003).

Circle. *Paris Concert* (ECM, 1972).

Anthony Coleman. *Selfhaters* (Tzadik, 1996).

Ornette Coleman. *Something Else* (Contemporary, 1958).

———. *Beauty Is a Rare Thing: The Complete Atlantic Recordings* (Atlantic, 1993).

———. *Chautauqua Suite* (CBS, 1966).

———. *Science Fiction* (Columbia, 1972).

———. *Skies of America* (Columbia, 1972).

———. *Dancing in Your Head* (Horizon, 1977).

———. *Of Human Feelings* (Antilles, 1982).

Steve Coleman. *Black Science* (Novus, 1991).

————. *The Tao of Mad Phat* (Novus, 1993).

————. *Genesis/The Opening of the Way* (RCA, 1997).

————. *The Sonic Language of Myth* (RCA, 1999).

————. *Harvesting Semblances and Affinities* (Pi, 2010).

————. *The Mancy of Sound* (Pi, 2012).

————. *Functional Arrhythmias* (Pi, 2013).

Alice Coltrane. *Journey to Satchidananda* (Impulse, 1970).

————. *Universal Consciousness* (Impulse, 1971).

————. *Lord of Lords* (Impulse, 1972).

————. *World Galaxy* (Impulse, 1972).

————. *Radha-Krsna Nama Sankirtana* (Warner Bros., 1977).

————. *Transcendence* (Warner Bros., 1977).

————. *Turiya Sings* (Avatar Book Institute, 1982).

————. *Glorious Chants* (Avatar Book Institute, 1995).

John Coltrane. *The Complete Prestige Recordings* (Original Jazz Classics, 1991).

————. *The Heavyweight Champion* (Atlantic, 1995).

————. *Live at the Village Vanguard* (Impulse, 1962).

————. *Live at Birdland* (Impulse, 1963).

————. *Crescent* (Impulse, 1964).

————. *A Love Supreme* (Impulse, 1965).

————. *Transition* (Impulse, 1965).

————. *The Major Works of John Coltrane* (Impulse, 1965).

————. *Sun Ship* (Impulse, 1965).

————. *First Meditations* (Impulse, 1977).

————. *Expression* (Impulse, 1993).

————. *Stellar Regions* (Impulse, 1995).

————. *One Down, One Up* (Impulse, 2005).

Chick Corea. A.R.C. (ECM, 1971).

————. *Return to Forever* (ECM, 1972).

Marilyn Crispell. *Gaia* (Leo, 1988).

Connie Crothers. *Perception* (Inner City, 1976).

————. *Music from Everyday Life* (New Artists, 1996).

Stephan Crump. *Rosetta* (Papillon Sounds, 2006).

Anthony Davis. *X: The Life and Times of Malcolm X* (Gramavision, 1992).

Bill Dixon. *Intents and Purposes* (RCA, 1967).

————. *Vade Mecum* (Soul Note, 1994).

Eric Dolphy. *Last Date* (Fontana, 1964).

Hamid Drake and Bindu. *Reggaeology* (Rogue Art, 2010).

Marty Ehrlich. *Sojourn* (Tzadik, 1999).

Jewlia Eisenberg. *Trilectic* (Tzadik, 2001).

Duke Ellington. *Black, Brown & Beige* (Columbia, 1999).

————. *The Blanton-Webster Band* (RCA, 1986).

————. *Concert of Sacred Music* (RCA, 1965).

————. *Second Sacred Concert* (Prestige, 1968).

————. *The Afro-Eurasian Eclipse* (Prestige, 1971).

————. *Third Sacred Concert* (RCA, 1973).

Kahil El'Zabar's Ritual Trio. *Big Cliff* (Delmark, 1995).

Ellery Eskelin, *The Sun Died* (Soul Note, 1996).

————. *Vanishing Point* (Hatology, 2001).

Ethnic Heritage Ensemble. *Dance with the Ancestors* (Chameleon, 1993).

Far East Side Band. *Caverns* (New World, 1994).

David Fiuczynski. *Jazz Punk* (Fuzelicious Morsels, 2000).

Erik Friedlander. *The Watchman* (Tzadik, 1996).

David Friesen. *Color Pool* (Muse, 1979).

————. *Inner Voices* (Global Pacific, 1987).

Charles Gayle. *Homeless* (Silkheart, 1988).

————. *Repent* (Knitting Factory, 1992).

————. *Touchin' on Trane* (FMP, 1993).

————. *Kingdom Come* (Knitting Factory, 1994).

————. *Look Up* (ESP, 2012).

Dizzy Gillespie. *The Complete RCA-Victor Recordings* (Bluebird, 1995).

————. *Volume 11 1947 Complete Edition* (Masters of Jazz, 2001).

Dennis Gonzalez. *Hymn for the Perfect Heart of a Pearl* (Konnex, 1991).

————. *Catechism* (Music & Arts, 1996).

————. *The Earth and the Heart* (Music & Arts, 1996).

————. *Old Time Revival* (Entropy Stereo, 2003).

Milford Graves. *Bäbi* (IPS, 1977).

————. *Grand Unification* (Tzadik, 1998).

Grant Green. *Feelin' the Spirit* (Blue Note, 1963).

Burton Greene. *Klezmokum* (Bvhaast, 1992).

Vince Guaraldi. *At Grace Cathedral* (Fantasy, 1965).

Charlie Haden and Hank Jones. *Steal Away* (Verve, 1995).

Herbie Hancock. *Maiden Voyage* (Blue Note, 1965).

————. *Mwandishi* (Warner Bros., 1971).

————. *Head Hunters* (Columbia, 1973).

Julius Hemphill. *Dogon A.D.* (Mbari, 1972).

————. *Coon Bid'ness* (Arista, 1975).

————. *Big Band* (Elektra, 1988).

Shelley Hirsch. *O Little Town of East New York* (Tzadik, 1995).

Fred Ho. *We Refuse to Be Used and Abused* (Soul Note, 1987).

————. *The Underground Railroad to My Heart* (Soul Note, 1993).

————. *Once Upon a Time in Chinese America* (Innova, 2001).

————. *Snake-Eaters* (Mutable, 2011).

Dave Holland. *Conference of the Birds* (ECM, 1973).

Paul Horn. *Jazz Suite on the Mass Texts* (RCA, 1965).

Human Arts Ensemble, *Whisper of Dharma* (Universal Justice, 1972).

Jason Kao Hwang. *The Floating Box: A Story in Chinatown* (New World, 2005).

———. *Stories Before Within* (Innova Records, 2007).

Abdullah Ibrahim. *African Space Program* (Enja, 1973).

———. *The Journey* (Downtown Sound, 1977).

———. *Africa—Tears and Laughter* (Enja, 1979).

———. *Echoes from Africa* (Enja, 1979).

———. *African River* (Enja, 1989).

Vijay Iyer. *Solo* (ACT Records, 2010).

Jon Jang. *Tiananmen!* (Soul Note Records, 1993).

———. *Two Flowers on a Stem* (Soul Note Records, 1995).

———. *Paper Son, Paper Songs* (Soul Note Records, 2000).

Joseph Jarman. *Song for* (Delmark, 1967)

Keith Jarrett. *The Köln Concert* (ECM, 1975).

———. *The Survivors' Suite* (ECM, 1977).

———. *G.I. Gurdjieff—Sacred Hymns* (ECM, 1980).

Keith Jarrett and Charlie Haden. *Jasmine* (ECM, 2010).

Darius Jones. *Man'ish Boy* (AUM Fidelity, 2009).

Scott Joplin. *Treemonisha* (Olympic, 1975).

Fred Katz. *Folk Songs for Far Out Folks* (Reboot Stereophonic, 2007).

Rahsaan Roland Kirk. *Left and Right* (Atlantic, 1969).

The Klezmatics. *Rhythm & Jews* (Flying Fish, 1991).

David Krakauer. *Klezmer Madness* (Tzadik, 1995).

Steve Lacy. *School Days* (Hatology, 2003).

———. *Lapis* (Saravah, 1971).

———. *The Way* (Hat Hut, 1980).

———. *Remains* (Hat Art, 1992).

———. *Vespers* (Soul Note, 1993).

Oliver Lake. *NTU: Point from Which Creation Begins* (Arista, 1976).

Adam Lane. *Zero Degree Music* (CIMP, 2005).

Yusef Lateef. *Prayer to the East* (Savoy, 1957).

———. *Part of the Search* (Atlantic, 1974).

———. *African-American Epic Suite* (ACT, 1994).

Babatunde Lea. *Suite Unseen: Summoner of the Ghost* (M.A.T., 2010).

Lacy and Joelle Leandre, *One More Time* (Leo Records, 2005).

George Lewis. *Plays Hymns* (Milneburg, 1999).

———. *Jazz at Vespers* (OJC, 1993).

George E. Lewis. *Homage to Charles Parker* (Black Saint, 1979).

———. *Les Exercises Spirituels* (Tzadik, 2011).

Abbey Lincoln. *People in Me* (Inner City, 1978).

The Mahavishnu Orchestra. *The Inner Mounting Flame* (Columbia, 1971).

Shelly Manne. *Steps to the Desert* (Contemporary, 1963).

Wynton Marsalis. *In This House/On This Morning* (Columbia, 1994).

———. *Blood on the Fields* (Columbia, 1997).

———. *All Rise* (Sony, 2002).

Masada. *Alef* (DIW, 1994).

———. *Beit* (DIW, 1994).

———. *Gimel* (DIW, 1994).

———. *Bar Kokhba* (Tzadik, 1996).

Kalaparusha Maurice McIntyre. *Humility in the Light of the Creator* (Delmark, 1969).

Francisco Mela. *Tree of Life* (Half Note, 2011).

Myra Melford. *The Same River Twice* (Gramavision, 1996).

———. *The Whole Tree Gone* (Firehouse 12, 2010).

Charles Mingus. *Ah Um* (Columbia, 1959).

———. *Presents Charles Mingus* (Candid, 1960).

———. *Passions of a Man: The Complete Atlantic Recordings* (Rhino, 1997).

———. *The Black Saint and the Sinner Lady* (Impulse, 1963).

———. *Music Written for Monterey* (Sunnyside, 2006).

———. *Let My Children Hear Music* (Columbia, 1972).

Nicole Mitchell. *Xenogenesis Suite* (Firehouse 12, 2008).

Roscoe Mitchell. *Sound* (Delmark, 1966).

———. *Congliptious* (Nessa, 1968).

———. *Nonaah* (Nessa, 1977).

Lawrence D. "Butch" Morris. *Current Trends in Racism in Modern America* (Sound Aspects, 1985).

———. *Testament: A Conduction Collection* (New World, 1995).

Oliver Nelson. *Afro-American Sketches* (Prestige, 1962).

New Klezmer Trio. *Melt Zonk Rewire* (Tzadik, 1995).

Pan Afrikan Peoples Arkestra. *Flight 17* (Nimbus West, 2006).

Evan Parker. *After Appleby* (Leo, 2000).

William Parker. *Flowers Grow in My Room* (Centering, 1994).

———. *In Order to Survive* (Black Saint, 1995).

———. *Sunrise in the Tone World* (AUM Fidelity, 1997).

———. *Mass for the Healing of the World* (Black Saint, 2003).

Ivo Perelman. *En Adir—Traditional Jewish Songs* (Music & Arts, 1997).

———. *Sad Life* (Leo, 1997).

———. *The Seven Energies of the Universe* (Leo, 2001).

———. *Soulstorm* (Clean Feed, 2010).

Prana Trio. *The Singing Image of Fire* (Circavision, 2009).

Sun Ra. *Super-Sonic Jazz* (Saturn, 1957).

———. *Visits Planet Earth/Interstellar Low Ways* (Evidence, 1992).

———. *We Travel the Spaceways/Bad and Beautiful* (Evidence, 1992).

———. *Other Planes of There* (Evidence, 1992).

———. *The Heliocentric Worlds of Sun Ra, Vols. 1 & 2* (ESP, 1965–66).

———. *Cosmic Tones for Mental Therapy* (Saturn, 1967).

———. *Black Myth/Out in Space* (MPS, 1971).

———. *The Creator of the Universe* (Transparency, 2007).

———. *Soundtrack to Space Is the Place* (Evidence, 1993).

———. *Pathways to Unknown Worlds* (Impulse, 1975).

Return to Forever. *Hymn of the Seventh Galaxy* (Polydor, 1973).

———. *Light as a Feather* (Polydor, 1973).

———. *Where Have I Known You Before?* (Polydor, 1974).

Marc Ribot. *Yo! I Killed Your God* (Tzadik, 1999).

Sam Rivers. *The Complete Blue Note Sessions* (Mosaic, 1996).

———. *Streams* (Impulse, 1973).

———. *Crystals* (Impulse, 1974).

———. *Portrait* (FMP Records, 1997).

———. *Inspiration* (BMG, 1999).

Max Roach. *Deeds Not Words* (Riverside, 1968).

We Insist! Freedom Now Suite (Candid, 1960).

———. *Percussion Bitter Sweet* (Impulse, 1961).

———. *Lift Every Voice and Sing* (Atlantic, 1971).

———. *M'Boom* (Columbia, 1980).

———. *Chattahoochee Red* (Columbia, 1981).

Matana Roberts. *Coin-Coin Chapter One: Gens de Couleur Libres* (Constellation, 2011).

———. *Coin-Coin Chapter Two: Mississippi Moonchile* (Constellation, 2013).

Sonny Rollins. *The Freedom Suite* (Riverside, 1958).

———. *The Complete RCA Victor Recordings* (RCA, 1997).

Ned Rothenberg. *The Lumina Recordings* (Tzadik, 2006).

———. *Power Lines* (New World, 1995).

———. *Inner Diaspora* (Tzadik, 2007).

George Russell. *Stratusphunk* (Riverside, 1960).

———. *Ezz-Thetic* (Riverside, 1961).

———. *Electric Sonata for Souls Loved by Nature* (Flying Dutchman, 1971).

———. *The African Game* (Blue Note, 1985).

Hal Russell. *The Hal Russell Story* (ECM, 1993).

Paul Shapiro. *Midnight Minyan* (Tzadik, 2002).

Archie Shepp. *Four for Trane* (Impulse, 1964).

———. *Fire Music* (Impulse, 1965).

———. *On This Night* (Impulse, 1965).

———. *Live in San Francisco* (Impulse, 1966).

———. *Mama Too Tight* (Impulse, 1966).

———. *The Magic of Juju* (Impulse, 1968).

———. *Yasmina, A Black Woman* (BYG, 1969).

———. *Things Have Got to Change* (Impulse, 1971).

———. *Attica Blues* (Impulse, 1972).

———. *The Cry of My People* (Impulse, 1973).

Archie Shepp and Horace Parlan. *Goin' Home* (Steeplechase, 1977).

Matthew Shipp. *Circular Temple* (Infinite Zero, 1992).

———. *Symbol Systems* (No More, 1995).

———. *By the Law of Music* (Hat Art, 1997).

———. *Harmony and Abyss* (Thirsty Ear, 2004).

Wayne Shorter. *The All-Seeing Eye* (Blue Note, 1965).

———. *Super Nova* (Blue Note, 1969).

———. *Without a Net* (Blue Note, 2013).

Ben Sidran. *Talking Jazz: An Oral History* (Rhino Records, 2006).

Horace Silver. *Silver n' Percussion* (Blue Note, 1978).

Wadada Leo Smith. *Kabell Years 1971–79* (Tzadik, 2004).

———. *Divine Love* (ECM, 1979).

———. *Human Rights* (Kabell, 1986).

———. *Procession of the Great Ancestry* (Nessa, 1983).

———. *Kulture Jazz* (ECM, 1993).

———. *Tao-Njia* (ECM, 1996).

———. *Light Upon Light* (Tzadik, 1999).

———. *Tabligh* (Cuneiform, 2008).

———. *Ten Freedom Summers* (Cuneiform, 2012).

Omar Sosa. *Across the Divide: A Tale of Rhythm and Ancestry* (Half Note, 2009).

William Grant Still. *Afro-American Symphony* (Naxos, 2005).

Horace Tapscott. *Songs of the Unsung* (Interplay, 1978).

———. *The Dark Tree* (Hat Art, 1995).

———. *Dissent or Descent* (Nimbus, 1998).

Cecil Taylor. *Jazz Advance* (OJC, 1956).

———. *Trance* (Black Lion, 1996).

———. *Unit Structures* (Blue Note, 1966).

———. *Air Above Mountains* (Enja, 1973).

———. *Garden 1 & 2* (Hat Art, 1990).

———. *For Olim* (Soul Note, 1987).

———. *Erzulie Maketh Scent* (FMP, 1989).

———. *The Tree of Life* (FMP, 1998).

Richard Teitelbaum. *Golem* (Tzadik, 1995).

Oluyemi Thomas. *Before the Beginning* (Recorded, 2002).

———. *The Power of Light* (Not Two, 2007).

———. *Beneath Tones Floor* (NoBusiness, 2010).

McCoy Tyner. *Expansions* (Blue Note, 1969).

———. *Sahara* (Milestone, 1972).

———. *Enlightenment* (Milestone, 1973).

Various Artists. *From Spirituals to Swing* (Vanguard, 1959).

———. *Spiritual Jazz: Esoteric, Modal + Deep Jazz from the Underground, 1968–77* (Now Again, 2009).

———. *Afro-Cuba: A Musical Anthology* (Rounder, 1994).

———. *American Piano, Vol. 4: Rhythmic Movements* (Premier, 1994).

Tom Varner. *The Mystery of Compassion* (Soul Note, 1993).

Greg Wall. *Later Prophets* (Tzadik, 2004).

David S. Ware. *Flight of i* (DIW, 1992).

———. *Third Ear Recitation* (DIW, 1993).

———. *Earthquation* (DIW, 1994).

———. *Dao* (Homestead, 1996).

———. *Godspelized* (DIW, 1996).

———. *Shakti* (AUM Fidelity, 2009).

———. *Saturnian* (AUM Fidelity, 2010).

James Weidman. *Three Worlds* (Inner Circle, 2009).

Mark Whitecage and the Bi-Coastal Orchestra. *BushWacked* (Acoustics, 2005).

Mary Lou Williams. *Black Christ of the Andes* (Smithsonian Folkways, 2004).

John Zorn. *News for Lulu* (Hat Art, 1988).

———. *Kristallnacht* (1993).

———. *Madness, Love and Mysticism* (Tzadik, 2001).

———. *Songs from the Hermetic Theatre* (Tzadik, 2001).

———. *IAO* (Tzadik, 2002).

———. *Book of Angels, Vols. 1–9* (Tzadik, 2005–8).

BOOKS, BOOK CHAPTERS, AND ARTICLES

Ake, David, Charles Hiroshi Garrett, and Daniel Goldmark, eds. *Jazz/Not Jazz: The Music and Its Boundaries*. Berkeley: University of California Press, 2012.

Albanese, Catherine L., ed. *American Spiritualities: A Reader*. Bloomington: Indiana University Press, 2001.

———. *A Republic of Mind and Spirit: A Cultural History of American Metaphysical Religion*. New Haven, Conn.: Yale University Press, 2008.

Allen, Ray. *Singing in the Spirit: African-American Sacred Quartets in New York City*. Philadelphia: University of Pennsylvania Press, 1991.

Armstrong, Lil Hardin. "Satchmo and Me." *American Music* 25, no. 1 (Spring 2007): 106–18.

Atkins, E. Taylor. "Sacred Swing: The Sacralization of Jazz in the American Baha'i Community." *American Music* 24, no. 4 (Winter 2006): 383–420.

Attali, Jacques. *Noise: The Political Economy of Music*. Minneapolis: University of Minnesota Press, 1985.

Austerlitz, Paul. *Jazz Consciousness: Music, Race, and Humanity*. Middletown, Conn.: Wesleyan University Press, 2005.

Ayler, Albert. "To Mr. Jones—I Had a Vision." In *The Cricket: Black Music in Evolution!!!* edited by Amiri Baraka, 27–30. Jihad Productions, 1969.

Bailey, Derek. *Improvisation: Its Nature and Practice in Music*. New York: Da Capo, 1993.

Baraka, Amiri. "The 'Blues Aesthetic' and the 'Black Aesthetic': Aesthetics as the Continuing Political History of a Culture." *Black Music Research Journal* 11, no. 2 (Autumn 1991): 101–9.

Barber, Benjamin. *Jihad vs. McWorld: How Globalism and Tribalism Are Reshaping the World*. New York: Ballantine, 1996.

Barnes, Julian. *The Sense of an Ending*. New York: Knopf, 2011.

Barthes, Roland. "The Grain of the Voice." In *The Sound Studies Reader*, edited by Jonathan Sterne, 504–10. New York: Routledge, 2012.

Bartlett, Andrew W. "Cecil Taylor, Identity Energy, and the Avant-Garde African American Body." *Perspectives of New Music* 33, nos. 1/2 (Winter–Summer 1995): 274–93.

Barzel, Tamar. "An Interrogation of Language: 'Radical Jewish Culture' on New York City's Downtown Music Scene." *Journal of the Society for American Music* 4, no. 2 (May 2010): 215–50.

Becker, Judith. "Tantrism, *Rasa*, and Javanese Gamelan Music." In *Enchanting Powers: Music in the World's Religions*, edited by Lawrence E. Sullivan, 15–60. Cambridge, Mass.: Harvard University Press, 1997.

Bell, Catherine. "Performance." In *Critical Terms for Religious Studies*, edited by Mark C. Taylor, 205–24 (Chicago: University of Chicago Press, 1998).

Bender, Courtney. *The New Metaphysicals: Spirituality and the Religious Imagination*. Chicago: University of Chicago Press, 2010.

Berg, Chuck. "The Fox Is Big on Bop." *Jazz Education Journal* 39, no. 2 (October 2006): 59, 61–63.

Berkman, Franya J. "Appropriating Universality: The Coltranes and 1960s Spirituality." *American Studies* 48, no. 1 (Spring 2007): 41–62.

———. *Monument Eternal: The Music of Alice Coltrane*. Middletown, Conn.: Wesleyan University Press, 2010.

Berliner, Paul F. *Thinking in Jazz: The Infinite Art of Improvisation*. Chicago: University of Chicago Press, 1994.

Bivins, Jason C. *The Fracture of Good Order: Christian Antiliberalism and the Challenge to American Politics*. Chapel Hill: University of North Carolina Press, 2003.

———. "'Only One Repertory': American Religious Studies." *Religion* 42, no. 3 (2012): 395–407.

———. *Religion of Fear: The Politics of Horror in Conservative Evangelicalism*. New York: Oxford University Press, 2008.

Bleckmann, Theo. "The Voices of My Voice: Three Working as One." In *Arcana III: Musicians on Music*, edited by John Zorn, 34–44. New York: Hips Road, 2008.

Bohlman, Philip V., Edith L. Blumhofer, and Maria M. Chow, eds. *Music in American Religious Experience*. New York: Oxford University Press, 2006.

Borgo, David. "Negotiating Freedom: Values and Practices in Contemporary Improvised Music." *Black Music Research Journal* 22, no. 2 (Autumn 2002): 165–88.

Brackett, John. *John Zorn: Tradition and Transgression*. Bloomington: Indiana University Press, 2008.

Brennan, Timothy. *Secular Devotion: Afro-Latin Music and Imperial Jazz*. New York: Verso, 2008.

Brown, Candy Gunther. "Touch and American Religions." *Religion Compass* 3, no. 4 (July 2009): 770–83.

Brown, David P. *Noise Orders: Jazz, Improvisation, and Architecture*. Minneapolis: University of Minnesota Press, 2006.

Brown, Leonard L., ed. *John Coltrane and Black America's Quest for Freedom: Spirituality and the Music*. New York: Oxford University Press, 2010.

Brubeck, Dave. "Dave Brubeck: His Music Keeps Us Here." *Jazz Education Journal* 34, no. 3 (November 2001): 38–45.

Bruns, Roger A. *Preacher: Billy Sunday and Big-Time American Evangelism*. New York: Norton, 1992.

Bryant, Clora, Buddy Collette, William Green, Steve Isoardi, and Marl Young, eds. *Central Avenue Sounds: Jazz in Los Angeles*. Berkeley: University of California Press, 1998.

Budds, Michael J. "The Art Ensemble of Chicago in Context." *Lenox Avenue* 3 (1997): 59–72.

Butler, Judith. *Gender Trouble: Feminism and the Subversion of Identity*. New York: Routledge, 2006.

Callahan, Allen Dwight. *Talking Book: African Americans and the Bible*. New Haven, Conn.: Yale University Press, 2006.

Castledine, Jacqueline. "Gender, Jazz, and Justice in Cold War Freedom Movements." In *Freedom Rights: New Perspectives on the Civil Rights Movement*, edited by Danielle L. McGuire and John Dittmer, 223–46. Lexington: University of Kentucky Press, 2011.

Chase, Christopher. "Prophetics in the Key of Allah: Towards an Understanding of Islam in Jazz." *Jazz Perspectives* 4, no. 2 (August 2010): 157–81.

Classen, Constance. *Worlds of Sense: Exploring the Senses in History and Across Cultures*. New York: Routledge, 1993.

Cohen, Harvey G. *Duke Ellington's America*. Chicago: University of Chicago Press, 2010.

Coleman, Steve. "The Lunation Cycle as a Point of Departure for Musical Ideas." In *Arcana II: Musicians on Music*, edited by John Zorn, 56–61. New York: Hips Road, 2007.

———. "Regarding the Sonic Symbolism of When and Where." In *Arcana V: Music, Magic and Mysticism*, edited by John Zorn, 33–97. New York: Hips Road, 2010.

Collins, Steven. *Selfless Persons: Imagery and Thought in Theravada Buddhism*. Cambridge: Cambridge University Press, 1990.

Corbett, John. *Extended Play: Sounding Off from John Cage to Dr. Funkenstein*. Durham, N.C.: Duke University Press, 1994.

———, ed. *The Wisdom of Sun Ra: Sun Ra's Polemical Broadsheets and Streetcorner Leaflets*. Chicago: WhiteWalls, 2006.

Corbett, John, Anthony Elms, and Terri Kapsalis, eds. *Pathways to Unknown Worlds: Sun Ra, El Saturn, and Chicago's Afro-Futurist Underground 1954–68*. Chicago: WhiteWalls, 2006.

Corrigan, John, ed. *Religion and Emotion: Approaches and Interpretations*. New York: Oxford University Press, 2004.

Cox, Christoph, and Daniel Warner, eds. *Audio Culture: Readings in Modern Music*. New York: Continuum, 2004.

Cox, Harvey. *Fire from Heaven: The Rise of Pentecostal Spirituality and the Reshaping of Religion in the Twenty-first Century*. New York: Da Capo, 1995.

Cross, Brian. *It's Not About a Salary...: Rap, Race and Resistance in Los Angeles*. New York: Verso, 1993.

Crumpacker, Bunny, and Chick Crumpacker. *Jazz Legends*. Layton, Utah: Gibbs Smith, 1995.

Dalachinsky, Steve, and Matthew Shipp. *Logos and Language: A Post-Jazz Metaphorical Dialogue*. Paris: Rogue Art, 2008.

Damon, Maria. "Jazz-Jews, Jive, and Gender: The Ethnic Politics of Jazz Argot." In *Jews and Other Differences: The New Jewish Cultural Studies*, edited by Jonathan Boyarin and Daniel Boyarin, 150–75. Minneapolis: University of Minnesota Press, 1997.

Davis, Francis. *Bebop and Nothingness: Jazz and Pop at the End of the Century*. New York: Schirmer, 1996.

———. *In the Moment: Jazz in the 1980s*. New York: Da Capo, 1996.

———. *Outcats: Jazz Composers, Instrumentalists, and Singers*. New York: Oxford University Press, 1990.

Dean, William. *American Spiritual Culture: And the Invention of Jazz, Football, and the Movies*. New York: Continuum, 2006.

Deleuze, Gilles, and Félix Guattari. *Mille Plateaux: Capitalism and Schizophrenia*. Minneapolis: University of Minnesota Press, 1987.

Dessen, Michael. "Improvising in a Different Clave: Steve Coleman and AfroCuba de Matanzas." In *The Other Side of Nowhere: Jazz, Improvisation, and Communities in Dialogue*, edited by Daniel Fischlin and Ajay Heble, 173–92. Middletown, Conn.: Wesleyan University Press, 2004.

DeVeaux, Scott. *The Birth of Bebop: A Social and Musical History*. Berkeley: University of California Press, 1999.

Diggins, John Patrick. *The Lost Soul of American Politics: Virtue, Self-Interest, and the Foundations of Liberalism*. Chicago: University of Chicago Press, 1986.

Duckworth, William. *Talking Music: Conversations with John Cage, Philip Glass, Laurie Anderson, and Five Generations of American Experimental Composers*. New York: Da Capo, 1999.

Ellison, Ralph. *Shadow and Act*. New York: Vintage, 1995.

Ellwood, Robert S. *The Sixties Spiritual Awakening*. New Brunswick, N.J.: Rutgers University Press, 1994.

Emerson, Ralph Waldo. *The Selected Writings of Ralph Waldo Emerson*. New York: Modern Library, 1940.

Enstice, Wayne, and Janis Stockhouse. *Jazzwomen: Conversations with Twenty-One Musicians*. Bloomington: Indiana University Press, 2004.

Evans, Curtis J. *The Burden of Black Religion*. New York: Oxford University Press, 2008.

Evans, Sara M., and Harry C. Boyte. *Free Spaces: The Sources of Democratic Change in America*. Chicago: University of Chicago Press, 1992.

Fischlin, Daniel, Ajay Heble, and George Lipsitz. *The Fierce Urgency of Now: Improvisation, Rights, and the Ethics of Cocreation*. Durham, N.C.: Duke University Press, 2013.

Fitzgerald, Frances. *Cities on a Hill: A Brilliant Exploration of Visionary Communities Remaking the American Dream*. New York: Simon and Schuster, 1987.

Fitzgerald, Timothy. "Experience." In *Guide to the Study of Religion*, edited by Willi Braun and Russell T. McCutcheon, 125–39. London: Cassell, 2000.

Fledderus, Francine May. "The Function of Oral Tradition in 'Mary Lou's Mass' by Mary Lou Williams." Master's thesis, University of North Texas, 1996.

Floyd, Samuel A. *The Power of Black Music: Interpreting Its History from Africa to the United States*. New York: Oxford University Press, 1996.

Frankiel, Tamar. "Ritual Sites in the Narrative of American Religion." In *American Spiritualities: A Reader*, edited by Catherine Albanese, 23–55. Bloomington: Indiana University Press, 2001.

Freeman, Phil. *New York Is Now! The New Wave of Free Jazz*. Brooklyn, N.Y.: Telegraph Company, 2001.

Fujino, Diane C., ed. *Wicked Theory, Wicked Practice: A Fred Ho Reader*. Minneapolis: University of Minnesota Press, 2009.

Fuller, Robert. *Spiritual but Not Religious: Understanding Unchurched America*. New York: Oxford University Press, 2001.

Gabbard, Krin. *Jammin' at the Margins: Jazz and the American Cinema*. Chicago: University of Chicago Press, 1996.

——, ed. *Jazz among the Discourses*. Durham, N.C.: Duke University Press, 1995.

Gannon, Sharon. "Yoga and Music." In *Arcana V: Music, Magic and Mysticism*, edited by John Zorn, 133–50. New York: Hips Road, 2010.

Garcia, David F. "'We Both Speak African': Gillespie, Pozo, and the Making of Afro-Cuban Jazz." *Institute for Studies in American Music Newsletter* 38, no. 1 (Fall 2007): 1–2, 13–14.

Giddins, Gary. *Weather Bird: Jazz at the Dawn of Its Second Century*. New York: Oxford University Press, 2004.

Gillespie, Dizzy, and Al Fraser. *To Be or Not . . . to Bop*. New York: Da Capo, 1985.

Gilroy, Paul. *The Black Atlantic: Modernity and Double Consciousness*. Cambridge, Mass.: Harvard University Press, 1995.

——. *Darker Than Blue: On the Moral Economies of Black Atlantic Culture*. Cambridge, Mass.: Belknap, 2011.

———. *Small Acts: Thoughts on the Politics of Black Culture*. New York: Serpent's Tail, 1994.

Gioia, Ted. "The Black Primitivist Myth." *Musical Quarterly* 73, no. 1 (1989): 130–43.

Glaude, Eddie, Jr., ed. *Is It Nation Time? Contemporary Essays on Black Power and Black Nationalism*. Chicago: University of Chicago Press, 2002.

Goodman, John F. *Mingus Speaks*. Berkeley: University of California Press, 2013.

Gordon, Allan M. "The AEC as Performance Art." *Lenox Avenue* 3 (1997): 55–58.

Graves, Milford. "Book of Tono-Rhythmology." In *Arcana II: Musicians on Music*, edited by John Zorn, 110–17. New York: Hips Road, 2007.

———. "Music Extensions of Infinite Dimensions." In *Arcana V: Music, Magic and Mysticism*, edited by John Zorn, 171–86. New York: Hips Road, 2010.

Griffin, Farah Jasmine. "When Malindy Sings: A Meditation on Black Women's Vocality." In *Uptown Conversation: The New Jazz Studies*, edited by Robert O'Meally, Brent Hayes Edwards, and Farah Jasmine Griffin, 102–25. New York: Columbia University Press, 2004.

Griffith, Jennifer. "Mingus in the Act: Confronting the Legacies of Vaudeville and Minstrelsy." *Jazz Perspectives* 4, no. 3 (2010): 337–68.

Gura, Philip F. *American Transcendentalism: A History*. New York: Hill and Wang, 2007.

Handy, D. Antoinette. "Conversation with Mary Lou Williams: First Lady of the Jazz Keyboard." *Black Perspective in Music* 8, no. 2 (Autumn 1980): 194–214.

Heble, Ajay. *Landing on the Wrong Note: Jazz, Dissonance, and Critical Practice*. New York: Routledge, 2000.

Heffley, Mike. *Northern Sun, Southern Moon: Europe's Reinvention of Jazz*. New Haven, Conn.: Yale University Press, 2005.

Hentoff, Nat. *Jazz Is*. Montclair, N.J.: Limelight, 1984.

Hermes, Will. *Love Goes to Buildings on Fire: Five Years in New York That Changed Music Forever*. New York: Faber & Faber, 2011.

Hobson, Wilder. *American Jazz Music*. New York: Da Capo, 1976.

Hodgkinson, Tim. "Holy Ghost." In *Arcana V: Music, Magic and Mysticism*, edited by John Zorn, 191–226. New York: Hips Road, 2010.

Hulse, Brian, and Nick Nesbitt, eds. *Sounding the Virtual: Gilles Deleuze and the Theory and Philosophy of Music*. Farnham: Ashgate, 2010.

Isaac, Jeffrey C. "Oases in the Desert: Hannah Arendt on Democratic Politics." *American Political Science Review* 8, no. 1 (March 1994): 156–68.

Isoardi, Steven L. *The Dark Tree: Jazz and the Community Arts in Los Angeles*. Berkeley: University of California Press, 2006.

Iton, Richard. *In Search of the Black Fantastic: Politics and Popular Culture in the Post–Civil Rights Era*. New York: Oxford University Press, 2008.

James, William. *The Varieties of Religious Experience: A Study in Human Nature*. Rockville, Md.: Manor Classics, 2008.

Janeczko, Jeffrey Matthew. "'Beyond Klezmer': Redefining Jewish Music for the Twenty-first Century." PhD diss., University of California, Los Angeles, 2009.

Janus, Cicily. *The New Face of Jazz*. New York: Billboard, 2010.

Jolly, Kenneth S. *Black Liberation in the Midwest: The Struggle in St. Louis, Missouri, 1964–1970*. New York: Routledge, 2006.

Jones, Olive, and George Russell. "A New Theory for Jazz." *Black Perspective in Music* 2, no. 1 (Spring 1974): 63–74.

Joseph, Peniel. *Waiting 'Til the Midnight Hour: A Narrative History of Black Power in America*. New York: Henry Holt, 2007.

Jost, Ekkehard. *Free Jazz*. New York: Da Capo, 1974.

Kastin, David. "Fred Ho and the Evolution of Afro-Asian New American Multicultural Music." *Popular Music and Society* 33, no. 1 (2010): 1–8.

Kelley, Robin D. G. *Africa Speaks, America Answers: Modern Jazz in Revolutionary Times*. Cambridge, Mass.: Harvard University Press, 2012.

———. "Dig They Freedom: Meditations on History and the Black Avant-Garde." *Lenox Avenue* 3 (1997): 13–27.

———. *Thelonious Monk: The Life and Times of an American Original*. New York: Free Press, 2009.

Kent, Stephen A. "Hollywood's Celebrity Lobbyists and the Clinton Administration's American Foreign Policy Towards German Scientology." *Journal of Religion and Popular Culture* 1 (Spring 2002).

Kernodle, Tammy. "Freedom Is a Constant Struggle: Alice Coltrane and the Redefining of the Jazz Avant-Garde." In *John Coltrane and Black America's Quest for Freedom: Spirituality and the Music*, edited by Leonard L. Brown, 73–98. New York: Oxford University Press, 2010.

———. *Soul on Soul: The Life of Mary Lou Williams*. Boston: Northeastern University Press, 2004.

———. "This Is My Story, This Is My Song: The Historiography of Vatican II, Black Catholic Identity, Jazz, and the Religious Recompositions of Mary Lou Williams." *U.S. Catholic Historian* 19, no. 2 (Spring 2001): 83–94.

Kofsky, Frank. *Black Nationalism and the Revolution in Music*. New York: Pathfinder, 1970.

Kripal, Jeffrey. *Mutants and Mystics: Science Fiction, Superhero Comics, and the Paranormal*. Chicago: University of Chicago Press, 2011.

Kun, Josh. *Audiotopia: Music, Race, and America*. Berkeley: University of California Press, 2005.

LaBelle, Brandon. "Auditory Relations." In *The Sound Studies Reader*, edited by Jonathan Sterne, 468–74. New York: Routledge, 2012.

Lateef, Yusef. "In the Name of God the Gracious the Merciful." In *Arcana V: Music, Magic and Mysticism*, edited by John Zorn, 248–53. New York: Hips Road, 2010.

Lateef, Yusef, with Herb Boyd. *The Gentle Giant: The Autobiography of Yusef Lateef*. Irvington, N.J.: Morton, 2006.

Lee, Shane, and Philip Luke Sinitiere, eds. *Holy Mavericks: Evangelical Innovators and the Spiritual Marketplace*. New York: New York University Press, 2009.

Lees, Gene. *Cats of Any Color: Jazz, Black and White.* New York: Da Capo, 1995.

Leonard, Neil. *Jazz: Myth and Religion.* New York: Oxford University Press, 1987.

Levine, Lawrence. *Black Culture and Black Consciousness: Afro-American Thought from Slavery to Freedom.* New York: Oxford University Press, 2007.

Levitin, Daniel J. *This Is Your Brain on Music: The Science of a Human Obsession.* New York: Plume, 2006.

Lewis, George E. "Gittin' to Know Y'all: Improvised Music, Interculturalism, and the Racial Imagination." *Critical Studies in Improvisation* 1, no. 1 (2004): 1–33.

———. "Omar's Song: A (Re)construction of Great Black Music." *Lenox Avenue* 4 (1998): 69–92.

———. *A Power Stronger Than Itself: The AACM and American Experimental Music.* Chicago: University of Chicago Press, 2008.

———. "Teaching Improvised Music: An Ethnographic Memoir." In *Arcana: Musicians on Music,* edited by John Zorn, 78–109. New York: Hips Road, 2000.

Lipsitz, George. *Dangerous Crossroads: Popular Music, Postmodernism, and the Poetics of Place.* New York: Verso, 1994.

———. *Footsteps in the Dark: The Hidden Histories of Popular Music.* Minneapolis: University of Minnesota Press, 2007.

———. *The Possessive Investment in Whiteness: How White People Profit from Identity Politics.* Philadelphia: Temple University Press, 1998.

Litweiler, John. *The Freedom Principle: Jazz After 1958.* New York: Da Capo, 1984.

———. *Ornette Coleman: A Harmolodic Life.* New York: William Morrow, 1992.

Lock, Graham. *Blutopia: Visions of the Future and Revisions of the Past in the Work of Sun Ra, Duke Ellington, and Anthony Braxton.* Durham, N.C.: Duke University Press, 1999.

———. *Chasing the Vibration: Meetings with Creative Musicians.* Exeter: Stride, 1994.

———. *Forces in Motion: The Music and Thoughts of Anthony Braxton.* New York: Da Capo, 1988.

———, ed. *Mixtery: A Festschrift for Anthony Braxton.* Exeter: Stride, 1995.

Looker, Benjamin. *"Point from Which Creation Begins": The Black Artists' Group of St. Louis.* St. Louis: Missouri Historical Society Press, 2004.

Mackey, Nathaniel. *Bedouin Hornbook.* Los Angeles: Sun and Moon Classics, 2000.

———. "Sound and Sentiment, Sound and Symbol." In *The Jazz Cadence of American Culture,* edited by Robert G. O'Meally, 602–28. New York: Columbia University Press, 1998.

Maffly-Kipp, Laurie. *Setting Down the Sacred Past: African-American Race Histories.* Cambridge, Mass.: Harvard University Press, 2010.

Marable, Manning. *Malcolm X: A Life of Reinvention.* New York: Viking, 2011.

Marini, Stephen A. "Hymnody and History: Early American Evangelical Hymns as Sacred Music." In *Music in American Religious Experience,* edited by Philip V. Bohlman, Edith L. Blumhofer, and Maria M. Chow, 123–54. New York: Oxford University Press, 2006.

Maxile, Horace J. "Churchy Blues, Bluesy Church: Vernacular Tropes, Expression, and Structure in Charles Mingus's 'Ecclusiastics'." *The Annual Review of Jazz Studies* 14 (2009): 65–81.

McKay, George. *Circular Breathing: The Cultural Politics of Jazz in Britain.* Durham, N.C.: Duke University Press, 2005.

Melford, Myra. "Aural Architecture: The Confluence of Freedom." In *Arcana: Musicians on Music,* edited by John Zorn, 119–35. New York: Hips Road, 2000.

Mercer, Michelle. *Footprints: The Life and Music of Wayne Shorter.* New York: Tarcher, 2004.

Metzer, David. "Shadow Play: The Spiritual in Duke Ellington's 'Black and Tan Fantasy'." *Black Music Research Journal* 17, no. 2 (Autumn 1987): 137–58.

Milbank, John. "A Closer Walk on the Wild Side." In *Varieties of Secularism in a Secular Age,* edited by Michael Warner, Jonathan Van Antwerpen, and Craig Calhoun, 54–82. Cambridge, Mass.: Harvard University Press, 2010.

Miller, James. *Examined Lives: From Socrates to Nietzsche.* New York: Picador, 2011.

Mingus, Charles. *Beneath the Underdog: His World as Composed by Mingus.* New York: Knopf, 1970.

Mizelle, Dary John. "The Sacred Power of Music." In *Arcana V: Music, Magic and Mysticism,* edited by John Zorn, 260–64. New York: Hips Road, 2010.

Modirzadeh, Hafez. "Aural Archetypes and Cyclic Perspectives in the Work of John Coltrane and Ancient Chinese Music Theory." *Black Music Research Journal* 21, no. 1 (Spring 2001): 75–106.

Monson, Ingrid. *Freedom Sounds: Civil Rights Call Out to Jazz and Africa.* New York: Oxford University Press, 2007.

———. *Saying Something: Jazz Improvisation and Interaction.* Chicago: University of Chicago Press, 1996.

Monson, Ingrid, Daniel Fischlin, and Ajay Heble, eds. *The Other Side of Nowhere: Jazz, Improvisation, and Communities in Dialogue.* Middletown, Conn.: Wesleyan University Press, 2004.

Moreno, Jairo. "Bauza-Gillespie-Latin/Jazz: Difference, Modernity, and the Black Carribean." In *Afro-Latin@ Reader: History and Culture in the United States,* edited by Miriam Jimenez Roman and Juan Flores, 177–86. Durham, N.C.: Duke University Press, 2010.

Morris, Joe. *Perpetual Frontier: The Properties of Free Music.* Stony Creek, Conn.: Riti, 2012.

Morris, Lawrence D. "Butch." "The Science of Finding." In *Arcana II: Musicians on Music,* edited by John Zorn, 169–73. New York: Hips Road, 2007.

Munoz, Tisziji. "Death: The Father of Creation." In *Arcana V: Music, Magic and Mysticism,* edited by John Zorn, 269–85. New York: Hips Road, 2010.

Murchison, Gayle. "Mary Lou Williams' *Black Christ of the Andes (St. Martin de Porres)*: Vatican II, Civil Rights, and Jazz as Sacred Music." *Musical Quarterly* 86, no. 4 (Winter 2003): 591–624.

Murray, Albert. *Stomping the Blues*. New York: Da Capo, 1989.

Nachmann, Ron. "Radical Jewish Culture: John Zorn's Tzadik Label." *Tikkun* 20, no. 1 (January/February 2005): 78–79.

Nagavajara, Chetana. "On the Power, Powerlessness and Omnipotence of Language: From Oral Culture Through Written Culture to Media Domination." *Silpakorn University International Journal* 7 (2007): 89–111.

Nielsen, Aldon Lynn. *Black Chant: Languages of African-American Postmodernism*. Cambridge: Cambridge University Press, 1997.

Niles, John J. "Shout, Coon, Shout!" *Musical Quarterly* 16, no. 4 (October 1930): 516–30.

Nisenson, Eric. *Ascension: John Coltrane and His Quest*. New York: Da Capo, 1995.

Oliveros, Pauline. "Harmonic Anatomy: Women in Improvisation." In *The Other Side of Nowhere: Jazz, Improvisation, and Communities in Dialogue*, edited by Daniel Fischlin and Ajay Heble, 50–69. Middletown, Conn.: Wesleyan University Press, 2004.

O'Meally, Robert, ed. *Living with Music: Ralph Ellison's Jazz Writings*. New York: Modern Library, 2001.

O'Meally, Robert, Brent Hayes Edwards, and Farah Jasmine Griffin, eds. *Uptown Conversation: The New Jazz Studies*. New York: Columbia University Press, 2004.

Orsi, Robert A. *Between Heaven and Earth: The Religious Worlds People Make and the Scholars Who Study Them*. Princeton, N.J.: Princeton University Press, 2005.

———. Introduction to *The Cambridge Companion to Religious Studies*, edited by Robert A. Orsi, 1–13. Cambridge: Cambridge University Press, 2012.

———. "When 2 + 2 = 5." *The American Scholar* (Spring 2007): 34–43.

Owsley, Dennis. *City of Gabriels: The History of Jazz in St. Louis, 1895–1973*. St. Louis: Reedy, 2006.

Patchen, Kenneth. *Collected Poems*. New York: New Directions, 1968.

Peters, Gary. *The Philosophy of Improvisation*. Chicago: University of Chicago Press, 2009.

Peterson, Lloyd. *Music and the Creative Spirit*. Lanham, Md.: Scarecrow, 2006.

Piekut, Benjamin. *Experimentalism Otherwise: The New York Avant-Garde and Its Limits*. Berkeley: University of California Press, 2011.

Pike, Sarah M. *Earthly Bodies, Magical Selves: Contemporary Pagans and the Search for Community*. Berkeley: University of California Press, 2001.

———. *New Age and Neopagan Religions in America*. New York: Columbia University Press, 2006.

Pinn, Anthony B. *Varieties of African American Religious Experience*. Minneapolis: Fortress, 1998.

Pitzer, Donald E. *America's Communal Utopias*. Chapel Hill: University of North Carolina Press, 1997.

Porter, Eric. "'Born Out of Jazz…Yet Embracing All Music': Race, Gender, and Technology in George Russell's Lydian Chromatic Concept." In *Big Ears: Listening* for *Gender in Jazz Studies*, edited by Nichole T. Rustin and Sherrie Tucker, 210–34. Durham, N.C.: Duke University Press, 2008.

———. "Jeanne Lee's Voice." *Critical Studies in Improvisation* 2, no. 1 (2006): 1–14.

———. *What Is This Thing Called Jazz? African American Musicians as Artists, Critics, and Activists.* Berkeley: University of California Press, 2002.

Porter, Lewis. *John Coltrane: His Life and Music.* Ann Arbor: University of Michigan Press, 2000.

Pratt, Ray. *Rhythm and Resistance: The Political Uses of American Popular Music.* Washington, D.C.: Smithsonian Institution Press, 1990.

Radano, Ronald. "Jazzin' the Classics: The AACM's Challenge to Mainstream Aesthetics." *Black Music Research Journal* 12, no. 1 (Spring 1992): 79–95.

———. *Lying Up a Nation: Race and Black Music.* Chicago: University of Chicago Press, 2003.

———. *New Musical Figurations: Anthony Braxton's Cultural Critique.* Chicago: University of Chicago Press, 1993.

Ramsey, Guthrie P., Jr. *Race Music: Black Cultures from Bebop to Hip-Hop.* Berkeley: University of California Press, 2003.

Rasula, Jed. "The Media of Memory: The Seductive Menace of Records in Jazz History." In *Jazz among the Discourses*, edited by Krin Gabbard, 134–62. Durham, N.C.: Duke University Press, 1995.

Ratliff, Ben. *Coltrane: The Story of a Sound.* New York: Farrar, Straus and Giroux, 2007.

———. *The Jazz Ear: Conversations over Music.* New York: Times, 2010.

Reitman, Janet. *Inside Scientology: The Story of America's Most Secretive Religion.* New York: Mariner, 2013.

Rogovoy, Seth. *The Essential Klezmer.* New York: Algonquin, 2000.

Roof, Wade Clark. *Generation of Seekers: The Spiritual Journeys of the Baby Boom Generation.* New York: HarperSanFrancisco, 1993.

Rosenthal, David. "The Big Beat!" *Black Perspective in Music* 14, no. 3 (Autumn 1986): 267–89.

———. *Hard Bop and Black Music, 1955–1965.* New York: Oxford University Press, 1992.

Ross, Alex. *Listen to This.* New York: Farrar, Straus and Giroux, 2010.

———. *The Rest Is Noise.* New York: Farrar, Straus and Giroux, 2007.

Rudolph, Adam. "Music and Mysticism, Rhythm and Form: A Blues Romance in 12 Parts." In *Arcana V: Music, Magic and Mysticism*, edited by John Zorn, 327–35. New York: Hips Road, 2010.

Rusch, Robert. *Jazztalk: The Cadence Interviews.* Fort Lee, N.J.: Lyle Stuart, 1984.

Santoro, Gene. *Dancing in Your Head: Jazz, Blues, Rock, and Beyond.* New York: Oxford University Press, 1994.

Saul, Scott. *Freedom Is, Freedom Ain't: Jazz and the Making of the Sixties.* Cambridge, Mass.: Harvard University Press, 2003.

Schafer, R. Murray. *The Soundscape: Our Sonic Environment and the Tuning of the World*. Rochester, Vt.: Destiny, 1993.

Schleifer, Ronald. *Modernism and Popular Music*. Cambridge: Cambridge University Press, 2011.

Schmidt, Leigh Eric. *Hearing Things: Religion, Illusion, and the American Enlightenment*. Cambridge, Mass.: Harvard University Press, 2002.

———. *Restless Souls: The Making of American Spirituality*. Berkeley: University of California Press, 2012.

Sharp, Charles. "Seeking John Carter and Bobby Bradford: Free Music and Community in Los Angeles." *The Black Music Research Journal* 31, no. 1 (Spring 2011): 65–83.

Small, Christopher. *Music of the Common Tongue: Survival and Celebration in Afro-American Music*. New York: Riverrun, 1987.

Smith, Jonathan Z. *Imagining Religion: From Babylon to Jonestown*. Chicago: University of Chicago Press, 1982.

———. *To Take Place: Toward Theory in Ritual*. Chicago: University of Chicago Press, 1987.

Smith, Leo. "(M1) American Music." *The Black Perspective in Music* 2, no. 2 (Autumn 1974): 111–16.

Smith, Theophus. *Conjuring Culture: Biblical Formations of Black America*. New York: Oxford University Press, 1995.

Spellman, A. B. *Black Music: Four Lives*. New York: Schocken, 1970.

Spencer, Jon Michael. "Overview of American Popular Music in a Theological Perspective." In *Theomusicology: A Special Issue of Black Sacred Music*, edited by Jon Michael Spencer, 205–17. Durham, N.C.: Duke University Press, 1994.

Steinbeck, Paul. "'Area by Area the Machine Unfolds': The Improvisational Performance Practice of the Art Ensemble of Chicago." *Journal of the Society for American Music* 2, no. 3 (2008): 397–427.

Stephenson, Gene, and Andrew Cyrille. "Dialogue of the Drums." *Black Perspective in Music* 3, no. 1 (Spring 1975): 53–57.

Stevens, Wallace. *The Collected Poems of Wallace Stevens*. New York: Vintage, 1990.

Stowe, David W. "Both American and Global: Jazz and World Religions in the United States." *Religion Compass* 4, no. 5 (May 2010): 312–23.

———. *How Sweet the Sound: Music in the Spiritual Lives of Americans*. Cambridge, Mass.: Harvard University Press, 2004.

Such, David G. *Avant-Garde Musicians Performing "Out There."* Iowa City: University of Iowa Press, 1993.

Sullivan, Denise. *Keep On Pushing: Black Power Music from Blues to Hip-Hop*. Chicago: Chicago Review Press, 2011.

Sullivan, Lawrence. Introduction to *Enchanting Powers: Music in the World's Religions*, edited by Lawrence Sullivan, 1–14. Cambridge, Mass.: Harvard University Press, 1997.

Sylvan, Robin. *Traces of the Spirit: The Religious Dimensions of Popular Music.* New York: New York University Press, 2002.

Szwed, John. "Antiquity of the Avant Garde." In *People Get Ready: The Future of Jazz Is Now!* edited by Ajay Heble and Rob Wallace, 44–58. Durham, N.C.: Duke University Press, 2013.

———. *Crossovers: Essays on Race, Music, and American Culture.* Philadelphia: University of Pennsylvania Press, 2005.

———. *Space Is the Place: The Lives and Times of Sun Ra.* New York: Pantheon, 1997.

Tapscott, Horace. *Songs of the Unsung: The Musical and Social Journey of Horace Tapscott.* Durham, N.C.: Duke University Press, 2001.

Taves, Ann. *Fits, Trances, and Visions: Experiencing Religion and Explaining Experience from Wesley to James.* Princeton, N.J.: Princeton University Press, 1999.

———. *Religious Experience Reconsidered: A Building-Block Approach to the Study of Religion and Other Special Things.* Princeton, N.J.: Princeton University Press, 2009.

Taylor, Arthur. *Notes and Tones: Musician-to-Musician Interviews.* New York: Da Capo, 1993.

Taylor, Mark C. *About Religion: Economies of Faith in Virtual Culture.* Chicago: University of Chicago Press, 1999.

Thomas, J. C. *Chasin' the Trane.* New York: Da Capo, 1975.

Toop, David. *Sinister Resonance: The Mediumship of the Listener.* New York: Continuum, 2010.

Troupe, Quincy, and Ben Riley. "Remembering Thelonious Monk: When the Music Was Happening Then He'd Get Up and Do His Little Dance." In *The Jazz Cadence of American Culture,* edited by Robert G. O'Meally, 102–10. New York: Columbia University Press, 1998.

Tucker, Bruce. "Narrative, Extramusical Form, and the Metamodernism of the Art Ensemble of Chicago." *Lenox Avenue* 3 (1997): 29–41.

Turner, Richard Brent. *Jazz Religion, the Second Line, and Black New Orleans.* Bloomington: Indiana University Press, 2009.

Van DeBurg, William L. *New Day in Babylon: The Black Power Movement in American Culture 1965–1975.* Chicago: University of Chicago Press, 1993.

Varga, George. "Quincy Jones: A Profile." *International Association of Jazz Educators Journal* 34, no. 4 (January 2002): 2–3, 5–6.

Veal, Michael. "Starship Africa." In *The Sound Studies Reader,* edited by Jonathan Sterne, 454–67. New York: Routledge, 2012.

Versace, Angelo D. "The Evolution of Sacred Jazz as Reflected in the Music of Mary Lou Williams, Duke Ellington, John Coltrane, and Recognized Contemporary Sacred Jazz Artists." PhD diss., University of Miami, Coral Gables, 2013.

Voelz, Johannes. "Improvisation, Correlation, and Vibration: An Interview with Steve Coleman." *Critical Studies in Improvisation* 2, no. 1 (2006): 1–18.

Walden, Daniel. "Black Music and Cultural Nationalism: The Maturation of Archie Shepp." *Negro American Literature Forum* 5, no. 4 (Winter 1971): 150–54.

Wall, Greg. "Horn O' Plenty." In *Arcana V: Music, Magic and Mysticism*, edited by John Zorn, 396–400. New York: Hips Road, 2010.

Walser, Robert, ed. *Keeping Time: Readings in Jazz History.* New York: Oxford University Press, 1999.

Watts, Jill. *God, Harlem, U.S.A.: The Father Divine Story*. Berkeley: University of California Press, 1992.

Weinstein, Norman. *A Night in Tunisia: Imaginings of Africa in Jazz*. Montclair, N.J.: Limelight, 2004.

———. "Steps Toward an Integrative Comprehension of the Art Ensemble of Chicago's Music." *Lenox Avenue* 3 (1997): 3, 5–11.

Weiss, Jason. *Always in Trouble: An Oral History of ESP-Disk', The Most Outrageous Record Label in America*. Middletown, Conn.: Wesleyan University Press, 2012.

———. *Steve Lacy: Conversations*. Durham, N.C.: Duke University Press, 2006.

Welch, Sharon. *Sweet Dreams in America: Making Ethics and Spirituality Work*. New York: Routledge, 1998.

Whitehead, Kevin. *Why Jazz? A Concise Guide*. New York: Oxford University Press, 2010.

Whiticker, Michael. "Morton Feldman: Conversation Without Cage." *Ossia: A Journal of Contemporary Music* 1 (Winter 1989): 6–9.

Widener, Daniel. *Black Arts West: Culture and Struggle in Postwar Los Angeles*. Durham, N.C.: Duke University Press, 2010.

Wilmer, Valerie. *As Serious as Your Life: The Story of the New Jazz*. New York: Serpent's Tail, 1992.

———. *Jazz People*. New York: Da Capo, 1970.

Wittgenstein, Ludwig. *Philosophical Investigations*. Saddle River, N.J.: Prentice-Hall, 1973.

Wright, Josephine R. B. "Conversation with John Birks 'Dizzy' Gillespie." *Black Music Research Journal* 4, no. 1 (Spring 1976): 82–89.

X, Malcolm. "I Don't Mean Bananas." In *The New Left Reader*, edited by Carl Oglesby. New York: Grove, 1969.

Yancy, George, ed. *Cornel West: A Critical Reader*. Cambridge: Wiley-Blackwell, 2001.

Index